The Limitation of Conflict

A THEORY OF BARGAINING AND NEGOTIATION

L.N. RANGARAJAN

ST. MARTIN'S PRESS
NEW YORK

© 1985 L.N. Rangarajan
All rights reserved. For information, write:
St. Martin's Press, Inc., 175 Fifth Avenue, New York, NY 10010
Printed in Great Britain
First published in the United States of America in 1985

Library of Congress Cataloging in Publication Data

Rangarajan, L.N.
   The limitation of conflict.

  Bibliography: p.
  Includes index.
  1. Diplomatic negotiations in international disputes.
2. Negotiation. 3. Conflict management. I. Title.
JX4473.R36   1985   327.2   82-60908
ISBN 0-312-48675-8

28961

THE LIMITATION OF CONFLICT

CONTENTS

List of Figures
List of Tables
Abbreviations
Preface
Prologue

Part One: Dissatisfaction, Vulnerability, Conflict and Negotiation

1. On Limiting Conflicts by Negotiation   1
2. Conflict, Aggression, Bargaining and Negotiation   19
3. Dissatisfaction and Vulnerability   37
4. Uncertainty of Perception   53
5. Environment, Memory and Time   71

Part Two: A Theory of Bargaining

6. The Theoretical Framework   89
7. On Buying Potatoes   96
8. Linkages, Trade-offs and Package Deals   119
9. Numbers, Coalitions and Collusion   139
10. The Theory So Far   159

Part Three: Four Aspects of Negotiation

11. Escalation, Enlargement and Expansion   167
12. Bargaining Power   184
13. Political Will   207

Part Four: On Peaceful Change

14. The Rule of International Law   223

| 15. Making, Obeying and Disobeying Rules | 238 |
| 16. Conciliation, Mediation, Arbitration and Adjudication | 257 |

Part Five: The Limitation of Conflict

17. Conflict–Limitation: a Summary	279
18. World Order and Conflicts: the Next Fifteen Years	291
Epilogue	309
Appendix: Additional Material on the Theory of Negotiation	310
Index	316

FIGURES

2.1	Aggression, Conflict, Negotiation and Order	28
5.1	Bargaining Space and the Environment	78
6.1	Making a Choice	93
7.1	Three Possible Outcomes: two negotiants/ one dimension	98
7.2	Negotiants' Perceptions at Three Different Times	101
7.3	The Negotiating Process: two person/ one dimension — Breakdown	103
7.4	Seven Types of Negotiations: two persons/ one dimension	104
7.5	Poker-type Negotiation: two persons/ one dimension	107
7.6	Negotiation with Unequal Bargaining Power: two person/ one dimension — B superior	108
7.7	See-saw Type Negotiation at the Time of the Outcome	110
7.8	Buying a House	113
7.9	Residue of Dissatisfaction	117
8.1	Functional Relationships Between Dimensions: sale of house and fittings	126
8.2	Functional Relationships Between Dimensions: ICAs	127
11.1a	Stages of Enlargement	172
11.1b	Stages of Expansion	172
12.1	Voting Power in the International Monetary Fund	204
13.1	Causes of Breakdowns in Negotiations	209

TABLES

7.1	Negotiating Times for Different Types of Negotiations: two persons/one dimension	111
7.2	Division of Teesta Waters	115
8.1	Phases and Duration of Multidimensional Negotiations up to Alignment of Priorities	134
8.2	Types of Two-dimension Negotiations After Identifying High-priority Dimensions	135
8.3	Phases and Minimum Duration of Multidimensional Negotiations	137
9.1	Coalition-formation — three negotiants/three dimensions	149
12.1	Number of Commissioners in the Commission of the European Communities	200
12.2	Voting Power in the Council of Ministers of the European Communities	202
16.1	Third-party Intercession: the four techniques compared	258-9

जठरेऽग्निस्तिष्ठतु ।   हृदये शिवस्तिष्ठतु ।

To
Joyce
whose contribution to this book
can never be adequately acknowledged

ABBREVIATIONS

ABM	—	Anti-ballistic missile (defence system)
CAP	—	Common Agricultural Policy
ECSC	—	European Conference on Security and Co-operation
EEC	—	European Economic Community
GATT	—	General Agreement on Tariffs and Trade
IATA	—	International Air Transport Authority
ICA	—	International Commodity Agreement
ICJ	—	International Court of Justice
IMF	—	International Monetary Fund
IMO	—	International Maritime Organisation
MFA	—	Multi-Fibre Agreement
mfn	—	most favoured nation
MIRV	—	Multiple independently targetable re-entry vehicle
NANs	—	Negotiations about negotiations
NATO	—	North Atlantic Treaty Organisation
NIEO	—	New International Economic Order
OAS	—	Organisation of American States
OAU	—	Organisation of African Unity
OECD	—	Organisation for Economic Co-operation and Development
OPEC	—	Organisation of Petroleum Exporting Countries
PLO	—	Palestine Liberation Organisation
PPI	—	Purchasing Power Index
PRC	—	People's Republic of China
RPI	—	Retail Price Index
SALT	—	Strategic Arms Limitation Talks
START	—	Strategic Arms Reduction Talks
SWAPO	—	South-West Africa People's Organisation
TSB	—	Textiles Surveillance Body
UN	—	United Nations
UNCLOS	—	UN Conference on the Law of the Sea
UNESCO	—	UN Educational, Scientific and Cultural Organisation
UK	—	United Kingdom (also referred to as Britain)
US	—	United States of America
USSR	—	Union of Soviet Socialist Republics (also referred to as Russia)

PREFACE

This book is the result of many years of labour. From the beginning, I have been sustained by the constant encouragement of Joyce, my wife, and Susan Strange, Professor of International Relations at the London School of Economics.

The ideas in this book, particularly those relating to a new theory of bargaining and negotiation, have been discussed with many people, all of whom gave their time unstintingly and shared readily with me their knowledge and experience. I owe a special debt of gratitude to the participants in two seminars. At the first, organised by Susan Strange, my thanks go to Barry Buzan of Warwick University, Michael Donelan of the London School of Economics, Christopher Mitchell of the City University (London), Michael Nicholson, Director of the Richardson Institute of Conflict at the University of Lancaster, Max Steuer of the London School of Economics, and Roger Tooze of the North Staffordshire Polytechnic. The second was organised by Uma Shankar Bajpai at the India International Centre, New Delhi, and my thanks go to Virendra Laroie, S. Satyabhama, K. Subrahmanyam, Director of the Institute for Defence Studies and Analysis, and K. Subramaniam of the Department of Economic Affairs.

I have also had the benefit of personal discussions with many. I thank Mrinal Datta-Choudhry, Director, Delhi School of Economics, for his encouragement and perceptive comments. I learnt a great deal from the Rev. Michael Hollings of St Mary's Presbytery, Bayswater. Dharma Kumar of the Delhi School of Economics was, as usual, a constant source of encouragement. I had a fortuitous and valuable meeting with Roger Fisher, who has devoted many years to the study of conflicts and negotiations. Chithamparanathan of the UN University, Tokyo and N.R. Ranganathan of the Institute of Mathematical Physics, Madras are two friends whose advice was always constructive.

My thanks to Vijay Pande, then of the Ford Foundation, for generously offering me Foundation assistance and to Carolyn Elliott, who pursued it with vigour: I was unable to make use of it due to governmental restrictions.

Karen Lee Abu Zeid, Joyce Rangarajan and B.P.R. Vithal read

Preface

the entire book in manuscript and made many valuable suggestions in addition to improving the language and the style. I am deeply grateful to them.

I am indebted, for typing the manuscript, to Ram Charan who did it as a labour of love. My thanks also to Manimekalai, H.S. Chatterjee and Sujata Chatterjee for proof reading the manuscript.

It is unusual to acknowledge the debt to authors of books which one has read. However, in my case, a number of books have been a source of inspiration. Though I have acknowledged my debt at appropriate places in the book, I would like to mention especially the following: J.L. Brierly, *The Law of Nations*; P.B. Medawar, *The Art of the Soluble*; Michael Nicholson, *Conflict Analysis*; Anatol Rapoport, *Fights, Games and Debates*; Thomas Schelling, *The Strategy of Conflict*; M.D. Vernon, *The Psychology of Perception*; Norbert Weiner, *The Human Use of Human Beings*; and Solly Zuckerman, *Nuclear Illusion and Reality*. The fact that I have been helped and inspired by so many does not mean that they bear any responsibility for the views expressed by me in this work, the demerits of which are entirely mine.

I have also to add the disclaimer that the Government of India, whose servant I am, is in no way responsible for the opinions expressed or the courses of action adumbrated in this book.

Lastly, my thanks to David Croom for all his help and consideration.

L.N. Rangarajan
Khartoum, Eid al-Fitr, 30 June 1984

PROLOGUE

Why do you and I and so many other people rebel so violently against war? Why do we not accept it as another of the many painful calamities of life?... We react to war in this way because everyone has a right to his own life, because war puts an end to human lives that are full of hope, because it brings individual men into humiliating situations, because it compels them against their will to murder other men and because it destroys precious material objects which have been produced by the labours of humanity.

It is my opinion that the main reason why we rebel against war is that we cannot help doing so. We are pacifists because we are obliged to be for organic reasons.

>Sigmund Freud, in reply to
>Einstein's circular letter on war
>to leading thinkers,
>Vienna, September 1932

PART ONE

DISSATISFACTION, VULNERABILITY, CONFLICT AND NEGOTIATION

Riots are the language of the unheard.
        Dr Martin Luther King

The highest title to glory is to kill war with words of negotiation instead of killing men with the sword.
        St Augustine, quoted by
        Pope John Paul II in his homily,
        21 May 1982

1 ON LIMITING CONFLICTS BY NEGOTIATION

The second blow makes the fray. The second word makes the bargaine.
> Francis Bacon,
> *Of the Colours of Good and Evil* (1597)

And through the heat of conflict, keep the law
In calmness made.
> William Wordsworth,
> *The Character of the Happy Warrior*

The two rails of the track on which this book will run are first, a study of conflicts, particularly conflicts between states; and second, an analysis of the process of negotiation. It must, however, be emphasised at the outset that all conflict situations are not necessarily bargaining situations. Individuals, groups of people and nation states may resort to violent action for a variety of reasons. An example of anarchic violence, not susceptible to negotiation, is the reported case of a group of Hell's Angels who challenged another group to prove itself by 'taking out' (i.e. killing) at least two total strangers. Likewise, a country determined to go to war for territorial aggrandisement is unlikely to be moved by pleas to settle a dispute peacefully. On the other hand, many conflicts between individuals and between nations are settled peacefully. One aim of this book will be to find out which types of conflict can be prevented from becoming violent by encouraging negotiation among the disputants.

Conflicts

Three extracts from newspaper reports will serve as examples of certain types of conflict which resulted in a violent event.

Woman 'snapped' after 44 years of 'Victorian' marriage
A loyal wife put up with a loveless marriage of slavery for 44 years before she snapped and killed her 'Victorian' husband

when he admitted being a homosexual. ... Almost throughout her marriage she had been treated more like a slave than a wife.[1]

The Champion who died a Dacoit
During the late fifties and early sixties, Subedar-Major (Pan Singh Tomar) was national champion in the 5000 metres and the gruelling 3000 metres steeplechase ... On his retirement [from the Army] he discovered to his chagrin that his ancestral land had, in his absence, been usurped by a neighbouring landlord, Babu Singh, and his family. Initially he took recourse to litigation which proved a futile expense. ... Appeals to former sports officials were also of no avail. ... An embittered man, Pan Singh ... in sheer desperation and rage ... sought justice through the barrel of the gun. He killed Babu Singh.[2]

Car workers go on a rampage
Why did a group of about 300 workers surge through the Longbridge plant of British Leyland leaving behind them a trail of vandalism? Mr Brian Mathews, regional secretary of the TGWU ... says 'the situation inside the plant is so bad that many workers quite literally hate the management' ... The spokesman for the Joint Staff Unions Committee said: 'In all my time I have never known men so angry. The place is literally like a pressure cooker.'[3]

Words like 'slavery', 'subjugation', 'bitterness', 'hate', 'frustration' and 'desperation' recur in these extracts. Bottled-up emotion is clearly one cause of violence erupting suddenly. Collective violent behaviour can also be prompted by feelings of insecurity and fear. After the first murder by a group which feels vulnerable, violence takes its own escalating course. Repetitive killings by two groups, each scared of the other, become the pattern.

Nations also go to war because of insecurity, fear or vulnerability. Some in the United States advocate a violent takeover of the Gulf oil-fields, because dependence on oil imports makes them feel insecure. Some grievances last centuries; later in the book we shall cite the example of the Iran—Iraq War, the causes of which have been traced to dissatisfaction and grievances as far back as AD 637!

Not all conflicts and disputes end in violence. There are many divorces with the erstwhile partners parting as friends, while others leave a legacy of bitterness and hate; many labour—management disputes are settled amicably, while some lead to strikes and lock-outs. If poverty, unemployment and consequent social deprivation lead to riots in some cities, there are other much poorer parts of the world where the underprivileged are not in a constant state of turmoil. Among nations, not every boundary or river dispute ends in the countries fighting each other. In short, we have to ask the question, 'Why is there not *more* violence in this world?'

In an excellent article examining the difference between coercive and voluntary submission to law, Professor Hilding Eek cautions against the mistake of studying inter-state relations by assuming that these must concern, in the first instance, or only, existing or potential conflicts between power-seeking states: 'The study of the reasons why nations do not constantly live in a state of war is being neglected just as, within a society, criminology is looked upon as more interesting than the study of the reasons why law and order prevail.'[4]

Conflict Resolution and Conflict Limitation

The term 'conflict resolution' has become not only common but commonplace; it has gained a respected place in academic thinking, and entire journals are devoted to it. The media, of course, use it indiscriminately, talking of 'resolving' conflicts as if they ended totally and cleanly. It is my view that *no* conflict is ever resolved irrevocably or totally.

Suppose a branch of my neighbour's tree hangs over my garden and suppose too that he rejects my repeated requests to have it cut down. I can take him to court, get an injunction and succeed in having the offending branch removed. The specific conflict of the overhanging branch appears to be resolved; but it is bound to affect our relations so long as we remain neighbours; our perceptions of each other will be coloured by this history. The Treaty of Versailles (1919) was hailed as a 'peace' treaty. Most historians, however, agree that it was responsible in large part for the much larger second world war 20 years later. These are just two examples to illustrate the point that, while some conflicts may appear to have been resolved at a particular time, they may well contain the seeds of a future conflict.

A so-called resolution of a conflict is sometimes made possible only by the disputants agreeing to postpone some aspects of it for future negotiations. This is especially true in multilateral negotiations, where some intractable problems are swept under the carpet. Others are resolutions in name only; President Nixon proclaimed the Smithsonian Agreement on exchange rates as the 'Agreement of the century' — it was nothing of the kind, and lasted only a few weeks! Media exaggeration, politicians' rhetoric and, to some extent, academic wishful-thinking have led to a futile pursuit of conflict resolution.

A conflict can evolve in many ways. We can imagine the course of a conflict as having a compass bearing. Actions by one or the other of the parties, actions by third parties, or even chance events, can move the needle towards violence or away from it. An action which limits a conflict is one which, in all probability, and as far as one can predict, directs its future evolution away from a violent end and towards the possibility of accommodation by peaceful negotiation.

The Process of Negotiation

While we shall be studying negotiation for its relevance to conflict-limitation, I must emphasise that the process itself is neutral. Two criminals planning a bank robbery may negotiate about how they will divide the loot if the crime pays; two people may negotiate about how to divide their time so that a sick person is never left unattended; two nations may negotiate about how many divisions each will contribute in attacking a third, or how to share the waters of a river to mutual advantage. 'Jaw-jaw is better than war-war' is true only if the purpose of negotiation is to prevent a dispute from becoming a war. The part of this book dealing with the development of a theory of negotiation will be solely concerned with it as a *process* and not on whether its objective is a morally laudable one.

Negotiation is an integral part of every human activity. We may not realise it, but we all enter negotiations many times a day, whenever we have to accommodate a different point of view. Children, without any conscious coaching on how to negotiate, bargain a chocolate for bubble-gum. More important for the limitation of conflict, 'negotiations on matters great and small of common concern to modern governments are ubiquitous and continuous.'⁵ In peace, governments have to negotiate trade agreements and postal conventions; in conflict, they may start to fight while negotiating a boundary dispute but, if their leaders are prudent, they will continue to negotiate even as they go to war. Every method of settling disputes between two governments involves negotiation. Any dispute strictly between two governments can be settled by themselves through bilateral diplomatic negotiation. If they accept conciliation or mediation by a third party, they first have to agree, by negotiation, to adopt this method and then to agree on an individual or a state as the mediator or conciliator. If they agree to refer the dispute to arbitration, they have to agree, by negotiation, on the names of the arbitrators and also on the precise question which is to be referred to them.

A negotiation is not an auction. The psychology of the bidders, with an auctioneer jogging the bidding up, is one of pure competition. I emphasise this because of its relevance to the nuclear arms race between the two super-powers. In an interesting article ('When Both the Bidders Lost at a Stupid Game'), Samuel Gorovitz has described his experience of auctioning dollar bills; the only unusual condition he imposed was that, while the winner got the dollar by paying the amount of his bid, the second-highest bidder also had to pay Gorovitz the amount of his bid, though he got nothing in exchange. The auctioneer always made a tidy profit because the bidding always went 'well above $1, sometimes as high as $5 or $6'. Such irrational behaviour, known as entrapment, is found whenever people, in pursuit of an objective, invest more than what they themselves in other circumstances would consider sensible.⁶ Gorovitz recommends that, however difficult arms control agreements may be, it is better to invest in negotiations than continue irrationally piling up more horrendous nuclear weapons.

It is not merely matters of high moment like bringing sanity to the nuclear balance of terror that are susceptible to negotiation. As an example of peaceful negotiation of a very complex problem, one can cite the Third UN Conference on the Law of the Sea (1973-82) in which over 150 countries participated, each of which perceived many questions as affecting their vital national interests.

Like conflicts, negotiations also have two polarities; every event can either move them towards an agreement or towards a breakdown. We know that, in real life, negotiations often end in breakdown. Michael Nicholson, in his pioneering book *Conflict*

Analysis points out that 'The most important question that a theory of bargaining, whose basic purpose is to describe behaviour, would attempt to answer is not where a bargain *should* be concluded but where, in fact, it *is* concluded' (Nicholson's emphasis).[7] It is necessary to add that, for negotiations in real life, we must also try to answer *when* it is concluded.

If we are to understand people's behaviour when negotiating, we should not assume that it is a totally rational process: there is always a mixture of rationality and irrationality. Even when a negotiator wants to reach an agreement, he also fears that the agreement reached may turn out to be unfavourable to him. In analysing the process of negotiation, we shall assume that it is a rational process indulged in by people who may often behave irrationally. During the course of this book, we shall cite examples to substantiate this assumption.

Conflicts and Negotiations

Thomas Schelling has explained why most conflicts are essentially bargaining situations: 'They are situations in which the ability of one participant to gain his end is dependent to an important degree on the choices or decisions that the other participant will make.'[8] If we exclude those conflicts in which there is no common interest whatsoever between the antagonists, we shall find that most conflicts are a mixture of competition and co-operation.

The examples given at the beginning of this chapter show that some conflicts become violent either because dissatisfactions turn into frustrations or because people feel threatened and fear makes them strike out. Fairness and unfairness, security, vulnerability and vital interests are expressions which will occur often. In Chapter 2, we shall postulate two sequences, starting respectively with dissatisfaction and dependence, that are likely to end in violence and disorder. From a study of the two sequences, we shall be able to delimit the boundaries of negotiation, with violence and disorder at one extreme and absence of conflict at the other.

Between the boundaries, negotiations can take place for a variety of reasons. Perception of a conflict of interest may induce people to negotiate about it in order to reduce uncertainty and create greater order; negotiations may continue right up to the outbreak of violence and will resume after the violent phase is over. The area covered by conflict and negotiation is, therefore, very large. It is not enough to confine oneself, as many strategists of conflict do, to only that extreme which is concerned exclusively with deterrence and brinkmanship. The other extreme, concerned with creating order, at the other end, is important for understanding why there is not more violence in this world.

Though the areas of conflict and negotiation overlap we must be aware that any conflict has a much longer history than the negotiations which may take place about it from time to time.

Dissatisfaction, Utility and Game Theory

Until recently, the theoretical approaches to bargaining and negotiation have been based on game theory. Game theory will be repeatedly mentioned in the earlier chapters of this book because it is widely known, having been developed with elegant mathematics. Though much intellectual effort has been lavished on it, I find it inadequate for a number of reasons. A fundamental assumption of game theory is that all bargaining takes place between people who behave strictly rationally, an assumption we know not to be true in real life. The theory is also concerned only with those negotiations which are assumed, *a priori*, to end in an agreement; if a theory of bargaining cannot explain why some negotiations break down, it loses touch with reality. Furthermore, the theory cannot explain why negotiations start and can give no credible reason for such a common phenomenon as 'splitting the difference'.

My approach is based on treating negotiations as a human process happening in real time. In Chapter 3, I shall argue, citing many examples, that dissatisfaction is a more useful concept for understanding negotiations. Only by using dissatisfaction can we explain why any negotiation *starts*. A long-running saga in international negotiations is Britain's demand for a rebate in the contributions it makes to the European Community Budget. It is very difficult to argue that the negotiation between Britain and the other (then) eight members began because they all saw, spontaneously, that to negotiate on this question would increase their individual and collective satisfaction! In fact, the history of the negotiations shows precisely the opposite. The bargaining began because one party was dissatisfied with its place in the agreed framework of the Community. When the problem was first mooted, there was no indication that an agreed solution was even possible. The Britain/EEC Budget dispute will be cited in almost every chapter, since it exemplifies many of the aspects of the theory of negotiation proposed in this book.

In the real world, there is a fundamental asymmetry of information in almost all bargaining situations. The seller of a product is probably better endowed with information than the buyer; in fact, one could argue that the purpose of negotiation itself is to redress the imbalance by working towards a symmetry of information. Nicholson has discussed disputes between labour and management as follows:

> The bargaining situation is asymmetrical and in the employer's favour. The firm makes the positive act of handing out the wages — the workers are involved in the passive act of receiving them. The union cannot directly force the management to hand out a higher wage and, prior to an agreement, the situation is always heavily in favour of the employer.[9]

The moment we take into account inequalities in bargaining power, we recognise the existence of asymmetry. The assumption of symmetry, implicit in the game theory approach to bargaining, has also been questioned by authors like Schelling.[10]

The concept of utility is now an essential part of thinking in economic theory. In advocating an approach for the study of negotiation based on dissatisfaction, I am not jettisoning utility altogether. Clearly, at the end of every negotiation, the bargainers must derive some satisfaction — this may include satisfaction on the issues under negotiation, as well as satisfaction at reaching agreement without recourse to violence. I shall, however, argue that, notwithstanding the satisfaction or utility gained, every negotiation also leaves behind a residue of *dis*satisfaction. Any agreement, in itself, has a utility which is the 'value' of the agreement. In short, dissatisfaction is an *extension* of the concept of utility and the two are related to each other at the point of agreement.

Uncertainty of Perception, Environment and Time

The concept of dissatisfaction is also useful for understanding why an agreement is reached, *where* it is reached. I shall propose, in Chapter 3, a new hypothesis — perception of equality of dissatisfaction — as a key for answering the questions, where and when agreements are reached in negotiations.

The word 'perception' has already been used in this chapter a number of times. How well the parties involved in a negotiation understand each other's communications is an essential element of feedback in the negotiating process. But, however much we may try to place ourselves in someone else's position, we can never be totally he or she; there will always be some uncertainty in the way we understand any communication made to us. What the other person intends conveying is also warped by our own perceptions and judgements. Uncertainty not only affects perception but also makes people feel insecure. I believe that most people, individually and collectively, desire greater order. This may be for no better reason than that it makes life simpler and easier to manage. To the extent that people can predict with reasonable assurance how others will behave, to that extent their feelings of vulnerability are reduced and feelings of security strengthened.

One reason why conflicts are never resolved with any finality is that people, both individually and collectively, have memories. The 'resolution' of one phase of a conflict is only an event in a continuing history of which this event is also a part. An individual can opt out of a conflict. For example, if I find my neighbour too obstreperous, I can move house. But, countries cannot totally opt out of the international community: even isolationist countries, like Albania or Burma, have some dealings with the outside world; nor can countries run away from problems like boundary disputes or the rights of minority nationalities within their borders.

The environment in which a negotiation takes place also affects every aspect of the negotiating process; it provides reference points for comparison. In labour disputes, dissatisfactions arise from labour in one industry comparing its wage rates with labour in another. Countries enter arms races by comparing their arsenal with their neighbours'. Further, disparities in bargaining power can only be understood by referring to the inherent power an entity has in the environment. Political will — that is, the will to engage in a negotiation and to reach an agreement — is primarily a judgement made by a party about his status in the environment.

Nor can we afford to assume that in real negotiations time is irrelevant. The mere fact that a negotiation takes place by exchange of communication implies the passage of time during which significant changes may occur: a negotiation nearing agreement may break down, or a conflict may erupt into violence.

Chapters 2 to 5 are devoted to an examination of dissatisfaction, uncertainty of perception, environment, memory and time, using many examples from real life. A constant reference to real negotiations is necessary to avoid idealising it by making unwarranted assumptions. We must avoid the temptation of being Procrustean and chopping or stretching our facts to fit our theory, which we can then parade as a paradigm. The insistence on referring back to real life will necessarily mean some vagueness in the early chapters. This vagueness will, however, be eliminated when we develop a theory of negotiation in Part Two, and examine four of its aspects in Part Three.

Theory of Bargaining

Having criticised the theory of games for its shortcomings, I must explain how these are avoided in the approach adopted in this book. We shall incorporate irrationality and differing perceptions by looking at the negotiating process through the eyes of different negotiators (e.g. a buyer and a seller). We shall show how the perceptions and the expectations of the negotiators are modified by exchange of information between them, and graphs will be included to show how these changes can be plotted against time.

We shall start by examining how a person makes a choice. Though this is not a negotiation, it will help us to understand the concept of equality of dissatisfaction. We shall then take the simple case of buying potatoes in an oriental market — that is to say, a bargaining situation between two persons on a single issue. The analysis will show why some negotiations break down while others end in agreement. The where and when questions raised earlier can be answered by using equality of dissatisfaction, which will also provide an explanation for 'splitting the difference'. From two negotiators bargaining over a single issue, we shall extend the theory in two directions. The problem of negotiations involving more than one issue raises interesting questions such as the priority different negotiators attach to different issues and the functional relationships (i.e. linkages) between the issues. The analysis will lead to a clearer understanding of the well-known phenomena of 'trade-offs' and 'package deals'. The second extension of the theory covers negotiations with more than two parties. The analysis in Chapter 9 devoted to numbers will assist in understanding why coalitions form. Collusion, which is quite common in actual negotiations but rarely touched on in theories of bargaining, will also be examined.

Just as conflicts can be escalated, negotiations can also become more complex either by the addition of more issues or by the addition of more participants. The addition of new issues to a negotiation — called 'enlargement' in this book — has quite different effects on the negotiation compared with the increase in the number of participants, for which we shall use the term 'expansion' of the bargaining population. Any increase in the complexity of a negotiation makes an agreement less likely. We shall, therefore, consider the converse phenomena of contraction and reduction as vital steps for the limitation of conflicts.

Chapter 12 is devoted to bargaining power, because few theories of bargaining give it any importance, usually taking it for granted. We shall examine disparities in bargaining power as well as changes in it, because these affect the perceptions of the participants and influence the course of a negotiation. We shall also attempt to measure bargaining power. If dissatisfactions are to be ameliorated and vulnerabilities assuaged in order to limit conflicts, then the will to negotiate and the will to conclude agreements has to exist or has to be created; this is the subject of Chapter 13.

Because we shall treat time as a real dimension, we shall be able to identify the different phases of the negotiating process and understand why different negotiations break down at different times for different reasons.

A question normally posed is whether the proposed theory is normative, prescriptive, predictive or simply explanatory. From the emphasis I have laid on studying negotiations in real life, it is apparent that the theory is empirical. In erecting the basic structure of the theory, I shall first give some contrived examples, but then use everyday bargaining situations or examples from real negotiations. If, in the process, a generalised theory of bargaining emerges, well and good. To the extent that this general theory does not depart from reality, it will be predictive; otherwise, the aim of this study of bargaining is to derive lessons for the limitation of conflict, especially conflicts between states.

At this point it is necessary to say how the concepts employed in this book were developed. I did not select a variety of bargaining situations and then study them deductively until the concepts crystallised; nor did I first postulate them and then search for examples which would fit them. The process is as Medawar defined it: 'The activity that is characteristically scientific begins with an explanatory conjecture which at once becomes the subject of an energetic critical analysis.'[11]

Negotiating Situations

In this introductory chapter we have already used as examples a variety of situations (conflicts between individuals, labour disputes and international problems). I believe we can learn why governments employ certain tactics in negotiating an International Commodity Agreement (ICA) by analysing the bargaining in an oriental market. This is not to say that buying potatoes and onions is of the same importance and complexity as, say, states agreeing on quotas in a UN conference. However, similarities do exist. I therefore propose to use a wide spectrum of human relationships in the study of the bargaining process.

Seven different types of situation will be used. The first four are: (i) the oriental market; (ii) relationships within a family; (iii) relationships within an institution; and (iv) disputes between labour and management.

Whether it is buying carpets in Teheran, brass lamps in Tangier or even potatoes in India, every foreign tourist is earnestly advised to bargain when he goes to the 'mysterious' East. It is a process the rules of which are well understood.[12] Because it is so widespread and exemplifies many of the tactics of bargaining, we shall use it in the early stages of developing the theory.

In general, the scenario runs something like this. The seller is assumed to demand a price which is much higher than the price at which he is ultimately expected to part with his goods. Equally, the prospective buyer is expected to offer a price lower than what he is eventually prepared to pay. The process of bargaining consists of successive communications between the two which have the result of narrowing the difference between the initial bid and offer. The bargaining comes to an end when the exchange takes place at an agreed price or when both parties realise that there is no sale. There may be enactment of dramatic sub-scenes — pretended breakdowns, walking away, calling back, assurances of special favour, even pretended anger, appeals for sympathy to bystanders — every trick in the book can, and often is, used. All these tactics are also used by governments in negotiations![13]

Books on conflict and on game theory often use domestic situations as illustrative examples. Rapoport's *Fights, Games and Debates* has, in the chapter 'Friend and Foe', an example of a husband and wife with different preferences (mountains, seaside, ocean voyage) about where to go for their holiday.[14] The bargainers, being both friend *and* foe, have many things in common but also have some differences. Many negotiations between states are of this kind; there will be many co-operative linkages but also some issues where a conflict of interest is perceived. There is a lot in common between negotiating for a bride in the Ivory Coast and the kind of haggle which happens in the European Community over the price of dairy products or pig meat.

For most people, the next level where they negotiate continually (on sharing work, deciding who will go on holiday when, determining corporate policy, etc.) is the workplace. This is less tightly bound than a family, but is characterised by a clear-cut decision-making hierarchy. There are two reasons why such intra-institutional negotiations should be examined. When an organisation (the management) negotiates with another (the union), there is no unique participant, but, conceptually, we have to think of them as a single negotiating entity. Negotiating positions taken by collective bodies are usually the result of another set of negotiations between conflicting pressure and interest groups, some urging hostility and others peaceful settlement. The second reason for studying institutions is to try to understand what happens when there is no command structure or ultimate arbiter — a situation which obtains in international relations today.

The economic order inside a modern industrialised company depends on the extent to which it functions undisrupted by labour disputes. The environment plays an important role in negotiations between labour and employers. These disputes can end in a negotiated settlement, with or without the help of third parties, or there may be a strike followed by negotiations. In this sense, they resemble different kinds of negotiations between states — peaceful bilateral negotiation, settlement with mediation or conciliation and negotiation after a war. The crucial difference between the two is, of course, that labour disputes occur within a well-understood framework of national laws, while there is no such framework in international disputes.

I propose to divide negotiations between governments into three types. Negotiations between two governments ought to be the simplest, since there are only two parties; however, this is far from being true. No one would claim that a bilateral negotiation between the US and the USSR on arms limitation has the same level of simplicity as, say, the negotiation of a cultural agreement between France and the Ivory Coast. The other two types of negotiations are both multilateral, namely, those with more than two participating countries. I shall make a distinction between those occurring within an agreed treaty framework and those without one. GATT, ICAs, the North Atlantic Treaty and the Law of the Sea are only a few of the long list of multilateral treaties. A particularly important group is the set of treaties establishing the European Communities. The existence of a treaty framework implies the creation of a rule-system and the purpose of negotiations within them is to maintain the order so created.

But many multilateral negotiations also take place without the umbrella of an agreed treaty. Sometimes these are undertaken for the purpose of creating new rule-systems, a point of importance to increasing order by reducing uncertainty. Because we are concerned with the political economy of inter-state relations, I shall use both political and economic conflicts as illustrations. Two economic examples, the Britain/EEC Budget dispute and ICAs, will be used often. Many of the examples are from Britain and the United States, because of the availability of more information in English about conflicts in these countries and not because of any prejudice or predilection. If some judgements seem harsh, particularly in the chapters on violation of international law, it is because these countries are judged against the standards they proclaim to follow. This may be unfair but, inevitably, countries are judged by the standards they set for themselves. India, the country of Mahatma Gandhi, cannot complain if its recovery of Goa by military action evoked a greater shock than the total desecration and destruction of a centuries-old way of life in Tibet by China. Israel, after the Sabra and Chatila massacres, was judged by itself, and by others, against a much higher standard than the one used for its neighbours.

The International Order

The breakdown of any rule-system in the international political and economic order signifies a collapse of a part of that order. Small and big wars between states indicate a collapse of the international political order, locally, regionally or globally. Likewise, the collapse of the fixed exchange-rate system of the Bretton Woods Agreement indicated a failure of that part of the international economic order.

Most people do not think about international law, except when a political event happens — for example, the invasion of Grenada by the United States in 1983 prompted questions about the legality of intervention (whether it was in accordance with the OAS Treaty, and whether the Governor-General of a Commonwealth country had the legal right to invite a non-Commonwealth power to intervene). The questions were quickly forgotten and attention was again directed to international law only when another event happened — the use of chemical weapons in the Iran—Iraq War.

It is simplistic to assume that states will stop going to war if only we had a better international order which would give them what they 'deserve' without having to fight for it. First of all, states often go to war because they want something, not because they deserve what they want. Secondly, no two states agree on what is 'just'; justice too is a subjective concept. Thirdly, power is an important factor which states are tempted to use if they have it. Redressal of grievances will, of course, help to limit conflicts, but so long as the three conditions persist there can be room only for a conflict-limitation process, and not for one aiming at a stable universal peace.

However surprising it may seem, international law is obeyed by states most of the time. But the areas in which the law is obeyed, though extensive, are unexciting. Today, we take it for granted that letters posted in one country will be delivered in another; we can make transnational telephone calls and send telexes; trade takes place in ever-increasing volume between nations; ships carry cargoes, aircraft cross national boundaries carrying millions of passengers. We need to remind ourselves that all this activity could not happen without elaborate rule-systems and more or less consistent rule-obedience.

More international rule-systems have been created in the last 70 years than ever before; this is a consequence of growing interdependence. Susan Strange has described this succinctly:

> whereas it was once perceived that the only important issue likely to penetrate the shell of the nation state and directly affect the lives of individual men and women within it was war and peace — the order/disorder issue — it is now perceived that practically the whole range of political issues affecting the lives of individuals is subject to developments in the world system, especially in what has now become a world-wide system of production geared to the demands of a world market.[15]

The world of the 1980s is one of two contradictory forces. On the one hand is the desire for increasing order, particularly with the threat of nuclear war hanging over our heads. On the other, is the strong feeling of exclusive nationalism with its historically entrenched pattern of hostility. How willingly do states obey international law? When do they obey it? Why and how often do they violate it? These are all questions important for the maintenance of international order. Amicable settlements of disputes arising from dissatisfactions and grievances can be promoted by third-party intercession, such as mediation, conciliation, binding arbitration and adjudication. We shall, therefore, study in Part Four making and maintaining rule-systems as well as peaceful methods of settlement of disputes.

In Chapter 17 we shall summarise the lessons learnt from the study of the process of negotiation that could be of help in limiting conflicts. A theoretical study is of little value if we do not then proceed to apply the lessons to the conflict-ridden world of the last 15 years of the twentieth century. Chapter 18 is devoted to an analysis of the current environment, the conflicts that beset us (particularly the super-power nuclear arms race and the North—South conflict) and to suggestions on how we may attempt to limit them.

Some Observations and Reservations

Every book on political economy is a product of its time; this one is no exception. In conflict analysis, Schelling's *Strategy of Conflict* was written when the temperature of the Cold War was at its lowest; consequently he concentrated on deterrence, bluff, threats, and the game of 'chicken'. This book is the product of an environment of imminent nuclear holocaust, of the widening gap between the rich and poor nations, and the rise of absolutism in many parts of the world.

There are no simple solutions offered, no miraculous panacea that will make aggression, violence and war disappear. Complex phenomena involving human fears and hopes do not have ready-made solutions. There is an excitement about violence. Whether it is a football game or war, people want 'their' side to win. The reaction in Great Britain after the naval task-force steamed towards the Falklands and the reaction after the US marines landed in Grenada are proof of the suspension of critical faculties. 'My country, right or wrong' is the dominant emotion once a war is declared, even if most people are only passive spectators. Hatred of the perceived enemy is then easy to preach, hysteria easy to whip up. There is no need to cite examples — every religious, linguistic or territorial conflict has enough people ready and willing to escalate the violence.

The excitement violence produces makes the work of those who believe in its reduction more difficult. Fanatics are better able to propagate their views than those aware of shades of grey. French newspapers reported that, in a national television appearance, M. Le Pen, the leader of the National Front, came across better preaching racism than those who were opposed to him, partly because his opponents were aware of the complexity of the race question in France. Limitation of conflict does not have the kind of appealing simplicity that out-and-out belligerency or pure pacifism have.

The development of the theory of strategic deterrence in the US in the 1950s and 1960s owes a great deal to the concepts of active warfare. In this kind of conflict analysis the approach is confrontationist, the motivation is to extract compliance and the means, actual or threatened use of force. Roman Kolkowicz has pointed out an unfortunate consequence of concentrating on acute bipolar conflicts with a high potential for great violence: there ensued a poverty of theoretical deveopment on conflicts below the strategic and bipolar level.[16] In adopting negotiation as a mechanism for limiting some conflicts lower on the threat scale, the approach is conciliatory, the motivation is reduction of dissatisfaction and vulnerability and the means adopted is communication.

This book covers a wide spectrum of subjects: human aggression, psychology of perception, communication theory, cybernetics, arbitration and international law are merely the major ones. The justification for straddling so many disciplines is provided by Susan Strange, quoting Karl Popper (with Popper's emphasis): '*We are not students of some subject matter but students of problems.* And problems may cut right across the border of any subject matter or discipline.'[17]

Notes

1. News item, *Guardian*, 6 Sept. 1980.
2. Novy Kapadia, *The Hindustan Times Sunday Magazine*, 25 Oct. 1981.
3. News item, *Guardian*, 12 Jan. 1981.
4. Hilding Eek, 'Coercion vs. Voluntary Submission to the Law', *Thesaurus Acroasium*, vol. IV (*Modern Problems in International Law and Philosophy of Law: Miscellanea in Honour of Professor D.S. Constantopoulos)*, (Thessaloniki, Institute of International Public Law and International Relations, 1977), p. 205.
5. F.S. Northedge and M.D. Donelan, *International Disputes: The Political Aspects* (London, Europa Publications for the David Davies Memorial Institute for International Studies, 1971), p. 278. The rest of the paragraph owes a great deal to Chapter 12 of this book, pp. 278-96.
6. Samuel Gorovitz, *International Herald Tribune*, 16 Aug. 1983.
7. Michael Nicholson, *Conflict Analysis* (London, The English Universities Press, 1970), p. 76.
8. Thomas C. Schelling, *The Strategy of Conflict* (London, Oxford University Press, paperback edn, 1973), p. 5.
9. Nicholson, *Conflict Analysis*, p. 4.
10. Schelling, *Strategy of Conflict*, Appendix B, pp. 267-90.
11. P.B. Medawar, *The Art of the Soluble* (Pelican Books, 1969), p. 172.
12. For a perceptive but amusingly written description, see Jill Tweedie, 'Oh, you have to bargain . . . That's how they do things over there', *Guardian*, 8 May 1980.
13. In the arms control talks with the USSR, for a 'build down' of long-range weapons, the proposal of the US called for each side to scrap *two* old missile warheads for *one* new ICBM warhead, *a* bomber for *a* bomber, and *three for two* for new submarine-launched warheads. The US proposal was clearly an opening bid asking for more proportionate destruction of land-based missiles (of which the USSR had more) than submarine-based ones (of which the US had more). Had the USSR made a counter-proposal, it could have been similar to a buyer's offer, with proportionately more destruction of submarine-launched warheads than land-based ones. See *The Economist*, 17 March 1984.
14. Anatol Rapoport, *Fights, Games and Debates* (Ann Arbor, The University of Michigan Press, 1960), Chapter V, 'What if the Opponent is Both Friend and Foe?', pp. 166-79.
15. Susan Strange, 'Looking Back — But Mostly Looking Forward', in *Millenium: Journal of International Studies.* vol. II (1982) no. 1, p. 44.
16. Roman Kolkowicz, 'US and Soviet Approaches in Military Strategy: Theory vs. Experience', *Foreign Affairs*, Summer 1981, in *Strategic Digest* (New Delhi, Institute for Defence Studies and Analyses), vol. 11, no. 11, pp. 887-8.
17. Strange, 'Looking Back', p. 47. The quotation is from Karl Popper, *Conjectures and Refutations: The Growth of Scientific Knowledge*.

2 CONFLICT, AGGRESSION, BARGAINING AND NEGOTIATION

Eka Draviyabilashi, Dveshi.
(Enmity is born when the same wealth is coveted [by many].)
Sanskrit saying

Also where there is any lacke of ordere, nedes must be perpetuall conflicte.
Sir Thomas Elyot,
Boke Called the Governour (1531)

Conflict, bargaining and negotiation are words in such common currency that it might be thought superfluous to discuss what exactly we mean by them. But the fact that a word is widely used is no guarantee that its usage and comprehension are the same for everyone. An example is the word 'war'. Malinowski has defined war as an 'armed conflict, between two independent political units, by means of organized military force, in the pursuit of a tribal or national policy'.[1] By this definition, the state of armed conflict between Britain and Argentina over the Falkland Islands in May 1982 was war; but the British government, steadfastly denying that it was in a state of war with Argentina, described the action as 'hostilities', a 'dispute', etc. Another example is the term 'political will', which is often used to explain the failure of a negotiation: there was a 'lack of political will'. Any negotiation fails due to a variety of factors, and the complex interrelationship between them. To lump them all under the term 'will' is merely a case of a definition masquerading as an explanation. In order to make it easier to define such difficult terms, we have to start by being clear about the basic concepts.

Clausewitz is often misquoted as having said that war was a continuation of diplomacy by other means. A more accurate translation of his dictum would be, 'War is nothing more than the continuation of *state policy* by other means' (emphasis added). There is a lot of difference between furthering a state's political objectives by violent means and achieving them by diplomacy. War, far from being a continuation of diplomacy, is the result of the failure of diplomacy. Recently, the blurring of the distinction between war and non-aggression has become even more pronounced. Covert intervention by a great power in the internal affairs of another country is a hostile aggressive act, and is a kind of war — though it is rarely acknowledged as such. Words like 'weapon' are often used loosely: oil has become a 'weapon'; some people in the USA advocate the use of food as a 'weapon'. But the term 'Cold War', in spite of its apparent contradiction, has, with good reason, passed into the vocabulary because it expresses a state of affairs pithily, conveying an impression of glowing embers covered with ash that can be fanned into flames by a puff of wind — a delicate balance between apparent peace and conflagration. Is this state of conflict a prelude to negotiation or a prelude to war? Is the activity called 'threat of war', a prelude to the beginning of hostilities or is it a 'negotiating tactic' to avoid the hostilities? In short, where does negotiation end and violence begin?

Conflict

Examining what a theory of the strategy of conflict should deal with, Schelling says: 'The theory degenerates at one extreme if there is no scope for mutual accommodation, no common interest at all even in avoiding mutual disaster; it degenerates at the other extreme if there is no conflict at all and no problem in identifying and reaching common goals.'[2] Schelling calls this mixture of conflict and common interest a 'precarious partnership' and 'incomplete antagonism'. Unfortunately, his subsequent analysis is solely concerned with deterrence, 'the exploitation of potential force'. In my view, the area of conflict, co-operation and negotiation is much wider than the limited segment where there is an imminent threat of the use of force.

A better definition is given by Michael Nicholson: 'A conflict exists when two people wish to carry out acts which are mutually inconsistent.'[3] We shall adopt this definition with the understanding that 'people' also includes their collective institutions, organisations and nation states.

Some authors have tried to subdivide common interests into various categories; others have made a distinction between constructive conflicts and destructive ones. Creative tension is a form of conflict. We must also accept that conflict motivates innovation and change, though innovation sometimes produces high-yielding seeds and sometimes multiple independently-targeted nuclear missiles.

It seems to me that it is more useful to distinguish between voluntary and involuntary conflicts to understand the two ends of the spectrum. A buyer who wants to pay the lowest price and a seller who wants the highest attainable, want to carry out a mutually inconsistent transaction. But entering voluntarily into a conflict and bargaining situation for trading is not the same as, say, a wife faced with a demand for a divorce from her husband. Between states, negotiating a cultural agreement or tariff reduction are bargaining situations voluntarily created; a boundary dispute is not. However, in many conflict situations, one of the parties at least will be happy with the *status quo* and is drawn into the conflict by a demand for change from someone else.

While recognising the existence of different types of conflicts, we shall concern ourselves only with those which, even if they are not actually violent and disruptive, have a potential for becoming so. Violent disruptive action, in this context, will include all activities which have similarities with battles — a fight over market shares, a takeover battle waged by one company for another, strikes and lockouts, and civil war. All these involve defeating an 'enemy'. Before the disputants plunge into the battle, they would have been, in Rapoport's words, in a 'friend *and* foe' situation.

Bargaining and Negotiation

The terms 'bargaining' and 'negotiation' are considered synonymous in this book. The processes are identical, though usage may indicate a difference in the area of human activity. Bargaining is usually associated with trade and commerce, while negotiation is generally used for inter-state dealings. But this distinction is not always kept: we negotiate bills of exchange, we also talk about 'wage bargaining' and, at the same time, 'negotiations between employers and trade unions'.

Nicholson attempts a subtle distinction between bargaining and negotiation: 'The activity whereby two contending parties decide between themselves what actions to take, when some are better for one than for the other, is called bargaining. When it is done by explicit verbal communication, we refer to it as negotiation.'[4] In his view, negotiation is one aspect of the bargaining process, which may include other types such as 'tacit bargaining'. We shall not make such fine distinctions, but shall find room for 'tacit bargaining' elsewhere in our theory.

In his *Economics of Bargaining*, Cross defines bargaining as 'the voluntary process of distributing the proceeds from cooperation'.[5] Iklé defines negotiation as 'a process in which explicit proposals are put forward ostensibly for the purpose of reaching agreement on an exchange or on the realization of a common interest where conflicting interests are present'.[6] I give below the definitions for bargaining and negotiation from the *Oxford English Dictionary* (the definitions in *Webster* are very similar). These tell us more about the bargaining process than the definitions given above.

> Bargain: An agreement between two parties settling how much each gives and takes, or what each performs and receives in a transaction between them.
> Negotiation: To hold communication or conference (with another) for the purpose of arranging some matter by mutual agreement; to discuss a matter with a view to some settlement or compromise.

There are some crucial ideas embedded in the dictionary definitions. The process of bargaining or negotiation must have an element of give and take; there must be communication between the participants, implying a passage of time between the stages of the process.

What is the objective of the participants in entering into negotiations? Nicholson says, 'The goals of the parties are initially incompatible and the process of bargaining is to make them compatible.'[7] This is too wide, and begs the question of the type of goals in mind — short-term or long-term? Physical, philosophical or moral? For example, if the ultimate goal of the USSR is a universal socialist state based on Marxism—Leninism, an agreement on arms limitation will not make it compatible with the American goal of the universal pursuit of happiness by free competition. For limiting conflicts, we do not need to solve every single ideological or philosophical problem; most negotiations have the objective of arriving at an agreement in a limited area of activity.

Any definition of negotiation and bargaining has to include the following elements. *It is a peaceful process, entered into by two or more negotiants. The objective is to arrive at an agreement in a specified area of activity in which a conflict of interest is perceived. The process involves repeated mutual communication, conference or discussion, over a period of time. It may result in an agreement on an exchange or on a course of action comprising a set of activities which each will follow, or it may break down. If any participant perceives as unsatisfactory the results of the course of action agreed upon, further negotiations may follow.*

The definition is not succinct; nor is it meant to be. There is need for each of the elements. Even though there is a conflict of interest between the participants, the process of accommodation has to be peaceful, a better word than 'voluntary'. I have deliberately brought into the definition 'perception' and 'dissatisfaction' for reasons which will become clear in the next two chapters. I have used the word 'negotiant' to describe a participant in the process in preference to the more common 'negotiator'. A 'negotiant' may be an individual, organisation, institution or government; negotiators, in this book, are always individuals, representing either themselves or an organisation, and with varying competence and skills.[8] There is a final proviso to the effect that the agreement arrived at in any negotiation is maintained only for the period for which it is perceived to be satisfactory by the participants. The reason for this proviso is explained in Chapters 3 and 5.

Limits of Negotiation — Violent Disruption

War, in the sense of active armed hostilities, is *not* negotiation because it lacks two aspects central to negotiation: (i) during the hostilities, there is no consultation or discussion of the main issues which provoked the conflict — in fact, the parties are no longer negotiants but combatants; (ii) there is no element of give and take during a war; trying to beat the other party into submission does not include any element of concession by either. The objective of hostilities is to change the environment and the relative bargaining power.

To say that war, or similar disruptive activity, is not negotiation does not mean that no negotiations take place between the combatants. The combatants may engage in a number of limited negotiations. During a contested divorce, a couple can still negotiate on who will use the car on a given day; during a strike, there may be negotiations on maintenance of essential equipment. Local agreements to remove the dead and wounded or exchange prisoners are examples from wars between states. The negotiations which take place for limited objectives during a limited period of time are not central to the causes and objectives of the war itself; these occupy much smaller bargaining spaces compared with the much larger bargaining space in which the negotiations failed.

We now have the phenomenon of negotiations seeming to take place in one venue while the war is being fought elsewhere. The UN Security Council was publicly debating the Falkland Islands (Malvinas) while Argentina and Britain were fighting an actual land, sea and air war. The negotiations in the UN in such circumstances were either propaganda exercises or, at best, limited in bringing about a ceasefire in the hope of arranging later negotiations on the substantive issues.

I do not want to imply that the demarcation between the beginning of violent action and the end of negotiation is clear-cut and precise. Often, the petering-out of negotiation is accompanied by escalation towards violence. The steps by which the British government moved towards war while negotiating for the withdrawal of the Argentinian force were: sending a naval taskforce, declaring an exclusion zone, enforcing a siege, sinking an Argentinian cruiser, air raids, and eventually the actual landing on the Islands. In labour disputes, work-to-rule, go-slows and overtime bans may be used while negotiations continue. Sporadic violence and civil commotion may occur before civil war actually breaks out.

The border area between failure of negotiations and the outbreak of violence has fascinated most writers on conflict, especially in the context of nuclear deterrence. If war is not negotiation, is threat of war a part of the negotiating process? Or is it a signal of the end of negotiations? An ultimatum clearly signals the end of negotiations and is a call for a particular course of action without giving the other party any opportunity to negotiate about it. It implies: 'If you do not submit to my demands, I'll forcibly change the environment so that you'll have to accept them after losses.' A recent example was Iraq's demand, in the early stages of the Iran—Iraq War, that negotiations could take place only if Iran conceded to Iraq sovereignty over the Shatt-el-Arab river and contiguous areas. An unfulfillable precondition cannot fall within the definition of negotiation. An even more interesting example is the reported statement of an Argentine official: 'Sovereignty over Malvinas is neither a condition nor a precondition; it is outside the negotiations.' The military takeover of the Islands by Argentina was intended to achieve precisely this objective — the removal of the issue from the bargaining space by accomplishing a fact on the ground. Argentina having failed to achieve this, it is now Britain's turn to insist that sovereignty cannot be part of the negotiation.

The problem of deciding whether negotiations have collapsed becomes more complicated when we consider deterrence, especially nuclear deterrence. In so far as the aim of a policy of deterrence is the *prevention* of war, it must belong to the negotiating process. It is still a communication, even if it means: 'Whatever my losses, your losses will be unacceptable to you.' From a policy of deterrence to one of brinkmanship, one traverses an area where the end of negotiation and the beginning of hostilities becomes unclear. It is in this area that accidents and mistakes in perception may tilt it from one to other. While it is important to study this area, it is well-tilled ground. I believe it is equally important to explore the other end of the spectrum — the area where dissatisfaction about an agreed set of rules leads to their deliberate violation.

Limits of Negotiation — Agreed Rules

If violent disruption lies at one extreme of the area covered by negotiation, voluntary obedience lies at the other. (By voluntary obedience is meant the implementation of the course of action agreed upon in a rule-system governing a specific activity.) Most people obey rules not merely because of the threat of punishment (the coercive aspect) but also because they feel, instinctively, that it is 'right' to do so (the submissive aspect).[9] I have qualified obedience with the adjective 'voluntary' because there can be other kinds of obedience — unwilling obedience, and obedience under duress. The best example of voluntary obedience is the defence services in volunteer (i.e. not conscripted) armies; one does not question an order in the Army even if it carries the danger of loss of life. Discipline in the forces is born out of a sense of collective security, habit, training and the psychology of the group.

At the other extreme, slavery is obedience under constant

duress. If obedience is procured solely by coercion, there is no negotiation between the power-holder and the coerced. In Chapter 1, I cited the example of a long-suffering wife suddenly ending her subjugation by hitting her tyrannical husband with a heavy object. This is not a lone example: newspapers often report such acts of violence under these headlines: 'Student killed "bullying" father for kicking dog'; 'Slave son who shot dead his parents given freedom to start new life'; 'Sisters stabbed drunken and violent father.'[10]

In addition to violence and negotiation, a third course is also available; one can run away from a conflict. To take a not entirely hypothetical example, consider a dictatorial husband who threatens his wife: 'If my tea is not on the table when I get home from work, I'll wallop you!' If a wallop does follow the first few transgressions, the wife's subsequent obedience is obtained under duress.[11] If the wife's suppressed unhappiness continues to increase, she may (i) remonstrate with her husband (enter into negotiations); (ii) hit him on the head with a heavy object (become violent); or (iii) run away from home. Unfortunately, the choice of running away from a conflict becomes difficult for institutions with continuing relationships, and for governments. An employer can, perhaps, 'run away' from a labour dispute by declaring bankruptcy; but the trade union, even after a strike, has to come back to the same employer. Countries cannot remove themselves from geophysical problems, although there have been a few cases (e.g. Albania and Burma) of nations trying to remove themselves from the international arena. Rare though it may be, sometimes a conflict between two communities is temporarily avoided by exchange of population; the transfer of populations between Greece and Turkey after 1925 is one example. But such moves only give rise to new conflicts, though the subsequent ones may be less violent than the one averted.

Just as there is a grey area between the end of negotiations and the beginning of violence, there is also a grey area between complete voluntary obedience to a rule and the beginning of negotiation to change that rule. This is the area of a series of steps expressing dissatisfaction with the operation of the rule, sending signals, negotiations about negotiations and, eventually, violations of the agreed rule. Except for negotiations about negotiations, the rest are what Schelling calls 'tacit bargaining', 'bargaining in which communication is incomplete or impossible'. The examples he gives are: 'limited war, ... limited competition, jurisdictional manoeuvres, jockeying in a traffic jam, or getting along with a neighbour one does not speak to'.[12] None of these can be called bargaining as we have defined it. Since communication is an integral part of the negotiating process, there is no negotiation when there is little or no communication. War is war, whether limited or otherwise, and the objective of limited war or jockeying for position is to change the environment and bargaining power before entering into negotiations. Only by stretching logic to its breaking point can we say that jockeying in a traffic jam is 'bargaining' — tacit or accompanied by oaths and imprecations!

The Area of Conflict and Negotiation

Acceptance of the *status quo*, changing it by peaceful negotiation, taking violent action to change it by force and opting out are the four courses of action open to parties who perceive a conflict between themselves. These are represented schematically in Figure 2.1. (For obvious reasons, one cannot represent running away from a problem in it.)

In Figure 2.1, three areas are identified, with the state of the entities (violent disruption, commotion, obedience) at the top. The nature of the action (war and similar acts, brinkmanship and negotiation) is shown at the bottom. The area to the extreme right, called peaceful change, is one where most people are satisfied with the existing order and rules are maintained by punishing the infrequent transgressor. There is order of a kind under subjugation; there is so-called peace at the end of violent hostilities. But clearly, the middle area is the area of conflict and negotiation. Within this area lie the conflicts which, if not pushed towards peace by negotiation, will lead to aggressive action.

The area of conflict is also one where the feelings of the participants are likely to be dissatisfaction, insecurity, frustration, vulnerability and desperation. We see from the figure that there can be different kinds of dissatisfaction. The unhappiness of a coerced individual or population is quite different from the dissatisfaction of a member of a treaty with one of the agreed rules. The latter could be alleviated by rational negotiation; in the former, both the coercer and the victim will have deep emotional antagonisms. Likewise, as one moves in the process of negotiation to war

28 *Conflict, Aggression, Bargaining and Negotiation*

Figure 2.1: Aggression, Conflict, Negotiation and Order

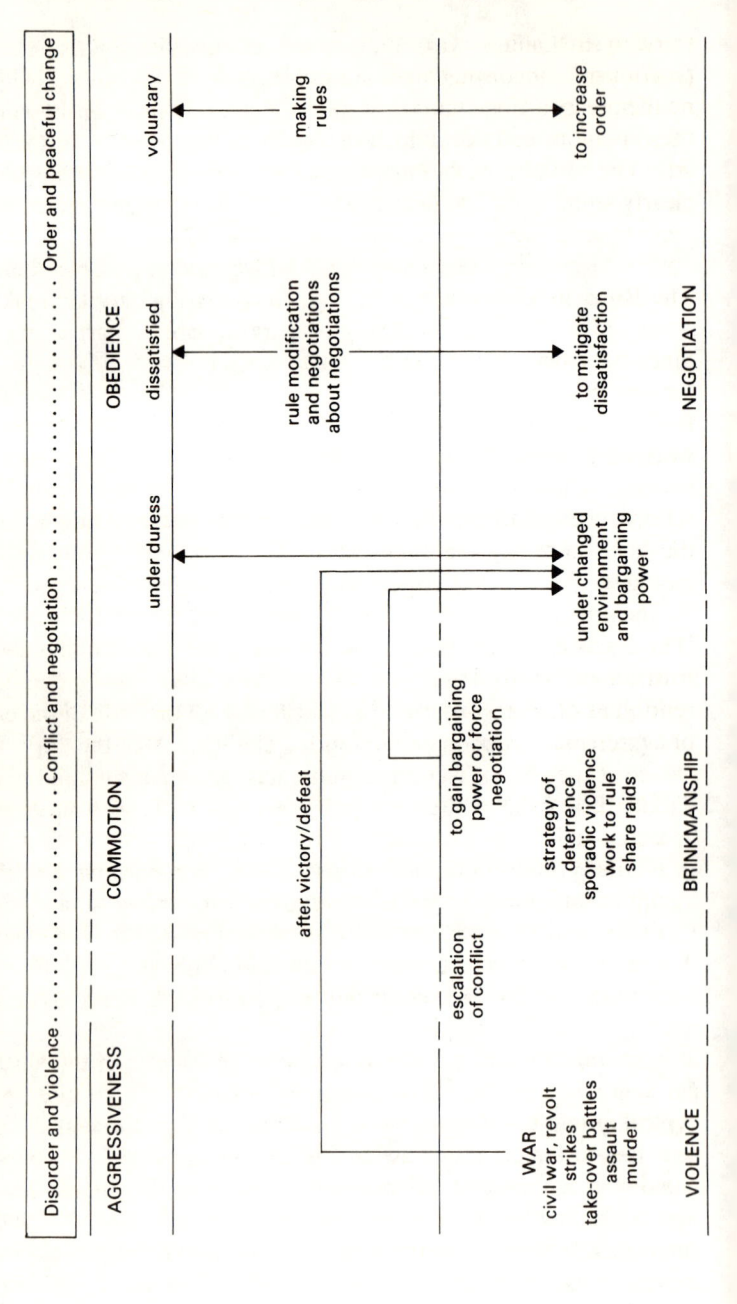

Disorder and violence .... Conflict and negotiation .... Order and peaceful change

AGGRESSIVENESS	COMMOTION	OBEDIENCE	
	under duress	dissatisfied	voluntary

escalation of conflict

after victory/defeat

to gain bargaining power or force negotiation

strategy of deterrence
sporadic violence
work to rule
share raids

under changed environment and bargaining power

rule modification and negotiations about negotiations

to mitigate dissatisfaction

making rules

to increase order

WAR
civil war, revolt
strikes
take-over battles
assault
murder

VIOLENCE — — — BRINKMANSHIP — — — NEGOTIATION

through the stage of brinkmanship, more and more emotion (patriotism, jingoism, hysteria) enter into the conflict. Though neither reason nor emotion is ever totally absent in any conflict, there is more emotion and less reason as we move from right to left. The mixture of rationality and irrationality in negotiation is clearly seen.

The Road to Violence

Since we intend to analyse the techniques, however imperfect, for limiting conflicts, we have to digress briefly into the controversial field of human aggression. Starting with Konrad Lorenz's classic work on aggression,[13] many theories for the causes of aggressive or violent behaviour have been propounded. Basically, the two schools of thought are the 'frustration—aggression hypothesis' and the 'man is biologically an aggressive animal' hypothesis. Sociobiologists like Edward Wilson take a middle position.[14]

The frustration—aggression hypothesis can be put as follows: 'The occurrence of aggression always presupposes the existence of frustration. Frustration produces instigations to a number of different types of response one of which is an instigation to some form of aggression.'[15] On the other hand, Anthony Storr holds that:

> The theory that aggression is nothing but a response to frustration is no longer tenable in the light of biological research.... It is vitally important that we finally discard the kind of futile optimism which is implied in the frustration—aggression hypothesis, and face the fact that, in man, as in other animals, the aggressive drive is an inherited constant, of which we cannot rid ourselves and which is absolutely necessary for survival.[16]

It is an unfortunate sign of our times that the more popular works on aggression all favour the biological imperative hypothesis. A typical example is Robert Ardrey's *Territorial Imperative.* The violent behaviour of groups in football matches is now serialised in Sunday magazines as an example of biological warfare on the sports ground. Whether the writer intends it or not, in such popular writings there is a justificatory or exculpatory element. Human beings cannot help being violent; therefore, people are not responsible for their violent behaviour and the consequent harm they cause to others. However, Storr's criticism of the frustration—aggression hypothesis as 'futile optimism' is valid because there is the imputation that if only frustration were removed, there would be no human aggression.

The biological imperative theory also has its critics, a cogent and convincing exposition being Ashley Montagu's *The Nature of Human Aggression*.[17] I shall mention here only two arguments which seem to me to be important. The biological imperative theory underestimates the value people attach to order and also ignores the spiritual dimension of human existence — man is not just an aggressive, competitive, territorial animal. It needs no elaborate justification to prove that human beings are also motivated by charity, altruism and self-sacrifice. To ignore a few millennia of philosophic and mystical experience is to do us all an injustice.

In adjusting to living in societies, human beings accept not only laws but also codes of ethical behaviour. They are willing to accept some constraints in their individual goals for the sake of something perceived as the 'collective good'. For the purpose of analysing how to limit conflicts, we can say that there is some validity in both the frustration—aggression and the biological imperative hypotheses. We can agree that people react violently when they are frustrated, but we need not agree that all frustrations have to end in violence. From the other theory, we may accept that aggression has other causes apart from frustration. Violent action may be due to psychological reasons born out of fear, anger or greed, the insecurity which breeds them sometimes having biological origins.

At the risk of some simplification — and with a number of reservations — I suggest that we may consider the following two sequences as those likely to result in violent behaviour:

Dissatisfaction ⟶ Frustration ⟶ Desperation ⟶ Violence
Dependence ⟶ Vulnerability ⟶ Fear ⟶ Violence

I do not assert that these are the only two sequences and that all aggressive behaviour, both individual and collective, can be fitted neatly into one or the other. For example, it is said that many parents who batter their children were themselves battered when *they* were children. There are also cases of killings without any reason, especially by mass murderers. We do, however, need to understand that violence has its own sequence. Vendetta killing and Mafia-type gang warfare have their own logic of escalation. I need quote only two examples to show that an unstoppable pattern of violence can become established in communities.

> The Provisional IRA announced on Thursday 23 January 1981 that they had killed the former Speaker of the Northern Ireland Parliament, Sir Norman Strong ... The attack was clearly direct retaliation for last week's gun attack on the former Westminster MP, Mrs Bernadette McAliskey and her husband Michael. ... The McAliskey attack followed the murder of a number of leading Republicans during the last year.[18]

We shall have to go far back to find out when and how this sequence started.

The second example is a brief extract from Robert Fisk's account of the sequence of massacres in Lebanon:

> On 18 January 1976 the Phalangists ... moved into Karantina [near Beirut] and slaughtered thousands of inhabitants ... gunning down women, children and old men as they stood. ... Two days later, the first Palestinian units broke into Damour as thousands of inhabitants fled to the beaches. ... But at least 350 Christians stayed behind. ... [All but 20] were civilians, families for the most part with three or four children ... The civilians were lined up against the walls of their own homes and sprayed with machine-gun fire. ... Seven months later the Phalange too had their revenge for Damour, breaking into the Beirut Palestinian camp of Tel al-Zaatar. They killed up to four thousand Palestinians.[19]

Where there is such an entrenched pattern of repeated violence, the conflict-limitation approach advocated in this book will be applicable — if at all — only in the very long run; if the cycle of violence can be arrested, if one can then go back one step to the causes of fear, if we can then build a modicum of trust, and then go back still further and remove the causes of insecurity — it is a long and forbidding series of 'ifs'.

Nations become violent because they want something, because they are afraid, or because they perceive a real or imagined affront to their 'national honour'. A curious additional cause — boredom with peace — is given by J.B. Priestley as a reason for Britain going to war in the Crimea: 'The people of all classes, except the Quakers and a small group of Liberal pacifists, wanted a war; they demanded glory, excitement, wonderful news, bloodstirring events. There had been close upon forty years of peace, and they had enough of it. ... John Bull was now hysterical.'[20] So long as people find certain types of violence exciting, the two sequences proposed above can account only for a part of aggressive behaviour.

Another reservation about the two sequences is that everything that is true of individual aggressive behaviour need not necessarily be true of collective aggression. Individual acts of violence have complex psychological causes. Collective acts of violence, like riots and massacres, may sometimes have spontaneous irrational causes. Wars between states, on the other hand, are assumed to have some rationality — nations may fight out of anger or pique, but reason is never supposed to be totally absent.

There is also no inevitability in the progression from one stage to the next in the two sequences. Individuals are sometimes said to lead lives of 'quiet desperation'. Subject people too may suffer frustration and desperation for generations before erupting into violent behaviour. How much force is used to back intransigence determines the rate of regression towards violence. The repression of the black community under apartheid in South Africa prevents one kind of violence from erupting by the use of another kind of violence. A last reservation — to be explained later — is that the two sequences are not really independent.

The Two Sequences

The first sequence, from dissatisfaction to violence, is an extension of the frustration—aggression hypothesis, to the extent we have accepted it as valid. Since human beings, living in a society, prefer order, they accept rules. But in the application of any rule, someone is bound to feel dissatisfied with the fruits obtained. Strongly-felt dissatisfaction is often voiced, and if nothing is done about it, frustration sets in. If no notice is taken of the frustration, some of those affected may become so desperate that they resort to violence. An example is the dissatisfaction, voiced over many years, by the people of the Indian north-eastern state of Assam at the influx of 'foreigners' (people from other parts of India and from neighbouring Bangladesh). The dissatisfaction was primarily an economic one, based on the perception that the foreigners were taking away jobs that could have gone to native Assamese. Since the free movement of people within India could not legally be obstructed, little could be done to ameliorate their frustration. Eventually this turned into desperation, particularly among university students, who felt the threat of unemployment after graduation most keenly. The desperation finally erupted into violence. Up to the time of writing this passage (May 1984), no solution has been found which could take cognisance of the frustration of the Assamese while, at the same time, preserving the right of all Indian citizens to live where they please.

The sequence from dissatisfaction to disruptive action (i.e. a strike) is clearly seen in labour disputes. The workforce becomes dissatisfied with prevailing wages either because they find other workers getting higher wages or because they perceive a drop in real income due to inflation. Discontent at not being given adequate wage rises becomes frustration if the workers feel that they have been losing steadily over the years with every wage settlement. They resort to work-to-rule, go-slows, one-day stoppages, and eventually to a complete strike. It is often argued that the additional wages gained *after* a strike fail to compensate for the wages lost *during* the strike. Such arguments rarely carry much weight with the strikers; when an aggressive action occurs as a result of deep-seated frustration, rational arguments cease to have an impact. When the Royal College of Nurses, by tradition averse to strike action, was forced to contemplate it, the change came about because of the frustration at having fallen behind other health workers over many years, and the perception that their self-denial was being exploited.

The second sequence, from dependence to violence, may appear less obvious but is, nevertheless, quite common. There are many examples of dependence inducing feelings of vulnerability and fear in groups of people or states. A classical historian has pointed out that Pericles founded the city of Thurii in southern Italy in the 440s because the forest of Sila in the hinterland was a valuable timber source; the Athenians launched their invasion of Sicily in 415 because they faced a timber-supply crisis.[21] The action of the OPEC countries in quadrupling the price of oil brought home suddenly to the industrial nations how dependent they had become on imports for their energy supplies from an area perceived as unstable. This dependence made them feel vulnerable and there were immediate outcries against 'cartelisation' (i.e. foreigners 'ganging up' against them). Because OPEC had been successful, they feared that other raw material-producing nations would form similar organisations, though there was little likelihood of this. Not only the media, but academics and prestigious international organisations all exhibited symptoms of hysteria. Power changes in Iran further worsened this fear, and from this arose the demand for war-like action to take over the oilfields in the Gulf.

The dependence of the poor countries on the rich industrialised countries is well known.[22] Many poor countries are dependent for their export earnings on one or two commodities, whose markets shrink continuously and whose prices either fluctuate widely or fall steadily. Very often a multinational company, belonging to one of the rich countries, controls the production, distribution and marketing; sometimes speculators in far-off countries wreak havoc on the markets. If the developing countries try to escape the servitude of being only raw materials exporters by increasing their exports of industrial products, they find themselves thwarted. The poor are always the victims of any upheaval in the system. When powerful OPEC confronts the equally powerful OECD countries over the price of oil, the main sufferers are the non-oil-producing, developing countries. The poor countries have to depend on the rich for aid from the governments and loans from the banks; increasing interest rates mean they have to pay back far more for their borrowings than they had planned. This vulnerability makes them feel insecure. This is a conflict which has not yet reached the stage of violence on an international scale, though there are some rumblings of disruptive action in the suggestion that the developing countries with very large debts should collectively repudiate them — an action fraught with grave consequences for the international economic order.

The violence in Northern Ireland, in which the insecurity of two groups of people, and their mutual fear, plays a major part, and the aggressive acts of Israel against its neighbours are only two examples of the close relationship between aggressive behaviour and feelings of vulnerability. The theories of deterrence in US strategic thinking also clearly demonstrate the close connection between aggressive behaviour and feelings of vulnerability. A Rand Corporation study stated: 'Deterrence stability (hence security) is best served by a strategic environment of mutual vulnerability.'[23] This is almost an equation: mutual vulnerability = mutual security. This leads to MAD (mutually assured destruction) doctrines. I find it difficult to accept that the best means of reducing feelings of insecurity is to *increase* the vulnerability of the parties.

Earlier I remarked that the two sequences are not really independent. The case of the Assamese students can either be seen as frustration born out of dissatisfaction due to shrinking job opportunities, or as a case of fear at the threat to their way of life due to the different culture brought in by the foreigners. The super-power conflict can be seen either as frustration born out of an inability to exercise unfettered power over other nations, or as a case of fear of a threat to their way of life. The rational and the irrational, the pragmatic and the psychological, are usually mixed up.

As a human activity, negotiation is a peaceful method for accommodating a perceived conflict of interest. We cannot pinpoint exactly when a conflict will erupt into disruptive aggression; it is precisely these borderline areas which are sensitive to small changes. When dissatisfaction is greatest, a small negative change may swing the conflict towards violence. A small dissatisfaction, in the vicinity of an agreed rule, can possibly be ameliorated through the negotiating process. In Chapter 3 we shall examine the concept of dissatisfaction in greater detail.

Notes

1. Bronislaw Malinowski, 'An Anthropological Analysis of War', *American Journal of Sociology*, 46 (1941): 521-50.
2. Thomas C. Schelling, *The Strategy of Conflict* (London, Oxford University Press, 1973), p. 15.
3. Michael Nicholson, *Conflict Analysis* (London, The English Universities Press, 1970), p. 2.
4. ibid., p. 67.
5. J.G. Cross, *The Economics of Bargaining* (New York, Basic Books, 1969).
6. Fred Charles Iklé, *How Nations Negotiate* (New York, Harper & Row, 1964), pp. 3-4.
7. Nicholson, *Conflict Analysis*, p. 4.
8. To cite an example from a labour dispute, the *Times* management and the NGA (the National Graphic Association, one of the unions involved in the dispute) were the two negotiants; the managing director of Times Newspapers Ltd and the chapel father were the negotiators.
9. See Hilding Eek, 'Coercion vs. Voluntary Submission to the Law', *Thesaurus Acroasium*, vol. IV (*Modern Problems in International Law and Philosophy of Law: Miscellanea in Honour of Professor D.S. Constantopoulos*) (Thessaloniki, Institute of International Public Law and International Relations, 1977), p. 205. Professor Eek cites a number of authors: 'Timasheff ... has

36 *Conflict, Aggression, Bargaining and Negotiation*

maintained that coercion is ... only one root of the efficiency of the law; the other is socio-economic pressure. ... Leon Petrazhitsky goes further, denying that sanctions belong to essential elements of law; apprehension of punishment is not the reason why the great majority of people do not commit crime but inner motivations ("law convictions").'

10. Headlines from *Guardian*, 11 Feb. 1982; *The Times*, 26 March 1983; and *Guardian*, 18 Jan. 1980.

11. See *Observer*, 30 May 1982, p. 11. In the case of Mrs X, who brought a private prosecution in Scotland against three youths who raped and then mutilated her, the newspaper reporting on the trial added; 'She had a row with her boyfriend [now her husband] because his tea wasn't ready. There was a "bit of a skirmish", she said, in a neighbour's flat, during which a hatchet was produced.'

12. Schelling, *Strategy of Conflict*, p. 53.

13. Konrad Lorenz, *On Aggression*, reproduced in Edwin I. Megargce and Jack E. Kokason (eds), *The Dynamics of Aggression* (New York, Harper & Row, 1970; and New York, Harcourt, Brace & World, 1966).

14. Edward O. Wilson, *On Human Nature* (Bantam Books, 1979): 'The clear perception of human aggressive behaviour as a structured, predictable pattern of interaction between genes and environment is consistent with evolutionary theory. It should satisfy both camps in the venerable nature—nurture controversy' (p. 108).

15. J. Dolland, L.W. Doob, N.E. Miller, O.H. Mowrer and R.R. Sears, *Frustration and Aggression* (Yale University Press, 1939).

16. Anthony Storr, *Human Aggression* (Pelican Books, 1970), p. 148.

17. Ashley Montagu, *The Nature of Human Aggression* (London, Oxford University Press, 1976).

18. Newspaper reports c. 23 Jan. 1981.

19. Robert Fisk, 'Damour: The Story of Lebanon Now', *The Times*, 10 Sept. 1983.

20. J.B. Priestley, *Victoria's Heyday* (London, Heinemann, 1972).

21. *The Times*, 12 Sept. 1983. The item refers to Robert Meiggs, *Trees and Timber in the Ancient Mediterranean World.*

22. The literature is extensive. 'Partners in Development', the Report of the Pearson Commission and the Brandt Commission Reports are well-known. For *dependencia* and related theories, see authors like Carlos F. Diaz-Alejandro. The documents of UNCTAD, especially the conference documents, have many papers on inequality and asymmetry in North—South relations.

23. Quoted in Roman Kolkowicz, 'US and Soviet approaches in Military Strategy: Theory vs. Experience ', *Foreign Affairs*, Summer 1981, in *Strategic Digest* (New Delhi, Institute for Defence Studies and Analyses), vol. 11, no. 11, pp. 887-8.

3 DISSATISFACTION AND VULNERABILITY

> Game theory leads to some genuine impasses, that is, to situations where its axiomatic base is shown to be insufficient for dealing with certain types of conflict situations. These impasses set up tensions in the minds of people who care.
> Anatol Rapoport,
> *Fights, Games and Debates* (p. 242)

There are a number of reasons why I consider dissatisfaction to be a useful concept in my approach to a theory of bargaining. We noted earlier that dissatisfactions could be tackled more rationally when these occur near the area where order prevails. By the time a feeling of dependence gives way to a feeling of insecurity or vulnerability we are obliged to look for psychological remedies too.

Satisfaction may accrue to the negotiants when there is a successful conclusion to a negotiation. But, in my view, there would have been no need for the bargaining to begin unless there was a dissatisfaction in at least one of the potential negotiants. I am also not convinced that total and complete satisfaction results at the end of any negotiation. More often than not, there is a residue of dissatisfaction in the negotiants; this residue has consequences for the future. This is really paraphrasing the point made in Chapter 1 about total and complete resolution of any human conflict being a chimera. Likewise, complete satisfaction for all negotiants is a myth or, at best, a mathematical convenience.

I mention mathematical convenience because the approach of economists to bargaining has been based on 'utility' or satisfaction. When von Neumann propounded his game theory, it was, indeed, revolutionary[1], that it has become a widely-accepted approach in bargaining, statistics and military science is a tribute to its originality and power. If I disagree with its application to the human activity called bargaining, it is only because I find that, beyond a point, it becomes unproductive.

Since the evolution of a conflict is affected by a breakdown as well as by an agreement we shall consider the levels of dissatisfaction at the end of a negotiation whatever the nature of the outcome as well as the hypothesis that equalisation of dissatisfaction determines when a negotiation ends in an agreement.

The Commencement of Negotiations

Rapoport, in his *Fights, Games and Debates*,[2] has discussed extensively the limitations of game theory for constructing models of human behaviour in conflict situations. One of his examples, referred to briefly in Chapter 1, described the situation where a husband and wife enjoy each other's company but their preferences about where to spend their annual holiday differ. The wife, let us say, likes to take her holidays in the mountains, the husband prefers an ocean voyage; the seaside is the second choice for both. Rapoport has analysed the problem with three different assumptions and the conclusions are as follows:

> (i) If the couple discuss the problem rationally, the 'fair' compromise is the obvious one of the holiday being taken at the seaside; neither gets the first or last preference, both plumping for the second option.
> (ii) If the husband is not interested in a compromise but simply announces that he has booked a cruise, irrespective of whether the wife chooses to accompany him or not, then the wife can cut her losses and go on the cruise, or she can call his bluff by stating equally firmly that she has booked a holiday in the Alps. Rapoport concludes: 'The game has been reduced to a battle of wills not wits.'
> (iii) If the two do not discuss the problem but make their own arrangements independently, two outcomes are possible: both can reason to themselves that the 'fair' solution would be the second option and thus come to the same conclusion as if they had discussed it rationally beforehand, or, they can make a sacrifice. If they love each other deeply, each can try to please the other by going on a holiday that he or she least prefers. Rapoport calls this 'misplaced altruism'.

Although Rapoport has given a game theory veneer to his analysis by starting off with an arbitrary matrix of pay-offs, the situation is not really susceptible to such analysis. Only when the two behave totally rationally — either by discussing beforehand or by reasoning independently what the other would like or dislike — does the matrix yield a 'correct' solution. If one behaves irrationally by an overbearing attitude, the game deteriorates into a battle of wills. If either or both behave altruistically, their behaviour has little to do with the utility ordering of the choice of holiday. We also note that the 'correct' solution is the one which most people would consider a 'fair' solution. We can never get away from fairness and unfairness in conflict situations.

Let us look at the same situation another way. For both husband and wife, there is an element of dissatisfaction in *every* choice. If the husband goes to the mountains and the wife does not go with him, they are both dissatisfied at the loss of the other's company. If they adopt the 'preferred' middle solution, they are both still dissatisfied at not having gone to their most favoured location. It is the very existence of the set of dissatisfactions that gave rise to the conflict in the first place. We also see that, at the end of the negotiations, on reaching agreement, there is a residue of dissatisfaction in one or both the parties.

The negotiations between Britain and the other partners in the European Community on the level of Britain's contributions to the EEC Budget, began only because Britain was dissatisfied and voiced this loudly. At first, France refused even to discuss the question. The Commission of the Communities, which may be assumed to have a somewhat objective view of the good of the group as a whole, could not perceive even the *existence* of a solution, let alone propose one. There was no question, at that stage, of assigning 'utilities' to the outcome of the negotiations when even the beginning of substantive negotiations was in doubt. Instead of attempting the impossible job of assigning utilities to a negotiation that was yet to begin, it is better to accept that before any negotiation can commence, dissatisfaction must be present in at least one of the potential negotiants.

This hypothesis is applicable to the other five types of bargaining situations used in this book. In all commercial transactions, the archetype of which is the oriental market, we can see that the buyer at least has a dissatisfaction — he wants or needs the product he sets out to buy. It is not necessary to argue that the seller also has a dissatisfaction in wanting to dispose of his stock, though that may also be true. In the case of other everyday negotiating situations, particularly in the workplace, there are always elements of dissatisfaction. Distributing workloads often has to be done because one employee feels that he or she is doing more than a 'fair' share. Even policy decisions at the level of a company's board of directors start because different members may be unhappy with different aspects of the company's performance — its market share, its profitability, or with its acquisitions and disposals.

Most labour disputes begin with a *demand* from labour, an indicator of their dissatisfaction. While the dissatisfaction may be about the actual level of their own emoluments, very often it is about their wages in relation to those of other workers. The importance of differentials (the take-home wages of one group of workers as compared to another group within the same establishment or type of industry) was amply demonstrated in *The Times* dispute when machine managers insisted on the differential being maintained between themselves and the machine assistants. Demands for changes in work practices arise from a dissatisfaction of the management about productivity levels not being adequate to maintain a competitive position.

Many kinds of bilateral inter-governmental negotiations — visa abolition agreements, extradition treaties, trade and transit agreements — have dissatisfaction as a cause. A commercial agreement — say, exchanging tariff preferences — has as a cause the perception that the existence of import duties reduces the market in the other country. One type of treaty which gives rise to some difficulty is the conclusion of cultural exchange agreements, providing for exchange of academics, books, cultural troupes, films, etc. It is a situation where the negotiants appear to be aware of an increase in total welfare before the negotiation commences.[3] If the negotiants perceive the possibility of an increase in welfare, not attaining it induces a dissatisfaction.

The idea that absence of an attainable goal creates dissatisfaction is not far-fetched. Expressions like 'keeping up with the Joneses', 'rising expectations' and 'demonstration effect' prove that it is widespread. Advertising has as its aim the creation of a want, dissatisfaction arising from which is alleviated only when one goes out and buys. Differentials in wage structures and 'keeping up with the Joneses' are examples of dissatisfactions arising from comparing one's lot with others' in the same environment. Such a comparison is the cause of arms races and nuclear proliferation.

The classic exposition of arms races is by Lewis Richardson and it is unnecessary to repeat its arguments here. Were he alive today, nuclear proliferation would have provided him with the best example. If the US makes an atom bomb, the Soviet Union follows suit; therefore, China has to have one too. If Britain is a nuclear power, France wants to become one. Because China has the bomb, some Indians feel they have to have it also. It follows that some Pakistanis feel insecure without it. If Israel has the technology to make the weapon, some Arab countries want to acquire that technology. Such a competitive reaction is also true of vertical proliferation. If the United States develops a hydrogen bomb, because the Soviet Union had already caught up with it in making an atom bomb, the USSR also goes in for thermo-nuclear weapons — and China, Britain and France follow suit. If the US puts multiple warheads in a nuclear missile, so does the USSR. If, then, the US independently targets the warheads (MIRVs), the USSR follows. If one side has nuclear submarines, the other builds them too. The dismal saga of nuclear proliferation — both horizontal and vertical — is an unrelieved history of keeping up with the Joneses. The dissatisfaction in these cases is more vulnerability and fear; the two sequences, described in Chapter 2, are inseparable.

Negotiations about Negotiations

The most interesting example of dissatisfaction being the cause of multilateral negotiations without an overall agreed framework is the so-called North—South dialogue on the new international economic order (NIEO). The developing countries collectively perceive the existing international economic order as an unfair one, because they feel that the gains from it are distributed inequitably. The developed industrialised nations, on the other hand, deny the existence of any such in-built unfairness. Since the early 1960s, the two groups have been talking about whether there is really any need for change. To date, the dissatisfaction of the developing countries has not even been recognised as being legitimate and needing corrective action.

In this dialogue, the two groups are clearly not negotiating about the same thing. The developing countries have proposed sweeping changes in every sector of the international economic order — commodity trade, industrial development, transfer of technology, development assistance, shipping and the institutions which supervise the order. The reply of the industrialised countries is, in essence, that there is no need to negotiate in these bargaining spaces at all; they are quite happy with the way things are. However, in order that they may not appear too intransigent, they propose preconditions about 'not interfering with the autonomy of existing institutions'. Put more clearly, this means discussing the international monetary system in the IMF, development assistance in the World Bank, trade in GATT, and so on. The rich countries want to confine the negotiations to those bargaining spaces where they already have superior bargaining power.

The developing countries often deplore the lack of progress in these talks and attribute it to a 'lack of political will'; many commentators in the developed countries echo them. The disappointment of all these people will at least be tinged with realism if they perceive that there is no agreement on what the bargaining spaces ought to be. The dialogue is, therefore, a negotiation about a negotiation. Since this phase of the negotiating process will be referred to often, we shall call it NAN.

I am not suggesting that whenever there is a disagreement about bargaining spaces, this is always equivalent to a permanent refusal to negotiate. Sometimes it is a tactic to postpone negotiations. In the case of the British dissatisfaction with the EEC budget contributions, the first reactions of France and West Germany to Britain's complaints were to deny that there was any budgetary imbalance at all, and to claim that, even if there were one, it was strictly in accordance with the Treaty of Rome and the Treaties of Accession and Renegotiation. In other words, the reactions were: 'What problem?' and 'It's all legal anyway.' The period between the election of the Conservative government in the UK in June 1979 and the Dublin Summit in the winter of that year could be said to have been spent in getting the other eight members to agree to negotiate: 'The problem has been recognised' was how this was headlined in the British newspapers. This example suggests that, even if the potential negotiants are convinced that negotiations will eventually have to take place, they can still buy time by shifting the bargaining space from the main issue to NANs.

Refusal to negotiate is also common in most other types of bargaining situations. In inter-personal relations, 'I don't want to talk about it!' is quite common between husband and wife, lovers and friends. In commercial transactions, the board 'fixed price' indicates the seller's refusal to bargain. Within institutions with a hierarchy, refusal to negotiate does not last too long since a dissatisfied negotiant can appeal to a superior authority who can either decide the question or order that a negotiation must take place. In industrial bargaining, total rejection of the employees' demands is a refusal to negotiate and an attempt to postpone both the negotiation and the inevitable higher wages which will follow. Takeover bids are similar to annexation by conquest; quite often the victim refuses to negotiate. In bilateral negotiations between governments, one can reject a protest note, delay sending a reply, make an unacceptable counter-proposal, take the matter to the International Court — do anything *except* negotiate.

We can now identify some stages in the negotiating process. Sending signals and similar tactics of so-called tacit bargaining constitute a stage before NAN because, when there is no communication, it is not a negotiation. The perception-influencing stage may be followed by a phase when some of the potential negotiants refuse to negotiate either because they have superior bargaining power or because they want to buy time. Next come NANs to determine the bargaining spaces. This is true negotiation, the objective being to agree on what to negotiate about.

Game Theory and the Concept of Utility

Since this is not a book on game theory, I have to assume some familiarity on the part of the reader with its basic elements.[4] Some of its terminology, at any rate, has passed into common currency, albeit in a grossly oversimplified form. A zero (or constant sum) game is one in which whatever one party gains is matched by the other party's loss. A non-zero sum game is one where both may gain (or lose), though not equally. Games have 'strategies', namely an appropriate mixture of choices which could maximise the pay-off to the parties, provided both are assumed to act rationally. From the two-person zero-sum game, which has an elegant mathematical solution (the 'maximin' or 'saddle' point) the theory was extended to the non-zero sum variety and from two to many participants.

All developments of game theory dealing with bargaining are mathematical developments of non-zero sum games. In this approach to bargaining, the analysis of every problem begins with a matrix of pay-offs (always arbitrary), denoting the utility to each player of different outcomes. The arbitrary assigning of values is justified on the grounds that, in a purely theoretical approach, it is the analysis which is important and not the actual values. But this is precisely the problem central to applying the theory to real-life negotiations. To use it in practice, we must know in advance the utility attached to each of the different outcomes by the participants. For most real-life situations this is impossible. In a bargaining situation, we not only have to know the utility function for each participant; we must also be able to compare them. In other words, we need an absolute scale of utility; such a scale, valid for all those involved in a negotiation, does not exist. An example from Rapoport is the well-known rationalisation of physical violence used by many parents: 'This hurts me more than it hurts you.' This is meaningless; there is no way of comparing the hurts of two individuals.[5] Some theoretical attempts have been made to devise means of comparing utilities. Since each theory gives a different answer, one must conclude that the answers are implicit in the assumptions underlying the theories.

Other difficulties crop up when the theory is applied to human situations. Is utility transferable? Can it be conserved, that is, does the total utility remain the same during the negotiation? These questions are not simply theoretical, as the following well-known example shows.[6] Luke and Matthew share a flat; Luke likes to play classical music on his piano but Matthew, the trumpet player, is a jazz fan. If they can both practise only during the same one hour in the evening, how can they divide the evenings so that both get the maximum utility? Before we jump to the solution that the evenings should be divided equally, we have to know their preferences. Maybe Matthew likes to hear Luke play; maybe both prefer some music to total silence. In applying game theory to such problems, either we have to assume that their satisfactions are transferable, or we have to have some definition of what is 'equitable' in the circumstances. To assume transferability would mean believing that the loss of any specific pleasure, like music-making, can be compensated by something else; serious musicians cannot always be bribed not to play. The second objection is a more serious one; if we could find acceptable definitions for equity and fairness, most conflicts would never arise.

A fundamental problem about utility as a basis is the assumption that there is a fixed point which is the solution. Once we find it, the problem is solved once and for all. I have emphasised earlier that no conflict is ever resolved totally, except by the extinction of the conflict itself. In the above example, either Luke or Matthew can move and find himself a single flat or a more congenial companion. If, however, they continue to stay in the same flat, then many things may happen to change their utilities. For example, Luke can plead sympathy on the grounds that he has to learn a concert piece within a week; during that week, Matthew's utilities will be different and he may agree to forgo all his practice sessions. Later, of course, he may extract a price for the sacrifice; the utilities change again. This example also shows that, at the end of every negotiation, there is a residue of dissatisfaction in one or the other negotiant; the residue then becomes a part of future negotiations.

Two assumptions implicit in game theory — rationality and symmetry — have been referred to in Chapter 1. If all parties in a negotiation behave rationally, then each can argue: 'If I do this, he will do that, and then I can do that'; in other words, each player can calculate the risk involved in making a particular move. This kind of behaviour is least likely in many conflict situations, especially war. There was no use telling Britain that buying out 1800 Falkland Islanders could have proved much cheaper than fighting a war costing thousands of millions of pounds. 'They do not know when they're beaten', 'He's dead but doesn't know it', expressions like these imply that, if only the opponent were to behave rationally, he would surrender. While all negotiations are a mixture of rationality and irrationality, the *one* assumption we cannot afford to make is that there is *total* rationality in all the participants. The concept corresponding to dissatisfaction in the psychological plane is vulnerability.

In the husband and wife example we found that altruism had no place in game theory; nor do equity, fairness, morale or welfare. The theory also has no place for memory; in it every game starts afresh with a new set of pay-offs. But every conflict *does* have a memory and does *not* start afresh. It may be argued that memory as well as psychological, moral or ethical values are all subsumed in the matrix of pay-offs. If 'utility' is a bottomless basket into which we can dump everything, then this concept is just a convenience, and of little practical 'utility'.

Much of this criticism is well known. For example, Dorfman, Samuelson and Solow say: 'Economists have long since become reconciled to the conclusion that the utilities derived by two or more persons from a social situation is not summable. What, then, becomes of the constant-sum game? Answer: It must go by the board.'[7] If even the most basic theorem of game theory has to go by the board, what happens to all its extensions to non-zero sum games or many-person games? These three eminent economists conclude that, in the many years that have elapsed since the publication of the theory of games, there has been no important application to concrete economic problems.

Dissatisfaction

People feel dissatisfaction more easily than they perceive utility; this is because there are always reference points in the environment readily available for comparison. Further, dissatisfaction persists in the memory and affects future courses of action. A couple of examples will suffice to illustrate these points.

The Conservative Party in Britain, soon after taking over power in 1979, introduced a purchasing power index (PPI) in an attempt to sell the concept of utility. Mrs Thatcher's government thought that, in an inflationary situation, the normally-used retail price index (RPI) made people unhappy because the rise in prices was perceived by them as a reduction in living standards. The PPI was intended to convince them that, taking both tax cuts and inflation into account, they were really better-off under the Conservative government. The experiment was a failure; even Mrs Thatcher's government has now drawn a discreet veil over its pet index. The failure was partly due to the government finding itself unable to sustain the theory that people were better-off; sometimes the maligned RPI showed a rosier picture than the PPI! I believe another reason could be that people knew when they were worse-off and dissatisfied. To prove that they are really more satisfied than they think they are is beyond the powers of any government.

International commodity agreements (ICAs) provide the best example of the existence of reference points in the environment. In most of these negotiations, the countries exporting the commodity try to divide up the market by apportioning quotas. One would think that the calculation would be fairly straightforward; each country can estimate its exportable surplus and, after totalling up all the surpluses, relate it to total demand and then simply divide the market *pro rata*. It rarely works like that; there is always the problem of comparison. In the sugar negotiations countries argue that, if Australia gets x tonnes, for example, they must have y

tonnes. In the International Coffee Agreement, if Brazil has a particular quota, Colombia has to have the next highest and a differential has to be maintained between all the participating countries right down almost to the smallest one. In such a negotiation it is not merely each country's quota that counts, but also what each gets *in relation to* other countries. 'My earnings are important, but I want to know what others earn', is as true of countries as it is of provincial bus drivers comparing themselves with London bus drivers.

Dissatisfaction is not simply the other side of the coin of utility; if utility is measured on a positive scale, we cannot call it dissatisfaction by simply ascribing a negative sign to it. For one thing, while a negotiant may know that he is dissatisfied, he would have no idea, at the beginning of a negotiation, how much satisfaction he is going to get, if any. The satisfaction depends on other negotiants who must first agree to start the bargaining. Further, even if the negotiation ends successfully, there is no guarantee that everyone gets optimum satisfaction. More often, it is not what one gets for oneself that matters, but what one gets *out of* the other parties.

From Figure 2.1 we saw that there are at least three kinds of dissatisfaction. The unpredictability of an existing situation may prompt individuals or institutions to want to create a set of rules. Starting negotiations voluntarily to create order is a kind of dissatisfaction different from the suppressed dissatisfaction of entities under duress or coercion. Being that much nearer violence, the reactions of the discontented are more governed by feelings of fear and possibly hatred. A third kind of dissatisfaction is the one present after forcible change — after a strike, takeover by another company, or defeat in war. Any dictated agreement, after a victory, is one between the victor and the vulnerable victim.

Residue of Dissatisfaction

If dissatisfaction is the cause of negotiation, what happens when there is a refusal to negotiate? If negotiations do take place, what is the residue left at the end in the case of agreement and in the case of breakdown?

In cases where refusal to negotiate is a time-buying tactic, it is reasonable to assume that the level of dissatisfaction will rise during the period of negotiations about negotiations (NAN). When the refusal is prolonged, dissatisfaction eventually finds an outlet in other ways. Failure to increase soldiers' pay scales comparable to wages elsewhere in the economy leads to a fall in recruitment. Failure to raise wages in controlled economies leads to mounting dissatisfaction, work stoppages which are considered illegal in these societies, and eventually to sabotage. In April 1984, all the doctors in the Sudan government service, over 2000 of them, resigned *en masse* because their pay and conditions had not improved despite years spent seeking revision.

If there are no outlets at all, discontent simmers with the lid kept tightly shut; dissatisfaction becomes frustration with the consequences for aggression mentioned in Chapter 2. This is also the likely result when there is a breakdown in the negotiations. When negotiations fail to produce any amelioration, the dissatisfaction of a negotiant who originally voiced it must become worse. Not only is he deprived of any satisfaction, he has tried and failed, and the resulting feeling can only be one of frustration. The bitterness that remains in some cases of failed marriages and contested divorces is well known. Periodically one sees reports, in any country, of either a father or a mother 'snatching' a child from the custody of the other parent.

I have argued earlier that there is a residue of dissatisfaction even after an agreement is reached. It is a common experience after bargaining in an oriental market for the buyer at least to be left with a remnant of dissatisfaction. This is due to the lingering doubt that the price he paid was, in fact, the lowest he could have paid. It may be that there was no such thing as the lowest possible price; the residual feeling is entirely due to psychological uncertainty. The buyer usually blames himself, his wife or the environment: 'If only I'd started with a lower offer ...', 'If I'd had more time to look around ...', 'If *you* hadn't been so impatient. ...', etc. The seller too may be left with a dissatisfaction: 'I ought to have asked more, he being an Arab ...', 'Had there been more customers, I wouldn't have wasted so much time ...', 'That tourist guide is a scoundrel ...', and so on.

In the two examples of inter-personal relationships used in this chapter (husband and wife, the two musicians) we have established that there was a residue of dissatisfaction, even if the solution arrived at was the best possible under the circumstances. In the workplace also residues of dissatisfaction are quite common, as the following illustrative remarks show:

Work-sharing: 'I filled in for you when you went to the dentist last week.'
Vacation times: 'You took your holiday in August last year.'
Executive perks: 'Every time there is a trip to France, John gets it.'
Policy decisions: 'We have been saying no to too many of Tom's proposals; we don't want him to become too unhappy.'
Takeover bids: 'We didn't have to raise the price but we had to give them a Vice-Presidency.'

Industrial bargaining ending in an agreement is similar to bargaining in a market; neither the employer nor the workers get what they originally wanted. In all three kinds of settlement — peaceful, arbitrated, or after a strike — there is a residue of dissatisfaction in both negotiants. In the first case, the dissatisfaction is not knowing whether the best deal has been struck. Could the employer have done better if he had declared a lockout, threatened to sack the workers' leader, waited till Christmas? Could the employees have done better if they had gone on strike, canvassed for support from other unions? Nobody will ever know the answers to these questions and the hard-liners within the two groups will ensure that the dissatisfaction against those who settled is kept alive. In the case of an arbitrated settlement, the mere fact of arbitration implies that both negotiants have had to accept a settlement beyond their last stated position. The dissatisfaction left behind after a strike is deeper. One of the two negotiants is seen to have lost the battle; this always leaves wounds which become scars and get etched into the memory to affect all future negotiations.

In all cases of inter-governmental negotiations, there is a residue of dissatisfaction which is inherent in the nature of the negotiating positions adopted by them. These are the result of a compromise between conflicting interest groups within the country. In that compromise itself there are seeds of dissatisfaction. When, as a result of negotiations between states, the agreement is less than the initial negotiating position, those groups within the states, who were already dissatisfied, will be given an opportunity to say, 'You've given away too much!'

An example is provided by the controversy in the United States on the SALT II Agreement. There are always some in that country who are hostile to any kind of arms limitation agreement with the Soviet Union; there are others who reluctantly agree to a negotiation but have little hope that it will preserve or enhance US security. When the Carter administration started negotiations with the USSR, the range of dissatisfactions in the US was already very wide. When a draft treaty was finally agreed upon, the US negotiators must have thought that they had fully protected American national interest; but the erstwhile critics thought that too much had been given away. The dissatisfied became more numerous, the balance shifted, and SALT II was never submitted to the Senate for ratification. What tilted the balance between ratification and repudiation was the residual dissatisfaction of those who were originally sceptical.

Equality of Dissatisfaction

A major shortcoming of game theory is that it is static. The theory cannot say *when* an agreement will be reached, even if it can be said to predict what the agreement should be. For example, in Nash's theory of bargaining, it is assumed that there is a fixed point at which the utilities of the participants are optimised.[8] We have argued that utilities change with time, due to changes in the environment or as a result of communication between the negotiants. There cannot be a fixed point for a solution, because the utility curves themselves keep changing. If a theory cannot predict when a solution will be reached in a process in which time is an essential component, then its prediction about what the solution should be will have little validity. I shall now give an example (not contrived but based on an actual experience) to show that dissatisfaction can give us an insight into when an agreement is likely to be reached.

Suppose an owner wants to sell her flat in order to move into the country to start a kennel. The price she first puts on her flat has a direct relationship to its 'utility' to her. If there are no buyers at that price, she will have to lower the price. The 'utility' of the flat has come down because her dissatisfaction at not being able to be with her dogs reduces the 'worth' of staying on in town. She keeps dropping the price until a buyer appears; but with every drop in price she is also more unhappy because she is forced to sell below what she first thought the flat was worth, and because she has less capital to start her kennels. When the flat is sold, she has two dissatisfactions — losing money on the flat and delaying starting her kennels. The two dissatisfactions become equal. This example is artificial only to the extent that it was concerned with only one person. In a negotiation there are a minimum of two parties and equality of dissatisfaction in such cases will be elaborated in Part Two.

Utility and Dissatisfaction

The emphasis on dissatisfaction does not mean that the negotiants do not perceive any satisfaction when there is an agreement. In all types of bargaining situations considered in this book there is some measure of satisfaction on reaching an agreement; some negotiants may even achieve satisfaction when there is a breakdown, short-lived though it may be in many cases. If a seller and a buyer agree on the sale and purchase of a house, both obtain satisfaction — one gets the house and the other the money. When a strike is settled there is some satisfaction: 'we have got the best deal we could', is a perception of optimality. It is unnecessary to add more examples. In fact, we have implicitly recognised the existence of satisfaction by saying that, even when a negotiation ends in an agreement, there is a residue of dissatisfaction. The word 'residue' can only mean that the original dissatisfaction has been alleviated to some extent by satisfaction.

When a negotiation results in an agreement, the outcome is itself an expectation of the value of the agreement. The negotiants expect some benefits to flow, and are equally prepared for the costs thereof. This expectation, which may be financial, emotional or psychological, is the 'utility' of the agreement. This utility is quantifiable to the extent that we can calculate the difference between the original expectations and the actual outcome in the various dimensions (issues) of the bargaining space. How this is done will be shown in Part Two.

One criticism which needs answering is that no one sets out to equalise someone else's dissatisfaction. This is true only if we assume that the motivation in entering into a negotiation is to equalise dissatisfaction. A point repeatedly stressed in this chapter is that a call for a negotiation starts with the voicing of a dissatisfaction by a potential negotiant. When another potential negotiant has to do something to ameliorate this dissatisfaction by agreeing to a change in the *status quo, he* faces the possibility of a dissatisfaction himself. It is these two sets of dissatisfactions which need to be equalised. The concept of equality of dissatisfaction is, therefore, forced on the negotiants.

In this chapter I have used words such as perception, uncertainty, time, environment and bargaining space freely. It is to these we now turn.

Notes

1. John von Neumann and Oskar Morgenstern, *Theory of Games and Economic Behaviour* (Princeton, N.J., Princeton University Press, 1953).
2. Anatol Rapoport, *Fights, Games and Debates* (Ann Arbor, The Michigan University Press, 1960).
3. Even in such cases there is an element of dissatisfaction induced by the environment. One can imagine a Chinese ambassador telling Beijing: 'The Russians, under the Cultural Agreement have sent the Bolshoi Ballet and the President of the Republic attended the first performance. If we had a cultural agreement, we can send the Beijing Opera and invite the President.' In the author's experience, such comparisons are often made by ambassadors to persuade their governments to adopt particular policies.
4. See Rapoport, *Fights, Games*, for clarity of exposition; and R.D. Luce and H. Raiffa, *Games and Decisions* (New York, John Wiley, 1957), for the definitive and comprehensive treatment.
5. Rapoport, *Fights, Games*, p. 125
6. ibid., pp. 182-94. This example was first suggested by R.B. Braithwaite.
7. Robert Dorfman, Paul A. Samuelson and Robert M. Solow, *Linear Programming and Economic Analysis* (New York, McGraw-Hill, 1958, International Students' edn), pp. 445, 468.
8. John F. Nash, Jr, 'The Bargaining Problem', *Econometrica*, 18 (1950), 155-62: 'We may think of one point in the set of the graph as representing a solution' (p. 158).

4 UNCERTAINTY OF PERCEPTION

'That dog has five legs.'
'Then it must have had five legs. I only paint what I see.'
L.S. Lowry, painter

'Where are you going?'
'To Minsk.'
'Shame on you! You say this to make me think you are going to Pinsk. But I happen to know you *are* going to Minsk.'
Anecdote to Rapoport's
Fights, Games and Debates (p. 105)

Utility has an engaging nuance of being impersonal, something abstract. If it had been called satisfaction, it would have been seen as a feeling. Dissatisfaction, on the other hand, has no such semantic ambiguity and is clearly a feeling — subjective, personal and individually perceived. We can communicate to others the fact of our being dissatisfied, but we cannot convey the degree of dissatisfaction with any great precision; in fact, we cannot quantify it even to ourselves. Am I more dissatisfied today when I did not get a raise in salary than I was as a boy at not scoring a goal? This is a fruitless question, since I am not even comparing like with like, I am only comparing my present dissatisfaction with my memory of a past dissatisfaction. 'I have never been so unhappy in my life', is meaningless as a *scale* of one's unhappiness; it is meaningful only as a verbal communication of the intensity of *present* feeling.

How does a listener react to statements like this? 'Don't be silly', could easily be one of the reactions. From this to 'I know how you feel', there exists a series of graded responses, all of them signifying the perception of the listener to the communication received. If the everyday expressions quoted seem far removed from negotiations between governments, we only have to compare British ministerial pronouncements on the EEC Budget question which said, in effect, 'We have never been so unhappy in our life within the Community.' The French reaction was 'Don't be silly!' and the Italian one was, 'We know how you feel.' These responses depended on (a) how serious France or Italy thought Britain's dissatisfaction to be, and (b) what tactics they judged most appropriate to deal with it.

We perceive our own dissatisfaction, which is real to us, but perceive it in an inchoate way. We perceive the dissatisfaction of another, but with an uncertain degree of accuracy. This uncertainty of perception is the theme of this chapter. Since the uncertainty persists in a negotiation even after repeated communication, we shall also have to examine the role of communication in reducing uncertainty. Lastly, we shall look into reduction of uncertainty as a means of promoting order.

Problems of Perception

It is not my intention to set out a comprehensive thesis on human perception nor to go into psychological theories. These are vast subjects and much work has been done on them, with children as well as adults. While a large part of the experimental work has been concerned with perception of shape, colour and movement, some has been concerned with motivation — rewards and punishments, success and failure, likes and dislikes, as well as values. For the most part, I shall confine myself to quoting from Professor Vernon's fascinating book, *The Psychology of Perception*.[1] I must emphasise that Professor Vernon's conclusions have been derived from experiments with individuals on motivation in perceiving shape, etc., and she bears no responsibility for my trying to apply them to collective perceptions in an entirely different area of human activity.

Professor Vernon refers to a large group of experiments designed to investigate the effect on perception of material likely to produce considerable emotion of a conflicting type in the observers. These were mainly material with a sexual connotation. The results of the experiments were very variable and often disagreed with each other. 'One explanation of this disagreement is ... that the reactions of different people to objectively the same situations may be different, not to say diametrically opposed.'[2] I think we can safely take this conclusion as being valid for conflict situations which are also bargaining situations. In these, the negotiants want to reach an agreement but fear reaching one that may turn out to be unfavourable to them.

How the same fact is perceived differently by negotiants can be seen in river water disputes with the upper riparian arguing that the available supply is adequate for all uses, and the lower riparian claiming that the total quantity available is insufficient and seeking to limit its use by the other. In the negotiations between exporters and importers in ICAs, the first conflict of interest in determining the annual quotas for different exporters is in fixing the size of the total available market. The importers usually propose a high figure in order to ensure that enough of the commodity enters the market to keep prices low. The exporters on the other hand, propose a low figure, in order to keep the market tight and prices high. In a negotiation, the quantum of water in a river or the size of the world market are no longer objective, verifiable facts, but figures distorted by perception (including perceptions of self-interest) and judgement.

Another well-known example is the terms-of-trade controversy between the North and South. The developing countries argue that, since 1945, their terms of trade have been deteriorating: they have to export more of their products (coffee, tea or tin) to buy the same quantity of their imports from the developed countries (steel, machinery, fertilisers, drugs and chemicals). The developed countries vehemently deny any such deterioration. Both sides parade eminent economists in support of their positions. Terms of trade ought to be clearly definable and factually verifiable; not so, when it becomes the basis for the developing countries demanding a change in the international economic order and the rich countries refusing to countenance change.

The reasons why different people perceive the same objective situation differently are many and varied.

> The individual in a state of need is more likely to perceive something which will satisfy his need, if he thinks it will probably be there. If the perceptual situation is ill defined he may imagine for a time something appropriate to his need; but he ceases to do this after prolonged frustration. ... In an experiment on adults, hungry and thirsty observers perceived pictures of articles of food and drink as being relatively brighter than those of objects unrelated to food or drink. The estimates of brightness increased steadily in amount until the observers had been eight hours without drinking. They were then allowed to drink all they wanted; and immediately the estimated brightness

of the pictures fell to the same value as it had at the beginning of the experiment.[3]

We can adapt these experimental results to negotiation as follows. A negotiant who wants an agreement badly may perceive something which the other negotiant did not intend to convey. When this perception is later proved wrong, he suffers frustration. An example is found in President Carter's memoirs. At the first private meeting with Prime Minister Begin during the Camp David tripartite negotiations, Carter was encouraged by Begin promising *full* autonomy to the West Bank Palestinians. However, as the negotiations progressed, 'I pushed him on how much freedom they would have. He replied that the only powers they would not be able to exert would be those relating to immigration of Palestinian refugees and the security of Israel. This sounded good but later the Israelis would seek a veto over almost anything of substance the Palestinians could decide, even claiming that road construction and water supplies affect the security of Israel.'[4] Carter mentions that he later accused Begin of subterfuge. The interesting point is that, even at the beginning, Carter could have chosen to distrust Begin's assurances of full autonomy. Was Carter's trust influenced by his desire to have an agreement? Did he believe something that he wanted to believe? In spite of all the mutual knowledge states have, the perceptions of individual negotiators or mediators still remains unpredictable.

Another possible reason for differences in perception in different people is the distortion which can occur in the observer. Professor Vernon reports that 'distortions occurred during the process of deliberation over the judgement, rather than in the original perception. It is not possible, however, to arrive at any definite conclusion on this point.'[5] At least some of the experiments dealt with individuals' social values and the attributes of social groups. It is, therefore, not unlikely that negotiants might also distort their perception in the process of judgement rather than in the act of perception itself. In Chapter 2, we referred to the fear induced in the industrialised countries by the display of power by OPEC. The media and the leaders of the industrialised countries often excoriate OPEC for what amounts to, in their eyes, almost original sin — the cartelisation of an essential source of energy. Simultaneously, uranium producers in the United States, Canada, Australia and Great Britain were happily running a cartel and fixing markets and prices. The existence of this cartel would not even have become known but for one US buyer of uranium filing a suit for damages for illegal price-fixing. Except for the US, the other governments knew very well what was going on, because some of the companies were state-owned or controlled. Also, when the US courts ordered all the companies to produce documents, the Australian, British and Canadian governments rushed to pass laws prohibiting their companies from providing any information to the US courts. The objective situation in both OPEC and the uranium cartels was the same; both involved price-fixing by a cartel on an energy source. A cartel was obviously not perceived as one if it involved one's own interests. The conjugation is: 'I am protecting my interests; you are bending the rules; he is a crook.'

A very good example of perceptions colouring judgements was given in an article in *Le Monde* on how a certain action by President Giscard d'Estaing was reported in the French media favourably, while identical action by President Mitterand was reported critically.[6] The media in western countries object strenuously to the poor countries talking about a new international information order in UNESCO. The complaint of the poor countries is that these media report events in the Third World not factually, but with their judgements coloured by the developed world's perceptions and prejudices. The fact that the media treat events inside their own countries similarly is no consolation to the victims, who rarely find any organ reporting anything favourable about them. The balance available in domestic news from different publications is absent in international news.

International relations afford plenty of examples of the use of different expressions for the same type of action when it is performed by an ally or by a perceived enemy. Pol Pot, whose regime was responsible for the extermination of between 1 and 3 million Cambodians, is now, to China and South-East Asian countries, a valiant fighter who tries to free his country from invaders. The subtle distinction made by Mrs Jeanne Kirkpatrick (the United States representative in the UN) between 'authoritarian' and 'totalitarian' regimes is well known; one doubts whether they look any different to the victims of either type of regime. To Britain, the right of 1800 Falkland Islanders to live in their own island was one to be preserved at all costs; but a similar number of Diego Garcians were uprooted against their will from their island so that it could be handed over to the United States to be converted into a naval base. Such distortions are not confined to any one ideology; countries in the capitalist, communist or non-aligned group are all capable of distorting their perceptions in the interests of perceived national interest.

One man's 'terrorist' is another man's 'freedom fighter'. In an interesting piece in the *Guardian*, the Diarist showed how the same fact was reported differently by sections of the British press during the Falklands War.[7] Sea Harriers (British) were *lost* or *shot down*; Mirages and Sea Hawks (Argentinian) were *blown out of the sky*. Argentinian gunboats were *blasted to smithereens*, while British ships were only *sunk*. Britain's brave planes carried out bombing raids or strafed enemy ships; Argentinian pilots, by contrast, embarked on *desperate suicide missions* or carried out *merciless air attacks*. Whether the journalists who wrote these really saw them differently or were influenced by their judgement is a moot point.

Another kind of distortion that can occur in the perception of communications is due to the personality of the negotiator. A part of the difference may be due to differences in their individual psychological make-up. However, we cannot be sure how much distortion is caused by the values of the social group to which the individual belongs.

Rewards and punishments also affect perception. This is, perhaps, not very relevant to our consideration of institutional negotiants, particularly when these are governments. They may apply to individual negotiators. The question 'Did Kissinger become a better negotiator after getting the Nobel Peace Prize?' may be fascinating, but whether the improvement in his competence — if any — was good for limiting conflicts is an entirely different matter. When a negotiator has a vested interest in his own aggrandisement, another distortion is added to his perceptions.

The influence of success or failure is more relevant for our purposes. 'It is not surprising to find that success or failure in a task has some effect on the performance of the task itself, and may also affect tasks performed immediately afterwards.'[8] Would success in negotiating an ICA, say, on coffee make the conclusion of an agreement on cocoa more likely, particularly if a Cocoa Conference is held immediately afterwards? I think it is easier to prove the converse: if the Coffee Agreement fails, it makes the conclusion of a Cocoa Agreement that much harder. For example, hard-line opponents of any kind of commodity agreement in the

US Congress would find their hands strengthened, making the US administration less enthusiastic about embarking on negotiations in another commodity. Professor Vernon adds: 'The most interesting of the ... experiments ... showed that after success or failure people might not only be quicker or slower, more or less correct, in their perceptions; but also that the *actual nature of what they perceived might be affected*' (emphasis added).[9]

Discussing the overthrow of the Shah of Iran, Carter says that he, like other presidents before him, considered the Shah a good ally. After the proclamation of martial law in September 1978 and the shooting of several hundred demonstrators, 'the Shah was trying to decide whether to set up an interim government, set up a military government or even abdicate. We encouraged him to stand firm and to count on our backing.'[10] When things deteriorated and 'the Shah was no longer functioning as a strong leader ... I knew that he needed all the support the US could properly give him, short of direct intervention. I sent him a message stating that whatever action he took, including setting up a military government, I would support him.' Ayatollah Khomeini in Paris was calling for general strikes, the overthrow of the Shah and the establishment of a republic, yet there was no question in Carter's mind that the Shah deserved his 'unequivocal support'. However, 'we knew little about the forces contending against him, but their anti-American statements were enough to strengthen our resolve to support the Shah.' Having supported the Shah so unequivocally, was it a surprise that those who opposed him would be anti-American? The very anti-Americanism which was provoked by the unflinching US support itself became a reason for 'strengthening the resolve'. Thus do perceptions and judgements tend to reinforce each other.

Perception and Trust

The conclusion that individual perception was affected by social values seems to be true also for groups of people and nations. For complex historical reasons, the British distrust the motivations of the French, the Algerians of the Moroccans, the Turkish-Cypriots of the Greek-Cypriots, the Vietnamese of the Chinese and so on. It seems easier to reinforce a mistrust than a trust. Where there is no trust, every action by a negotiant is viewed with deep suspicion and a search for malign motives. This is now well recognised even in grave conflict situations; the Helsinki Conference on European Security and Co-operation did seriously negotiate about confidence-building measures.

It is in the context of trust that we must consider the case of the 'Prisoners' Dilemma', a staple of all books on conflict and bargaining. The anecdote from which this two-person non-zero sum game derives its name is as follows. There are two suspects, A and B, both under detention for a serious offence (for example, robbery with violence). The District Attorney (DA), who is quite sure they are guilty, cannot prove the most serious indictment but can prove one carrying a lesser sentence (say, in our example, breaking and entering). The DA, who can plea-bargain under the American legal system, offers A and B the same deal: each of them can either confess or not confess; if they both confess to the more serious offence they get convicted for it but get a mitigated sentence because of the confession; if one confesses and the other does not, the confessor is promised freedom but the other gets the maximum sentence for the serious offence. Both A and B know that, if neither confesses, they can only be convicted of the lesser offence and thus both get a lesser sentence. If we assume that the maximum sentence for robbery with violence is 20 years, the mitigated one is 12 years and the sentence for the lesser offence is 5 years, the utility matrix, in game theory, will be as shown below (the minus sign indicates that it is a loss, i.e. a loss of freedom).

A's options	B's options	
	Confess	Not confess
Confess	$-12, -12$	$0, -20$
Not confess	$-20, 0$	$-5, -5$

(first figure is A's utility)

How should A and B, acting independently, decide? If there is total trust and there is no uncertainty whatsoever about each other's integrity (i.e. honour among thieves), both do well by *not* confessing. But supposing A has some lingering doubts about B, he can argue: 'If I do not confess, and B does, I get 20 years. But if I confess, and he does not, I go free. If he also confesses, I still get only 12 years. I am better-off confessing.' The trouble with this line of reasoning is that B can do the same. So they both confess and get 12 years each. What they should have done was not to confess and get only 5 years each. Lack of mutual trust, coupled with 'rational' considerations, leads to disaster.

The trouble arises precisely because of the rationality assumption. 'Trust' is not a rational judgement; it is an emotion in which there is always an element of uncertainty. If A trusts B he is, in effect, taking a gamble on his own judgement. In another approach to this problem, Amartya Sen points out that the prisoners arrive at the best solution for both only if they ignore their own self-interest and instead choose to *maximise the welfare of the other.*[11] A can then argue: 'If I confess, B gets either 12 or 20 years. If I do not confess, B gets only 5 years or goes free. It is in B's interest that I do not confess!' In other words, altruism helps both when self-interest produces only the worst result.

It is my view that the 'Prisoners' Dilemma' has no relevance to bargaining. A crucial assumption in the anecdote is that there is no communication between A and B; only the DA can communicate. This makes it a problem of two separate negotiations between three negotiants, two of whom are asked to gamble on their judgements. The whole set cannot be treated as a single bargaining problem.

The problem has fascinated a lot of people and learned articles have been written on various 'experiments' connected with it. It is supposed to illuminate conflict resolution because this kind of strategic thinking became academically fashionable during the Cold War. The diversion of intellectual effort into tacit bargaining, prisoners' dilemmas and similar contrivances in which the participants do not communicate with each other is of little use to us in trying to understand how to limit conflicts.

Threat, Intimidation and Bluff

These tactics play an important part in the thinking of strategic theorists concentrating on the precarious area of brinkmanship, shown at the left-hand extreme of the area of conflict in Figure 2.1. The use of threat or intimidation is particularly dangerous in these circumstances because there is a great deal of uncertainty about how an antagonist perceives such tactics.

There can be four possible reactions to a threat. Take the case of a parent threatening a child, 'If you do it again, I'll spank you!' What the child makes of this depends on its perception of the action which followed the previous such threats. If the parent is a 'paper tiger', the threat has little value in conditioning future action. If past history shows that the threat is always implemented by resort to physical violence, the child may be deterred, albeit feeling more embittered and hostile. A third possibility is that past history may be ambiguous; spanking may or may not have occurred after every threat, though the transgression may have been repeated. In this case, the child may be tempted to take a risk and try it once more. The last possibility is defiance; when the child is old enough, the threat of physical violence may only produce the reaction, 'Try it and see!'.

The uncertainty about reaction to threats is even worse in interstate relations. No two situations are so identical that action in one can be said to be an unambiguous pointer to action in another. For the threats of a nation to become totally credible, it should not only utter them often but also follow them up each time by the threatened punitive action. This seems to me to be horrible advice to give the world on the brink of nuclear war.

An example of this kind of uncertainty is the 'reaffirmation of commitment' made by President Carter to Pakistan, following the invasion of Afghanistan by the Soviet Union. Calling this reaffirmation the 'Carter doctrine', William Safire, a columnist of the *New York Times*, enquired,

> If more Soviet soldiers are killed, the Russians may move to 'clean out the sanctuaries' inside Pakistan. In that event, what is the Carter doctrine's 'commitment'? — to complain again to the United Nations? To send in the 82nd Airborne? Precisely what? ... Under the Carter doctrine would the United States help the Pakistanis crush a Baluchi rebellion? What if the Soviet troops in neighbouring Afghanistan came to the[ir] aid ...? Would the United States join only in moral condemnation? Reply with an air strike? What?[12]

The precise extent of Carter's commitment to Pakistan confused even an experienced US political columnist. What would the USSR have made of it? The reaction of the Russian leadership could well be defiance. Those who make threats rarely seem to take into account the likelihood of defiance as a response. When it happens, as in the case of Britain's reaction to the Argentine military takeover of the Falkland Islands, it comes as a great surprise to the threatener.

A bluff, by its very nature, is meant to deceive; its purpose is to reinforce uncertainty. When a bluff is called, the credibility of the bluffer is adversely affected — even if it is all right to do it in poker, where it is a part of the rules of the game. Since negotiations between institutions or governments take place in an environment with a great deal of information, a bluff is unlikely to have a long lifespan. It is not a tactic to be indulged in by responsible negotiants in the interests of their own credibility.

Communication and Competence

Uncertainty clouds every aspect of negotiating and conflict situations. Nevertheless, further study of this concept is not fruitless. I believe that uncertainty in social relations can be reduced; that the greater the reduction of uncertainty the nearer one will be to creating a rule; and that the more the rules, the greater the predictability in a system. Communication plays a decisive role in the reduction of uncertainty.

What I have called 'uncertainty', Norbert Wiener calls 'incomplete determinism' in his classic and wide-ranging work *The Human Use of Human Beings*.[13] Though cybernetics is no longer a 'buzz word', and computers have become ubiquitous, Wiener's powerful arguments are as fresh and valid today as they were 30 years ago. His basic thesis was that though in the universe as a whole disorganisation (entropy) tended to increase, there were local enclaves where there was a limited and temporary tendency for organisation (order) to increase. In his view, communication and control (in the sense of information feedback controlling the actions of a person or machine) are essential aspects of order.

The following are some of Wiener's conclusions that could be applied to the negotiating process. A cliché has no information; in order to convey information, a message must have something new and not anticipated by the recipient. Every message is likely to suffer a loss of information in its transmission. Feedback is a method of controlling a system by reinserting into it the results of past performance. Though human perception is partly a function of the nervous system and synaptic threshold, emotions also control learning and similar processes.

The process of negotiation is one of repeated communication and conference between the negotiants, with the aim of influencing the perception of other negotiants. Except when it is intended to deceive (as in a bluff), the objective is to convey to other negotiants a clearer picture of the communicator's position. In this sense, communication in a negotiation serves to reduce uncertainty. Therefore, if a communication carries no information it achieves no positive purpose in a negotiation. We must be careful when we say that there is no information content in a communication. Repetition of an earlier position is not devoid of information; the additional information conveyed is: 'I have not changed my position, though time has elapsed and though I have heard and assimilated what you have had to say.'

The problem of loss of information in transmission is relevant to international negotiation because negotiators from different countries speak different languages. In reacting to Carter's warning to the USSR, containing his commitment to Pakistan, the USSR may not have understood all the nuances of the original. Somebody must have translated the statement into Russian, which was then read and understood in the light of the reader's experience of his own language and the experience of previous communications. We have all read with incomprehension, and with some amusement, the long and involved slogans which the Chinese leadership provides for its people. They must convey, in Chinese, much more than is apparent in a literal English translation. It is not clear to many outsiders what the Chinese mean when they say 'We will not stand idly by!' Will the idleness be terminated by rhetoric, limited war, or nuclear weapons? In fact, what the Chinese government means to convey is that they are not to be ignored as mere bystanders, but should be included in the bargaining population.

Linguistic difficulties sometimes produce insuperable political problems. At the Geneva Conference of 1954, the French and the Vietnamese signed a ceasefire agreement, one of the provisions of which was the creation of an 'International Commission for Supervision and Control'. The Vietnamese always understood *controle* in the French sense of 'inspection', whereas the Americans thought it meant 'to regulate'. Regulation implied that the Commission had the power to direct a government to do something or prevent it from doing something else; one who merely inspects need not have such powers. This misunderstanding was responsible, to some extent, for the US always blaming the Commission as an ineffective organisation.

The loss of information in transmission due to the language barrier is not always acute. People gradually acquire an approximate understanding of what others mean. Professor Vernon comments: 'people do acquire a special vocabulary of words relating to the topics in which they are interested, and for that reason are able to perceive such words more easily.'[14] One commentator on the Northern Ireland conflict says: 'Words such as "institutional" and "constitutional" have highly charged special meanings within the vocabulary of Northern Ireland politics.'[15] When a Northern Ireland politician meets these words in an ordinary context, he attaches one set of meanings to them; in the context of his own politics, he attaches another set, charged with emotion.

Such acquisition of special knowledge, due to past history and memory, is feedback. Without it, there can be no negotiation. In a bargaining situation, negotiators seek from each other more and more information on attitudes and intentions in order to build up, by successive approximation, a less uncertain picture of the other negotiant's position. It is, however, evident that, even with the maximum of communication, there can be only an approximate understanding. The series converges towards full information but is never equal to it. One of the roles of a mediator is to assist in the feedback process, especially in situations with little trust between the participants. President Carter's role in the Camp David negotiations is an example of a mediator acting as a channel of communication and feedback, although these would have been filtered through his own perceptions.

Since feedback helps to reduce uncertainty, its importance to conflict limitation is obvious. Secrecy in negotiation plays the opposite role, since it increases uncertainty. There is no paradox in a negotiant who wants to reach an agreement also making it more difficult by being secretive. The need for an agreement may be perceived rationally; but secrecy is partly induced by fear and insecurity.[16] Secrecy in refraining from conveying full information about one's own position is also used to prolong a negotiation. President Reagan's understanding of the negotiating process is as follows: 'In a negotiation ... impatience can be a real handicap ... patience strengthens your bargaining position. If one side seems too eager or desperate, the other side has no reason to offer a compromise and every reason to hold back, expecting that the more eager side will cave in first.'[17]

On the question of group values, experienced international negotiators have detected significant variations in the approach of negotiators from different countries. Iklé compares typical national attitudes to negotiations thus: 'French diplomats are prone to elaborate historical-philosophical themes as a background to their negotiating strategies .... German and American negotiators at times place greater emphasis on legal aspects than the diplomats of many other Western countries ... [Soviet negotiators] ask for the whole loaf when they could get half-a-loaf and wind up with nothing.'[18] A former high Indian official has this to say: 'The Japanese are tough negotiators and can be blunt at times. Russians exhaust your patience but sometimes exhaust themselves in the process. Indians are always anxious to negotiate a deal successfully and in the process are generous and perhaps give away too much sometimes.'[19] Another example is from Carter's memoirs: 'Vance [then US Secretary of State] told me that [the Egyptians] had a reputation of being the most contentious of all Arabs in international negotiations.'[20] These are random quotations no doubt influenced by the perceivers' own predilections. On the whole, it is quite difficult to find out what many countries think about the negotiating tactics of others.

Even if we grant the existence of identifiable national traits, it is difficult to conclude that all negotiators from a country behave exactly the same way. Nobody would claim that the tactics of Daniel Patrick Moynihan, as the US representative in the UN, were the same as those of Adlai Stevenson. The competence of individual negotiators varies widely. Expressions such as 'he drives a hard bargain' testify to a recognition of superior bargaining skill. Are some people better negotiators because they perceive more clearly or because they communicate better? Can bargaining skills be learned? We know far too little about such questions.

We know even less about how a negotiator functions under stress. During the final hectic stages of the negotiations with Iran over the release of the American hostages, it was reported that Warren Christopher, the American negotiator in Algiers, went without sleep for two days! In the White House, President Carter 'had not been to bed since early Sunday, and ... was discouraged and almost exhausted.'[21] And he did not get any regular sleep till he handed over the presidency at noon on Tuesday, 20 January

1981. If exhaustion is a problem, the grave illness of a leader at a critical time is a more serious one (e.g. Sir Anthony Eden at the time of the Suez crisis).

Every government negotiator has had the experience of international negotiations going through a frenzied period of activity in the last days of a conference, with the final session going on right through the night. The Council of Ministers of the European Community has now acquired the habit of 'stopping the clock' — a pretension that a deadline had not been breached by ignoring it. Are negotiators in the best position to make rational judgements after sleepless nights? This is not an idle query. One possible scenario about the build-up to a nuclear war is that tensions would gradually increase during the previous days and weeks. Many world leaders would have spent much of this time sleepless and under great stress. Would they then be in the best condition to decide about nuclear war?

On Reducing Uncertainty

In spite of the difficulties in comprehending the phenomenon of perception, I suggest that it is necessary to reduce uncertainty in conflicts in order to limit them. Reduction in uncertainty increases predictability and helps to create order.

In all cases of buying and selling, uncertainty is eliminated if either the seller or the buyer refuses to bargain. The advice to a tourist, 'Don't go to the market; go to the Government Handicraft Store; you don't have to bargain there', is advice to save him the later dissatisfaction of wondering whether he had paid too much. In a supermarket, the buyer's choice is limited to buying or not buying at the quoted price; the supermarket owner has reduced his uncertainty over every transaction by taking the risk that a sufficient number of people will buy at his price to make it worth his while. He is, no doubt, betting on his judgement, but he is not acting irrationally; his gamble is based on probability theory and risk analysis.

Today, taxis everywhere have fixed rates; the individual user does not have to bargain over the fare for each trip; order has been created out of a large number of disorganised bargaining situations. But this gives rise to a higher-order negotiating situation. When the majority of taxi drivers become dissatisfied with the rates, they collectively negotiate with the concerned authority for a rise. One might say that instead of individual negotiations happening all the time, they have been collapsed into a single negotiation held periodically.

The agglomeration of a large number of individual negotiations into a single larger one has also happened in wage-bargaining. In less organised societies, each employee negotiates wages and conditions of employment with the employer, who generally acts independently of other employers. As society becomes more complex, the uncertainty involved in a large number of separate bargains is reduced by resorting to rules of various kinds. Firms advertise wage-levels and working conditions; the offer is on a 'take it or leave it' basis and negotiations, if any, are within narrow limits. Collective bargaining means precisely that; employers and employees collapse a large number of negotiations into (normally) an annual one. A great deal of uncertainty (on the part of the employee on the level of his wage packet from week to week, and on the part of the employer on the level of his costs) are eliminated, and order created for a period.

I am not suggesting that such continuous upward agglomeration is always a good thing. Too much of it produces a different set of dissatisfactions on the shopfloor where the workers may feel alienated from the union leadership at the national level. A recent example is the refusal of miners in some regions in Britain to go on strike, in spite of pressures on them from the national leadership. Merely increasing the size of the bargaining space does not eliminate all dissatisfaction.

The need to create a medium of exchange seems to arise when the number of negotiants exceeds a critical limit, even when there are no problems of exchange of dissimilar goods. I have seen such a medium evolve, almost spontaneously, in a highly modern society. A group of mothers in a university town in the United States started a baby-sitting group on the principle that one parent would sit for another, in exchange for a similar service later to the same or a third member, subject to an equality being achieved over a period of time. This was not even a case of barter; what was being exchanged was the same commodity — one's time today for someone else's time tomorrow. Very soon the dissatisfaction level in the group increased; somebody had to maintain the complicated accounts, there were disagreements about time expended, some were too much in credit and a few were seen as taking advantage.

The group, therefore, evolved a 'token' system. Every member started with a supply of tokens, which were 'paid' out for babysitting done — one token per hour. Uncertainty was eliminated and dissatisfaction reduced significantly by this group of educated American women spontaneously rediscovering the limited circulation of money.

It is more difficult to find examples of rule-making to reduce uncertainty in inter-personal relationships within a family. The group is too small and the rules are, more often than not, tacit understandings rather than explicit rules. A possible example of rule-making is the weekly pocket money given to children in order to avoid a negotiation between parent and child every time the child wants to buy sweets or a comic. One set of uncertainties is removed, only to create a different type of dissatisfaction: 'Tom gets a pound a week; why do I get only 50 pence?' Eliminating uncertainty and creating order does not always lead to eliminating all dissatisfactions; the new order may create its own set.

The purpose of citing examples from the four non-governmental types of bargaining situation is to prove that people prefer to reduce uncertainty and create order. Governments, too, try to follow a policy of creating order out of disorder. Since the second world war, there has been an acceleration in the movement to create more international rule-systems. The role of order in international relations is dealt with in Part Four.

When a negotiator acts on his own behalf, we need to take into account only his perception. However, when he acts on behalf of an institution or government, we have to take note of two sets of perceptions — his own and the collective perception of the institution. Many of those who influence the collective perception of the institution may not be involved actively in negotiation and gain their information second-hand from the negotiator. These other actors in the environment are also influenced by considerations wider than a particular negotiation (e.g. senators in the US voting on arms control or the Panama Canal Treaty). We have also referred in this chapter to the effects of past history on trust and to the importance of time. How environment, history and time affect negotiations is analysed in the next chapter.

Notes

1. M.D. Vernon, *The Psychology of Perception* (Pelican Books, 1962).
2. ibid., p. 212.
3. ibid., pp. 197, 204.
4. Jimmy Carter, *Keeping Faith* (Bantam Books, 1982). Extracts quoted here from *Time Magazine*, 11 October 1982.
5. Vernon, *Psychology of Perception*, p. 201.
6. Jean-Marie Colombani, *Le Monde*, reproduced in the *Guardian Weekly Review*, 17 April 1983, p. 11. 'Giscard d'Estaing [when he was President] took France out of the European Monetary System (EMS) without any hullabaloo. Is Mitterand thinking of doing the same? The simple supposition right away becomes the threat of a cataclysm. ... Ten days went by between the second round of the municipal elections in 1977 and the resignation and later the constitution of Barre's second government. Nine days elapsed between the second round of the municipal elections in 1983 and the resignation and nomination of Mauroy's third government. During this time in 1977, Giscard was reflecting. As for Mitterand in 1983, he was wavering, if he hadn't actually left executive authority vacant. The former, as is normal, consulted; the latter gave in to pressures.'
7. *Guardian*, 27 May 1982.
8. Vernon, *Psychology of Perception*, p. 207.
9. ibid., p. 209.
10. All quotations in this paragraph from *Time Magazine*, 18 Oct. 1982.
11. Amartya Sen, *Choice, Welfare and Measurement* (Oxford University Press, 1983), p. 66.
12. William Safire, *New York Times*, reproduced in the *International Herald Tribune*, 15 Jan. 1980.
13. Norbert Wiener, *The Human Use of Human Beings* (Boston, Houghton Mifflin Company; The Riverside Press Cambridge, 1954).
14. Vernon, *Psychology of Perception*, p. 199.
15. Peter Jenkins, *Guardian*, 17 Dec. 1980.
16. We shall refer later to the role of secrecy as a means of handling negotiations *within* institutions so that opposition to a negotiating position is not given an opportunity to build up. Secrecy is often used against one's own people.
17. President Reagan's address to the World Affairs Council of Los Angeles, 31 March 1983 (official USIA text).
18. Fred Charles Iklé, *How Nations Negotiate* (New York, Harper & Row, 1964), pp. 225-6, 234.
19. Triloki Nath Kaul, *Diplomacy in Peace and War* (New Delhi, Vikas, 1979).
20. Carter, *Keeping Faith*, *Time Magazine*, 11 Oct. 1982.
21. ibid.

5 ENVIRONMENT, MEMORY AND TIME

> Fate, Time, Occasion, Chance and Change —
> To these all things are subject ...
> Percy Bysshe Shelley

The world is ever with us. It is not only outside impinging on our activities, but it is also within us, in the form of our perception of it. Our perceptions of today's world are distorted by all our past perceptions. The world is ever-changing and three factors — environment, memory of past history and time — exert a significant influence on the negotiating process.

The Environment and the Bargaining Space

The whole world is not the environment for each negotiation: when I buy potatoes in the market, I am not thinking about the nuclear holocaust. But aspects of my current life may affect my perceptions and my negotiating position. For example, if I am on strike and have only strike pay to spend and not my regular wages, I may bargain harder and also have more time to spend bargaining. On the other hand, if I have quarrelled with my wife about who should do the shopping, I might be willing to pay more just to get it over with. These are part of my immediate psychological make-up and are perception-distorting influences. They are different from the actual environment of the potato-buying exercise; the environment is the 'market' with many buyers and many sellers, governed by the laws of demand and supply for the specific product.

Any market, whether an oriental one or the international trade in coffee, sets the limits of negotiation: both the buyer and seller are aware of the market price. This need not be perceived as an exact figure, but is at least perceived as a range. An example of the environment setting limits to a negotiation can be found in the annual negotiations in an ICA when importers and exporters agree on the quantities of the commodity to be placed on the market in the ensuing year. Though the exporting countries usually want a smaller annual quota than the importing ones, the two cannot be very far apart. A typical illustration in the case of coffee would be when the available market is estimated at about 45–46 million bags. The exporting countries will start by suggesting a quota of 43 million bags, and the importing countries one of 49 million bags. The eventual agreement will fall somewhere in this range, depending on the relative bargaining power of the two groups. The environment has set the limits of the bargaining space, and both groups have perceived that 40 million or 55 million bags are outside the range.

From this we may conclude that the bargaining space is finite. And this is true for even the most complex and intractable of conflicts. At present, the Middle East conflict is, perhaps, the least limitable. An essential aspect of this particular conflict is Israel's perception of its need for guaranteed security, but in its demand for such a guarantee, Israel cannot, and does not, demand the total demilitarisation of all Islamic countries from Morocco to Indonesia. To state it in this extreme form is to see its absurdity.

We can try to see where the boundary lies by narrowing down both factors — the geographical extent and the degree of demilitarisation. If the demilitarised region is not to extend from Morocco to Indonesia, is it to be from Algeria to Malaysia, Libya to Bangladesh ...? If not total demilitarisation, how partial? Police weapons only, or 'defensive' weapons only? What are defensive weapons? As we continue this process, we may at first have a rough, and then an increasingly clearer idea of where the boundaries lie. I say might, because we can never know precisely where the boundary lies. Indeed, it is doubtful whether such a thing as a precise boundary exists. Even within Israel, different people have different ideas on what would guarantee their security. That judgement depends on the person's perception, the degree of trust that he is willing to place in others, and a host of other factors that make for uncertainty.

The fact that we may not know exactly where the boundary lies does not contradict the conclusion that the bargaining space itself is finite: we can perceive the finiteness of a space without being able to draw a precise line. This is analogous to the problem of defining a bald man. Is a man bald when he has 368 strands of hair on his head but not 369? We cannot be that precise, but we still recognise a bald man when we see one! Line-drawing is a difficult exercise in many problems, especially those in which the change between one state and another is continuous. It becomes even more difficult when there are many interrelated issues and the position of the boundary in one dimension affects the position in another. These aspects will be examined in more detail in Part Two.

The environment not only prescribes the boundaries of the dimensions in a bargaining space but also makes the negotants aware of their existence. In the example of the International Coffee Agreement, the initial demand was influenced by an assumption of what was practicable and negotiable. Any demand perceived to be out of line with the reality imposed by the environment is usually called a non-starter. This limitation applies even to negotiations with no mutual trust, and in which the starting point is only the irreducible minimum of agreeing to negotiate on the issue at all (e.g. the SALT negotiations between the US and the USSR). Even in SALT, neither of the two negotants could claim a 5:1 or 10:1 superiority over the other; such a demand was a non-starter and was, in fact, implicit in the two countries agreeing to negotiate. Subsequently, of course, US policy underwent a dramatic change when Ronald Reagan became president. Proposals, like the zero option were made, though these were clearly non-starters. One such proposal (demanding that the Russians do something now, in return for the USA *not* doing something in the future) was characterised by an American negotiator as 'pay now, buy later'.

The fact that a proposal is a non-starter does not prevent a negotant from making it. It is a tactic similar to 'refusal to negotiate'. Just as a potential negotant can delay the beginning of a negotiation by putting forward impossible preconditions, a negotant can also put forward impossible proposals whilst negotiating. We have to view this as a dismantling of the agreement about the boundaries of the bargaining space; what follows is a new negotiation, with the previous one becoming a part of history.

Finiteness and uncertainty of precise location apply to every dimension of a negotiation, however complex. A negotiation to conclude an ICA is usually concerned with a number of interrelated issues — the total quantity to be traded, its division among various exporting countries, maximum and minimum prices, the division of the price range into sectors, the action to be taken when the market price moves from one sector to another, buffer stocks, distribution of shortfalls, etc. But these are only those concerned with quantities and prices; there will also be a host of other issues ranging from reporting and enforcement provisions, to voting power. Every dimension, however, has it own boundary, imprecise but delimited by the environment. It may be the state of the art, financial constraints or public opinion, but there is always a limiting factor. In the SALT example, the number of delivery vehicles and throw-weight (the explosive power of the warheads) are the principal interrelated dimensions, analogous to quantities and prices in commodity trade. But these are not just two dimensions; delivery vehicles may be bombers or ballistic missiles; the range inter-continental or intermediate; they could be submarine-launched or cruise-launched; the warheads single or multiple, a cluster or independently targeted; they could be thermo-nuclear or neutron bombs. There are other important dimensions including surveillance, enforcement, anti-missile defence, future development, and so on.

The picture we have evoked is that bargaining space is like a cloud, suspended in the environment, and moving through time. I find this simile helpful because it graphically conveys a picture of nebulousness, of imprecise and ever-changing shapes and an indeterminate configuration far removed from any mathematical precision — just like negotiating situations in real life.

The Immediate Environment

What constitutes the immediate environment is a question that has different answers for different negotiations, and different answers at different times. In buying vegetables, the market is the immediate environment; the trucks which bring in the vegetables are normally part of the more distant environment, unless the truck-drivers decide to go on strike. A change in the incumbency of the President of the United States affects the immediate environment for SALT negotiations, but less so for ICAs. In international conflicts, the death of a leader assumes great importance. Take the case of Salazar. His removal from power in Portugal affected a number of international conflicts — the independence movements in Mozambique and Angola (where an internal armed conflict was generated), the future of negotiations on Southern Rhodesia, and the international negotiations on the independence of Namibia. Salazar was very much a part of the immediate environment for anything that happened in Southern Africa, a fact which became dramatically apparent only when he had a stroke. We shall revert to this example in Chapter 12, when the impact of an act of God on bargaining power will be analysed.

It is not necessary to give details of the immediate environment for two of the seven types of negotiating situations. Where close personal relationships are involved, at home or in the workplace, we know what our immediate environment is at any given time. The case of labour disputes is, however, worth a closer look, mainly because we can see how parts of the environment, which are normally remote, become more immediate. In describing the influence of the environment on labour disputes, I am, of course, referring only to democratic societies.

In labour disputes, the immediate environment is clearly the labour market, which is governed by a number of factors, including the availability of other local sources of employment and the wages paid to comparable groups of workers. The somewhat distant environment includes the national economy, particularly the rate of inflation, public opinion and the government.

Other workers in the immediate environment affect the perceptions of the labour involved in a negotiation in two ways — in terms of 'comparability' and of 'differentials'. Though both involve comparison with other workers, the motivation is quite different. In the case of comparability, a worker demands as much as X gets, because he sees himself and X as doing comparable jobs. Until recently, comparability with the private sector was the basis for determining the pay of civil servants in Britain; now, the pay of Members of Parliament has been pegged to that of a specific level in the civil service. In the case of differentials, maintenance of a hierarchy and preservation of prestige motivate a worker to demand that he get *more* than Y, because Y has always been paid less. The almost perpetual conflict in Fleet Street between newspaper managements and men in one union demanding that they get more than printing workers in another union is well known.

The existence of other unions in the immediate environment may also affect labour disputes. To the extent that one union involved in a dispute can command the support of other unions in a strike, the negotiating union's bargaining power is strengthened. On the other hand, a striking union may fail to win the support of other unions on the same site and may then have to expand the conflict to the national level. We shall describe an example in Chapter 11.

Other employers are also reference points. If most newspapers in Fleet Street negotiate wage agreements without demanding much in the way of the use of advanced technology, the position of the management of *The Times* in demanding electronic typesetting is made much weaker. Employers often band together and conduct industry-wide negotiations. The fear of one union leader gaining excessive power produced, among textile companies in Bombay, a very strong coalition which withstood a strike for over a year.

In an atmosphere of growing unemployment and recession, unions seek to preserve jobs and moderate wage demands; and women workers are less likely to seek equal pay for equal work. In extreme cases, the unions almost completely lose their bargaining power to protect the standard of living of their members to keep pace with inflation. Airlines in the US have recently successfully demanded that their employees should have their wages frozen or even cut. When the Chrysler Motor Corporation had to seek US government assistance, Congress insisted that its workers also make a 'contribution' to the recovery programme.

Another example of expectations being modified is the effect of regional variations, especially in large countries. One of the largest employers in the textile industry in the United States has an entrenched anti-union policy and has adopted every means available to prevent the unionisation of its workforce. It has been able to defy or circumvent even the orders of Federal courts partly because the environment in which it functions — the southern states of the United States — is favourable to such attitudes. The coal miners working in the pits of West Virginia are more unionised than the open-cast workers in the western states. In India, bonded labour is more likely to occur in those states where feudalism still persists.

The climate of public opinion in a country may not only be favourable or unfavourable to unions in general, but may be more or less sympathetic to particular groups of workers. This seems to be a matter of societal perception. In Britain coal miners until recently generated more sympathy than civil servants; in France, farmers and fishermen can disrupt everyday life without losing much public sympathy. President Reagan is said to have made an example of air traffic controllers by sacking 13,000 of them, because they were unlikely to evoke public sympathy. Dramatic shifts in public opinion against unions and labour in general are not very common; a possible example is the shift in public opinion in Britain after 'the winter of discontent' in 1978.

A government may be a benign or malign spectator; it can try to influence by jaw-boning. But it can also become an active participant by suggesting, or even imposing, arbitration. It can change the negotiating assumptions by offering or withholding money. It can make secondary picketing illegal and use the police in a manner which has direct bearing on the negotiations. It can bring in the armed forces to run 'essential' services (e.g. the fire service, the railways, the docks or even civilian air traffic control).

Since both business and unions have political influence in democratic countries, the political complexion of the government is relevant to labour disputes. If the President of the USA is a Democrat, it is assumed that he will be more sympathetic to labour. When Ronald Reagan became President it was correctly assumed that business interests would be supported if they 'stood up' to the unions. The power of the unions is further eroded if a pro-business party is elected specifically on an anti-union platform.

A commonsense way of describing the 'immediate' environment would be to say that it affects the bargaining process more intimately than the more distant environment, but this would be begging the question. Two possible answers suggest themselves. The immediate environment is that part from which the negotiants may be able to draw new dimensions into the bargaining space, that is to say, enlarge it. Or, they may be able to bring in new negotiants, and so increase the number. Since both phenomena are common in negotiations, we shall analyse them in greater detail in Chapter 11. Another aspect of the immediate environment relevant to conflict limitation is that it can provide arbitrators, mediators and conciliators; the role of such third parties is considered in Chapter 16.

The fact that we can differentiate among the immediate, remote and irrelevant environments does not mean that we can draw precise boundary lines between them. If we add the possibilities of expansion and enlargement to the bargaining space, we see that, like a cloud, it can change its shape and form; it can grow bigger or smaller, lighter or darker and more or less threatening. Figure 5.1 represents the bargaining space and the different parts of the environment.

Figure 5.1: Bargaining Space and the Environment

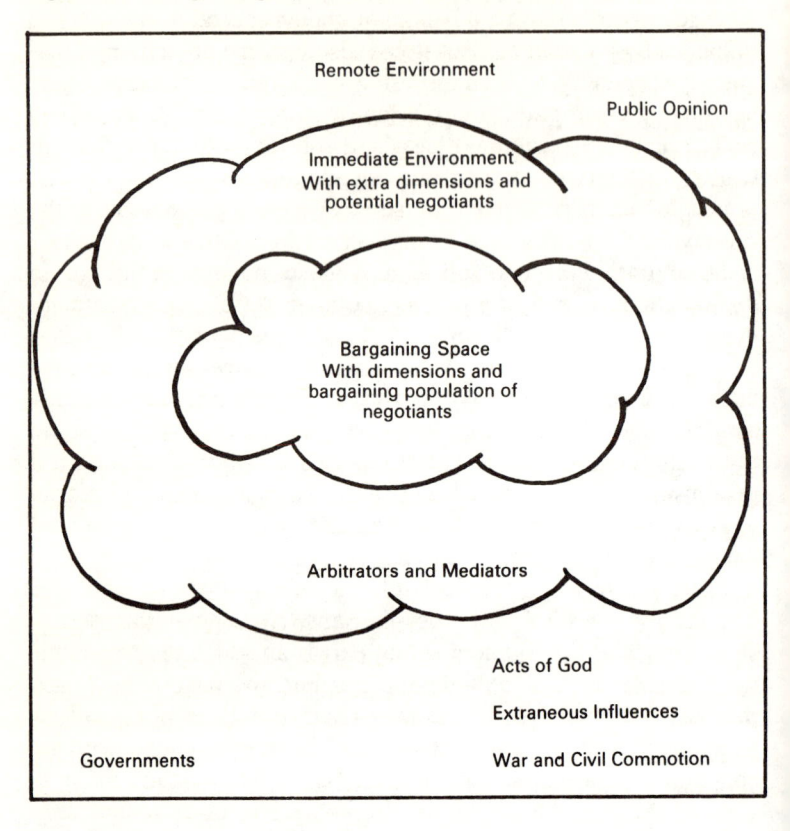

- Remote Environment
- Public Opinion
- Immediate Environment With extra dimensions and potential negotiants
- Bargaining Space With dimensions and bargaining population of negotiants
- Arbitrators and Mediators
- Acts of God
- Extraneous Influences
- Governments
- War and Civil Commotion

The Changing Environment

It would be convenient if we could make the assumption that the environment, at least, was fixed and unchanging. But it is only in situations where the time taken for negotiation is very brief that one can safely assume that the environment remains invariant. It may seem reasonable to do so when shopping for a kilo of potatoes in the market. But what happens if another customer arrives while I am bargaining? The seller's attention is diverted. He now has a choice of buyers, and his bargaining position is strengthened at my expense. Thus, even in short duration negotiations, chance or luck can introduce an extraneous element, changing a negotiation significantly. Chance events do not only affect the course of negotiations but also the implementation of an agreement. The more complex the transaction, the more probable is the occurrence of a chance event. In international trade, while a contract is being fulfilled, foreign exchange rates may change by an unexpected devaluation; governments may ban imports, levy an import or export duty, or demand import deposits; freight or insurance rates may go up; the exporter may have to pay a higher price for his raw materials; he may suffer a strike, a power shortage or similar interruptions in production; the buyer might have misjudged the market. When the buyer and seller conclude a contract, they do so on the assumption that the environment will continue unchanged. With this goes the tacit assumption that, if the environment does change, a renegotiation will be undertaken. It is said that law recognises an implied clause in judging contracts *rebus sic substantibus* (so long as things stand as they are). Because unpredictable changes can occur, most contracts contain a *force majeure* clause to protect the parties from the impact of events outside their control.

Since conflicts can arise while an agreement is being implemented, to stop examining the negotiating process as soon as the outcome is reached is not enough. A natural disaster is an act of God; the effect of frost on the coffee crop in Brazil, for example, is often cataclysmic for negotiations on coffee, whether these are for concluding an ICA or those arising during its implementation. Other factors which affect ICAs are: production cycles, natural disasters, commodity booms, inflation and recession in the importing countries, and the international monetary situation.

The death of Salazar was also an act of God. It is trite to say that one cannot predict death; neither can we predict natural disasters, riots, revolutions and *coups d'état*. The ousting of the Shah of Iran by Ayatollah Khomeini affected fundamentally a number of international conflicts, in addition to being one of the causes of the Iran—Iraq War. The point I am stressing is that analysing conflict and negotiations without taking into account unpredictable changes in the environment is a futile exercise. Negotiants behave as if they believed the environment to be immutable; but they must be aware that their belief may be proved false. This may be a contradiction, but it is part of the complicated nature of the perception of negotiants.

The environment can be changed forcibly. Any violent disruptive action, such as a war or a revolt, indicates a level of dissatisfaction or fear that presupposes a need to change the environment before negotiations can recommence. Another way of changing the environment is to create facts. The settlement of the West Bank by Israel is an obvious example. Another is the building-up of a record of sugar exports by the European Community before beginning to negotiate joining the International Sugar Agreement. A negotiator takes action to change the environment when he perceives the prevailing one as putting him in an inferior bargaining position. Bargaining power is thus a perception born of the environment.

Like bargaining power, political will is also affected by changes in the environment. The Falklands War intervened while one series of negotiations was going on in the Britain/EEC Budget dispute. Until then, Britain had been insisting on a 5-year agreement on Budget rebates. When the other members of the Community supported Britain in the war, Britain's will to accept a less favourable deal was strengthened; as a mark of gratitude, Britain accepted a 1-year arrangement, with the promise of a 5-year deal later. How changes in the environment affect bargaining power and political power are described in greater detail in Chapters 12 and 13.

Time and the Phases of Negotiation

Throughout this book, bargaining and negotiation are examined as *processes*. We are concerned with what happens *during* the process, because every event in it can push the negotiation towards an agreement or towards a breakdown. Time affects every one of the concepts examined in the preceding chapters. It has a direct impact on levels of dissatisfaction. Passage of time, with no action taken to alleviate a grievance, may have the effect of reducing gradually the prospects of success, leaving no choice but violent action for the aggrieved. During a period of refusal to negotiate, the dissatisfaction level of the aggrieved party increases; consequently, the one who delays the negotiation may have to make greater sacrifices. We have to take note of time, not from the time a negotiation begins, but from the moment a dissatisfaction is voiced.

In saying that the level of dissatisfaction may be higher at one period than at an earlier one, we are also saying that the outcome expected by the dissatisfied negotiator may alter. Indeed, one of the effects of the negotiating process is to modify the expectations of the negotiators by successive approximations towards what is attainable. We can take full note of the changes in perception over time only by taking 'snapshots' of perception at different points in time. These should show, not merely dissatisfactions, expectations and fears, but also the perceptions of the negotiators about their relative bargaining power, about potential negotiators who can be drawn into the negotiation, and about the environment.

Time has an impact in speeding up or slowing down negotiations. In the market, at the end of the day, the seller has an incentive to speed up the bargaining. His stock will be running low, he will expect to see fewer customers and he will be more anxious to pack up and go home. His will to reach an agreement is thus higher. (We have earlier referred to the phenomenon of the frenzied activity during the last minutes of any international conference and of the tactic of stopping the clock). Time, therefore, is not only a factor in the negotiating process, but is also an actual dimension in the bargaining space. It is necessary to emphasise that the 'time' we are discussing is 'real time'. In the real world, time is associated with gains and losses. There are costs and benefits in taking a supposedly rational economic decision at one time rather than at another. In most economic theorising, the analysis becomes extremely complex if real costs and benefits are to be included, and the assumption is made that these are not significant. We cannot afford the same luxury in dealing with bargaining. Because the process depends on communication which involves time, and because each communication is perceived by the recipient in the light of the situation at that time, the real costs and benefits automatically become part of the perceptions, which, in turn, influence the next communication.

We can now identify some of the phases of real-life conflicts and negotiations. The starting point is the *voicing* of a dissatisfaction, grievance or vulnerability. This could be an explicit communication. Sometimes an actor in a conflict makes his insecurity known by action — buying more arms, seeking the protection of an ally, or slackening work. The first phase, which we may call *encounter*, happens when the dissatisfied party confronts those who can act in some way to reduce the dissatisfaction. The others may then perceive that the amelioration of the voiced dissatisfaction or the reduction of the indicated vulnerability will involve some concessions or sacrifices on their part. Encounter, therefore, is the phase that runs from the voicing of a dissatisfaction by one potential negotiant to the perception of a conflict of interest by other potential negotiants.

The reaction of the other potential negotiants is rarely a decision to negotiate immediately. One tactic for postponing negotiations is *refusal to negotiate*. A more extreme form of this time-buying tactic is *refusal to recognise*. A classic example of this is Israel's refusal to recognise the PLO, even though it is obvious that the limitation of the Middle East conflict must involve negotiating with the representatives of the Palestinian people. If the Palestinians, and other Arab states, have decided that the PLO is the sole representative of the Palestinian people, then refusal to recognise the PLO is nothing but a persistent refusal to negotiate. Other examples are Morocco's refusal to recognise the Polisario Front in the dispute over the former Spanish Sahara, and South Africa's stubborn refusal to recognise the South West Africa People's Organisation (SWAPO) as a means of continuing her control over this former mandated territory.

In less extreme cases, the refusal phase is accompanied by communication between the parties. This sometimes merges into a third phase in a transition that is not clear-cut. In the Britain/EEC Budget dispute, for example, the refusal phase changed imperceptibly into a negotiation about the issues to be bargained over.

This third phase is *negotiation about negotiation* (NAN). The purpose of this is to agree on the dimensions of the bargaining space. While it looks, on the face of it, to be an attempt to answer the question 'What shall we negotiate about?', it is really an attempt to answer the question 'What shall we *not* negotiate about?' For example, Britain and the rest of the Community might not have been able to agree whether they should include, in addition to the actual Budget issue, fisheries policy, sheep meat and North Sea oil. But they did agree *not* to negotiate about tachographs, the weight of heavy lorries, Spain's application to join the Community and the Lomé Convention.

The inclusion or removal of some subjects from the substantive negotiations to follow is sometimes achieved by setting *preconditions*. 'We shall negotiate only if there are no preconditions' is itself a precondition; in this case, a negotiant does not want any issue removed from the bargaining space. The two examples of preconditions cited earlier were (i) Iraq's insistence in the early stages of the conflict with Iran that sovereignty over the Shatt-al-

Arab should be kept out of the negotiations, and (ii) a similar sovereignty demand by Argentina about the Falkland Islands. 'We shall not negotiate under threat' is also a precondition. This is simultaneously a demand that the other negotiant refrains from exercising his threat to use force to change the environment and a counter-threat to meet force with force. All preconditions are related to a determination of the dimensions of the bargaining space. Setting a precondition is equivalent to removing a dimension from the bargaining space, and removing one is agreeing to add that dimension in the negotiations which are to follow.

NANs are also negotiations and, as such, may end in agreement or breakdown. If there is agreement, the end of the phase is the telescoping of this negotiation into the next one. In addition, the exchange of information during this period has the effect of delimiting approximately the boundaries in each dimension. An example is the long-drawn-out Madrid negotiations in November 1981, on the review of the Helsinki Declaration. The participating countries were supposed to be discussing the agenda for the conference; they were, in effect, pre-empting a major part of the substantive discussions which were to follow, after the agenda had been agreed upon. The so-called discussions on procedural issues are never just that; one cannot talk about the procedure without talking about the substantive issues and without disclosing what any negotiant expects to get out of the subsequent negotiations.

If the negotiants agree on the bargaining space and on all the procedural matters, then substantive negotiations can begin. There will be further stages in the ensuing negotiation, but we can identify them only after considering other aspects of the process in Parts Two and Three.

If the negotiants agree on a course of action, we have called it *agreement*; if they fail, we have called it *breakdown*. If there are more than two negotiants, some may drop out leaving the rest to continue negotiating; we have called this *opting out*. All the possible terminations will, henceforth, be called *outcome*. All the emphasised words have their normal meanings and I have imputed no special or restricted meanings.

Past History and Memory

While we have made a distinction between 'negotiations about negotiations' and 'negotiations on substantive issues', both are negotiations — the process is the same. We have also pointed out how new negotiations can arise either out of residues of dissatisfactions or from new dissatisfactions. In short, every negotiation is part of a continuum of negotiations. At each point in time, there is a past history which affects the perceptions and judgements of the negotiants.

The Treaty of Versailles was perceived in Germany, in the 1930s, as an iniquitous settlement and one responsible for mass unemployment and hyper-inflation. The memory of the defeat in the first world war and the memory of the peace negotiations which followed became part of German perceptions thereafter. An article in *The Economist* (27 September 1980) on the Iran—Iraq War was titled 'It all goes back to AD 637', and traced the conflict back to the Battle of Qadiriya that year 'when Arab Moslems defeated Persian Zoroastrians'. Even if we do not go back that far, the dispute can still be traced to Iran's discontent with an agreement made in 1937 on fixing the boundary between the two countries as the low-water mark on the Iranian side of the Shatt-al-Arab. This gave the whole of the river (and a shifting one at that) to Iraq. In 1965, Iran denounced this treaty and the ensuing conflict was supposed to have been settled by the Algiers Agreement of 1975, which fixed the boundary as the mid-stream line. This left a discontent in Iraq which took the opportunity of the disturbed conditions following the Iranian revolution to take the river by force. The conflicts between India and Pakistan have origins which go back before the countries were divided. The origins of the conflict between Greek and Turkish-Cypriots may go as far back as the fall of Constantinople. The Middle East conflict did not start with the Balfour Declaration; nor did the troubles in Ulster begin with the Derry apprentices' march.

There are two reasons why I stress the obvious. First, all the examples have given rise to repeated violence. With the exception of Germany, the others are still simmering; and even in the German case, there are dissatisfactions arising from the division of the country after the second world war. It is difficult to be optimistic about any of these conflicts being limited in order to make violence less likely. In tackling conflict-limitation, we ignore past history only at our peril. Secondly, theorising without keeping in mind real-life situations is an unproductive endeavour. Such theories face insurmountable obstacles if they are applied to the far more complex reality.

Past history affects many aspects of negotiation, especially trust, credibility and amenability to threats. The Greek- and Turkish-Cypriots evidently do not trust each other; should we, therefore, abandon all attempts at peaceful limitation of conflict and stand by until violence erupts again? If distrust is a legacy left in the memory by past history, it should be possible equally to diminish distrust. That it can be done has been proved by the diminution of distrust between France and Germany, two nations with centuries of hostility behind them.

The combined effect of time and history is memory. Starting with an accumulated memory before a negotiation begins, every stage in the process adds to it. Perceptions and judgements are affected by the total memory, composed of the immediate past experience of the negotiation and the accumulated past history. We shall not be able to explain the alchemy between memory, perception and judgement, but at least we can be aware of the resultant perception.

PART TWO

A THEORY OF BARGAINING

There is a mask of theory over the whole of the face of nature.
          William Whewell

Scientific enquiry ... begins as a story about a possible world — a story which we invent and criticize and modify as we go along, so that it ends by being, as nearly as we can make it, a story about real life.
          P.B. Medawar

We shall see that there are several kinds of hypotheses, that some are verifiable and when once confirmed by experiment become truths of great fertility; that others may be useful to us in fixing our ideas, and, finally, that others are hypotheses only in appearance, and reduce to definition or conventions in disguise.
          Poincaré

(All quotations from P.B. Medawar, *The Art of the Soluble* or *Induction and Intuition in Scientific Thought.*)

6 THE THEORETICAL FRAMEWORK

> Postulates, axioms, premises (hypotheses, assumptions) etc. are statements of the same logical standing; they differ from one another in the ways in which they have come to be formulated and the degree of confidence they enjoy. We assert a postulate, and take an axiom for granted but hypotheses we merely venture to propose.
> P.B. Medawar,
> *Induction and Intuition in Scientific Thought*

The aim of the chapters in Part One was to argue the validity of some concepts as being central to the understanding of the negotiating or bargaining process. Of these, dissatisfaction is a crucial one; it has to be present before a negotiation commences; it is present throughout the process as a standard against which other negotiants' dissatisfaction is compared; and a residue remains even after an agreement is reached. Perception is also important because it is impossible to devise an absolute scale of value or utilities that will be applicable to all negotiants at all times. Because perception is subjective, we have to take note of inherent uncertainties. In the next three chapters, I shall attempt to develop the theory of negotiation without losing sight of the objective of limitation of conflicts.

Summary of Conclusions from Part One

A *conflict* has its origins when an individual, group or nation, having felt a dissatisfaction or vulnerability, perceives that there are others in the environment who can act to reduce the dissatisfaction or decrease the vulnerablity. On the aggrieved voicing a discontent, the others perceive a conflict of interest.

Negotiation or bargaining is a process, happening over a period of time and involving two or more entities (negotiants). It is a peaceful process and does not include subjugation or violent disruptive action or those who have opted out. Subjugation is obedience secured by duress and does not take note of increasing dissatisfaction in the coerced. Disruptive violence is any action designed to hurt and includes physical assault, strikes and lockouts, takeover bids, revolt within states and wars between states. Opting-out is withdrawal from the bargaining process by a negotiant physically or metaphorically removing himself; this includes actions such as running away from home, filing for bankruptcy and abstaining on a UN resolution.

The *objective* of engaging in negotiation is to arrive at a mutual understanding in a specified area of activity with a view to reducing the dissatisfaction or vulnerability in one or more of the negotiants. The aim may be achieved by reaching *agreement*; alternatively, the negotiation may end in a *breakdown.*

The *means* employed in the bargaining process are exchange of information about dissatisfactions, insecurities, expectations and limits by communication, conference or discussion. The process involves judgements made by each negotiator about the outcome, based on his perceptions.

Vulnerability, which can lead to violence, arises from a perception of excessive dependence or insecurity due to perceived threats. Prolonged vulnerability degenerates into fear, leading to desperation.

Dissatisfaction is perception of either (i) unfairness, inequity or injustice, or (ii) the feeling of absence of an attainable goal. Each negotiant perceives his own dissatisfaction as being real to himself but does so in an inchoate way. Each negotiant perceives the dissatisfaction of another with an uncertain degree of accuracy. Dissatisfaction is never totally extinguished; the residue may give rise to further negotiations. Sometimes one dissatisfaction leads to another; any agreement can also generate new dissatisfactions. Acute dissatisfaction is frustration, leading to desperation, which may erupt into violence. There is no objective and absolute scale of dissatisfaction. Every negotiant tries to estimate the dissatisfactions of others and, therefore, the process is dependent on perceptions.

The *perceptions* of negotiants are unpredictable; the reactions of different people to the same situation may be different and may even be diametrically opposed. Negotiators may also perceive what others did not intend to convey. Distortions occur in the act of perception as well as in the process of judgement. Time, individual traits, success or failure, and the satisfaction of a need are some of the factors which affect perception. Economic constraints, social conditioning and distortions in communication are other factors affecting perception. Because of such distortions, the perception of one negotiant never corresponds totally with what was meant to be conveyed; there is always uncertainty.

Uncertainty is due to imperfect feedback, linguistic difficulties, differences in competence, and semantics. Though uncertainty can never be completely eliminated, it can be reduced. Reduction is achieved by communication, improved skills and by agglomeration of a large number of individual negotiations into fewer, higher-order, periodic ones. Communication helps to reduce uncertainty by successive approximation. It is possible to diminish distrust by reducing uncertainty.

The greater the reduction in uncertainty, the more predictable the behaviour of others becomes. This reduces insecurity and promotes *order*. The higher the order, the nearer one is to creating a framework of *rules* for organised human activity.

There will always be *residues* of dissatisfaction, vulnerability and uncertainty. While these are related, there is no direct correspondence between them. Even when order is created, dissatisfaction will persist. Creating a rule does not end a conflict; it only brings it within a framework which may make it more manageable for purposes of limiting conflicts.

Bargaining takes place within the *environment* but the process includes only a limited number of agreed issues or dimensions. The set of dimensions is the *bargaining space*. The set of negotiants is the *bargaining population* in the space. The environment sets the limits of the bargaining space, but the boundaries in each dimension are uncertain. Negotiants may perceive the location of a boundary differently but there is an understanding about what lies outside the boundary.

The environment changes with *time*; the unpredictable often happens. Negotiants engage themselves in the bargaining process on two tacit assumptions: that the environment will either be invariant or vary predictably; and if the environment undergoes unpredicted changes, that the outcome of the previous negotiation will be subject to further negotiation.

Time has a direct impact on levels of dissatisfaction; affects perception and all other aspects of the negotiating process; and is required for communication. *Expectations* change with time. It is an irreversible dimension unlike the other dimensions that are perceived as part of the bargaining space by the negotiants.

No negotiation takes place in an historical vacuum and all negotiations are part of a continuum of negotiations. The combined effect of time and history is *memory*, which affects the perceptions and judgement of the negotiators at every stage of the process.

Though the negotiants achieve some satisfaction (*utility*) if a negotiation ends in an agreement, the process of reaching it also involves a consideration of what each can get out of others. Thus, the time at which agreement is reached is dependent on a perception of *equality of dissatisfaction.*

The phases that are relevant to conflicts, after the *voicing* of a dissatisfaction or vulnerability are: (i) the *encounter* which is a confrontation between an entity with a grievance and others who perceive that alleviating it will involve a sacrifice from them; (ii) *refusal to recognise* and *refusal to negotiate* which are the time periods when other potential negotiators indicate that the ameliorating actions required of them will not be forthcoming; (iii) *negotiations about negotiations* which is the stage concerned with agreeing on the dimensions of a bargaining space and approximately delimiting the boundaries in each dimension; and (iv) *the negotiation on the substantive issues.* At each stage, the participants have the option of turning the conflict away from a violent end. The *outcome*, signifying the termination of the continuum of negotiations, may either be an agreement or a breakdown. The *future of the conflict* will depend on the nature of the outcome; the negotiating phase becomes part of the past history of the conflict and of subsequent negotiations, if any follow.

The Trivial Case

The minimum number of negotiants required for a negotiation is two. Though there is no such thing as a one-person negotiation, an examination of this zero-order type will be helpful in laying the basis for a two-negotiant case.

In a one-person negotiation, there is no uncertainty of perception. The negotiant 'knows' his dissatisfaction, which is real to him at that moment. When comparing current dissatisfactions, he is 'thinking' or 'making a choice'. Any choice is still a matter of judgement involving rational and psychological factors, as in any true negotiation.

Let us take the choice between buying chicken or turkey at the supermarket, a place where I do not have to bargain. We assume that I have decided to buy food, when I would rather buy whisky, because my dissatisfactioin at having to go hungry is greater than my dissatisfaction at not getting drunk. (Alcoholics, like other addicts, may make a different choice.) Let us also assume that, though I prefer turkey to chicken, I normally buy chicken because it is cheaper. However, at Christmas (in England) or Thanksgiving (in the United States) I buy turkey even if it is dearer, because I am prepared to spend more money at certain times of the year. One reason may be that the idea of chicken every week of the year is quite sickening; another is the psychological satisfaction of marking the special nature of the occasion. The choice made on special occasions and during the rest of the year is schematically shown in Figure 6.1.

Viewed thus, my dissatisfaction at having to spend more on turkey has moved up to equalise my dissatisfaction at not having it. This example is used only to show that (i) dissatisfactions change with time, and (ii) if there is no perceptual uncertainty, we can think of choosing by an individual as equalising two dissatisfactions. We should also note that satisfaction accrues at both

Figure 6.1: Making a Choice

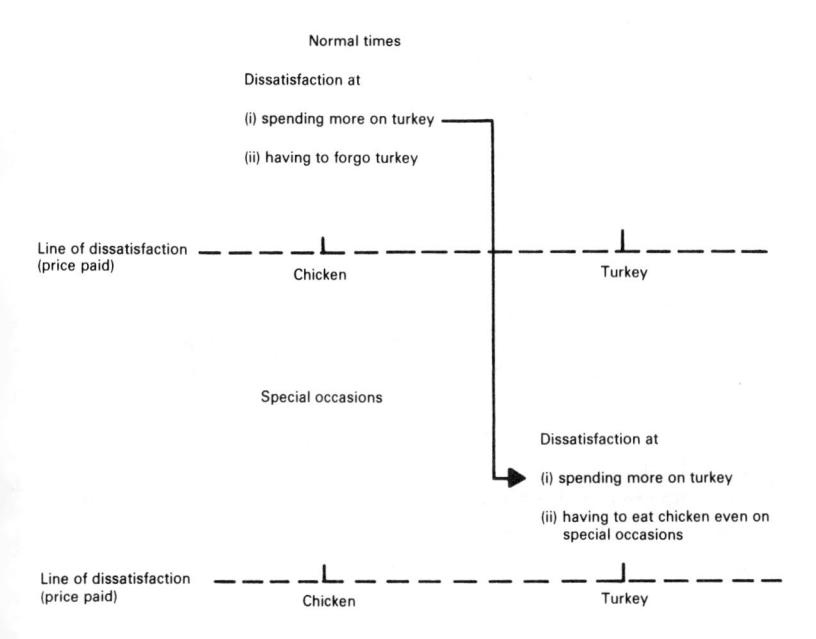

times; by buying chicken I satisfy my hunger, but by buying turkey I not only satisfy my hunger but also a psychological want. At this simplified level, the example can also be explained using utilities; dissatisfactions are used here only as a starting point for further development in the succeeding chapters.

Choice and Dimension

We have to make a clear distinction between making a choice among a set of possible courses of action and negotiating in different dimensions. To illustrate, suppose a couple are arguing about whether to go to Greece or Italy for their holiday, the two destinations are not two different dimensions; there is only one dimension with alternative choices. Suppose the husband prefers Greece and the wife Italy, this problem is insoluble as a negotiation if they have equal bargaining power. It is soluble if the husband says: 'Let's go to Greece this year; next year we'll definitely go to Italy.' At this point a new dimension has been added by the promise of future action. The negotiation has been enlarged and a trade-off has been offered. The agreement reached between the couple is a package comprising two things — something to be done immediately and a promise about potential action. Both are functionally related. If there is no functional relationship between the dimensions of a bargaining space, then such negotiations have to be independent of each other. Suppose the husband and the wife, while they are discussing their holiday plans, are also discussing when to hold the next dinner party, the two negotiations may be independent of each other, unless one or the other chooses to link them. The fact that the same two entities negotiate on different subjects simultaneously does not necessarily make them part of the same bargaining space. The British and French governments negotiate on a large number of subjects; while complex negotiations were going on about the Community Budget, the CAP and the fisheries policy, they could also have been negotiating about, say, the extradition of Lord Kagan. Neither government linked the latter negotiation with the ones on Community matters.

The distinction between choice and dimension has to be maintained even if the number of available choices is more than two. In the example examined in Chapter 3, the couple trying to decide had a choice of three different holiday venues. We arbitrarily described the example in such a way that the husband's first preference was the wife's last and vice versa, and both had a common middle preference. Because of this particular ordering, the couple managed to equalise their dissatisfaction within the one dimension. Had their order of preference been different, they could not have found an agreement within the dimension of that year's holiday destination. They would have had to find a trade-off by invoking another dimension. Trade-offs, package deals and functional relationships between dimensions are examined in Chapter 8.

What happens when there are more than two persons, faced with having to choose between different alternatives? For example, we could add to the argument between the couple, a grown-up son, with his own preference on the holiday destination. The complication arising from an increase in the number of negotiants is of a different kind from those arising from increasing the number of dimensions. Two of the three could form a coalition against the third. Adding negotiants is examined in Chapter 9.

In the next chapter we shall start with the simplest true negotiation — two negotiants and one dimension.

7 ON BUYING POTATOES

> I should, I think, be prepared to argue that, in a world ruled by uncertainty with an uncertain future linked to an actual present, a final position of equilibrium, such as one deals with in static economics, does not probably exist.
>
> John Maynard Keynes,
> *Collected Works*, vol. XXIX

Two-person Negotiations in One Dimension

The simplest true negotiation is the bargaining between two negotiants in a single-issue dimension, with a time dimension. Let us consider a seemingly real-life example — buying potatoes in a market where bargaining is the accepted practice. Since such a bargaining takes only a few minutes, we can assume that the environment does not change. We also assume that the buyer wants to buy only potatoes and nothing else. The two assumptions, an invariant environment and constant bargaining space, will be discarded in later chapters. The subject of the bargaining is the price for exactly one kilo of potatoes, thus avoiding the question of discounts if larger quantities are bought. We shall follow this negotiation step by step, at first assigning numerical values in order to make it easier to understand. A purely symbolic derivation, without assigning any arbitrary values, is explained later in the chapter.

The Limits of the Bargaining Space

Suppose the vegetable seller (hereafter seller or S) quotes 90 paise (90 p; 100 paise = 1 rupee) a kilo, and let the buyer (B) offer 50 p. Of course, the seller does not expect to get 90 p nor does the buyer expect to pay as little as 50 p, these are merely their opening gambits or initial offer of S and initial bid by B. This is not different from quota negotiations in ICAs; the initial inflated bids by various exporting countries are said to contain 'water in the quota', which needs to be squeezed out in later negotiations. In arms control negotiations also, inflated claims are put in by the parties on issues such as missile numbers, throw-weights and independent warheads.

Whatever their expectations, S and B each have a fixed point. There is the price below which S will not sell; it may be 65 p, 70 p or 75 p. Likewise, B will not pay more than his maximum. When the bargaining begins, S knows his own minimum price and his expectation; but the only thing he knows about the buyer is B's initial bid. From this, S concludes that the sale, if successful, will not be below 50 p. This sets one limit to the bargaining space. Likewise, B knows that he will not have to pay more than 90 p and that becomes the other limit of the bargaining space. This is true even if the negotiants have different expectations before the bargaining begins. For example, B might have been told by a friend, 'Do you know potatoes have gone up again? I paid a rupee a kilo yesterday!' and then might have come to the market expecting to pay about 1 rupee. Once B has heard the offer price of 90 p, he knows that he will not have to pay *more* than that. (In negotiations between institutions or governments these limits would have become apparent from the earlier stage of NAN.)

In general, the boundaries of a dimension in the bargaining space are the initial positions of the negotiants. This is subject to the simplifying assumptions made about the environment and bargaining space remaining unchanged during the negotiation. If the environment changes, the limits of the bargaining space may also change. One example should suffice. The expectation of the South African government — and consequently its limits — in the negotiations on independence for Namibia underwent a change as a result of the success of Ronald Reagan in the American presidential election in 1979 with South Africa raising its minimum. In this case, the bargaining space also changed; a new dimension relating to Cuban troops in Angola was added.

Notwithstanding the prices offered at the beginning of the bargaining, B knows that S will be prepared to sell for something less than 90 p, and S knows that B will be prepared to pay more than 50 p. But they do not know how much less or how much more. In the nebulous bargaining space, no details are visible at this stage. Only what is outside is clearly known.

The Nature of the Outcome

Let us now postulate the existence of an omniscient observer, a convenience we shall soon discard. The observer alone knows all the positions of S and B. Earlier, we did not specify a single figure for either S's minimum or B's maximum, but proposed, deliberately, a choice between three figures — 65, 70 or 75 p. Depending on where S's minimum and B's maximum fall on the price line, there are three possible outcomes: (i) S's minimum price is higher than B's maximum, (ii) S's minimum is lower than B's maximum, and (iii) both are equal. Our numerical example will be seen by the omniscient observer as in Figure 7.1.

The three possible outcomes are named, for obvious reasons, eventual breakdown, possible agreement and see-saw. The

Figure 7.1: Three Possible Outcomes: two negotiants/one dimension

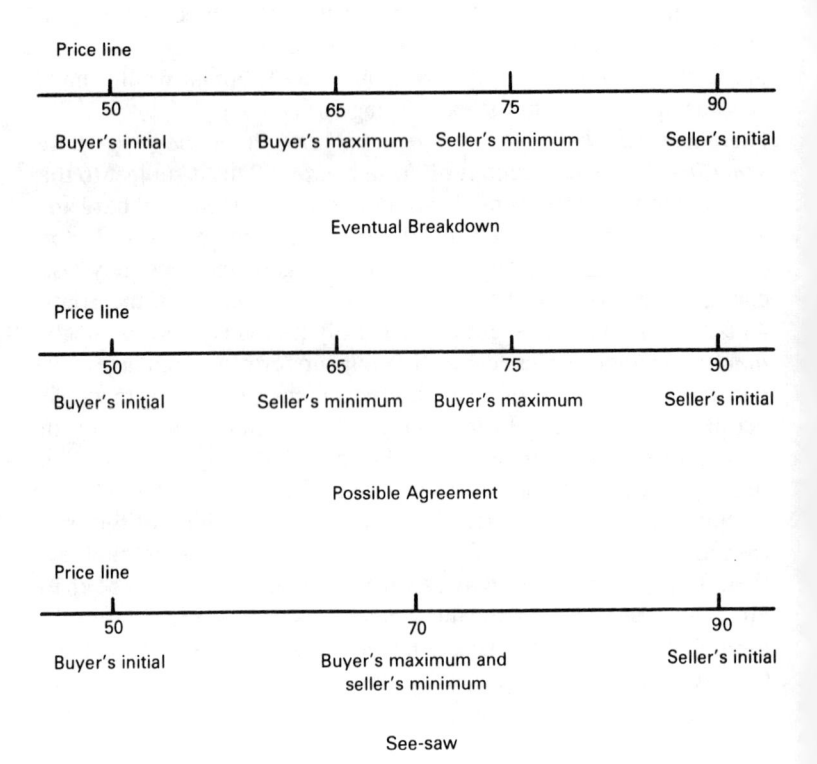

Price line

50	65	75	90
Buyer's initial	Buyer's maximum	Seller's minimum	Seller's initial

Eventual Breakdown

Price line

50	65	75	90
Buyer's initial	Seller's minimum	Buyer's maximum	Seller's initial

Possible Agreement

Price line

50	70	90
Buyer's initial	Buyer's maximum and seller's minimum	Seller's initial

See-saw

observer alone can see that (i) if the seller will not sell below 75 p, and the buyer will not pay more than 65 p, there can be no agreement however long the two may negotiate; (ii) an agreement is possible in the second type; and (iii) an agreement in the last type will be quite difficult.

I want to emphasise that, even in this elementary case, a breakdown is possible. One of my criticisms against other bargaining theories is that they assume *a priori* the existence of an agreement point, and never provide for the possibility of a breakdown. We have avoided that trap.

The observer has been introduced into the discussion only to illustrate the point that the relative positions of the minimum and maximum are crucial to the prospects of success of a negotiation. One might say that the outcome is almost pre-ordained provided, of course, the environment and the bargaining space remain unchanged. In the second type, the agreement point must fall between 65 p and 75 p. Agreement is possible in the see-saw type only when a kilo of potatoes changes hands at 70 p.

The Process of Negotiation

The three possible outcomes are what common sense tells us would happen if all negotiants had the kind of perfect knowledge which only the ominiscient observer has. S and B, however, have to bargain with imperfect knowledge. B, though opening the bidding with 50 p and being prepared to go up to his maximum, *expects* to pay a price between his maximum and his initial offer. At the beginning of negotiations, neither S nor B knows the other's *limit position* or *expectation*. But B knows that S knows that B will raise his offer, just as S knows that B knows that S will lower his asking price.

The process of negotiation is, therefore, concerned with communicating information about limit positions and changing expectations. In the second type, where an agreement is possible, S will reduce his initial offer fairly rapidly to 80 p, then to 75 p, and, somewhat later, to 70 p. As he approaches his minimum of 65 p, his concessions will become smaller and will also take longer to extract. Likewise, B's concessions, as he moves nearer 75 p, will become smaller and be made after longer intervals. Each negotiant automatically notes the time taken between one concession and the next; time *is* an integral part of the negotiating process.

The voicing of each bid or offer is a communication about current expectation; the totality of such communications, taking into account time spent, conveys information about limits.

Neither negotiant specifies clearly his minimum or maximum position. The reason is obvious. It is against S's interest to tell B that his minimum price is 65 p, since the sale would then take place only at that price. B cannot know with certainty that S's minimum price is 65 p; he can only guess, after some negotiation, that it is somewhere near it. Neither can B have a precise idea of S's expectation.

Negotiants keep the exact location of their limit positions and expectations secret, but convey information about them. The limit position and expectation are perceived by other negotiants uncertainly. At later stages, when there is more information, the uncertainty is reduced but not eliminated.

The description of the process also shows why expectations change. In the beginning, after making an initial offer of 90 p, S may expect to sell for 80 p. But when he hears B's opening bid of 50 p, S has to revise his expectation downwards. *Communication of information about expectation by one negotiant prompts the others to modify theirs.*

Throughout this discussion, we have described how S sees the situation and, separately, how B sees it. The process of negotiation, and the changes in perception that result from communication, are shown graphically in Figure 7.2 for breakdowns. The reasoning for the other two outcomes will be similar.

At time T_B, when the bargaining begins, B's and S's knowledge and perceptions (Figure 7.2a) have a large degree of uncertainty ('cloudy' area). After negotiating up to, say, time T_1, both S and B have a less uncertain idea of the changed expectation of the other and have also gained an insight into the other's break-off position (Figure 7.2b). Between T_B and T_1, B has revised his expectation upwards from 60 p to 62 p, and S has revised his downwards from 83 p to 80 p. There is less uncertainty, and B perceives S's minimum to be somewhere below 80 p while S perceives B's maximum to be somewhere above 62 p.

In subsequent periods of negotiation, the same phenomena of revision of expectations, reduction in uncertainty and clearer perception of limits recur. But the range of movement becomes smaller for equal time periods indicating to the other negotiant the approach of the limit position.

On Buying Potatoes 101

Figure 7.2a: Negotiants' Perceptions at Time T_B

B's perception

50	60	65	S's expectation	90
B's bid	B's expectation	B's maximum		S's offer

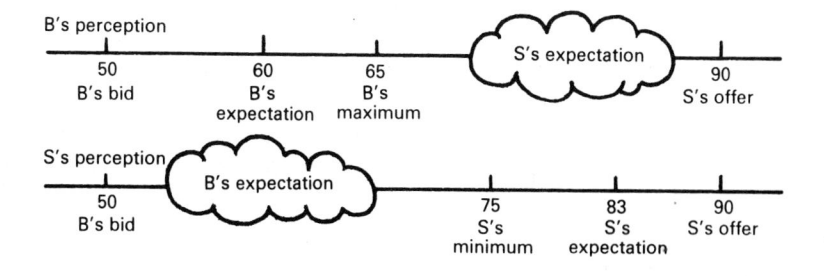

S's perception

50	B's expectation	75	83	90
B's bid		S's minimum	S's expectation	S's offer

Figure 7.2b: Negotiants' Perceptions at Time T_1

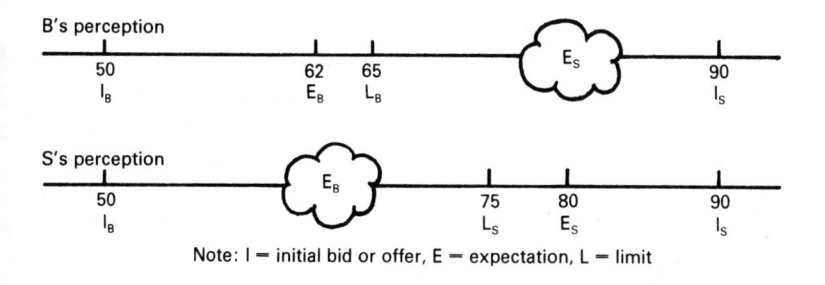

B's perception

50	62	65	E_S	90
I_B	E_B	L_B		I_S

S's perception

50	E_B	75	80	90
I_B		L_S	E_S	I_S

Note: I — initial bid or offer, E — expectation, L — limit

Figure 7.2c: Negotiants' Perceptions at Time T_0

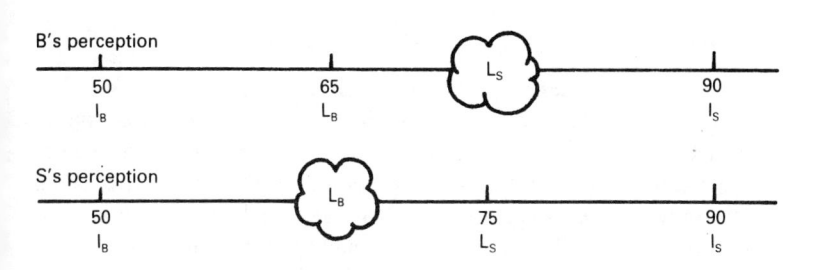

B's perception

50	65	L_S	90
I_B	L_B		I_S

S's perception

50	L_B	75	90
I_B		L_S	I_S

At time T_O when the outcome is clear (Figure 7.2c), the negotiants perceive an irreconcilable gap. What was obvious to the omniscient observer from the beginning is perceived by S and B only at time T_O.

Instead of looking at the negotiation at different moments in time (Figure 7.2a, b and c being 'snap shots' at times T_B, T_1 and T_O), the entire process can be shown in a plane diagram using time as a dimension (Figure 7.3). As before, there are two diagrams, one for S and one for B.

Types of Negotiations

In the negotiation illustrated in Figure 7.3, the buyer started with an expectation (E_B) between his initial bid (I_B) and his maximum (L_B—B's limit). As the negotiation progressed, E_B moved towards L_B. Likewise, S's expectation (E_S) moved towards L_S. In the see-saw type also, the expectations would have been in the segments between the negotiant's initial position and his limit position.

The second type — possible agreement — is different. Because the seller's minimum price is below the buyer's maximum price, their expectations can, logically, take five different positions. If we look at the price line, E_B can fall in either of two segments: between I_B and L_S or between L_S and L_B. Similarly, E_S can fall between I_S and L_B or between L_B and L_S. If both E_S and E_B fall in the middle segment, there are again two possibilities: $E_B > E_S$ or $E_S > E_B$. These five possibilities, along with the two types of breakdown and see-saw, are logically the only seven types of possible negotiations between two-persons in one-dimension (shown in Figure 7.4 with appropriate names for each).

The five sub-types where agreement is possible provide answers to two questions: (i) Why do some negotiations take longer than others? and (ii) why do some negotiations end in an agreement which is more favourable to one of the negotiants?

Negotiations with Inadequate Prior Knowledge

There are two interesting types which are logically possible, but somewhat implausible in real life. In the type called *quick agreement* B expects to buy a kilo of potatoes for 75 p, while S expects to get only 65 p — S's expectation is much lower than that of B! This may happen in a market, because the last time B bought potatoes he paid 80 p and he was unaware that, since then, there

On Buying Potatoes 103

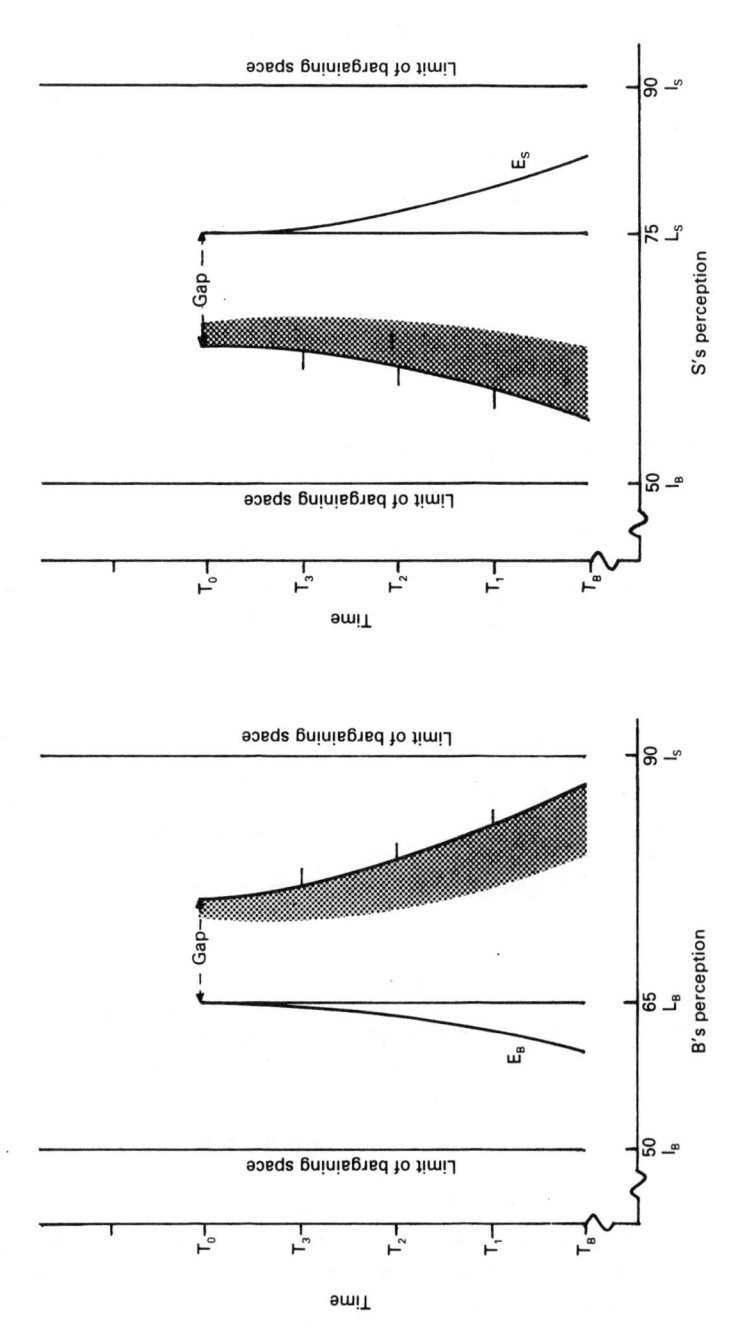

Figure 7.3: The Negotiating Process: two person/one dimension — breakdown

104 On Buying Potatoes

Figure 7.4: Seven Types of Negotiations: two person/one dimension

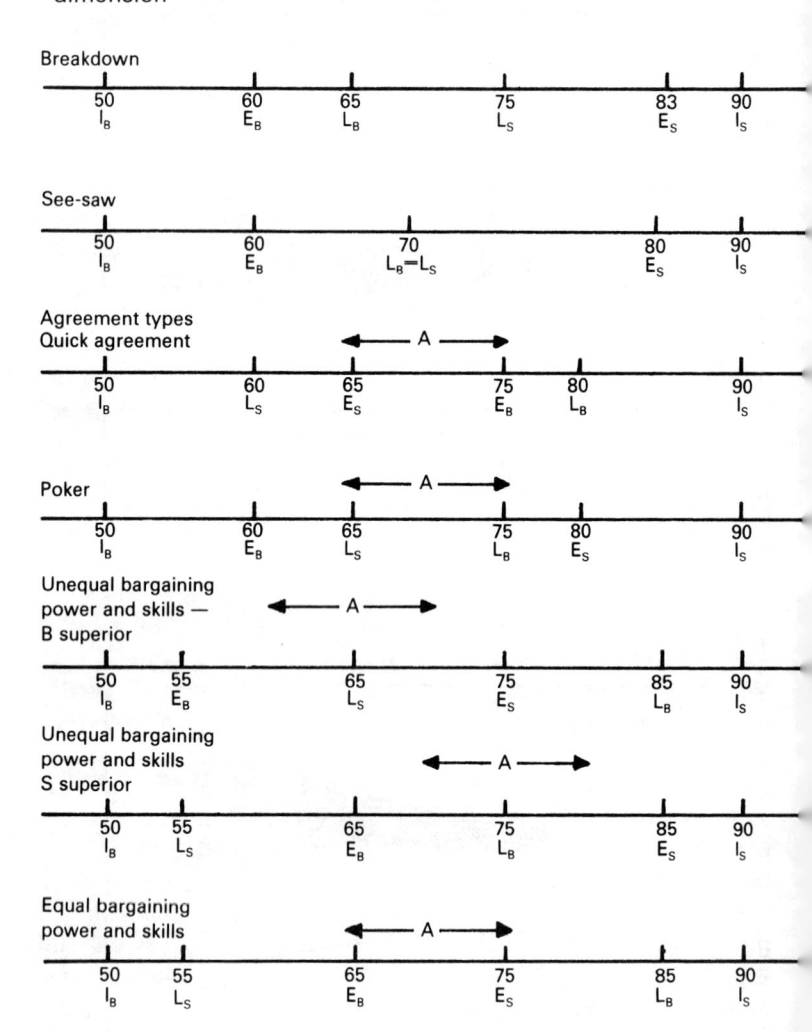

Breakdown

50	60	65	75	83	90
I_B	E_B	L_B	L_S	E_S	I_S

See-saw

50	60	70		80	90
I_B	E_B	$L_B = L_S$		E_S	I_S

Agreement types
Quick agreement ← A →

50	60	65	75	80	90
I_B	L_S	E_S	E_B	L_B	I_S

Poker ← A →

50	60	65	75	80	90
I_B	E_B	L_S	L_B	E_S	I_S

Unequal bargaining power and skills — B superior ← A →

50	55	65	75	85	90
I_B	E_B	L_S	E_S	L_B	I_S

Unequal bargaining power and skills S superior ← A →

50	55	65	75	85	90
I_B	L_S	E_B	L_B	E_S	I_S

Equal bargaining power and skills ← A →

50	55	65	75	85	90
I_B	L_S	E_B	E_S	L_B	I_S

had been a glut in the market which prompted S to lower his expectations.

S and B move rapidly in early stages, from their initial positions towards their expectations. S, therefore, will reduce his initial offer of 90 p substantially since he is going towards 65 p, and will get to B's original expectation of 75 p fairly soon. Likewise B, trying to move from 50 p to 75 p, will get quickly to S's original expectation of 65 p. Knowledge will suddenly dawn on both that their expectations were unduly pessimistic and both rapidly revise them upwards. Very soon, they arrive at an agreement somewhere between 65 p and 75 p (not necessarily at the precise midpoint). Lack of adequate knowledge makes it possible to arrive at a speedy agreement.

In the type called 'poker', B is prepared to pay up to 75 p, but makes an initial bid of only 50 p, hoping to settle for 60 p. He may pitch his expectations well below his maximum because he happens to have a high opinion of his own bargaining skill. S, too, may make an initial offer of 90 p, be prepared to settle for as low as 65 p, but expect to get 80 p by hard bargaining. Since their maximum and minimum are quite far from their expectations, S and B will play their cards close to their chests. Unlike the previous case, they will not approach their limits rapidly, but make only small concessions stretched over long periods. They may use such tactics as threatening to break off negotiations. The information communicated will be more limited and may even be misleading. Such negotiations will take much longer for agreement to be reached.

Bargaining Power and Bargaining Skills

Whenever the maximum price that B is prepared to pay is higher than the minimum S is prepared to sell at ($L_B > L_S$), an agreement is possible. However, in some negotiations B may expect to buy cheap and S may also have a low expectation. In the type called *B superior*, he expects to buy at 55 p, though the maximum he is prepared to pay may be as high as 85 p. The low expectation may be because he knows that S is anxious to dispose of his last few kilos and go home. For his part, S may be prepared to sell at 65 p, though he has some hopes, albeit faint ones, of getting more. The expectations of the two negotiants are clustered round S's minimum price. Because of the inequality in bargaining power, the eventual agreement will be nearer S's minimum than B's maximum. The environment has determined this by imposing either a glut on the market or an impatience to sell on S's part.

The converse case of S having superior bargaining power is also shown in Figure 7.4. In this case, the environment may impose a different set of constraints; either a scarcity in the market or B being in a hurry. Since the expectations are clustered round B's maximum, the eventual agreement will be more favourable to S. He will get a price much higher than his minimum while B will pay a price near his maximum.

The third possibility, also shown in Figure 7.4 is, obviously, one where the negotiants have equal bargaining power.

The five different sub-types, all resulting in agreement, can be shown graphically using plane diagrams, with time as a dimension. (For reasons of space, only two types, poker and unequal bargaining power are shown in Figures 7.5 and 7.6). In these figures the numbers used to illustrate the types have been omitted and the patterns are shown using symbols.

The See-saw

At the beginning of a one-dimension negotiation, the omniscient observer could discern agreement, breakdown or a state of prolonged negotiation, the last occurring when the maximum of one negotiant is also the minimum of the other. Both S and B start negotiating with expectations falling somewhere between their initial and limit positions. As the negotiation proceeds, each will perceive the other's expectation to be quite far from his own. Each negotiant will then gradually change his expectation nearer his own limit. Since both limits fall on the same point, each is bound to perceive that the other is also approaching it. But neither can be sure that the two points are identical, since each negotiant can perceive the other's position only uncertainly. There will always be some doubt about whether the limits coincide, or whether there is an unbridgeable gap, however tiny. This has two consequences. A lot of time will have to be spent ascertaining the presence or absence of a gap. Second, the negotiations will always be teetering on the balance between agreement and breakdown. If there is to be an agreement, it will call for a substantial reduction in uncertainty and almost total certainty. Achievement of certainty implies a high degree of trust, a factor vital to the limitation of conflict.

Agreement is also possible with mediation — an arbiter who can become the observer, if both parties trust him with information about their limits. Further, a breakdown can be averted if a trade-off can be found in some other dimension. Again, the environment itself might change, making an agreement or a clear-cut breakdown possible. Lastly, one of the negotiants may become impatient and simply opt out. The outcome in a see-saw case can be anything.

On Buying Potatoes 107

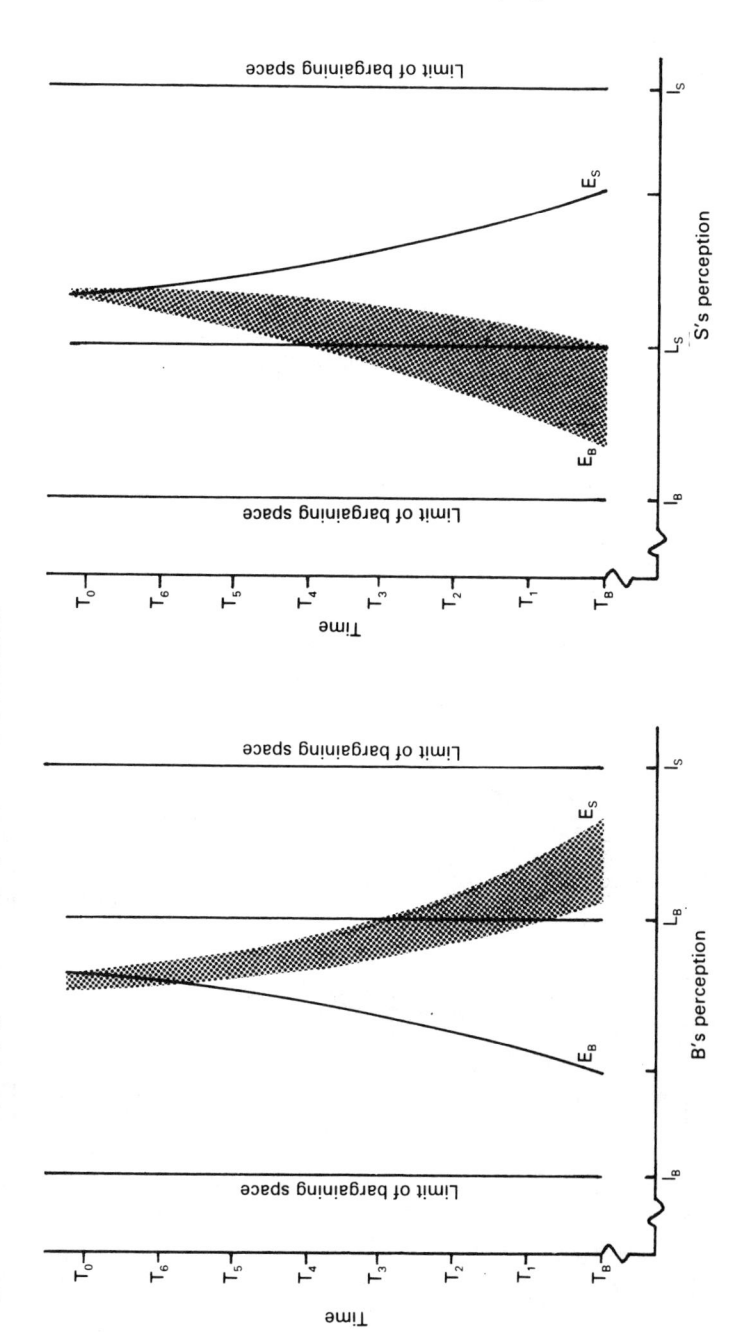

Figure 7.5: Poker-type Negotiation: two person/one dimension

108 *On Buying Potatoes*

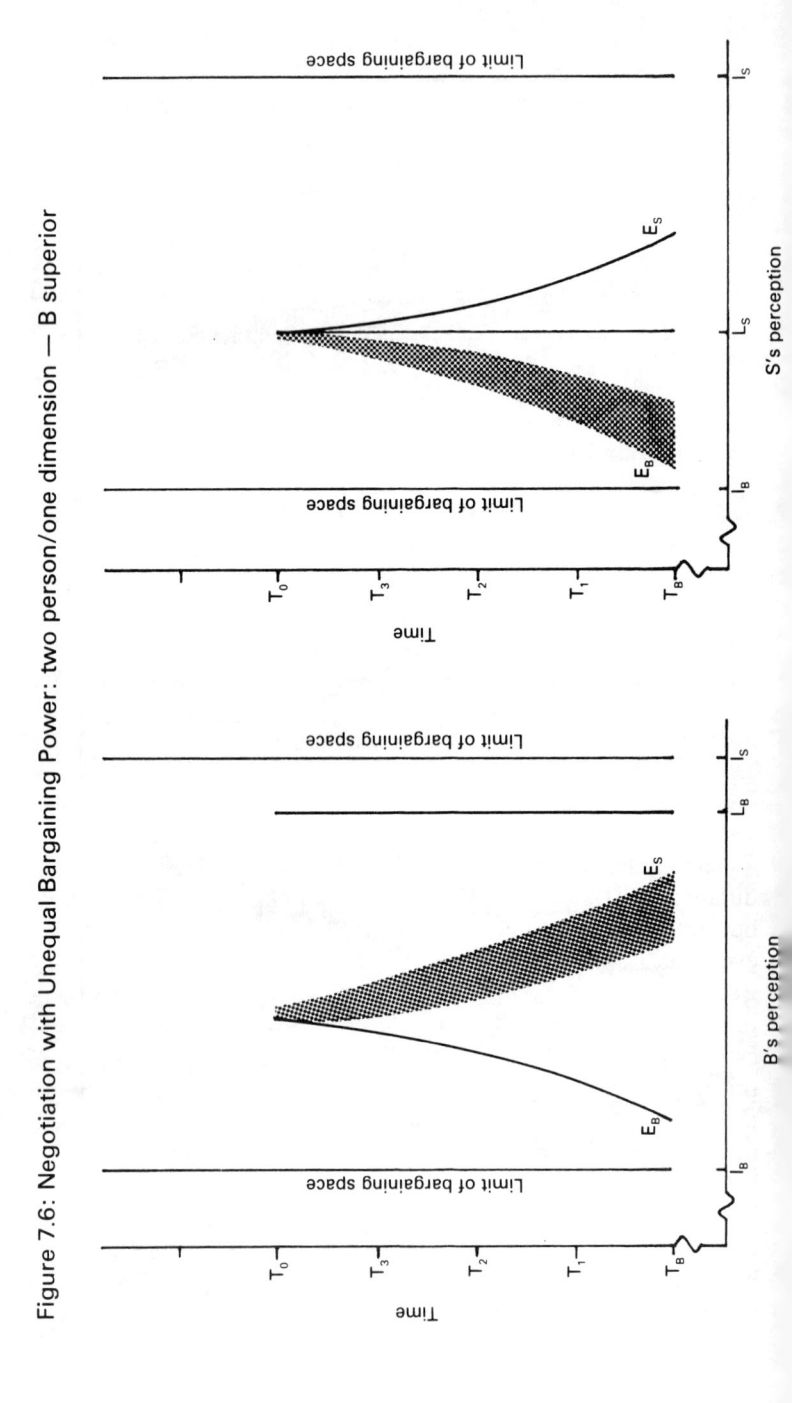

Figure 7.6: Negotiation with Unequal Bargaining Power: two person/one dimension — B superior

For the most part, the see-saw case proceeds like every other negotiation with information being exchanged about expectations and limits. The problem of teetering between breakdown and agreement arises towards the end of the negotiations when the uncertainties about expectations have been greatly reduced but not totally eliminated. We, therefore, have to look at the situation near the outcome point; it is as if we are enlarging the top section of Figures 7.5 and 7.6. Such an enlargement, as in Figure 7.7, shows an uncertain gap which will persist unless something else happens — a trade-off, arbitration, a change in the environment, or impatience.

The Duration and Phases of Negotiations

The seven types — breakdown, see-saw, and four types of agreement — differ from each other because of the relative position of the maximum and minimum of the negotiators and the relative positions of their initial expectations. The places in the bargaining dimension where the minimum and maximum fall determine the nature of the outcome — breakdown, agreement, or something between the two. I do not assert that, in real life, the negotiant's minimum and maximum never change with time. Within the assumptions of an invariant environment and a constant bargaining space, for a negotiation of short duration, there are only these seven types.

The nature of the types determines how long they take; i.e. the duration for T_B to T_O. Two negotiators who are close to agreement but are equally near a breakdown can, in theory, negotiate for ever; but, as pointed out earlier, this is unlikely in practice. As one would expect from common sense, a poker-type negotiation takes the longest to reach agreement. At the other extreme, the type called 'quick agreement' takes the shortest time; this again, in practice, is unusual and is due to ignorance of the environment on the part of at least one negotiant. The four types where an agreement is reached all take about the same time. A minimum duration is always required for the negotiators to convey information about limits, reduce the uncertainty in their perception of the other's limits, modify expectations and, in general, acquire a somewhat hazy comprehension of the whole picture. It is only at this stage that they can compute dissatisfactions.

Figure 7.7: See-saw Type Negotiation at the Time of Outcome

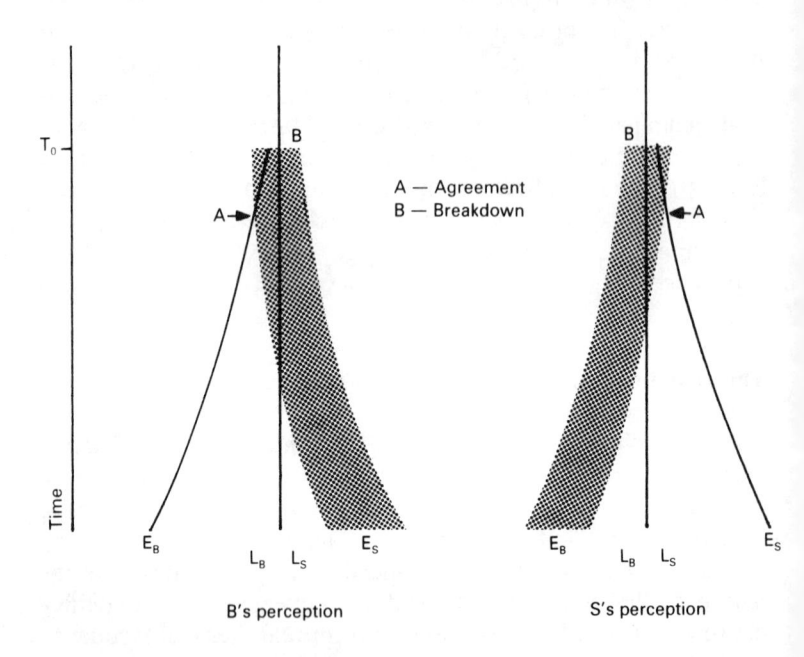

A — Agreement
B — Breakdown

B's perception

S's perception

We can now identify some phases of the negotiating process. Broadly, these are: (i) communication to ascertain initial expectations, (ii) modifying expectations, (iii) ascertaining limits, and (iv) determination of outcome based on a gap or on a perception of equality of dissatisfaction. The time required for different phases in each type is shown in tabular form in Table 7.1.

The last phase of the negotiation, just before the outcome, is worth noting. Prolonged uncertainty precedes outcome in the see-saw case and perception of a gap between limit positions in cases of breakdown. Where quick agreement is reached due to ignorance of the environment, both negotiants do better than they would have expected; the question of comparing dissatisfactions does not arise. In the other three cases we have to ascertain how the negotiants reach agreement.

On Buying Potatoes 111

Table 7.1: Negotiating Times for Different Types of Negotiations: two persons/one dimension

Time period	Outcome — agreement				Outcome — breakdown	Outcome — See-saw
	Quick agreement	Unequal power	Equal power	Poker type		
T_8 to T_1	←——— Communication to ascertain initial expectations ———→					
T_1 to T_2	←— Modifying expectations —→			Communication for more information	Modifying expectations	
T_2 to T_3	Perceiving better satisfaction than expected	Ascertaining limits and units of dissatisfaction		Modifying expectations	Ascertaining limits	Further modifying expectations
T_3 to T_4	Agreement	Perceiving equality of dissatisfaction		Further modifying expectations	Perceiving gap between limits	Ascertaining limits
T_4 to T_5		Agreement		Ascertaining limits and units of dissatisfaction	Breakdown	Further communication
T_5 to T_6				Perceiving equality of dissatisfaction		Outcome uncertain
T_6 to T_7				Agreement		Eventual breakdown

Equality of Dissatisfaction

A verbal description of dissatisfaction is easy; it is the difference between what a negotiant expects to get and what he actually gets. Symbolically, dissatisfaction = $E_S - O = E_B - O$. There are two difficulties in translating this definition to a real case. The process of negotiation is itself one of the negotiants modifying their expectations. These change with time and eventually merge with the outcome, becoming an expectation of the 'value' of the agreement. To measure dissatisfaction, we have to choose a point in time which is used by the negotiants to compare with the outcome. Is it the initial bid or offer? Is it the expectation at some other point between T_B and T_O? The second difficulty relates to the unit of dissatisfaction. Since it is a subjective concept, it needs a subjective unit of measurement. Though it is not necessary for each negotiant to use the same absolute standard, it must still be capable of being perceived by others.

The difficulties are not too great in the potato-buying example because of the simplifying assumptions of short duration, constant bargaining space and unchanging environment. We can safely ignore the buyer's initial bid and the seller's initial offer as not representing realistic expectations, since both know that the other's initial position was just that. Their only purpose was to establish the limits of the bargaining space. In most types of negotiation which end in agreement, the first phase of the bargaining process, communication to ascertain initial expectations, is achieved by time T_1; in a poker-type negotiation, it takes a little longer, up to T_2. Each negotiant works out his own dissatisfaction by computing the difference between his expectation at time T_1 (or T_2 in the poker type) and the outcome. By time T_1, each negotiant also has an uncertain idea of the other's initial expectation and can compute the other's dissatisfaction in relation to the outcome. In this simplified case, the unit of dissatisfaction is also clear; it is almost the same as the increase or decrease in price. For example, if the buyer initially expected to pay 65 p for a kilo of potatoes and the seller's initial expectation was 75 p, potatoes will, in all likelihood, change hands at 70 p if the bargaining powers are equal. This is only so in the special case of equal bargaining power where agreement is reached by 'splitting the difference'.

Two negotiants need not use the same standard for measuring dissatisfaction. Suppose S puts on the market a house worth about

£30,000, initially asking £35,000; let B make an initial bid of £26,000. Let us again assume that the environment does not change (e.g. interest rates do not go up, no new buyer emerges, etc.) and that the negotiation is only about the house and not about carpets or fixtures (i.e. there is only one negotiating dimension). S expects to sell for £30,000 but let us say he is prepared to go down to £29,000. B may be prepared to go as high as £31,000 because he likes the house, but he is in no hurry; he really expects to bargain with the expectation of buying it at £28,000. The price line will show the situation as in Figure 7.8.

Figure 7.8: Buying a House

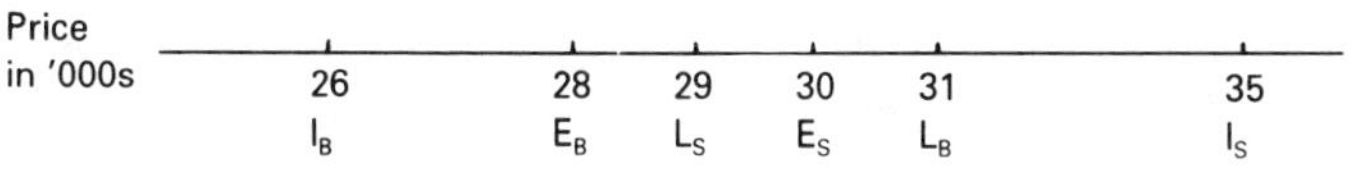

```
Price     ─────┼────────┼────┼────┼────┼──────────┼─────
in '000s      26       28   29   30   31         35
              I_B      E_B  L_S  E_S  L_B        I_S
```

The ordering of expectations and limits shows that this is a case of unequal bargaining power with B more powerful. S may be in a weaker bargaining position because he had already found another house, paid the deposit and is afraid of being 'gazumped' if he delays selling his own for too long.

During the negotiations from T_B to T_1, S will drop his price fairly rapidly to £30,000, while B will raise his by only £2000, from £26,000 to £28,000. When S reaches £30,000, he is only a £1000 away from his minimum, whereas B is still £3000 away from *his* maximum. In the next stage of negotiation, S's concessions will become fewer; he may drop his price only by a £100 each time. B, on the other hand, has still some way to go to his maximum and may increase his offer by as much as £300 each time. During this period the negotiants are conveying information about the limit position and, at the same time, also communicating information about their dissatisfactions. Each drop of £100 by S is equivalent to a rise of £300 by B.

Neither S nor B will perceive it as mathematically clear-cut as this. S will, however, perceive enough to know that a £100 dissatisfaction for him is equal to a dissatisfaction of between £250 and £350 for B. S will then have five units of dissatisfaction in dropping the price from £30,000 to £29,500 (by stages of £29,900, £29,800, etc.). S will also perceive that B has five units of dissatisfaction in raising the price in £300 steps from £28,000 to £29,500. The sale will take place at £29,500. In this specific example, S did not have to drop down to his minimum. Given a different choice of numbers, implying a different ordering of bargaining power, he might well have done so. The numbers used are not important. The example is used only to show that units of dissatisfaction are related to, but are not the same as, the unit of the dimension under negotiation; and that the process of communication also involves conveying information about units of dissatisfaction.

A mathematical presentation of the perception of equality of dissatisfaction is given in the Appendix. This also deals with the question of how to include impatience (i.e. the dissatisfaction at spending too much time negotiating). Put simply, impatience is a factor influencing the point at which agreement will be reached, and hence is a function of the total time spent negotiating.

Splitting the Difference

In one of the types in the potato-buying example, the buyer and seller were found to have reached agreement by 'splitting the difference'. This is a common occurrence but one for which there is no explanation in all the theories of bargaining so far propounded. If there is an agreement point exclusively predetermined by the objective conditions of the negotiation, then there is no need for the negotiants to abandon it in favour of another which, by definition, will give them less than optimum satisfaction. Splitting the difference becomes necessary beause of the uncertainty surrounding the perception by each negotiant of the other's position.

Any negotiation in one-dimension is either a case of making a choice between different courses of action or a case of 'division of the spoils'. If the negotiation is about agreeing on a course of action, an agreement is rarely possible without adding another dimension for finding a trade-off. This was shown in the example of a couple having to decide whether to go to Italy or Greece for their holiday; an agreement was possible only by adding a dimension about future action.

There are examples of negotiation about division of the spoils in international relations, a well-known one being the Yalta Conference between Roosevelt, Churchill and Stalin on dividing up the post-war world into respective spheres of influence. Another example of division clearly demonstrating splitting the difference is the negotiations between India and Bangladesh on the division of the waters of one of the many rivers common to them, the Teesta. One Bangladesh proposal and two Indian proposals are shown in Table 7.2, as reported in the Bangladesh press. The second Indian proposal is a clear case of splitting the difference between the first two proposals, keeping the Indian share constant.

Residue of Dissatisfaction

It is obvious that a substantial measure of dissatisfaction will remain after a breakdown — at least in the negotiant who voiced the original dissatisfaction. Why should there be a residue even after an agreement? The approach we have adopted for analysing negotiations shows why this happens.

In the example of the house sale, the price of the transfer for that specific numerical example was £29,500, the point at which both S and B perceived equality of dissatisfaction. But the perception of either S or B of the other's dissatisfaction has an element of uncertainty about it. S cannot be absolutely sure that equality of dissatisfaction was obtained only at £29,500; it could have been £29,600. Likewise, B cannot be sure that equality was possible only at the sale price and not at £29,400, say. The uncertainty leaves a feeling in both that the agreed price could have been £100 more or less. The range may be small, but there is still a residue of dissatisfaction arising out of uncertainty of perception.

The residue of dissatisfaction can be shown diagrammatically by looking at the negotiation at time T_0, as perceived by the two

Table 7.2: Division of Teesta Waters

	To Bangladesh	To India	Reserve
Bangladesh proposal	50	40	10
Indian proposal — 1	40	40	20
Indian proposal — 2	45	40	15

Source: *Ganaskantha, Ittefaq*, both from Dhaka, Bangladesh, 1 September 1982.

negotiants (Figure 7.9). We see that there are two uncertainties — one surrounding the opponent's initial expectation and the other around the agreement point. But for these uncertainties, either negotiant can compute equality of dissatisfaction precisely. The residue of dissatisfaction is due to a feeling that it could have been at any point over a range, however small. Like all perceptions, that of equality of dissatisfaction is also an uncertain one.

Expectation, Utility and Fair Bargains

In analysing a two-person/one-dimension negotiation we have assumed (except in one case) that the expectations of the negotiants were realistic. Only in the quick type of agreement were the expectations so unrealistic that the negotiants did better than their initial hopes. But what happens when the expectation of one negotiant is unrealistic, a non-starter?

Unrealistic expectations lead to negotiations which are different from the one supposed to be taking place on the substantive issues in the bargaining space agreed upon. One reason for a different negotiation is that the credibility of a negotiant with unrealistic expectations will be low, making it necessary for confidence-building negotiations. A negotiant with unrealistic expectations can scale them down only if he wants to engage in substantive negotiations, otherwise he can signal a temporary breakdown by a variety of means — waiting for a better time, enlarging the bargaining space, continuing NANs, waiting for a change in the environment or trying to change it by force. Therefore, negotiations with unrealistic expectations are a form of NAN, which can end in a breakdown or be followed by substantive negotiations.

In our graphical presentation, the agreement point is also on the line of expectations; it is the expectation realised by negotiation. This becomes the value of the agreement and is the satisfaction or utility obtained. The two examples analysed in this chapter both were the 'exchange' type, a house, or potatoes for cash. In the case of the house, the utility to the seller was £29,500, with a doubt that it could have been £29,600. For the buyer it was getting the house, with a doubt that he could have got it for £100 less. In neither case was the solution the optimum. Unlike other theories, *the approach based on uncertain perceptions does not produce an optimum solution, but the solution at time T_O plus or minus the residue of*

On Buying Potatoes 117

Figure 7.9: Residue of Dissatisfaction

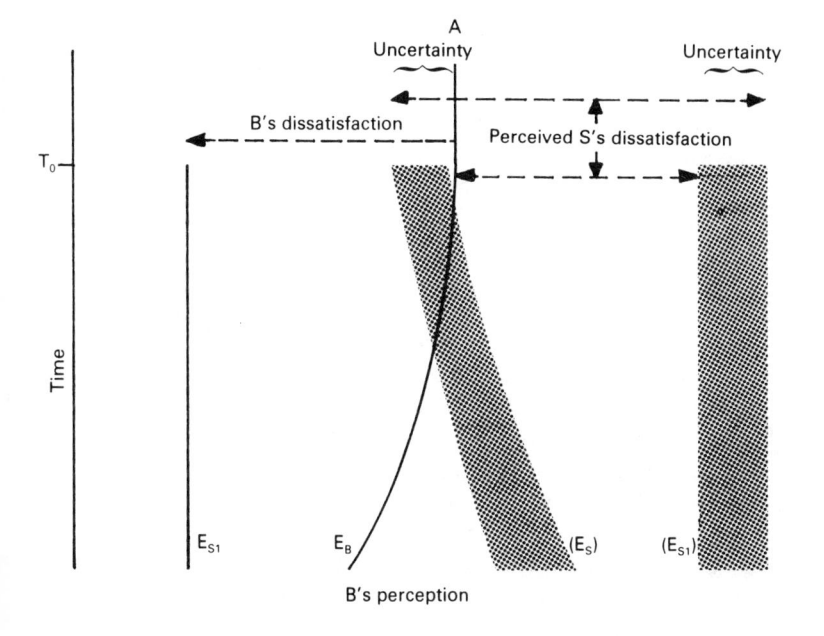

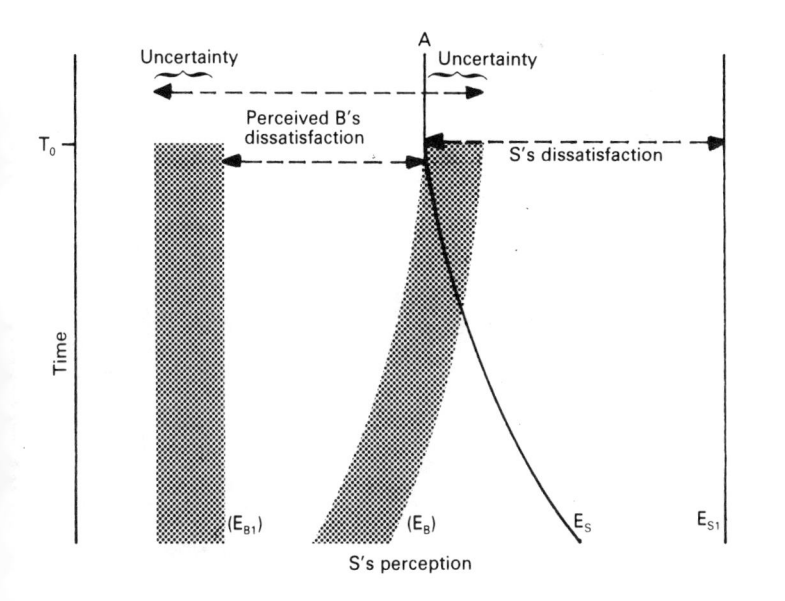

dissatisfaction. If the agreement had been reached at some other point of time, it could have been different. We therefore conclude that *the utility of an agreement depends on the time when it is reached.* If the one-dimensional negotiation is not a case of exchange but one to agree on a course of action, the utility of the agreement is also an expectation. Because the two negotiants have reached an agreement, each can argue thus: 'If I do this, then he has promised to do that'; predictability is improved and difficulties will arise only if one or the other fails to perform in accordance with the agreement.

One last question needs answering. In the four types of negotiation which end in agreement, is the achievement a 'fair bargain'? Fairness is a matter of perception, and each negotiant may have a different view on whether the agreement reached was fair. In all cases in which the negotiants mutually perceive equality of dissatisfaction, it is very probable that the result will be perceived as fair. In cases of unequal bargaining power, the negotiant in the superior position will perceive the agreement as fair while the one in the inferior position is unlikely to do so. Perception of fairness is also related to residues of dissatisfaction; the greater the residue in a negotiant, the less likely will he accept the agreement as a fair one. The approach to negotiation based on perception may or may not produce an agreement which would be judged fair by a disinterested outside observer. But this is not as relevant to conflict-limitation as whether the negotiants themselves perceive it as fair.

8 LINKAGES, TRADE-OFFS AND PACKAGE DEALS

> We might explore trade-offs between their interests and our interests. ... If you're suggesting that we should make further concessions to bring them to the table, NO! I think they would regard this as a matter of weakness.
> Edward L. Rowney,
> US arms control negotiator,
> 16 December 1983

Negotiations in Many Dimensions

One-dimension negotiations tend to be of short duration. The longer a negotiation takes, the more the chances of finding linkages, thereby increasing the possibility of adding more dimensions to the bargaining space. I do not imply that a multi-dimensional negotiation is in any way superior to a one-dimensional one — buying a used car is usually a negotiation in one dimension, often between strangers, but the sum involved could still be large. A quotation for the sale of a large computer or a secondhand aircraft for immediate delivery will result in a one-dimension negotiation between buyer and seller on the price; the fact of its being so confined does not make it trivial. However, as the money value of any contract increases, other dimensions tend to creep in — the amount of down-payment, repayment period, interest rates, etc. It is rare for negotiations between large organisations or governments to be confined to a single dimension.

When analysing a one-dimension negotiation on the choice of a holiday destination, we found that the addition of another dimension was necessary if a solution was to be found. In previous chapters, we have also used the expression 'finding a trade-off', implying a concession in one dimension to compensate for a gain in another. The quotation at the head of this chapter clarifies the distinction between trade-offs *during* negotiations and concessions made *prior* to beginning them. Mr Rowney was declining to make trade-offs or meet preconditions (such as the removal of Pershing or cruise missiles from Europe) during the stage of NAN.

Trade-offs and package deals imply that there is a functional relationship between the dimensions of a bargaining space. In the linked dimensions in a multidimensional bargaining space, some are likely to be more important than others. For example, in selling a house with furniture, the price of the house is clearly more important to both buyer and seller. This points to the existence of an order of priority among the dimensions.

When a negotiation is multidimensional, the increase in complexity is bound to make it last longer. There may well be more phases in the negotiating process. We must also answer the questions of when and how negotants reach agreement when there is more than one dimension. How do they perceive an equality of dissatisfaction?

Priority among Dimensions

That different dimensions in a negotiation will be seen by different negotants as being more important than others is common sense. In the case of a trade union negotiating with an employer, we can assume, without undue departure from reality, that the union is interested primarily in maximising the total earnings of its members. We can also assume that the employer, interested in minimising the additional impact of such an increase on his costs, looks for savings in the form of increased productivity. Neither side negotiates directly on these concepts — total earnings in the case of the workers and net additional cost in the case of the employer. The kind of topics that are likely to be on the negotiating table are: increase in basic wage rates, overtime rates, manning levels and paid holidays.

At the beginning of negotiations, the union's order of priority is usually: basic wage rates (which will include comparisons and differentials), followed by overtime rates, then paid holidays and, lastly, manning levels. The first three directly affect total take-home earnings. The union would have preferred not to negotiate on manning levels at all since any reduction may affect the workforce by making some redundant, restricting new recruitment, or a combination of both. It is in the bargaining space only because, without it, the employer would not have been willing to negotiate. The employer naturally attaches the highest priority to manning levels; if he knows how much he can save, he can calculate how high an increase he can afford on the others.

At the beginning, time T_B, after each negotiant has voiced his initial position in each of the dimensions, the order of priority of the two negotiants is:

Order of priority at T_B	of employer	of trade union
Basic wage rate	2	1
Overtime rate	3	2
Manning levels	1	4
Paid holidays	4	3

If the two were negotiating in only one dimension, they would then start communicating information about their respective expectations. With a quite different order of priority among the dimensions, there can be no progress in modifying their expectations. If the employer cannot form an idea of the kind of manning level changes that the union might accept, he cannot compute how to modify his own expectations on basic wage rates and overtime rates. The first step, therefore, is to *align* their orders of priority.

The process of *alignment* might proceed somewhat like this. Since both the union and the employer consider paid holidays to be least important, this can be relegated as the dimension of lowest priority. The main impact on total costs for the employer and on total earnings for the workforce will be from changes in basic wage rates and manning levels. Both sides might agree to give overtime rates a lower priority compared to the other two. After negotiating until time T_1, the order of priority will look like this:

Order of priority at T_1	of employer	of trade union
Basic wage rate	2	1
Manning levels	1	2
Overtime rates	3	3
Paid holidays	4	4

By this time, a substantial, but not total, alignment has been achieved. This degree of alignment should be adequate for the negotiating process to continue: complete alignment of priorities is neither necessary nor practical.

The next step in the negotiating process is modifying expectations. For this to happen, it is not necessary to go to the trouble of aligning the priorities accorded to the top two dimensions so long as the two negotiants agree that the two are closely linked (i.e. an agreement in one is impossible without an agreement in the other).

Complete alignment of priorities is also impractical because negotiants are generally most reluctant to give up their main objective and to relegate their most preferred dimension to lesser importance.

In this example, we have delineated a clearly-defined phase of aligning priorities as happening just after the negotiations begin. A study of other negotiations shows that the alignment phase can take place during NAN. Each negotiant will gain some knowledge of the expectations of the other in the NAN. For example, in the UK/EEC Budget dispute, Britain's initial position ('give me back my £1000 million') was clearly voiced before the substantive negotiations began. In such a case the negotiants would also have formed an idea of the relative priorities accorded by the different negotiants to the various dimensions to be included in the bargaining space. While Britain attached the highest priority to its actual amount of net contributions, France attached the highest priority to preservation of the elements of the CAP that increased the income of French farmers, and Germany accorded high priority to ensuring that the amount of money it had to contribute did not exceed pre-set limits and to evolving a common fisheries policy in order to assure access for German fishermen. Some other issues (like evolving a common energy policy) were also thrown in. However, by the time the substantive negotiations began, the number of important dimensions had been reduced to three and partial alignment of priorities had taken place.

There is also an example where alignment never took place with the result that a violent action, (a strike) was inevitable. Ronald Reagan, has described the course of a dispute between the Screen Actors' Guild and film producers as follows:

> In the first weeks of negotiations we haggled and bargained over minor changes in the contract until finally we had to say, 'Look, we're all kidding ourselves. None of the things we are settling means anything if we can't settle the big 'if'.' Then we were told by the men who ran the studios that they could not even discuss the issue with us.[1]

The big 'if' was the question of payments to actors and actresses for films shown on television but which, when they were produced, were meant to be shown only in cinemas. The interesting point is that both sides knew what the big 'if' was. The studios gave it the lowest priority; like the trade union not wanting to discuss manning levels, the producers were simply not going to discuss television payments. They were clearly informed by the Actors' Guild that if the main question was not settled, agreements on all other dimensions were to be considered inoperative. The refusal of the producers even to talk about the main question resulted in the performers going on strike. Negotiations therefore can end in a breakdown if one of the negotiants is unable or unwilling to realign his priorities: it is another form of 'refusal to negotiate'.

We must note an important psychological factor in this real-life case. The logical progression in a negotiation is to align the priorities among the dimensions, then to reach agreement on the most important two or three of the realigned dimensions and finally put together a package. The studios were either planning for or resigned to the performers going on strike. That the studios eventually had to give in and share television revenues did not prevent them letting the strike happen. People do not always behave rationally and are often prepared to push a conflict to a violent end, to test the validity of their perceptions about their opponent's unity and holding-power.

If total alignment of priorities is not necessary to prevent a breakdown, how much alignment is necessary? This question is really about how negotiants communicate information about expectations and limits in more than one dimension. Practical experience suggests that they can do so either *simultaneously* or *serially*. An employer and a trade union can communicate information simultaneously about basic wage rates and manning levels at each negotiating session; information in this case is conveyed in the form of 'if A, then B': 'if you don't agree to a reduction in the number of machinists on each machine, we can only afford a 2 percent increase in basic wage rate'; 'If you want to reduce the number of machinists, you'll have to put 20 percent on the table.'

This raises the interesting question of how many dimensions people can negotiate about simultaneously. By and large, it is difficult to comprehend more than two dimensions at the same time. If there are more than two dimensions, the conditional statements become very complex. (If A and B, then C; but if A and D, then E, or if F and B, then G, and so on.) Alignment of priorities is needed precisely because negotiations in three or four dimensions with each having a different functional relationship with the other entails complex communications, especially when it is all uncertainly perceived by the negotiants. Though eventually the complexity has to be perceived and understood, at this stage of negotiations alignment is a device by which negotiants break it up into more comprehensible sub-units.

Cases exist where alignment is found to be too difficult. The subjects covered in the European Conference on Security and Co-operation (ECSC) were eventually grouped under four 'baskets'. Of these, the western countries accorded the highest priority to the human rights basket (which itself contained a number of issues), while the Warsaw Pact countries gave it low priority according, instead, high priority to the basket on confidence-building measures. In the actual conference the negotiations gave an appearance of being held simultaneously only because different sets of people were talking about different subjects in different rooms at the same time. The chief delegates never had to consider more than one or two baskets at any given time. The extended nature of the negotiations made it possible to tackle them serially while preserving an appearance of simultaneity. It is interesting to note that the ECSC, after three years of negotiations, was reduced to only two baskets — human rights and confidence-building measures.

The serial solution to multidimensional negotiations without aligning priorities was clearly adopted by the Greek- and Turkish-Cypriot communities. In these talks, which went on for many months in 1980 and 1981, the negotiators met each week to consider one of the many problems (repopulation of Famagusta/Varosha, the nature of the federal constitution, economic questions and confidence-building measures) in turn. These were taken up in strict rotation so that no one subject was seen to be more important than any other. The degree of mistrust between the communities is shown by the following comment by Mr Isar Isik, a former Foreign Minister of Turkey: 'If the Turkish side agreed to give precedence to solving certain issues to which great importance is attached by the Greek side, then Turkey would have lost its negotiating ability.'[2]

When negotiators adopt a serial pattern or split up the bargaining space, the contracted spaces do not thereby become independent; there is either a tacit or an explicit agreement that the smaller spaces are interconnected and are integral parts of the total bargaining space. The prospect of dividing a complex negotiation into more manageable components is important for limiting conflicts. The examples described above show that this is no theoretical artifice, but is, in fact, how people negotiate in real life when confronted with a multidimensional bargaining space of high complexity.

Functional Relationship among Dimensions

In order to form part of the same bargaining space, the different dimensions must be linked. There are various types of functional relationships.

Suppose a seller is interested only in the total amount of money he gets from the sale of the house and its fittings (carpets and curtains, etc.). If he gets a higher than expected price for the house then he might be willing to lower the price of the fittings; the range may be fairly small since the price of the house is bound to be much higher than that of the fittings. The buyer, on the other hand, may not be interested in the fittings and may be willing to buy them only if he gets them cheaply enough, and if it is necessary to clinch the deal on the house. The functional relationship between the two dimensions for the two negotiants is:

For the seller: $[f(H,F)]_S: H + F = K$ H = price of the house
For the buyer: $[f(H,F)]_B: F = C$ F = price of fittings
                                          K, C = constants

We note that H and F have become a part of the negotiations only because S has made it so. B's attitude is likely to be: 'Let's discuss the house price first; we'll talk about the fittings later.' Since S is also interested in the sale of the higher valued house, he may well accept the serialisation of the negotiation in order to ascertain the buyer's expectation and limits. An alignment of priorities has taken place, but the functional relationship has not disappeared. This will become clear to the buyer when, after a tentative price agreement on the house looks likely, the seller says: 'Now, what about the carpets?'

The functional relationship between the dimensions, for S and B separately, is shown in Figure 8.1. There is nothing sacrosanct about S's and B's perceptions as shown; the positions could easily be reversed. S may not want to sell the fittings unless he gets a really good price for them and may be happy to take them to his new house. B may well want to save himself the bother of buying and installing carpets and curtains provided his total outgoings do

Figure 8.1: Functional Relationships Between Dimensions: sale of house and fittings

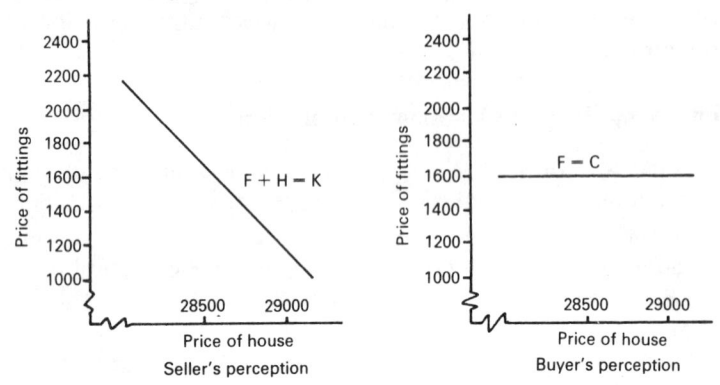

[Left graph: Seller's perception — Price of fittings (y-axis, 1000–2400) vs Price of house (x-axis, 28500–29000), showing downward sloping line labelled F + H = K]

[Right graph: Buyer's perception — Price of fittings (y-axis, 1000–2400) vs Price of house (x-axis, 28500–29000), showing horizontal line labelled F = C]

not exceed a certain figure. The two equations and the two graphs will be interchanged.

Two conclusions can be derived from this example: (i) the functional relationship between the same two dimensions may be different for different negotiants; and (ii) part of the negotiating process is concerned with each negotiant trying to perceive the functional relationship which holds good for the other negotiant. This phase can be called *ascertaining functional relationships*.

An example which will produce a different kind of graph is provided by the negotiations in an ICA between the group of exporting countries and the group of importing countries. The two major dimensions in such negotiations are the total quantity of the commodity to be placed on the market, expressed as total quota and the price, expressed usually as a range. Without entering into the details of the price range, consider the relationship between the floor price and the total basic export tonnage.[3]

The exporting countries, in general, will be more interested in their total realisation; the more the quantity they can legitimately export, the lower the price they may be willing to take, within the limits set by the environment. Since prices are usually expressed in round figures, the exporting countries may decide that they will accept a price P_1 for quantities around Q_1, a price P_2 for quantities around Q_2 and so on. The importing countries may feel that market conditions are such that only significant changes in the quantity committed for export will make a difference to the market price. They may envisage one level for the floor price for a whole range of quantities and a lower one for a sharply increased quantity. The two positions are shown diagrammatically in Figure 8.2. I may add that this situation is not at all theoretical and is one frequently encountered in international commodity negotiations.

Straight lines and step-like forms are only two possibilities for describing the functional relationships between dimensions. Sometimes the shape may not be precisely definable or be capable of being fitted into a mathematical expression. In the Camp David negotiations, Israel was negotiating on a number of dimensions which bore a complex inter-relationship. Simplifying somewhat, let us say that the dimensions were: protecting Israel's security, compensation for the loss of the Sinai oilfields, and the quantum of US military aid to Egypt. We ignore other important dimensions like the settlements on the West Bank and Palestinian autonomy, because these were, for Israel, low-priority dimensions in which it preferred the *status quo*. Even among the three chosen dimensions, the functional relationship was very complex. There could have been no unique perception of the functions among the Israeli negotiators; Menachem Begin would have seen it one way and Moshe Dayan another. There need have been no such thing as *the* Israeli set of functional equations. However, an inability to define any of the sets does not mean that there was no connection in Israeli minds between them. This connection was capable of being articulated and communicated so that other negotiants, and the

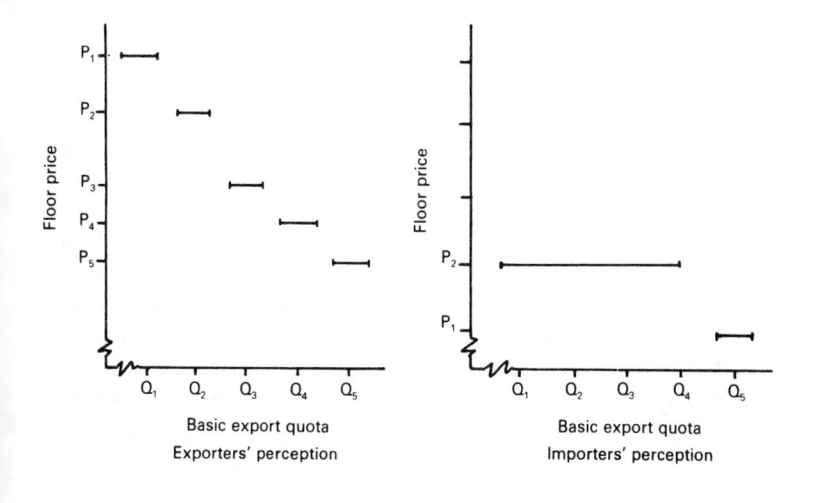

Figure 8.2: Functional Relationships Between Dimensions: ICAs

mediator, could perceive it. This is an example where verbal articulation and facial gestures communicate more, while precise mathematical formulations fail.

Whether we are able to draw lines on a piece of paper is not as important as noting the consequences of the existence of such functional relationships. One is that we can identify one more phase of the negotiating process — that of each negotiant trying to compute the functional relationships of the other. Without such perception, there is no possibility of trade-offs and package deals. With every addition of a negotiating phase, the total time from beginning to outcome increases and the assumption of constant environment becomes more difficult to sustain.

Trade-offs and Package Deals

Those who have actually bought vegetables in an eastern market will be familiar with the phenomenon of a seller 'throwing in' a handful of chillies or green coriander, after the bargaining is completed and the price settled. This is supposedly gratis but, in reality, bridges a very narrow gap in the equalisation of dissatisfaction between buyer and seller and is a 'payment' by the seller to the buyer for honouring him with his custom. There are precise words in some languages to describe the 'gratis equaliser' — in Tamil, *kosuru*, and in Arabic, *albia*. This is a trade-off.

Another everyday example is a parent saying 'You can have a *Coke*, if you tidy your room.' This becomes a trade-off if, prior to the introduction of *Coca Cola* as a new dimension, the negotiation had been entirely confined to whether the child was going to tidy his room or not before going out to play. 'If you don't tidy your room NOW, I'll smack you!', is a threat of violent action; 'If you don't tidy your room, you don't go out', is a punishment. But when *Coca Cola* is dangled as an incentive, it becomes a tactic equalising dissatisfactions — the child's dissatisfaction at having to do something he dislikes is equalised by the parent's dissatisfaction at having to give a *Coke* which she feels he doesn't deserve. We can superficially see this in game theory terms as an exchange of utilities. But this is not so: the negotiation did not arise spontaneously by both sides perceiving a way of maximising their utilities. The conflict started with the parent feeling dissatisfied at the state of the child's room, and the child perceiving a conflict of interest because he hates disturbing the chaos. Doing something to alleviate one dissatisfaction produced a counter-dissatisfaction: the trade-off was the *Coke*.

I have given an elaborate explanation for an every-day occurrence because it illustrates some crucial points. Trade-offs are essentially in different dimensions. The psychological value (unit of dissatisfaction) which the negotiants place on the concessions made in the different dimensions will be different. Without such an inequality, a perception of total equality of dissatisfaction will not be possible. It must, however, be emphasised that this does not require an absolute scale of dissatisfactions true for all negotiants. In the parent and child example, we do not have to worry whether a *Coke* is 'worth' the same to both. After all, they put it to different uses; one drinks it while the other only parts with it reluctantly. What we are interested in is whether each one perceives that the other is equally dissatisfied.

Trade-offs are common in complex negotiations because they help to shorten bargaining time. If two negotiants are very near agreement in a dimension, they can either prolong the negotiation until they achieve equality of dissatisfaction or they can find a trade-off from a proximate dimension. Suppose a trade union and an employer have reached a point when there was nearly an agreement on the two highest priority dimensions — basic wage rates and manning levels. The two sides may still not be satisfied that they had got the best out of the negotiations.

If such a gap is perceived as bridgeable by both sides, they turn to the dimensions lower in the order. Concessions in these dimensions (additional contributions to the workers' pension fund, taking fewer paid holidays than originally demanded, a compromise on tea-breaks, time off for union meetings, adjustments to dispute settlement procedures, etc.) can help bring about a perception of a totality of equality of dissatisfaction in all the dimensions.

From this example, we note that, for a trade-off to be effective in bringing about an agreement, there must be linkages available in the environment immediate to the negotiation. In other words, a controlled expansion of the bargaining space must be possible. This is why we defined the environment immediate to a bargaining space as one which has dimensions with linkages to any of the dimensions in the bargaining space and which can be introduced to enlarge it.

A trade-off can be combined with splitting the difference. Let us suppose that two negotiants have almost agreed on all but one dimension and also perceive that equality of dissatisfaction can be achieved by a trade-off. Instead of going on negotiating about this last dimension, they can cut short the time spent by simply splitting the difference. The impatience factor, discussed in the last chapter, affects the perceptions of both negotiants, hastening the conclusion of an agreement.

Trade-offs cannot only be foreseen but space can even be created for them by putting into the bargaining space a number of dimensions which are not meant to be negotiated on. Some dimensions will be abandoned during the negotiation, some kept in reserve and some even revived after being abandoned. In a trade union/employer negotiation, the union might well have demanded a variety of things in addition to the three main issues: car parking facilities, provision of special or safety clothing, discount on purchases of company products, improvement in canteen food, abolition of the executive dining room, the behaviour of the security staff, and so on. In reality, most of the demands will remain on paper (i.e. they will be placed in the immediate environment). The negotiation will concentrate on only those dimensions which rank high in the orders of priority of the employer and the union and the others will be picked up only when needed to make up the agreement package.

'Package deal' is a common expression that needs no definition. When the Camp David negotiations had almost broken down, President Carter prepared a unilateral document on the basic principles on which a Middle East peace structure could be erected. President Sadat declined to sign a document only with the United States and prepared to leave Camp David. He explained the reason for his decision to leave, by pointing to the danger in his signing an agreement with the US alone. Later, if direct discussions were ever resumed with the Israelis, they could use what the Egyptians had signed as the original basis for all future negotiations. President Carter acknowledged it as a telling argument and put forward his concept of the package deal: 'I told him that we would have a complete understanding that if any nation rejected *any* part of the agreements, *none* of the proposals would stay in effect.'[4]

The basic characteristic of a package deal is that an agreement in any dimension is tentative unless there is an agreement on all the dimensions. An implicit corollary is that any concession made in any dimension is deemed to be withdrawn unless the whole of the package is agreed to. The reason for the reservation is that when the negotiants fail to perceive total equality of dissatisfaction as a package, they may have to strive for equality by going back to the dimensions on which tentative agreement had been reached.

One way of wrapping up a package in multidimensional negotiations is for the negotiants to remove an issue from the bargaining space and postpone it for later negotiations. This is the converse of taking a dimension from the immediate environment in order to find a trade-off for equalising dissatisfactions. Such postponements are quite common in international negotiations, especially those which function within a rule-system. When the idea of instituting a strict reporting system for controlling exports was first mooted in the International Coffee Agreement, it was so new that it could be fitted into a package only after repeated postponements. Every time an issue is postponed, there is an increase in the residue of dissatisfaction of the negotiant who attaches priority to it; this affects the chances of success of future negotiations.

The concept of the package deal implicitly recognises that different negotiants attach different priorities to the dimensions. A small concession in a dimension to which a negotiant attaches high priority has to be matched by a larger concession by another negotiant for whom it has lower priority. Alternatively, a small concession in a dimension of high priority has to be matched by a small concession in a different dimension of equally high priority to another negotiant. The core of the long-running saga of the dispute between the London *Times* and the printing unions was the introduction of new technology, particularly the direct input of copy by journalists, bypassing a large part of the typesetting work. To the union, any concession carried considerable potential damage because, if they gave in on new technology in one paper, they would eventually have to do so for all Fleet Street newspapers. Thus, even a small concession by the union was seen as a breakthrough by the employer, who had to compensate it by large increases in pay or by hefty redundancy payments.

This example also shows that there is no way of invoking an absolute scale of dissatisfaction, just as there is no way of producing an absolute scale of utilities. In real-life negotiations, there is no *a priori* awareness of the satisfaction that would accrue when the total package is agreed upon. However, package deals are being negotiated all the time without the negotiants having preconceived or predetermined ideas of every element of the package. Negotiants can perceive equality of dissatisfaction — uncertainly and inchoately perhaps, but perceive it they do.

Types and Duration of Multidimensional Negotiations

In Chapter 7, we concluded that in a two-negotiant one dimension negotiation there were three major types — breakdown, see-saw and agreement, the last one divisible into four sub-types (poker, quick, unequal power and equal power). How many types are there when the bargaining space contains more than one dimension?

At the outset, we must note that there can be only two possible outcomes to any negotiation — an agreement or a breakdown. Even the special case of a prolonged negotiation see-sawing between the two must eventually end in one or the other. In this chapter, we have also identified two more phases of the negotiating process — alignment of priorities and ascertaining functional relationships; these came about only because of the existence of more than one dimension.

It is common sense to assume that if the negotiants are ignorant about each other in one dimension they are unlikely to know more in any other dimension in the same bargaining space. The lack of knowledge, brought about by little or no prior NANs, occurs when the negotiants have had no experience of dealing with each other. One might expect that such a profound lack of knowledge would be unlikely between sides with a past history of relations (unions/employer, or between governments). However, there are cases of governments entering into complex negotiations without adequate prior knowledge or preparation. Recent history is littered with examples of states signing economic integration agreements without having a clear idea of how to implement them. We shall return to this paradox of there being a will to negotiate without an understanding of each other's interests or vulnerabilities, when we consider political will in Chapter 13.

We can thus classify multidimensional negotiations into those with prior knowledge and those without it. Ignorance, of course, affects all aspects of the negotiating process — priorities among dimensions, functional relationships, expectations and limits. The phases of the process resulting either in alignment of priorities (at least to the extent of identifying the most important two dimensions) or in a breakdown are shown schematically in Table 8.1.

If the negotiants in a multidimensional negotiation succeed in identifying the most important dimensions, they will acquire enough knowledge on the functional relationships between them. These will have been deduced from the information available about priorities, initial positions and expectations. The negotiants then proceed to communicate further information on expectations and limits in the most important dimensions. At this stage, they will no longer be in a poker- or quick-type situation. If the bargaining space contains any dimension in which a quick agreement is possible, this will have been identified, a tentative agreement arrived at, and the dimension set aside, to be brought in at the 'wrapping-up' of the package.

When the negotiations continue, each of the major dimensions may take any of the three forms — breakdown, see-saw or agreement. Strictly for the purpose of determining the phases and duration of multidimensional negotiations, we can treat the unequal and equal power types as similar since the difference in power does not affect the nature of the outcome but only the points at which agreements are reached.

By logical extension of the theory in the one-dimension case, the two most important dimensions can take six forms — B—B, B—A, B—S, A—A, A—S and S—S (B = breakdown, A = agreement, S = see-saw). In each case, there are three possibilities: (i) both negotiants can agree to give one dimension high priority and also agree that an agreement on this dimension is essential for the package as a whole (e.g. the house dimension is essential but not the fittings); (ii) both agree on the order of priority but neither dimension is more important than the other (quotas and prices in ICAs); and (iii) both agree to deal with the two dimensions together since what is more important to one is less important to the other (basic wage rates and manning levels). Though in theory there appear to be 18 possible types, there are only 10 distinct types. The different outcomes are summarised in Table 8.2

If the negotiants succeed in reaching a tentative agreement on the high-priority dimensions, they can then tackle the lower-order ones. More often than not, these will result in agreements somewhat sooner than the time spent on the high-priority dimensions.

134 *Linkages, Trade-offs and Package Deals*

Table 8.1: Phases and Duration of Multi-dimensional Negotiations up to Alignment of Priorities

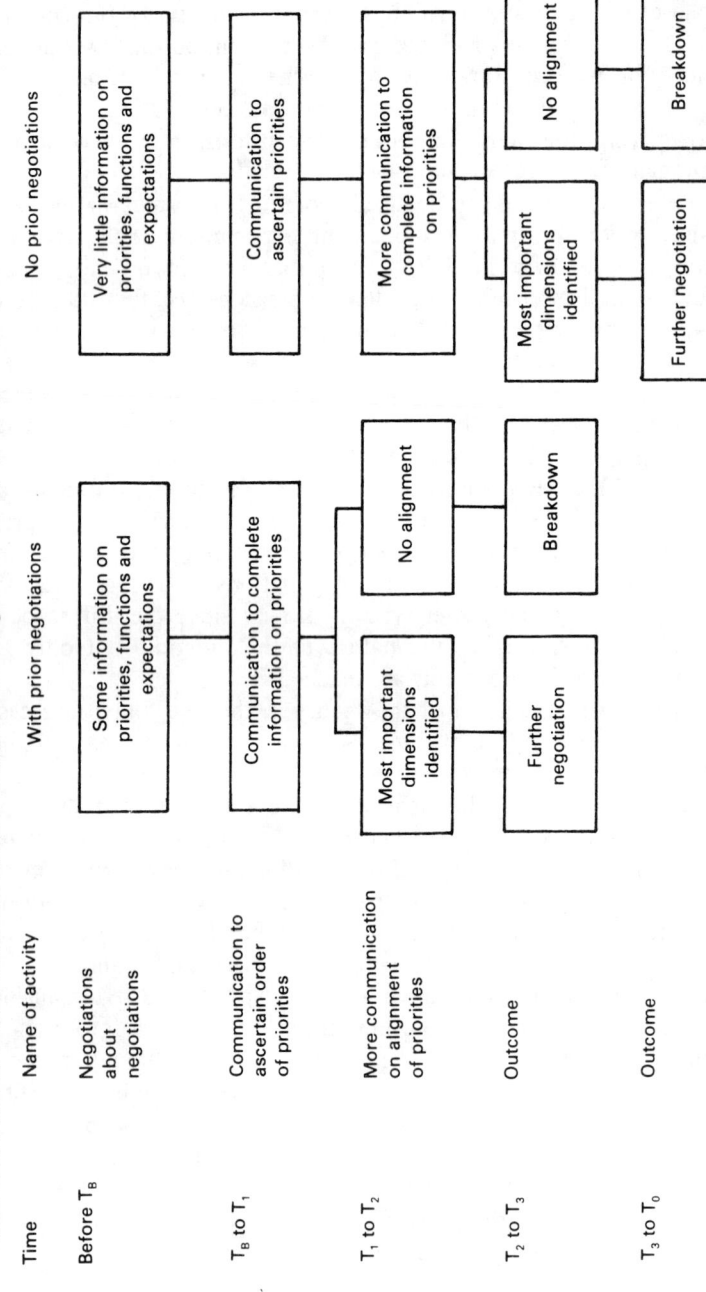

Time	Name of activity	With prior negotiations	No prior negotiations
Before T_B	Negotiations about negotiations	Some information on priorities, functions and expectations	Very little information on priorities, functions and expectations
T_B to T_1	Communication to ascertain order of priorities	Communication to complete information on priorities	Communication to ascertain priorities
T_1 to T_2	More communication on alignment of priorities		More communication to complete information on priorities
T_2 to T_3	Outcome	No alignment → Breakdown / Most important dimensions identified → Further negotiation	No alignment → Breakdown / Most important dimensions identified → Further negotiation
T_3 to T_0	Outcome		

Table 8.2: Types of Two-dimension Negotiations after Identifying High-priority Dimensions

Dimension 1	Dimension 2	Relative priority between dimensions	Outcome
Breakdown	Breakdown	Immaterial	Breakdown
Breakdown	See-saw	Immaterial	Breakdown
See-saw	See-saw	Immaterial	Breakdown
Agreement	Agreement	Immaterial	Agreement
Breakdown	Agreement	If 1 is high-priority	Breakdown
		If 2 is high-priority	Agreement, if a trade-off can be found
		If 1 and 2 are different priorities for different negotiants	Breakdown most likely; agreement after prolonged negotiation, only if trade-off can be found.
See-saw	Agreement	If 1 is high-priority	Breakdown
		If 2 is high-priority	Agreement, if a trade-off can be found
		If 1 and 2 are different priority for different negotiants	Breakdown most likely; agreement possible only after prolonged negotiation with trade-off.

The negotiants can then perceive the final 'package'. To be consistent, we must also consider the possibility that a package need not be perceived in all negotiations. Even if an agreement can be located in each of the dimensions of the bargaining space, an agreement in one may require modifying the tentative agreement in another and this may mean disturbing a third, and so on. The negotiations may become so prolonged that a breakdown is likely. During this time, changes in the environment may alter the conflict significantly. In the complex negotiations between the Greek- and Turkish-Cypriots, the fact that a tentative agreement could be reached in one or two dimensions (like the repopulation of Varosha) was no help in putting together an acceptable package.

When a package is perceived as attainable, the negotiants will also have acquired some knowledge about units of dissatisfaction in the different dimensions. Some final adjustments will still have to be made in order to bring about a perception of equality of dissatisfaction in the bargaining space as a whole. This is, on the face of it, a complex operation involving the agreement point in each dimension, the functional relationships among the dimensions, the different subjective units of dissatisfaction and an integration of all these. While analytically complex, real-life negotiators are able to do this. This is a stage at which the negotiations can still collapse if the negotiants are unable to perceive the equality (i.e. if all do not feel that they have *got out of the others as much as they have conceded*). If the negotiation survives this hurdle, the agreement is ready for signature.

Table 8.3, which is a continuation of Table 8.1, shows the remaining phases of multidimensional negotiations.

Equality of Dissatisfaction in Multidimensional Negotiations

In the one-dimension case, we identified time T_1 as the point from which expectation is to be reckoned in order to compute dissatisfaction. In multidimensional negotiations, an unambiguous stage is reached when the negotiants agree on the dimensions to be accorded the highest priority (time T_x in Table 8.3). By this time, they also acquire knowledge about the functional relationships between the dimensions; each negotiant has his own set of functions and perceives somewhat uncertainly the sets of the others.

Table 8.3: Phases and Minimum Duration of Multi-dimensional Negotiations

Time	Activity	Negotiating Process
T_x to T_{x+1}	Modifying expectations	Modification of expectations in high-priority dimensions
T_{x+1} to T_{x+2}	Ascertaining limits	Expectations further modified and limits ascertained in high-priority dimensions
T_{x+2} to T_{x+3}	Including low priority dimensions	Modifications of expectations and ascertaining limits in low-priority dimensions
T_{x+3} to T_{x+4}	Perception of a package	Potential package perceived and units of dissatisfaction ascertained — or — Package unattainable → Breakdown
T_{x+4} to T_{x+5}	Wrapping up a package	Final modification of expectations and dissatisfactions
T_{x+5} to T_{x+6}	Perception of equality of dissatisfaction	Package with total equality of dissatisfaction perceived — or — Equality unattainable → Breakdown
T_{x+6} to T_{x+7}	Outcome	Agreement

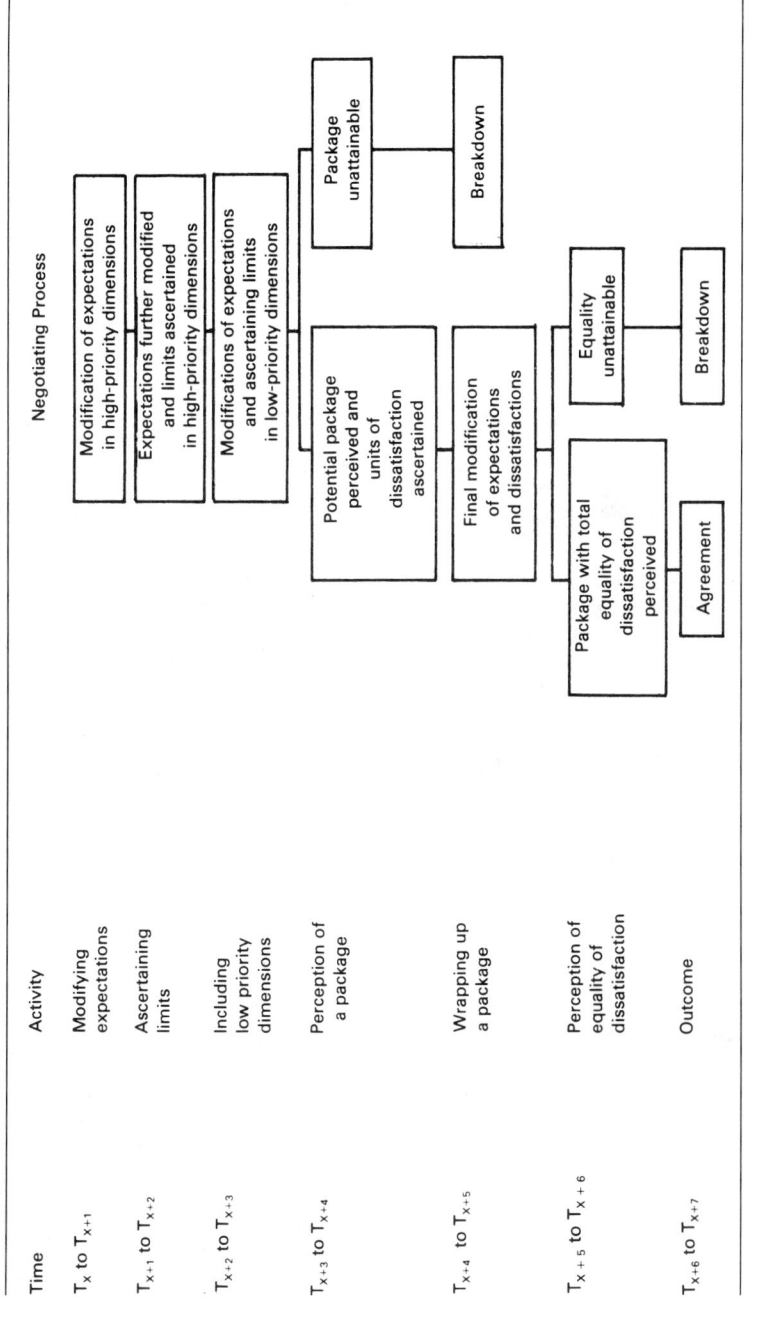

With all this knowledge, they would have modified their expectations to a realistic level.

A set of formulae for computing totality of dissatisfaction and equality of dissatisfaction is given in the Appendix. The mathematical formulae may look complicated, but, in real life negotiators are able to compute the total dissatisfaction for themselves, then to perceive uncertainly the total dissatisfaction of others and finally perceive an approximate equality between them.

Notes

1. *Observer*, 25 Jan. 1981. 'Reagan — Strike Leader', adapted from Ronald Reagan's autobiography, *My Early Life or, Where's the Rest of Me?* (London, Sidgwick & Jackson, 1981).

2. Isar Isik, former Minister of Foreign Affairs and Defence in Turkey, quoted in Athens News Agency *Daily Bulletin*, 17 Dec. 1980.

3. Price ranges in ICAs have a floor price and a ceiling price. If the market price drops below the floor, export quantities are restricted, and if it goes above the ceiling, all restrictions are removed. In addition, there may be sub-ranges within the price range. For example, if the ICA has a buffer-stock mechanism, there will be a lower range within which the buffer stock manager has to buy, a middle range when he will neither buy nor sell, and an upper range when he must sell. Further, as commodities are not always homogeneous and quality differences exist (e.g. unwashed Arabicas, mild Arabicas and Robustas in coffee) there has to be a formula for relating the actual market prices for different qualities to the price range inscribed in the ICA.

4. Jimmy Carter, *Keeping Faith* (Bantam Books, 1982). Reproduced in *Time Magazine*, 11 Oct. 1982.

9 NUMBERS, COALITIONS AND COLLUSION

> A king who is situated between two powerful kings shall seek protection from the stronger of the two; or from one of them on whom he can rely. ... A king shall make alliance with one of them who likes him and whom he likes; this is the best way of making alliances.
>
> Kautilya's Arthasastra, third century BC

Many Negotiants and Negotiators

Real-life negotiations with only two individuals are found exclusively in very limited, almost nuclear relationships: parent and child, husband and wife, an executive and his secretary and, occasionally, an employer with just a handful of workers. Any theory of negotiation has to take into account the possibility of there being more than two participants. There are two distinct categories — the number of participants may be more than two either because in a bilateral negotiation each negotiant is represented by more than one negotiator, or because there are three or more independent negotiants.

The number of cases where there are apparently only two negotiants are many: bargaining between a trade union and the management, negotiations between two companies, or between two ministries or departments of the same government or between two governments. In all these bilateral bargaining situations, the negotiants may be represented by one or more negotiators 'acting under instructions'. These instructions may be directives from the executive of the trade union, the board of directors of a company, briefs given by the Cabinet of a government or the decision of the president of a country. The expectations of an institutional negotiant are bound to be different in kind from those of an individual who only represents himself.

Many real-life negotiations also have more than two independent negotiators. For example, when the member states of the European Community negotiate among themselves on Community matters, there are currently 10 independent negotiants, soon to be increased to 12. In the UN Security Council there are 15 negotiants and, in the General Assembly, there are over 150. It is an observed fact that, when the number of negotiants increases, coalitions tend to form. Such coalitions, based on common interests, can be shown to arise from the different ordering of priorities among the dimensions for different negotiants.

Coalitions can also form for psychological or emotional reasons. In the Yalta Conference, which was concerned with the division of the post-second world war world into spheres of influence, there was a coalition between Churchill and Roosevelt based on emotional and cultural affinities, resulting in a shared antipathy towards the USSR. Since we cannot ignore psychological factors, a section of this chapter is devoted to this aspect.

Coalitions are not identical. The way most newspapers (and indeed many academics) write about the North—South dialogue, one would imagine that there was a cohesive entity called 'the developing South'. Nothing is further from the truth. We must also note that in any coalition some members will be more important than others. The cohesiveness or 'tightness' on which the survival of coalitions depends will also be examined in this chapter, and we shall examine collusion (which is an 'unnatural' coalition), because it will help to illustrate the relationship between the environment and the bargaining population.

A negotiation cannot keep on adding more negotiants without seriously jeopardising the possibility of an agreement. There is a limit beyond which meaningful negotiations become impossible. We shall examine empirically whether there is a number above which an agreement is made less likely.

The Institutional Negotiant

By institution is meant an organisation with a decision-making hierarchy, where internal conflicts of opinion can be adjudicated by a person in a superior position. These individuals, however, are not wholly independent decision-makers determining negotiating policy by themselves; they are, in effect, arbitrators between contending points of view and exercise their authority only to cut short internal negotiations and decide on courses of action.

Within an institution, conflicts arise because the participants pursue different objectives within the same overall policy objectives of the institution itself. Let us suppose that the board of directors of a company is meeting to determine the negotiating strategy for an imminent wage bargaining round with the trade union. Different directors may have different views on how to approach the negotiation, what offers to make, and what the limit should be. The industrial relations director may want to buy peace at any price; another director may want to 'teach the union a lesson'; the finance director may weigh up the relative costs of a strike against higher wages. The different views will either have to be reconciled or some overruled in order to evolve a collective institutional bargaining position and strategy.

Decisions made at a given time by a board of directors are not immutable. Depending on the progress of the negotiations, some directors may harden their attitudes and favour a showdown; others may want to reduce the expectations. The relative strength of the 'hard' and 'soft' factions will fluctuate over time. The consequence of such shifts in bargaining power between the different groups is that the expectations and limit positions of the institutional negotiant as a whole change with time.

These kinds of continuous subsidiary negotiations within a seemingly single negotiant also happen within governments. Take the example of a negotiation between two countries on the sharing of the waters of a common river. The different interests within the government of the upper riparian country are likely to be as follows. The Foreign Office may advocate a generous approach to sharing in the interests of placating a neighbour and possibly for fear of adverse international criticism; the Ministry of Irrigation will want to safeguard an adequate flow of water for agriculture; the Ministry of Power, on the other hand, may want to ensure an increased flow of water for a dam which they plan to build for generating power at some date in the future; the Ministry of Transport may want to preserve and improve inland water transport. The policy of the upper riparian country will be decided according to the priorities attached to these different interests; and may well be influenced by which minister is most powerful at that time. Since all objectives cannot be met equally, the prime minister or president will have to take the final decision on which interest and which minister can most safely be left dissatisfied. While the collective interest of the lower riparian country will be to get more water, there may be differences of opinion within the Cabinet of that country too. The Foreign Office may take a harder or softer line depending on how it views the international climate towards the 'justice' of its cause; the Law Minister may advocate abandoning negotiation in favour of lodging a case in the International Court of Justice; there may well be a minister whose portfolio has nothing to do with the dispute but who has a strong antipathy to the upper riparian. If he is also the leader of a minority party on whose support the survival of the coalition government depends, his views automatically become more important.

Some time ago, American newspapers were publicising a difference in approach between the State Department and the Defense Department (in particular, between Alexander Haig and Caspar Weinberger, the respective Secretaries) on US policy towards resumption of SALT negotiations. One need not doubt that both believed passionately in protecting the national security of the United States and its allies. Agreement on the basic objective did not mean that they agreed on when to start negotiating with the USSR, how to approach that country, or what agreement to aim for. They negotiated with each other personally during their weekly breakfast meetings, as well as through their respective hierarchies. Ultimately, however, the US position had to be determined by reference to a superior authority, namely the President, leaving Alexander Haig a very dissatisfied person.

The vicissitudes of SALT II negotiations also pinpoint the fact that an institution's policy towards a negotiation may undergo sudden and unpredictable changes. The limit position of the United States under President Reagan is distinctly different from that under President Carter.

Subsidiary negotiations within institutions for determining negotiating policy are generally confined to persons within the institution and are usually secret. One reason for the insistence on secrecy within institutions is the negotiators' desire to prevent the environment affecting the bargaining. Throughout its long negotiating period, the actual details of SALT negotiations were not available to the US public or Congress. It is reasonable to assume that the US administration felt that knowledge of negotiating details might strength domestic opposition to specific aspects of the package. A US senator, for example, might perceive a higher level of dissatisfaction compared to the US negotiator who would then be challenged even while he was negotiating with the USSR, resulting in the negotiator having to negotiate with the USSR and the US Senate simultaneously. By maintaining secrecy, simultaneous negotiations are avoided and made sequential. In the modern world, the main motivation for secrecy in governments is to keep information away from their own people.

Another reason is the judgement of the negotiator about his own competence. Negotiators generally believe that they are more competent to bargain on the subject than any one else and dislike having their competence questioned. By using specialised vocabulary, they also make negotiations seem more complex and esoteric than they really are. The admonishment of various US presidents that Congress should not interfere in the day-to-day conduct of foreign policy is composed in part of hubris and in part a desire to avoid looking over their shoulder when negotiating with a foreign government.

The larger the institution, the more difficult it is to maintain secrecy. This has nothing to do with espionage or other covert operations. Even if there were no spying, secrecy is difficult to maintain since interactions take place among many representatives of the negotiants, not all of whom are negotiators. It is no exaggeration to say that 90 percent of the information a governmental negotiator needs is available from the environment. For example, the governments of the United States and Japan often negotiate about 'voluntary restraint' on the export of cars from Japan to the US. However secret the actual negotiations within the US government may be, the Japanese know a great deal about the pressures brought to bear on the US government by American car companies, the United Auto Workers, congressmen from constituencies with car factories, and so on. The boundaries of an institution are not totally impermeable. Information seeps in — and out.

How does one ascribe an expectation to a negotiator which is a large organisation like a government? The answer is that the bargaining position and strategy of an institutional negotiator are the result of subsidiary negotiations within the institution itself modified to some extent by information available from the environment. As in the case of multidimensional negotiations, the problem is more easily comprehended by splitting up the negotiating process into its constituent subordinate negotiations. Within the big Russian doll of the institutional negotiator showing a single face, there are dolls of decreasing sizes.

The Formation of Coalitions

Rapoport, in his *Fights, Games and Debates*, gives the following example to illustrate one aspect of the difficulty of applying game theory to cases where there are more than two players.[1] Let us suppose that three men (A, B and C) are asked to divide one pound between them, the division to be determined by majority vote. The implication is that the three have equal bargaining power and any two can out-vote the third. The situation is ripe for forming coalitions, but what coalition? Suppose A and B form a coalition by agreeing to divide up the pound equally between themselves (50 pence each) freezing out C. When C finds out that he is to get nothing in this arrangement, he can approach B and offer him 60 pence as an inducement for forming a B/C coalition. C benefits because he gets at least 40 pence instead of nothing; B accepts because otherwise C can make the same offer to A, freezing B out. When A discovers this, he can out-bid C by offering B 70 pence to return to the original coalition. It may seem that B is in a happy state of the other two bidding for his alliance; this is not so, since A and C will soon find out that B is doing very well for himself! They then find it more profitable to freeze B out by agreeing to split the pound equally between them; they both get 50 pence instead of 40, 30 or 20 pence. Now B, who is left out, can offer A 60 pence and we are back where we started. Having fallen into the trap of circular reasoning, game theory cannot find a rational and optimal strategy for the three players.

An essential assumption in this example is that the players have equal bargaining power. This is rarely the case in real life. Let us take an even simpler, but more likely, everyday occurrence. Let us suppose there are two brothers and a younger sister with a packet of eight sweets to share between themselves. On the two assumptions that boys have more power than girls, and that the youngest has the least bargaining power, the probability is that the two boys will form a coalition against their sister. They might say to her: 'Here are your two sweets; now run along!' If they are more sophisticated, they might say, having earlier appropriated two sweets for themselves, 'Oh! there are six in the packet; we can have two each!' We cannot understand why and what kind of coalitions form if we ignore bargaining power.

In spite of the simplifications assumed in the two examples, we can draw one essential conclusion. Formation of coalitions involves negotiations, which may be subsidiary, supplementary or parallel to the main negotiation. For example, in dividing the sweets, the two brothers must first negotiate and agree between themselves before presenting that agreement as an accomplished fact to their sister. The example of dividing up the pound was nothing but a series of subsidiary but fruitless negotiations between any two of the three players. We can identify one more phase of the negotiating process. *In any bargaining situation with more than two negotiants, there is a phase of coalition-formation.* Any n-person negotiation can be broken up into a number of packets of negotiations with smaller numbers. The basic principle that agreement is possible only when there is a perception of equality of dissatisfaction, consistent with disparities in bargaining power, holds good for each of the subsidiary coalition-forming negotiations also. In the case of ICAs, though the exporters negotiate as a group with importers, their coalition has to divide up the total quota equitably. If any exporting country or group of countries is dissatisfied with the quota division, exporters as a whole cannot enter into meaningful negotiations.

The reason why the circular reasoning in the pound-division example gets nowhere is because the concept of equality of dissatisfaction is ignored. When three players have equal bargaining power, no coalition is stable because dissatisfaction cannot be equalised. The only solution which works, and can be perceived to do so by all three, is an equal division of the pound. After A, B and C go round and round for some time, eventually they will arrive at this conclusion — may be giving the odd left-over penny to the first who propounds this unique solution!

Coalitions and Ordering of Priorities

Let us imagine a family — father, mother and adolescent son — discussing how to spend the money they have saved. They could spend most of it on a trip to India and buy a new television set with what remains. Or they could take their holiday in Greece and use the balance for one of two things: (i) redecorating the house, or (ii) buying a second hand car for the son, trading in his motor cycle. A third choice is going to Blackpool. In this case, they can both redecorate the house and buy the car. The choice of three holidays and three ways of spending the balance is a negotiation in two dimensions — where to go on holiday and what to do with the remainder of the money. The two dimensions are functionally related by the total amount of money available.

Each member of the family will have his or her own preference. Let us assume that the son's burning ambition is to go to India and meet his guru and he does not care whether he has a car or a motor cycle. On the other hand, the mother wants him to give up his motor cycle which, in her opinion, is dangerous. The father prefers to redecorate the house since he is anxious to preserve the value of his investment. Both parents are tired of going to Blackpool every year and want a holiday abroad. Buying a new television set is least important for all. We assume that the three want to go on holiday together rather than going their separate ways. The priorities of the negotiants can now be set out as follows.

	First priority	*Second priority*
Father	Greece and redecorate house	Blackpool, redecorate and buy car
Mother	Greece and buy car	Same as father
Son	India	Doesn't care

They may all have third and lower priorities but these are not relevant. Because of the fairly close identity in the preferences of the parents, they are most likely to discuss it between them and decide that it would be best to go to Greece. They compromise on spending the rest of the money by agreeing to buy the car on condition that the house will be redecorated next year, that being the trade-off for the father. They justify their decision by arguing that getting a car for the son would be some compensation for the dissatisfaction he will feel in not going to India. It may appear that the mother has got her own way, but this may be some compensation owed to her for a past residue of dissatisfaction (she might have gone reluctantly to Blackpool the previous year).

We have reached this particular solution only because of the way we have set out the problem and the priorities we have attached to each one. Supposing the son was a do-it-yourself enthusiast, a coalition between father and son could form. The point to note is that, with three negotiants of equal bargaining power, an agreement between any two forming a coalition will become the agreement of the three.

We have analysed a domestic example in detail only to show

that a negotiation for coalition-forming is a negotiation like any other, and that the order of priorities plays a crucial role. Such an analysis can be made for any number of negotiants and any number of dimensions. I have done this for all possible combinations up to four independent negotiants and four dimensions. An additional example is given below. A generalised theory of coalition-formation can be worked out using the method of hierarchical clustering.

For three negotiants bargaining in three dimensions, consider the case of a board of directors discussing the introduction of a new product. The three dimensions they negotiate about are: (i) the quantity (Q) to be produced, (ii) the price (P) at which it is to be marketed, and (iii) the market share (S) they want to capture. Since the cost of production is related to the quantity produced, the sale price P is functionally related to Q. Since the higher the sale price, the lower the market share, P and S are related. Since there is little point in producing more than is saleable, S and Q are also related.

Of the three directors, the production director is most concerned with the quantity he can guarantee to manufacture while maintaining quality; in his view, this ought to determine the market share they should aim for. He is willing to let the others determine the sale price. The sales director, on the other hand, is most concerned with capturing a specific market share and knows the price that will make this possible. He wants the production to be adjusted to meet these targets. Let us suppose the finance director's main objective is the profit margin. He gives the highest priority to the sale price and then to the quantity which will give the best margin; if he can achieve this level of profitability, he is willing to accept the resulting market share. The discussion will not, of course, be as clear-cut as this; there will be sets of figures, each director preferring those sets which accord most closely with his own priority ordering. The order can be set out as:

| *Director* | \multicolumn{3}{c}{*Priorities*} |
	1st	2nd	3rd
Production	Q	S	P
Sales	S	P	Q
Finance	P	Q	S

There is no possibility of a coalition.

Suppose, however, that the finance director's priorities are somewhat different. He may well agree that capturing an adequate market share is more important in the long-term interests of the company, and may thus accept lower profit margins at least in the initial stages. The order of priorities will then look like this:

Director	Priorities		
	1st	2nd	3rd
Production	Q	S	P
Sales	S	P	Q ⎫
Finance	S	P	Q ⎭

Because the finance and sales directors both have the same order of priorities, there is a natural coalition between them.

The two cases of coalition and no coalition can be written more generally by calling the three directors negotiators N1, N2 and N3 and the three dimensions can also be numbered 1, 2 and 3. Schematically, the above example can be shown as:

	No coalition	Coalition of N2 and N3
Order of priority of N1	1 2 3	1 2 3
N2	2 3 1	2 3 1
N3	3 1 2	2 3 1

Though a coalition was formed in the above example when two of the negotiators had identical orders of priority, this condition is not always necessary. This can be shown theoretically by considering all possible combinations of negotiators bargaining in three dimensions. Eliminating all the combinations which are identical in form, we find that there are only 10 distinct types. The 10 types fall into five major classes as shown in Table 9.1

The proposition that coalitions are formed because of identity or similarity in the orders of priority among dimensions is a realistic one, since it is common sense that negotiators who share common interests will join together. For example, we have often referred to the coalitions of exporters and importers in ICAs. In the specific context of an ICA, the coalition formed may override affinities and antipathies. In the earlier International Wheat Agreements, the United States, Australia and Canada were in the exporters group while Britain was in the importers group; the close

Table 9.1: Coalition-formation: three negotiants/three dimensions

Class		Order of priority of			Type of Coalition Formed
Class 1	N1 N2 N3	1 1 1	2 2 2	3 3 3	Since all three negotiants have the same preference order, any coalition formed will be for reasons of psychological affinity.
Class 2	N1 N2 N3	1 1 2	2 2 3	3 3 1	Since two of the three have the same order of priority, there is an in-built incentive for N1 and N2 to form a coalition.
Class 3	N1 N2 N3	1 1 2	2 3 3	3 2 1	N1 and N2 can form a coalition by one of them interchanging his second and third priorities. A coalition between N2 and N3 is less likely since they disagree on the dimension to be accorded highest priority. Only if they have strong psychological ties, will they first negotiate with each other before beginning negotiations with N1.
Class 4	N1 N2 N3	1 3 2	2 2 3	3 1 1	A coalition between N1 and N2 is possible, but less likely than in Class 3, since, to begin with, they both disagree on which dimension should be considered the most important.
Class 5	N1 N2 N3	1 2 3	2 3 1	3 1 2	A coalition based solely on the importance attached to dimensions is quite unlikely; any coalition formed will be entirely for psychological reasons.

emotional affinities between Britain and the other three did not prevent Britain from forming a coalition with other importer countries. In the International Sugar Agreements, South Africa was admitted as an exporting member by other (mostly developing) exporting countries, all of whom detest South Africa's racialism.

An example of the variety of coalitions that can form, based on a perceived identity of interests, is shown by the Third United Nations Conference on the Law of the Sea. This Conference, a mammoth 9-year undertaking involving almost every country in the world, dealt with a wide range of subjects — territorial waters, the continental shelf, contiguous economic zones, fishing, mineral rights, deep sea mining, passage of ships, innocent passage of warships, marine research, marine pollution and others. The number of coalitions that were formed reflected the widely different priorities attached to different issues by various countries. By the time the fifth session was convened in 1976, the following distinct coalitions could be identified. The advanced countries and the maritime powers formed one group; this group included both the United States and the Soviet Union. Though the two super-powers are antagonists in many areas, their interests were identical when it came to safeguarding the right of passage for their warships! A second group was formed by 51 land-locked and 'geographically disadvantaged' countries. The usual 'have' and 'have-not' coalitions in international conferences are the group of developed countries opposed to the group of developing countries. In the Law of the Sea Conference, the haves were the coastal states and the have-nots the land-locked, with inherently weaker bargaining power because of their situation. A third group was formed as a counter-coalition against the second and had about 90 coastal states, excluding the maritime powers.

Even among the coastal states, those with a long coastline formed a separate coalition. The longer the uncontested coastline, the more sea a coastal state could acquire by extending its territorial waters to 12 miles, by calling an area covered by 200 miles from the coast an 'exclusive economic zone', and by defining the continental shelf in such a way that they could extend further their jurisdiction. On the question of the continental shelf, countries which had a gently sloping shelf formed a sub-coalition within the coalition of the coastal states. A separate coalition formed among archipelagic states like Greece and Indonesia, which shared an interest in enclosing large bodies of water as internal waters. A counter-coalition naturally formed among their neighbours who feared a loss of what they perceived as their legitimate rights. States near straits like Malacca or Hormuz formed a coalition because they perceived a need to control shipping through them in order to avoid oil spills and pollution. States which had large fleets of merchant ships, states which had the technology for deep sea mining, states which disapproved of the passage of warships too near their coast, states which preferred the median line as a boundary, states which found the median line to be a disadvantage — one could find as many coalitions in the Law of the Sea Conference as there were topics in which more than one country had an interest.

The perception of shared interest can also lead to temporary coalitions. In 1979, the dispute between the European Parliament and the Council of Ministers on the Budget of the Community, escalated into a constitutional crisis. The Parliament increased spending levels on regional development against the wishes of the Council. This Budget increase could have been overruled by the Council of Ministers if all of them had agreed to do so. But a temporary coalition of UK, Ireland and Italy prevented the Council from mustering the necessary majority. This coalition was not a stable or a permanent one within the Community; on other matters, such as dairy policy, Ireland shares a common interest with France and Germany and not the UK. Even on the Budget question, the following year the coalition did not materialise and Parliament also failed to intervene with the same effectiveness.

Coalitions and Psychological Affinities

We have frequently mentioned that coalitions can also form for psychological or emotional reasons. Within the big coalition of exporters in ICAs, sub-coalitions form for such reasons. For example, in the International Coffee Agreement, the two main exporters' sub-coalitions are the Latin American group and the African group. Within these the French-speaking African countries form one sub-coalition (OAMCAF — Organisation of Coffee Producers of Africa and Malagasy) and the Central American countries another.

If shared perceptions of vital interests promote coalitions, so do shared perceptions of vulnerability. An alliance is a coalition, backed by a written treaty, born out of shared fears. Alliances are not coalitions created for a specific negotiation, but are a consequence of a conflict situation. For example, NATO is a coalition of states who all share the perceptions that the Soviet Union threatens their security and way of life, and that in all negotiations involving the USSR priority should be accorded to the security dimension. Take the case of the proposal for increased purchases of natural gas by West Germany from the USSR. In theory, this was a purely commercial transaction. However, NATO in general, and the United States in particular, were concerned that too great a dependence by West Germany on Soviet energy imports would weaken the alliance. In the complex modern world, the security concerns of a military alliance are no longer limited to arms, armaments and military strategy; it embraces the whole gamut of economics and politics of its member countries. Without shared fears, an alliance cannot exist.

While a coalition within a continuing negotiation agrees on the dimensions which should be accorded priority, an alliance *excludes* certain dimensions in any current or future negotiation with the perceived antagonist. This is an *a priori* delimitation of bargaining space.

We should not underestimate the importance of psychological factors in the creation of military alliances. In the case of the ANZUS pact between Australia, New Zealand and the United States, the former two are not directly threatened by the Soviet Union in the way the countries of Western Europe feel they are threatened. They are members of the alliance because of the ancestry which many Australians and New Zealanders trace to Britain, of similar educational and cultural backgrounds, and the bonds of a common language. The alliance arises out of a feeling in the antipodean countries that they are part of the same cultural, 'western' world, a feeling no doubt intensified by the distance which separates them from the political and cultural centres of their world. So long as they perceive a common enemy, peoples of the same culture will form coalitions. Once the Arab countries of the Arabian Peninsula began to perceive revolutionary Iran as a threat, the Gulf Co-operation Council become a more coherent unit.

Inequality among Negotiants

If there are only two negotiants, the question of who is more important is shown by the relative bargaining power, which then influences the location of the agreement point. When the number of negotiants increases, and coalitions form, the relative bargaining power of the coalitions becomes the determining factor. However, as the number increases, a hierarchy is bound to develop among the negotiants.

In the case of ICAs, the relative importance of the members is clearly written down as the number of votes for each one, based on each country's market share, within the separate totals of 1000 votes for each coalition of exporters and importers. Thus, in the Coffee Agreement, Brazil, the largest exporter, has the highest number of votes among the exporters and the United States, the highest among the importers. Colombia has the second highest number among exporters. Since Brazil and Colombia rank much higher in importance than any of the other 60 or so exporting countries, the smaller ones tend to form coalitions among themselves.

It is unnecessary to add further examples to show that, when the number of negotiants increases, a pecking order is established amongst them. When the negotiations are conducted under the umbrella of a treaty, the voting strength displays this pecking order. If the negotiations take place without there being a written framework, the pecking order does not disappear: every negotiant knows which of the others is more important. The importance is derived in part from the negotiant's power in the environment and in part from the specific power on the issues under negotiation. We may not be able to write down a strict ranking of the negotiants, but we may be quite sure that every negotiant is aware of the existence of such an order.

How Many and how Few?

In the last chapter, I suggested that no more than a few dimensions can be comprehended adequately at the same time. The same proposition applies to the number of negotiants. The UN Law of the Sea Conference may have had more than 150 countries participating in it; but it is unrealistic to assume that every one of them took an equally active part, and that every subject was fully thrashed out by all of them sitting down together. Any one who has been a member of any committee (school governing bodies, voluntary organisations, clubs or associations) knows that decisions are rarely reached by full and thorough discussions of the whole committee. Whenever a subject of more than usual complication comes up, the discussion meanders, and becomes confused, sometimes heated and often boring with one or two tenacious members repeating what they have already said at length. At some point, a suggestion is made to 'form a sub-committee to look into the whole question and report back to the main committee'. This suggestion is accepted with relief by most members. The manoeuvre is intended to reduce the number of negotiants. A principle governing negotiations is: *too many negotiants cannot reach an agreement.*

This principle applies also to negotiations at the international level. Almost any large conference forms committees from the beginning. This is not of much help in inter-governmental conferences, since each country usually sends a representative to each committee, if only to hold a watching brief. At some point during a conference, a smaller group is formed. This may be called a 'drafting committee', 'rapporteurs group', 'the chairman's informal committee' or some such innocuous name. In the second UNCTAD held in New Delhi, this crucial negotiating group was simply called 'the Everest' because it had its meetings on the top floor of a hotel, well away from the conference venue where most delegates were continuing to orate. The purpose of forming these smaller groups is to reduce the number of negotiators to a manageable level so that a decision can be reached. The success of such a committee depends on their producing a decision or resolution which commands the least opposition. The smaller group does not ignore the rest, who continue to be part of the bargaining population, even though they are physically absent. The decision produced by the actual negotiators can never satisfy every negotiator; but it is formulated in such a way that all but the extremists are left more or less equally dissatisfied. The majority then overrides the extremists, being simply tired of the subject or because the conference cannot be extended any further.

However large the original population of negotiators, it will split up fairly soon into smaller coalitions, which will then sub-divide until the groups are reduced to a manageable size. In my experience, such a group never runs to double figures and usually numbers less than seven. (It is interesting to note that the high-powered economic summit of the western nations is restricted to seven.) Despite strenuous attempts to keep down the number, the North—South summit promoted by Chancellor Kreisky of Austria and President Lopez Portillo of Mexico had 22 members. The meeting at Cancun was clearly unproductive. It seems to me that the optimum number of individuals who can negotiate together and produce an agreement lies between four and seven.

Survival of Coalitions

A temporary coalition of the kind between Italy, Ireland and the UK for a few weeks in 1979, breaks up as soon as its purpose is accomplished. At the other extreme, a military alliance like NATO, concluded formally as an international treaty, survives many decades. Why do some coalitions survive longer than others? How long is the life of a coalition? When and why do they break up? The answers to these questions depend, in part, on the members of a coalition continuing to share the same interests and perceptions and, in part, on the tightness of the coalition.

It is obvious that some interests are more permanent than others. Irrespective of whether there is a functioning ICA or not, most exporting countries continue to be exporters, and importing countries remain importers.[2] The long-term identity of interests produces more lasting coalitions. Some of the coalitions formed during the Law of the Sea Conference are clearly limited to that context. Outside the treaty, there are not many issues on which archipelagic states will find common ground. On the other hand, the coalition of maritime powers is more likely to endure since they have common interests to defend in fora other than the Law of the Sea Conference (e.g. the IMO or UNCTAD). While interests may be short-term or long-term, hopes and fears generally have greater permanence, because attitudinal changes happen very slowly, if at all. So long as there is a perceived antagonist, coalitions based on such attitudes will survive. Linguistic affinities, religious loyalties, class or caste attachments and all 'isms', have the character of persistence.

In Chapter 1, I referred to three kinds of inter-state negotiations — bilateral, multilateral within an agreed framework and multilateral without a framework. An agreed framework (e.g. a treaty) not only provides a set of rules for members to negotiate among themselves on their mutual problems but also promotes a coalition for negotiations with states outside the treaty. The Rome Treaty of the European Communities is an example. While the members bargain as independent negotiators in all intra-Community matters (such as the Common Agricultural Policy, Industrial Policy, competition or harmonisation) they act as a coalition when facing the outside world (external trade, tariffs, foreign aid, relations with associate states). However, the Community is not a watertight coalition. The example of some member countries negotiating independent agreements to restrict car imports from Japan is a case in point.

The larger the coalition, the less cohesive it is likely to be. This is particularly true for the two overlapping coalitions of the developing countries each of which has over 100 members — the 'Group of 77', which had its origins in UNCTAD and the Non-Aligned Movement, whose origins were in the Cold War of the 1950s. It is unrealistic to expect any degree of tightness with such numbers. Cultural and linguistic affinities among the Latin American countries make them a distinct sub-group compared with, say, the African nations, who have their own forum in the Organisation of African Unity. The group of countries of the Islamic Conference form another sub-group which, at least in its richest members, overlaps with OPEC. On economic matters the interests of OPEC countries are often against the interests of the non-oil-exporting developing countries. It has become standard practice to refer to these countries as 'The South' or 'the Third World' as if they all belong to a watertight coalition with almost identical interests. Apart from ideological differences, they vary so much in size, population, natural resources and propinquity to great powers that it would indeed be surprising if the coalitions were stronger than they actually are. The loose groupings survive because of shared perceptions of vulnerability. They all perceive an excessive dependence on the advanced countries and are equally motivated by fears of coming too much under the control of one or the other of the super-powers.

The tightness of a coalition also depends on the atmosphere of a particular negotiation. The set of very complex negotiations held during the Conference on European Security and Co-operation (Helsinki, 1973—75; renewed in Madrid, 1980—83) were of vital importance for the limitation of conflict in the world. Unfortunately, they were held, from the beginning, in an atmosphere of confrontation rather than conciliation. This approach to negotiations makes it easier for coalitions based on shared antipathies to hold together. It was only the presence of some neutral countries (Sweden, Austria, Switzerland) that saved the Conference in Madrid from degenerating into unremitting confrontation. The fact that the few neutral countries shared many values with one of the two adversarial coalitions did not prevent them from striving to limit the conflict. I am pointing this out because a tight coalition by itself is no virtue if the consequence is not the limitation but escalation of conflict.

The survival of coalitions also depends on the degree of trust among their members. The concept of reciprocity ('If you support me on this, I'll support you on that') is common in many negotiations. In order to be effective, such promises of potential action must carry conviction. A negotiant will exchange present action for potential action only if he believes that the other will keep the promise. To be really effective, the potential action must also be seen to be a concession; it must involve some dissatisfaction on the part of the negotiant making the promise. A permanent alliance like NATO has to have history of past successful trade-offs. Trust-reinforcement and maintenance of credibility are as important for the survival of coalitions as they are for limiting conflict.

Before concluding this chapter, it will be useful to note the distinction between coalition and collusion. This is best illustrated by an example. At one of the annual meetings of the International Coffee Council (the body dealing with the operation of the ICA for coffee), a coalition of small exporters developed almost spontaneously because they were dissatisfied with the export quota decided by the biggest members, particularly Brazil and the United States. This coalition had little bargaining power; its only weapon was to threaten to withdraw *en masse* from the Agreement. If all small exporters had done so, it might have removed enough quantity from control to jeopardise the stability of the market. Since the disruption of the Agreement was not welcome to the most important members, the United States exerted political pressure on some of the smaller Central American countries, who then instructed their delegations to withdraw from the small exporters' coalition. This was perceived by the other small exporters as a case of 'collusion' with the 'enemy' (i.e. an importing country). The explanation can only be that the Central American countries in question valued their coalition with the United States on other matters so much that it was not worth sacrificing it for the sake of limited gains in the Coffee Agreement. One coalition involving long-term interests was seen to be more important than another of short-term validity. Thus, collusion is an apparently unnatural coalition between two negotiants in a specific negotiation in which their interests had placed them in different coalitions. A negotiant is charged with collusion when the other members of his coalition find that the colluder had not behaved in a manner consistent with the shared interest of their coalition.

Notes

1. Anatol Rapoport, *Fights, Games and Debates* (Ann Arbor: The University of Michigan Press, 1960), pp. 198-200.
2. Changes in status of countries in international commodity trade are exceptional. I can think of only two instances — the USSR which used to export wheat became an importer, and India emerged as an exporter of sugar in the 1950s.

10 THE THEORY SO FAR

> Induction ... is a process of inference; it proceeds from the known to the unknown.
> John Stuart Mill

By analysing the negotiating process both theoretically and by citing examples from real life, we have provided evidence for the concepts introduced in Part One. We have shown clearly, by plane diagrams, how time can be incorporated as a dimension in plotting the changing perceptions of the negotiants. We have also shown that, in general, the boundaries of a dimension in the bargaining space are the initial positions, so long as the bargaining space and the environment do not change. This supplied the explanation for why the negotiants know clearly what is outside the bargaining space, but have only an uncertain perception about what is inside. We now know that the specific purpose of communication in the negotiating process is to convey information, deliberately imprecisely, about expectations, limits and units of dissatisfaction. The voicing of each bid or offer is a communication about current expectations; the totality of such communications, taking into account the time spent, conveys information about limits. These, though perceived uncertainly by other negotiants, prompt them to modify theirs.

The main phases of the negotiating process are (i) communication to ascertain initial expectations; (ii) modifying expectations; (iii) ascertaining limits and units of dissatisfaction; and (iv) perceiving either equality of dissatisfaction or an irreconcilable gap between limits.

In a one-dimension case there are three distinct types — breakdown, agreement and see-saw. When there is a gap between the limit positions of the negotiants, there is a breakdown. When the limit positions coincide, the negotiation will teeter between agreement and breakdown. The impasse can be broken — and a definite outcome obtained — only by the intervention of an external event, such as (i) a substantial reduction in uncertainty caused by an increase in trust; (ii) a trade-off in another dimension; (iii) mediation; or (iv) a change in the environment.

Negotiations which result in an agreement take a shorter or longer time depending partly on the extent of mutual knowledge and partly on the degree of openness in the negotiants' approach to the bargaining. The point at which agreement is reached is influenced by differences in bargaining power and bargaining skills. Inequality in bargaining power, arising from the environment, manifests itself in the relationship between expectations and limits. If the expectations are clustered around one negotiant's limit, he is, *a priori*, the weaker.

Dissatisfaction is the gap between expectation and outcome. Units of dissatisfaction are related to, but are not the same as, the unit of the dimension under negotiation. There is no absolute scale of dissatisfaction applicable to all negotiants. In a one-dimension short-duration negotiation, the dissatisfaction is computed with reference to initial expectations. Because there is no perfect perception of equality of dissatisfaction there is always a residue of dissatisfaction. An agreement is also an expectation — that of the value or utility of the agreement.

Negotiations in Many Dimensions

In extending the analysis of negotiations from one dimension to many, we identified two new ideas — ordering of priority among dimensions, and the existence of their functional relationships. These are different for different negotiants. We have shown that the alignment of the order of priority is an important phase in the negotiating process. Complete alignment of priorities is neither necessary nor practical; it is enough if the negotiants agree on which are the two (at most three) most important dimensions. Generally speaking, the period immediately after the beginning will be devoted to aligning priorities. If, however, a negotiant is willing or prepared to have a show-down, he will refuse to discuss the dimension which is considered most important by another negotiant. We have also shown from examples that multi-dimensional negotiations are tackled in a variety of ways — serially, simultaneously or in 'baskets'. Functional relationships between dimensions can also take many forms, some of which are too complex to be presented in mathematical or diagrammatic form. However, the fact that the relationships cannot be expressed mathematically is no bar to their use in the negotiating process, since negotiants are capable of understanding, and articulating, complex interrelations.

We have shown that real-life negotiations deal with, at the most, two or three dimensions at a time. More complex negotiations are usually broken up into smaller, more easily manageable ones. The phases of the negotiating process in multidimensional negotiations have been identified (see Tables 8.1 and 8.3).

Negotiations in many dimensions can break down for a variety of reasons — if there is no alignment of priorities, if there is a breakdown or a see-saw in a high-priority dimension, if a package cannot be put together, and if equality of dissatisfaction cannot be perceived. On the other hand, we have also identified the conditions necessary for an agreement to be reached. Since, in real life, negotiations sometimes break down and sometimes end in agreement, understanding why negotiations break down is essential for limiting conflicts.

Because linkages exist between dimensions in the bargaining space and the immediate environment, trade-offs become possible. The concept of a package deal is implicit in any negotiation which has more than one dimension. By looking at negotiations through the eyes of the different negotiants, we can give content not only to these everyday phenomena but also to others, like 'splitting the difference'.

Coalitions and Alliances

In any negotiation with more than two negotiants, a hierarchy exists. In multilateral negotiations within an agreed treaty, the relative power is indicated by voting strength. Negotiation with a large number of negotiants may be reduced to a few negotiating groups by the formation of coalitions.

Coalition-formation involves negotiations which may be subsidiary, supplementary or parallel to the main negotiation. The principle that agreement is possible only when there is a perception of equality of dissatisfaction holds good for the coalition-forming negotiation also. Coalitions are formed between negotiants (i) who accord the same or similar order of priority to the dimensions in a bargaining space, (i.e. who share the same interests); and (ii) who share the same hopes or fears and are linked by psychological affinities. Coalitions break up when the motivating factor ceases to exist, though this is mainly true of coalitions based on shared interests.

Alliances last longer; these are coalitions which exclude some dimensions — usually security — from all current and future negotiations with a perceived antagonist. Cultural affinities promote the formation of coalitions so long as there are no specific interests that divide the parties. In such cases, coalitions can form even between normal antagonists. Just as no negotiation is independent of its past history, no coalition is independent of its past psychological history. Trust and credibility, built up by reinforcing actions, are essential for the survival of coalitions. The tightness of a coalition is indicated by the number of occasions when its members negotiate as a single negotiant compared with the number of occasions when they act independently.

Collusion is an apparently unnatural coalition between negotiants who are normally members of different coalitions among the bargaining population.

Large numbers of people do not seem able to arrive at any agreed decisions. A negotiation among more than seven is usually bound to end in an inconclusive outcome or in a breakdown. Inconclusiveness is avoided by forming smaller negotiating sub-groups.

Negotiations and the Limitation of Conflict

Both the theoretical and empirical approaches adopted so far have helped us arrive at some important conclusions. First, dissatisfactions, perceptions of vital interests, vulnerability and perceptions of threat influence every aspect of the process. Secondly, any negotiation, however complex, can be broken down into smaller segments — this is how negotiants operate in practice. Multidimensional negotiations, in fact, become negotiations in two or three dimensions, the maximum that people can comprehend and bargain on at a time. The negotiating policy or strategy of an institutional negotiant, like a government, can be understood by studying the negotiations between different interest groups within it. Any negotiation with a large number of negotiants can also be understood by analysing the coalition-forming negotiations. Thirdly, the desire for order finds its expression in evolving procedures for reducing the number of dimensions and the number of persons actually involved in a negotiation. All three conclusions are important for the limitiation of conflict.

Throughout Part Two, we have emphasised the close relationship between the bargaining space and the environment. The impact of the latter on the former is the subject of Part Three.

PART THREE

FOUR ASPECTS OF NEGOTIATION

Ita in vita ut in lusu alae pessima jactura arter corrigenda est.
As in life, so in a game of chance, skill will make something of the worst of throws.

Necessity never made a good bargain.
> Benjamin Franklin,
> *Poor Richard's Almanack*

Let us build a kind of United States of Europe.... The process is simple. All that is needed is the resolve of hundreds of millions of men and women.
> Winston Churchill,
> Speech in Zurich, 1946

11 ESCALATION, ENLARGEMENT AND EXPANSION

> In all sincerity, as a military man I can see no use for any nuclear weapons which would not end in escalation, with consequences no one can conceive.
> Lord Mountbatten,
> Speech at Strasbourg, 1979

The theory of negotiation has so far been developed under the assumptions of an unchanging environment and a constant bargaining space. These assumptions are not valid in real life. We have often alluded to the possibility of changes in the environment affecting every aspect of the bargaining process. Such environmental changes may both alter the bargaining power of the negotiants and affect the attitudes and perceptions of the negotiants. These consequences internalise into the bargaining space changes occurring outside it, without affecting either the number of negotiants or the number of dimensions. We shall examine these types of changes in Chapters 12 and 13.

Another change that may take place is that the bargaining space or the bargaining population may themselves be altered due to the initiative of one of the negotiants. New issues may be brought into the negotiation or new participants added to the existing number.

I make a distinction between the addition of a new dimension and the addition of a new negotiant because the resulting changes in the negotiating process are quite different. Suppose I am having an argument with my wife about where to spend Christmas and my wife says, 'Mummy wasn't too happy with what we did last year.' 'Mummy' is not physically present, but her sensitivity is a new dimension introduced into the existing set. A new order of priority is then perceived by the two negotiants. My wife thinks that her mother's feelings ought to have a high priority, whereas I may consider them unimportant, if not irrelevant. Alternatively, suppose that my wife's mother actually walks in while we are arguing; she is bound to join in and express her dissatisfaction. From a two-negotiant case, it is now a three-negotiant one, creating the potential for coalition-formation: my wife will no doubt form one with her mother. So there is no reason to think that the outcome with mother present will be the same as when her feelings are introduced as a means of increasing the number of dimensions in the negotiation.

In order to distinguish between the two types, we may call increasing the number of dimensions *enlargement of the bargaining space* and the addition of new negotiators *expansion of the bargaining population*. *Escalation*, a word in common use, embraces to some extent, the two phenomena. Since escalation implies a deliberate attempt by one participant to raise the level of conflict bringing it nearer to a violent end, we shall use it only with reference to conflicts.

The domestic example illustrates certain characteristics the two phenomena have in common. (i) There must exist in the immediate environment additional dimensions or potential negotiators capable of being introduced to the bargaining space or population; (ii) the addition is made at the initiative of one of the negotiators; and (iii) the addition must be accepted by others.

It is my view that any increase in the complexity of a negotiation by enlargement or expansion must make the achievement of a peaceful agreement more difficult. Since we are concerned in this book primarily with the limitation of conflict between states, we must consider the possibility of reducing the complexity in interstate negotiations, with a view to moving them away from a violent outcome and closer to a peaceful agreement. We shall call preventing a conflict from moving towards violence *containment*, and decreasing the number of dimensions *contraction* (i.e. the opposite of enlargement). Likewise, the opposite of expansion can be called *reduction*.

Enlargement

The existence of dimensions in the environment which can be brought into a current negotiation implies that the negotiators interact at other points in addition to those included in the bargaining space. If I bargain for a secondhand car with a stranger, there are not many avenues open to either of us to enlarge the bargaining space; there are few other linkages between us. It is obvious that in long-lasting, multifaceted relationships (such as those between husband and wife, trade union and employer, or between governments) there exist linkages which could be converted by one negotiant into a substantive dimension. In general, the longer the past history of relations between negotiants, the greater the number of linkages.

Recourse to enlargement can only be explained by using the concept of dissatisfaction. A negotiant feels impelled to add a new dimension because, in his perception, an agreement that equalises dissatisfaction is not possible within the existing set of dimensions — the bargaining space is seen to be too small. In the UK/Community Budget dispute, after the initial denial by other negotiants that there was a problem at all, let us suppose that everyone had agreed to limit the bargaining space to the Budget contribution alone. This would have resulted in a one-dimension negotiation, and equalisation of dissatisfaction would then have been achieved only by 'splitting the difference' — the rebate to the UK would have been exactly half of what was demanded. But when Mrs Thatcher dramatically rejected the 'half-a-loaf' formula, there was no way of achieving equality of dissatisfaction without resorting to enlargement. Lamb imports from France, the sharing of North Sea oil, fisheries policy, increase in farm prices for the following year — a variety of linkages were available in the immediate environment to make Britain contribute her share of dissatisfaction.

The addition of new dimensions can take place either during the period of NAN or during the course of substantive negotiations. We can visualise negotiations with enlargement as a series of boxes, one nesting inside another. This is quite consistent with the idea that all negotiations have a past history which is part of the collective memory.

But the demand for enlargement is a unilateral action; it still has to be accepted by the others. The process of gaining the acceptance of all other negotiants to the proposed enlargement also requires communication; it is part of the whole negotiating process.

Once enlargement has been agreed by all or most of the negotiants, the negotiation which ensues is not the same as before. This is not just a semantic point of defining when a negotiation becomes a new one. Just because a dimension is added at a later stage, it does not follow that it is the least priority for all negotiants. The immediate effect of enlargement is for the negotiants to try to realign the $d+1$ dimensions. In practice, the realignment would have been agreed to in the process of accepting the enlargement.

Imperceptibly, the negotiation in d dimensions merges into a negotiation d+1 dimensions: It may even go unnoticed by the negotiants.

This is important for understanding international conflicts with a view to limiting them. There is no such thing as *the* Middle East conflict, *the* Cyprus question or *the* Northern Ireland problem. As time changes, the environment and bargaining spaces change and the conflict is transmuted. There is a conflict in the Middle East and it is a continuing one. But the characteristics of the conflict have changed due to changes in the environment and bargaining power and due to the actions of the disputants. The kind of actions that would have limited the conflict in the Middle East in 1948 would have failed to do so in 1956 (when the combined British, French and Israeli forces attacked Egypt), or 1967 (when the Six-Day War erupted), or 1973 (when Egypt attacked Israel to regain lost territory) or 1983 (when Israel invaded Lebanon). As the conflict escalated, more dimensions were added; every additional annexation (Sinai, West Bank, the Golan Heights, Southern Lebanon) and every enlargement (West Bank settlements, Jerusalem) added a new complexity making limitation yet more difficult. I feel that we often make the mistake of assuming that a conflict remains the same in character irrespective of the passage of time.

Stages of Enlargement

The starting point is the perception by one negotiant that compensation in one specific dimension in the immediate environment is needed to produce equality of dissatisfaction. After this *identification of a dimension for enlargement*, the next stage is the communication of this perception to other negotiants by a *demand for enlargement*. This may be coupled with a warning that, unless enlargement is agreed to, the negotiations may end in breakdown. The third stage offers the other negotiants a choice between four courses of action: (i) they can alter their own positions, expectations as well as limits, to make additional concessions — i.e. the other negotiants can increase their own dissatisfaction in order to produce equality of dissatisfaction without enlargement. In the Community Budget example, Britain could have, notwithstanding earlier protestations, 'split the difference', if she did not want the enlargement demanded by the other Community members. (ii) Other negotiators can agree to the enlargement in the hope that the totality of dissatisfaction in d+1 dimensions will be equalised. (iii) Other negotiators can demand further enlargement as a condition for accepting the enlargement demanded by one negotiant — i.e., a counter-demand for enlargement to d+2 dimensions. (iv) At all times, the option of signalling breakdown is available to all the negotiants. The courses of action may be called *adjustment, acceptance, demand for further enlargement* or *breakdown*.

The stages of enlargement are shown in Figure 11.1a.

The Consequences of Enlargement

The possibility of further enlargement as a consequence of one enlargement is of special relevance to relations between nation states. It is difficult to find pure examples of negotiations between just *two* governments being enlarged, because there are always other governments in the immediate vicinity who become involved. A plausible, though not strictly accurate, example of enlargement in a bilateral negotiation is shown by the relationship between the United States and Mexico. There is a long-standing conflict between the two countries on the question of emigration of Mexicans across the border, who are often referred to in the US as 'illegal aliens'. When Mexico became a significant exporter of oil and gas, the question of the price to be paid by the US for purchases of Mexican gas became a matter for negotiation. The emigration question and the gas price question became linked, enlarging the negotiation to two dimensions. At this stage, a chance event introduced a third dimension. A blow-out in June 1979 at the Ixtoc I offshore exploratory oilwell resulted in the spilling of 2.4 million barrels, creating a massive oil slick which polluted beaches in Texas 500 miles away. The US then introduced the question of compensation for pollution, and the negotiations became three dimensional. The process need not have stopped there — Mexico could have further enlarged the negotiation by adding the demand for an increase in the quotas for textiles or shoes exported to the US, or seeking a change in US policy towards Central American countries. In fact, in July 1980, an unexpected new dimension was added when Mexico not only announced that it would arrest any tuna boat fishing within 200

172 *Escalation, Enlargement and Expansion*

Figure 11.1a: Stages of Enlargement

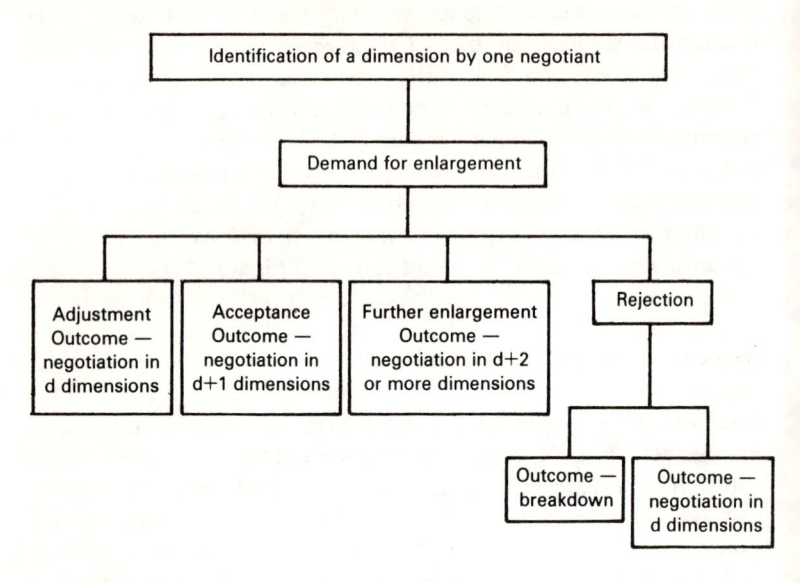

```
                 Identification of a dimension by one negotiant
                                       |
                            Demand for enlargement
          ┌──────────────┬──────────────────┬──────────────────┐
    Adjustment      Acceptance       Further enlargement    Rejection
    Outcome —       Outcome —          Outcome —              │
    negotiation in  negotiation in    negotiation in d+2      │
    d dimensions    d+1 dimensions    or more dimensions      │
                                                       ┌─────┴─────┐
                                                   Outcome —   Outcome —
                                                   breakdown   negotiation in
                                                               d dimensions
```

Figure 11.1b: Stages of Expansion

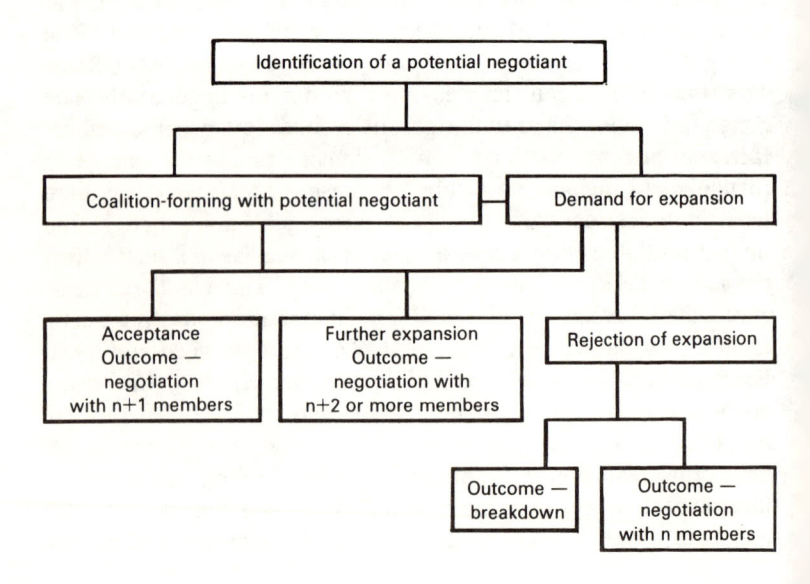

```
                      Identification of a potential negotiant
                                       |
        ┌──────────────────────────────┴──────────────────────────┐
    Coalition-forming with potential negotiant ── Demand for expansion
        ┌──────────────────┬──────────────────────┬──────────────────┐
    Acceptance         Further expansion        Rejection of expansion
    Outcome —          Outcome —                     │
    negotiation        negotiation with              │
    with n+1 members   n+2 or more members           │
                                                ┌────┴────┐
                                           Outcome —   Outcome —
                                           breakdown   negotiation
                                                       with n members
```

miles of its coast unless a fee was paid and a portion of the catch allocated to it, but actually arrested several US tuna boats, confiscated the catches and imposed heavy fines. The United States then imposed a ban on the import of Mexican tuna.

With so many linkages available between two neighbouring countries with a long land border, the possibilities of enlarging any negotiation by adding new dimensions are many. We must, however, also note that where there are many linkages, the prospects for finding trade-offs for achieving agreement are equally numerous.

Is a stage ever reached when no more new dimensions to the negotiation are available? The answer depends on what the negotiants perceive to be the immediate environment. In the United States – Mexico case, this could encompass emigration, natural gas imports, oil pollution, tuna fishing and foreign policy. In another case, the range may be more restricted, as, for example, in the annual negotiations within the Community for determining the CAP for the ensuing year. These negotiations sometimes reach a point when a veto on the whole package is threatened by one country. Let us suppose that France is dissatisfied with one element in the package (say, the price for liquid milk) and threatens a veto, without being dissatisfied with the other elements (e.g. the intervention price for wheat, the quota for sugar production and the sluice-gate price for pigs). The veto threat is made to convey to the others the French perception that the package contains less total dissatisfaction for the other member states than for France. The other eight may (i) increase their dissatisfaction by agreeing to higher prices for dairy products; (ii) increase everyone's dissatisfaction substantially by scuttling the entire CAP for the next year; (iii) enlarge the negotiation by demanding some other concession from France, such as a reduction in French state aid to agriculture; or (iv) find a compromise, say, a smaller rise in milk prices than the French demand coupled with some other concession. All these choices are confined within the CAP. But some members might be tempted to go outside it to find dimensions for enlargement. Britain could demand concessions on fisheries policy; Germany could seek a dismantling of production and price controls on steel products; Italy could ask for higher allocations for regional development. This not so hypothetical example is used only to illustrate the point that there is a limit to enlargement only if all the members agree that the negotiation should be kept within the bounds of the CAP. The delimitation of the immediate environment is easier in multilateral negotiations within an agreed framework. In open-ended multilateral negotiations, the possibilities of enlargement of the bargaining space are much wider.

Any enlargement takes the negotiation nearer a breakdown simply by adding to the complexity. This is primarily because even a perceptional judgement on equality of dissatisfaction becomes more difficult for the negotiants. If the United States reluctantly pays 10 ¢ more per 1000 cubic feet for natural gas, will that dissatisfaction be seen in Mexico as equalling the Mexican dissatisfaction about having to compromise on a human rights resolution in a conference of the OAS? This is not a contrived example; some newspapers reported that such a *quid pro quo* was offered. Governments do in practice make comparisons between dissatisfactions in widely different issues and make judgements on specific questions, keeping in mind the totality of relations with another country.

There is one exception to the rule that every enlargement takes a negotiation one step away from agreement. Trade-offs (the deliberate addition by mutual agreement of another dimension in order to achieve equality of dissatisfaction) represent *controlled enlargement*. This reduces the negotiating time required for reaching agreement.

Expansion

The significant difference between a negotiant wanting to enlarge the bargaining space and one wanting to expand the negotiating population is that the motivation for expansion is a perception of the need to augment one's bargaining power. A new participant is brought in only when the addition will enhance a negotiant's status by forming a coalition with the negotiant who brought him in, or by joining an existing coalition. In either case, the result is a change in the relative bargaining power of the negotiants and their coalitions. Attempts at expansion are made by negotiants in all types of negotiation. Even in the simplest two-person case of the oriental market, expansion is sometimes sought by the seller appealing to another customer or even a bystander with a plaintive, 'Tell me, sir, you seem a fair-minded man, isn't this gentleman offering a price which is unfair to a poor man like me?' When two siblings are bargaining about something, an appeal to a parent is not always a request for arbitration; often, it is an attempt to bring in a third negotiant for coalition formation.

In labour disputes, attempts to expand the negotiant population are quite common — 'one out, all out', sympathetic strikes, secondary picketing — the methods available are many. To take a specific example, during the construction of a large electricity generating plant in Britain, the sub-contractor, supported by the authority building the power station, refused to pay 26 laggers (insulation technicians) at rates out of line with the payments made to other workers belonging to other unions. The laggers then went on strike bringing construction to a halt. In other circumstances and in other disputes, one union can hope to obtain the sympathy of other unions; in this case, such a sympathetic coalition could not form since other workers on the same site did not want to be thrown out of work. Encouraged by the lack of support among the other workers, the contractor used workers belonging to a different union to do the lagging in direct contravention of inter-union agreements on demarcation. The weak bargaining position of the laggers could only be strengthened by escalating the conflict to the national level by raising the dispute about the employment of workers belonging to other unions at the national level with the Trade Union Congress. The laggers' union also threatened to bring out all laggers working on any project anywhere in the country, thus bringing a whole host of employers into the dispute. The number of negotiants had, by this time, been expanded to include: the General Council of the TUC, the Central Electricity Generating Board, the various contractors in the power station, construction companies throughout the country, the Ministry of Energy, the Ministry of Labour, and the Conciliation Service! A similar example, in the American context, was the national boycott of Californian farm produce successfully organised by Mr Chavez in order to bring about improvements in the conditions of farm workers, particularly migrant ones. In any labour dispute, whichever side feels weaker is tempted to bring more participants into the conflict and the negotiation.

The relationship between bargaining power and expansion of a negotiation in an international dispute is shown by the river water dispute between India and Bangladesh. The availability of adequate flows of water in the two main branches of the Ganges is important to both — to India for the survival of Calcutta as a port, and to Bangladesh for agriculture. There is enough water during most of the year to satisfy both requirements. But India has built a barrage on its own territory at Farakka to regulate the flow in the dry months. The use of the barrage has been the subject of negotiation between the two governments for many years. The main question is how to augment the flow in the dry months by diverting water from another source. The Indian proposal is to build a canal through Bangladesh to bring water from the Brahmaputra river. Bangladesh proposes that dams should be built in the upper reaches of the Ganges and its tributaries, some of which would lie in the territory of Nepal. Since the beginning of negotiations, Bangladesh has been pressing for the addition of Nepal to the negotiations, whereas India feels no need for expanding a bilateral negotiation into a three-negotiant one. Bangladesh probably perceives herself to be in a weaker bargaining position partly because of the relative sizes of the two countries, and partly because it is the lower riparian. The anticipation is that a coalition on the basis of shared fears will form between the smaller neighbours.

Just as the immediate environment has to contain linked dimensions to make enlargement possible, the environment also has to have potential negotiants to make expansion possible. By immediate environment, I do not mean just the geographically proximate. In the India—Bangladesh river water dispute, the third potential negotiant is a geographical neighbour because the dispute itself involves geography. For the laggers, the immediate environment available was other laggers throughout the country, not other workers on the same site. In inter-governmental negotiations, the potential negotiant may be an ally in the political or economic environment. In the case of the tuna fishing dispute between Mexico and the United States, the imposition of a 12-mile limit just for tuna affected US relations not only with Mexico but also with Canada, Costa Rica and Peru, in three distinct sea areas. When negotiations take place between the US and Mexico, the immediate environment from which a potential negotiant can be drawn will include all three countries, even if they do not all fish in the same waters.

As in the case of enlargement, expansion occurs at the instigation of one of the negotiants, who will choose the potential negotiant most likely to form the strongest possible coalition with him. In the tuna fish dispute, Mexico's first choice would probably be Canada. In practice, the coalition does not form immediately after the new negotiant joins; coalition-forming usually happens simultaneously with the negotiation (with other members of the existing bargaining population) for admitting the new member.

When one negotiant demands expansion, the others need not accept it. Why should they, when it is a move which reduces their relative bargaining power? Denial of expansion is also a negotiating move. In the Cyprus dispute, the Turkish-Cypriots, occupying 40 per cent of the territory but with only 18 per cent of the population of the island, are in a better bargaining position if the negotiations are strictly bilateral. However, in any international forum, their power is weaker. The Cyprus government is supported by the far more numerous non-aligned movement while the Turkish-Cypriots can depend only on Turkey, a few Islamic countries and the United States. Involvement of the non-aligned countries (the five-nation group on Cyprus) of the UN (the Secretary General's mediation efforts) is perceived by the Turkish-Cypriots as expanding the negotiation to their detriment. Hence the oft-repeated demand of the Turkish-Cypriots that the dispute be kept strictly bilateral and not 'internationalised'.

The arguments used to investigate whether there is a limit to enlargement can also be applied to the limits to expansion. The negotiants usually delimit the population in the environment to those who are potential negotiants and those who are not. In the case of multilateral negotiations within a treaty framework, expansion is more difficult because the treaty prescribes the conditions under which expansion can take place. For example, if an exporting country wants to become a member of an ICA, an export quota, acceptable to the new member and to all existing members, has to be negotiated. When Spain and Portugal applied to become members of the European Community, a complex accession treaty had to be negotiated. When there is no agreed framework, the position is less clear-cut; nevertheless, even in such cases, the possibilities of expansion are not endless.

Status of Negotiants

Expansion makes a negotiation more complex not only by the physical addition of another negotiator, but also because the status of the additional negotiant introduces a new set of complications. The most ludicrous example of a negotiation getting bogged down over status is the notorious 'shape of the table' controversy at the Paris talks on Viet Nam which held up the opening of the Paris talks for several weeks (*Keesing's Contemporary Archives*, 1969, p. 23, 551). The delay was caused by the refusal of the US and South Vietnamese governments to recognise the NLF (National Liberation Front of South Vietnam) and their insistence that the talks had to be regarded as two-sided; and the continued demand of the North Vietnamese government that the NLF be regarded as a party to the negotiation and the talks be four-sided. The North Vietnamese originally wanted the conference table to be square, symbolising the four-sided nature of the talks; the Americans preferred either an oblong table or two tables, one for each side. A few days later North Vietnam proposed that the delegations should sit at four tables placed an equal distance apart. Then Mr Vance, US Secretary of State, proposed that there should be either two semi-oval or semi-circular tables or two semi-circular tables separated by two rectangular tables for secretaries; whereupon the North Vietnamese suggested a round table cut into three with one half for the Americans and South Vietnamese and a quarter each for the North Vietnamese and the NLF, or a single circular table. After a month of wrangling, Mr Vance offered six alternatives: (i) a ring-shaped table with two small depressions on either side; (ii) a ring-shaped table with two tables for secretaries on either side; (iii) an oval table with a rectangular aperture in the middle; (iv) a ring-shaped table with a rectangular table in the open space in the middle; (v) a round table covered with a cloth divided down the middle in two contrasting colours; (vi) a ring-shaped table with a cloth on which two small patches of contrasting colour were let into either side. Still later the South Vietnamese delegation announced that it would accept a round table, provided that a wire was stretched across it to show that the conference was two-sided and not four-sided. Then Mr Vance proposed that there should be a round table divided by a narrow baize strip or by a line painted on it; both these suggestions were rejected by North Vietnam.

Agreement on the shape of the conference table was finally reached at a meeting on 16 January 1969, when it was decided that there should be an unmarked round table seating 24 people, with two small tables for secretaries and advisers placed on opposite sides of it.

From 2 December 1968 to 18 January 1969, while the Secretary of State of the United States and the Chief Delegate of

Escalation, Enlargement and Expansion 179

North Vietnam were disputing the shape of the table the war was going on, Americans and Vietnamese were being killed, and the country was being defoliated! This is yet another example of the tactic of 'refusal to negotiate' masquerading as a procedural dispute. The two sides, of course, justified their stands as a 'matter of principle'. The recognition problem was more important to the negotiators than making a genuine attempt at limiting the conflict. Indeed, one can only conclude that neither side had gone to Paris to negotiate the limitation of that conflict; they presumably went there to give an impression to international public opinion that something was being done to achieve a peaceful settlement.

Questions of recognition and status of participants continue to plague conflicts. A large part of the escalation of the Northern Ireland conflict, leading to the death of nine hunger-strikers in the Maze prison up to August 1981, was due to a conflict about recognition — the IRA prisoners demanding to be recognised as 'political prisoners' and the British government steadfastly refusing to grant them that status. The limitation of any conflict depends crucially on whether all those involved in it are recognised as legitimate participants. Expansion of the negotiating population to achieve this may assist in limitation while, at the same time, making the negotiation itself more complex.

Stages and Consequences of Expansion

A negotiation can undergo enlargement from d to $d+1$ dimensions imperceptibly, but the addition of a new negotiant cannot go unnoticed. With this difference, the stages of the process of expansion are otherwise similar to those of enlargement, except for the need for an extra stage. After a negotiant perceives the need for expansion, he and the potential negotiant have to bargain with each other on the conditions of participation; this is a coalition-forming neogitiation. The first two stages can be called *identification of a potential negotiant for expansion* and *coalition negotiations with a potential negotiant.* The next stage is the *demand for expansion* voiced by the negotiant seeking it. The $n-1$ negotiants already in the negotiation can (i) reject the demand, (ii) accept it without conditions, or (iii) accept it only if yet another negotiant is added so that the relative bargaining power is preserved. In the last case, the negotiating population increases to $n+2$. We must note that whatever the choice that is made by the $n-1$ negotiants, the result is to move the negotiation nearer a breakdown. If the demand for expansion is rejected, the negotiant seeking it is left dissatisfied and may either modify his expectations to compensate for it or withdraw from the negotiation altogether. If the negotiating population is expanded to n+1 or n+2, the level of complexity is raised. The stages of expansion are shown in Figure 11.1b.

The effect of expansion on the negotiating population can be demonstrated by referring to the accession of Greece to the European Community and the proposed further expansion to include Spain and Portugal. Though the accession of new members is called by the Community 'enlargement', we shall conform to our terminology and think of it as an expansion, because the main effect is to add additional institutional negotiators.

The accession of Greece brought into the Community a Mediterranean country, strengthening the bargaining power of Italy on Mediterranean agricultural products like olive oil and citrus fruit. The Greek accession also strengthened the power of the smaller countries as against that of the big four (France, Germany, Italy and Britain). On the question of regional development, Ireland and Greece share similar interests. Depending on the subject, every coalition existing in the Community of the Nine would have been affected by Greek accession. The consequences of Spanish accession will be even more significant, because of the size, population and resources of that country. The Mediterranean farming interests will gain further, substantially reducing the bargaining power of the Northern temperate farmers. The coalition seeking completely free movement of labour will be strengthened against the coalition of countries who want to restrict intra-Community migration. The net budgetary contribution that is expected of Spain will have an impact on all types of coalitions. The fact that a population of about 40 million from a Catholic country is added will have its repercussions on all coalitions on social questions. The few examples above are only indicative of the kind of change in coalitions that one can anticipate.

Containment, Contraction and Reduction

The proposition that a reduction in complexity moves a negotiation nearer to agreement is, unfortunately, more easily said than done. I should also add that the proposition is not true in all cases. The two exceptions are: (i) controlled enlargement as a means of finding a trade-off and (ii) exclusion of an essential negotiant. Though this reduces the number participating, it worsens the conflict.

An attempt at containing a conflict is described by Peter Jenkins in an article in the *Guardian* (17 December 1980) on the Northern Ireland problem. His article was prompted by the joint communiqué issued after a meeting in December 1980 in Dublin, between the British prime minister and the Taoiseach of Ireland. For the first time in a communiqué signed by the prime ministers of the two countries, references were made to the 'unique relationship' between them and to 'possible new institutional structures, citizenship rights, security matters, economic co-operation and measures to encourage mutual understanding'. The relationship is unique; geography, a commonly understood language, a shared though often antagonistic history, the presence of a large number of people of Irish extraction in Britain, a literary history whose strands cannot be separated are just a few of its facets. To these has now been added membership by both countries in the European Economic Community, with its in-built tendency to break down at least economic barriers. The problem really is how to recognise the validity of common long-term interests and use them to limit the conflict in Northern Ireland in the short term. To quote Peter Jenkins: 'Mrs Thatcher did not go to Dublin in the hope of "solving" the Irish problem. That is a task beyond her and Mr Haughey. What they both sought to do was to establish the framework of co-operation necessary for a long-term approach. . . . The policy agreed in Dublin is in essence a policy of *containment*.' (The emphasis is in the original; it could easily have been mine.)

Without underestimating the long history of the conflict between Greek-Cypriots and Turkish-Cypriots and its background in the centuries-old conflict between Greece and Turkey in general, we can say that a qualitative change occurred in the Cyprus conflict in 1974. That year, the military junta then ruling Greece made an abortive attempt to assassinate the President of Cyprus, Archbishop Makarios, who was forced to flee Cyprus. Turkey took advantage of the uncertainty which followed by invading the island. At first Turkish troops occupied 18 per cent of the area, approximately equal to the percentage of the population of Turkish origin. Finding the international climate favourable (and, some say, encouraged by Dr Kissinger, then US Secretary of State), Turkish troops extended their occupation to 40 per cent of the island, with the result that large numbers of Greek-Cypriots became refugees, whole towns like Varosha were depopulated, and Nicosia airport became unusable.

Prior to 1974, the negotiations between the two communities were about the degree of autonomy for the Turkish-Cypriots and the constitutional questions of how power was to be divided, and whether either community could exercise a veto. After the invasion, a whole new set of dimensions was added to the negotiation, some of which became more important than the subjects already under discussion. Return of the refugees, repopulation of Varosha and, most important, the territorial question became the priority dimensions, at least for the Greek-Cypriots. The number of negotiants, actual and potential, also increased dramatically. Apart from Greece, Turkey and the two island communities, Britain (the former colonial power and one of the guaranteeing countries) has always had an interest in the island, because of the sovereign bases it occupies there. The strategic importance of the bases means that NATO as a whole and the United States in particular have a vital interest in the conflict. This is further complicated by the US leaning towards Turkey in the interests of US global strategy which, in turn, prompted domestic opposition from the Greek-American community. Because the US and NATO had an interest in the continuance of the bases, the Soviet Union became involved in order to protect its strategic interests in the Eastern Mediterranean. Because Cyprus is a member of the non-aligned movement and the Archbishop was one of its respected leaders, and because the legitimate government of Cyprus was a victim of aggression, the entire movement became involved, at least to the extent of providing support in international fora. Soon after 1974, the problem became so multidimensional, and involved so many countries (including the super-powers), that it became almost insoluble. In February 1975, the Turkish-Cypriots proclaimed a Turkish Federated State, further reducing the chances of there being useful negotiations between the two communities.

The history of the attempts made since 1975 to get the two communities to negotiate seriously is a long and tortuous one. By the time the talks were resumed, six years after the invasion, many changes had taken place in the environment, affecting the attitudes and perceptions of all the interested parties. The main ones were

Escalation, Enlargement and Expansion 183

the lifting of the US arms embargo on Turkey (imposed in February 1975), partially in October 1977 and totally in September 1978 and the assumption of full control in Turkey by the military in September 1980.

Reference was made in Chapter 8 to how the inter-communal negotiations were conducted on a serial pattern—'concurrently, in rotation, at consecutive meetings'. The tortuous phraseology describing the procedure was meant to convey that all four subjects discussed were of equal importance. The two sides agreed on a 'federal solution of the constitutional aspect and a bizonal solution of the territorial aspect'. This form of words is one in which each side could read what it wanted. It was only when they tried to translate it into voting, taxation and revenue, policing and security, and similar specifics that the differences which needed bridging were brought into the open. Even so, in this round of talks the many dimensions had been contracted into four 'baskets'. The number of negotiants had also been reduced to a minimum — negotiators from the two island communities and a representative of the UN Secretary-General as a mediator. I do not imply that all other countries (Greece, Turkey and the United States, in particular) had lost interest in the problem and were content to let the two island communities come to their own agreement. They had only come to a tacit agreement to let the negotiations proceed. In spite of the degree of contraction and reduction achieved, the talks came to nothing. As the final draft of this book was being written in May 1984, the conflict had again been escalated by the Turkish-Cypriots declaring unilateral independence and Turkey recognising it as an 'independent' country.

The intractable Cyprus conflict teaches us two lessons. First, when a conflict escalates, the negotiations become more complex with too many dimensions, too many negotiants and too many outside powers involved. In this situation, even resuming substantive negotiations becomes very difficult and requires long NANs. Secondly, when negotiations do resume, the bargaining space has to be contracted adequately and the number of negotiants reduced, if any progress is to be made towards reaching a peaceful agreement. How to contain, and then de-escalate, is one of the crucial questions in the limitation of conflict.

12 BARGAINING POWER

> Just as an unbaked mud vessel struck by a similar one destroys them both, so war between two equal kings brings ruin to both. ... Like a stone striking an earthen pot, a superior king attains victory over an inferior king.
>
> Arthasastra, third century BC, VII: 3

The concept of bargaining power is well understood in everyday life: 'It's a buyer's market', 'The house owners are gazumping', 'The unions have become too powerful', 'The cards are stacked against him', 'OPEC can dictate the price of oil', 'Pick on somebody your own size' — these are just a random selection of common expressions indicating that one of the participants in a bargaining encounter is seen to be in a more powerful position than the others. We also imply that in these cases any eventual agreement will be more favourable to the stronger negotiator. In effect, the negotiants as well as outside observers estimate the approximate location of the agreement point in any dimension.

Bargaining power influences and is influenced by all the factors used in explaining the negotiating process. A negotiant with greater bargaining power enters into a negotiation with higher expectations and also pitches his limit position higher. The dissatisfaction of such a negotiant will be greater for smaller units than for a negotiant with less bargaining power, that is to say, the unit of dissatisfaction of a stronger negotiant will be a smaller quantum of the issue under discussion. A negotiant with greater bargaining power has a greater say about which of the dimensions should be accorded high priority; by virtue of his superior power, he can build and lead coalitions.

We can, therefore, define bargaining power as a factor, derived from the environment and past history, which (i) affects the perceptions of the negotiants regarding expectations, limits, priority among dimensions and units of dissatisfaction; (ii) influences coalition formation; and (iii) predetermines the range within which the agreement points will be located. As the factors affecting it change with time, so does bargaining power.

Aspects of Power

In the environment around any negotiation, the power of negotiants accrues to them for a variety of reasons. Individuals can have the power to give, withhold or deprive, the power to inflict pain, and the power to reward or to punish. Company management has the power to declare lockouts, close or relocate factories or declare bankruptcy. Workers have the power to disrupt production and to withdraw their labour. The seller who hoards anticipating a shortage, the speculator who buys or sells forward, a monopolistic company, a cartel — all exercise the bargaining power which the economic system gives them.

In Chapter 5, we described the influence of the environment on labour disputes. These included: the philosophy and complexion of the political party in power, the effect of public opinion, including its regional variations in large countries, the prevailing economic climate, the actions of other employers and other workers which give rise to perceptions of comparability and differentials and the extent of solidarity shown by other unions or employers. In addition, the bargaining power of an employer and his workforce is conditioned by its inherent strengths — in the case of the union, its finances, its cohesiveness and the quality of its leadership; in the case of the company, the ability to withstand a strike due to loss of production, markets and profits.

The three facets of a country's power are its political influence, its economic power and military might. A country may gain political influence from historical connections, a fortuitous geographical location or the prestige of its leader. In the Cyprus conflict, Turkey's proximity to the USSR gives it greater bargaining power with respect to the United States. In the 1950s, Jawaharlal Nehru conferred on India the power to influence international decisions, over and above its intrinsic power. Without disregarding such exceptional cases, we can say that area, population, natural resources, educational levels and technological ability place a limit on the power a country can acquire. Tiny island countries in the Caribbean or the Pacific can never hope to have the kind of power which countries with large land masses have. On the other hand, a small desert country, like the United Arab Emirates, has power conferred on it by the abundance of its natural resource — oil. This is all obvious; the only reason for my drawing attention to these facts is because of the by now almost universal tendency to talk about *the Third World*, as if all the countries so described had identical problems and identical means of solving them. The parameters for measuring the economic power of countries are well known and need not be recounted here.

On the face of it, the military power of a nation should also be easy to quantify. There are authoritative books, such as the annual reviews of strategic studies institutes and peace research institutes, which list the armaments of each country. But, military might is one area where judgements are subjective. We have become accustomed to periodic reports from the Pentagon or the CIA 'proving' that the USSR is getting stronger, and from the Soviet Union equally 'proving' that the United States is racing towards nuclear superiority. Every country can 'prove' that it is militarily weaker by comparing itself with a stronger nation. Afghanistan is afraid of Pakistan, which is afraid of India, which, in turn, is afraid of China, which is frightened of Soviet power that is in competition with US power. In Chapter 2, we noted that fear and vulnerability were starting points of a sequence which could ultimately lead to violence. When it comes to armed might, it is not so much the fire power which a country has that influences perception, but what someone else is seen as having. As in the case of machine-minders in a Fleet Street print room, it is the differential which is important and not the absolute value.

Power is not static; that of countries can rise and fall. In 1945, the United States was the most powerful state in the world; Britain, though weakened by the war, still had a far-flung empire; Germany, Japan and the USSR had their economies in ruins. Today, the world power structure looks quite different: the USSR has acquired nuclear parity with the US; new centres of economic power, such as Japan and the European Community, have emerged. Since 1973, the OPEC countries are perceived as being powerful in the energy and the international monetary sectors.

Power is cumulative. Sellers can form a cartel. OPEC is not the only one; either clandestinely or openly, cartels operate in uranium, electric power generation and transmission equipment, drugs and chemicals, rare metals and other industries dominated by only a few multinational companies. The control of production and prices in the steel industry by fiat of the European Commission has all the elements of a cartel. Countries can legitimately add to their power by integrating their economies or by forming alliances. Even co-ordination of policies can add to power; the summit of the seven richest countries, or the Group of Ten in the International Monetary Fund, the countries of the OECD when they negotiate with the developing countries — these are examples of the rich countries consolidating their power over the world economy by concerted action.

But the power of countries is not universally exercisable. With the exception of the United States, which is powerful in almost every sector, most countries have power only in some sectors or some regions. Even the super-powers sometimes encounter limits.

Power in international relations does not belong exclusively to governments. Multinational companies which control production, processing, marketing and distribution of a product (e.g. bananas) also have power over many small countries. It is not by accident that powerful multinationals originate in the rich countries; these companies derive their power from their economically and politically powerful home country and, in turn, add to the power of that nation. The Pope has power, an amalgam of religious belief, past history and the inherent power of an institution with a long history and extensive geographical spread.

Power can be a matter of perception. A senator in the US Congress can acquire power by long years of service; but someone like Senator Edward Kennedy has power because he is who he is. Brazil has almost the same land area and a higher gross national product than China; India has two-thirds the population of China and a more widespread technological base; yet, neither country is accorded in the world's perception a position in the power spectrum commensurate with these attributes. Such perceptions are not inexplicable; they are derived from perceptions of past history.

Possession, Dependence and Power to Disrupt

Countries with a dominant share in the export market of a commodity (e.g. Brazil in coffee, Cuba in sugar) and companies possessing a dominant market share have power. Possession of technology also confers power; the countries which have developed the technology for nuclear power generation have formed the so-called London Club with the main objective of denying technology to the poorer countries who are (inexplicably) assumed to be less moral, less stable and more war-like. Every lower riparian has less bargaining power than the upper riparian through whose territory the water flows.

In general, anyone who wants to change the existing order has less bargaining power than those who are happy with the *status quo*. This follows from the understandable reluctance to part with what one has. The only ways of obtaining a more equitable share without the use of force are to offer compensation in return, alleviate a fear, or point to the possibility of greater gain elsewhere. This is relevant to the demand of the poor countries for a new international economic order. The rich countries have control over the world economy, control all advanced technology, the markets which could be opened for exports from the poor, the resources for giving aid, and the banks which can lend. They are quite happy with the way things are, especially as they control all the crucial international institutions. Change requires something more than appeals to altruism.

If possession increases bargaining power, dependence weakens it. Though the most publicised example is the dependence of the developed countries on oil imports, there are other kinds of dependence. Within the family, financial dependence reduces bargaining power. Excessive dependence of a town or a region on one industry (Dundee in Scotland on jute, the Lorraine region of France on steel, Seattle on the Boeing Aircraft company) decreases the bargaining power of the unions in the area. Dependence weakens the bargaining power not only in the specific sector but in other sectors as well. For example, dependence on imported oil not only affects the bargaining power of the United States in the energy sector but in the Middle East conflict as well. But for the need to import natural gas from Mexico, the US could adopt different policies regarding Mexican immigration.

Dependence on exports is also a type of economic dependence. A single market reduces the bargaining power of the seller (e.g. a manufacturer selling all his output only to Marks & Spencer or Sears, Roebuck). Dependence on one or two commodities for their export earnings makes many developing countries susceptible to the vagaries of the market place and puts them at the mercy of speculators in London, New York or Chicago. Any nation dependent on another for financial assistance, political support or military hardware suffers a reduction in bargaining power and capacity for independent action. The fact that such freedom of action is often voluntarily sacrificed is not material to its effect on bargaining power. There can be conscious decisions to forgo bargaining power for the sake of security or for material benefits.

Dependence is a verifiable fact; but fear of dependence is a perception. The support given to Ian Smith's regime in Rhodesia was justified by some in the US as being necessary to avoid dependence on the USSR for supplies of chrome ore. The bargaining power of the US to bring about changes in Southern Africa was weakened by this perception. In the interest of national security, countries seek to avoid excessive dependence on foreign sources which could be disrupted in times of international tension or war. At its most basic, this is displayed in the protectionism for agriculture in every country, irrespective of the cost it entails. A corollary to the fear of dependence is the attempt by some countries to subjugate or at least bring under their influence the sources of raw materials or fuels. In Chapter 2, we referred to the Ancient Greeks conquering territory to secure their sources of timber and the demand in the United States for the military takeover of oil-fields in the Middle East. Having lost bargaining power through dependence, countries then seek to correct it by recourse to violent action.

If Germany were to increase the purchase of natural gas from, say, Algeria, it would not raise as much consternation as when it tries to buy it from the Soviet Union. While dependence by itself is perceived as a bad thing, dependence on the USSR is perceived as something worse. The perception of a country as an antagonist and the consequent feelings of fear and vulnerability are crucial factors in conflicts between nations.

Those who have possession have a stake in the preservation of the existing order; but those who are less powerful can also increase their bargaining power by threatening to disrupt the order. In Aristophanes' comedy, *Lysistrata*, the women of Athens and Sparta used their power to disrupt marital and amorous life as a bargaining counter to halt a war. In labour disputes, certain workers use their power to disrupt to maximum effect by timing their strikes — air traffic controllers and French lorry drivers choose the beginning of holiday periods and coal miners choose the winter.

Who has the power to disrupt? It is usually those who do not have a significant stake but at the same time are numerically large enough to be a nuisance. For example, a group of small countries in an ICA can disrupt its functioning by staying out; the countries with inherent market power have to reckon with this nuisance value. The effectiveness of this tactic is, however, open to question. It appears most effective when disruption is threatened. When disruption actually takes place, adjustments are often made which nullify the increase in the bargaining power of the disrupter.

The power of a small country to disrupt was shown by Malta in the ECSC negotiations in Madrid. After three years of hard negotiations, all states in the Conference were able to agree on a document. At this point, Malta refused to go along with it because its particular interest in convening a separate conference on Mediterranean security was not included in the final document. Though all the other countries did not see any utility in having such a conference, Malta was able to use the consensus principle to hold up the ECSC conference for many weeks. In the final analysis, Malta's bargaining power proved to be inadequate to drag on the conference until everyone else came round to her point of view. Eventually, the conference ended in September 1983, after exhausting the patience of all others.

The power to disrupt is most clearly seen in the additional bargaining power which a minority partner in a ruling coalition possesses. A well-known example is the switching of support by the Free Democrats, in the Federal Republic of Germany, from the CDU/CSU to the SDP and then back again. In a government coalition, the minority party can exercise power for a long time by threatening to deprive the majority partner of the power to govern. This is relevant to the way the negotiating positions of governments are arrived at, after initial negotiations between the different interest groups. The smaller religious parties in the Israeli coalition government were able to push Likud into adopting a harder stance on such matters as the settlements in the West Bank.

Like all other aspects of bargaining power, the power to disrupt is not permanent. While a major partner in a coalition may submit to pressure for a long time, a point may well be reached when the partner would rather forgo power than submit to unacceptable pressure.

Changes in Bargaining Power

Since bargaining power is derived from the environment, it changes with time and the environment. Changes in the environment may be man-made or acts of God; some may be more remote and affect a negotiation less than others; the same kind of event may not have the same effect at different times.

An external event which affects many negotiations in the international politico-economic system is the departure of a leader, either by death or by defeat in an election. Death, however certain in the long term is, in its timing, a chance event. Election to high office, however predictable about its timing, sometimes produces unpredictable changes.

A revealing example of how death and elections affect international negotiations is shown by the attitude of South Africa towards the negotiations for the independence of Namibia. In this case, a death affected the actual negotiations on the ground and an election affected attitudes and perceptions. Namibia, the former German colony of South West Africa, was mandated under the League of Nations to South Africa in 1919. After the second world war, trust territories throughout the world gained their independence. But South Africa refused to contemplate independence for South West Africa and took steps to integrate Namibia within its own territory. The policy of apartheid was adopted in the trust territory also. It was possible for South Africa to maintain this policy so long as it was surrounded by territories which were sympathetic to it — the Portuguese colonies of Angola and Mozambique and Southern Rhodesia under the control of a white minority.

In September 1968, the Portuguese President, Salazar, suffered a serious cerebral thrombosis and though he was to die twenty months later, he was no longer in direct control of the Portuguese government. Within six months, the first visit by a Portuguese prime minister to the African colonies was undertaken by Caetano, Salazar's successor, who was soon offering internal autonomy to the colonies. In April 1974, General Spinola took power in a *coup* and set in motion rapid changes. Within six months, Guinea-Bissau gained independence and Mozambique had an autonomous government as a prelude to independence. In 1975, Angola also became independent. Though Southern Rhodesia continued under a white minority regime for a few more years, the armed conflict there became more intense.

These changes were reflected in the degree of support given to South Africa. Until 1974, Portugal was the only country to vote consistently for South Africa in the United Nations. But in 1976, Portugal voted in favour of giving observer status in the UN to the

South West Africa People's Organisation (SWAPO). This vote went beyond even the policies of the United States and Britain, both of which abstained on the resolution.

With these changes, South Africa's attitude to independence for Namibia also had to change. In 1969, the high point of integrating Namibia into South Africa, control over coloured affairs and coloured education were transferred to Pretoria, which also started to create the so-called black homelands. But five years later, South Africa announced its readiness to discuss the political future of Namibia. In May 1975, the pass laws were repealed in that territory and it was announced that the people there could determine their own future. In November 1976, abolition of racial discrimination was proclaimed, and in June 1977 South Africa agreed to co-operate with the UN in holding elections.

For a few years after 1977 progress was made, albeit at an excruciatingly slow pace, for the holding of UN-sponsored elections. The negotiations to bring this about were pursued by a five-nation Western Contact Group comprised of the US, UK, France, West Germany and Canada. So long as Jimmy Carter was President of the United States, pressure was maintained on South Africa. But as the election of Ronald Reagan as President became more probable, the attitude of South Africa hardened. Originally, the Contact Group had intended that, at a conference to be held in January 1981, the details of a ceasefire and the timetable for elections would be settled. By that time, Reagan had been elected President and South Africa scuttled the meeting, anticipating, correctly, that US pressure would cease. Subsequent actions by the Reagan administration further encouraged South Africa to escalate the conflict, by attacking all its neighbours and embarking on a policy of destabilizing their governments.[1] If the death of Salazar moved the clock forward, the election of Reagan set it back again.

Clearly, South Africa's policies are dictated by her bargaining power, which is perceived by her as the degree of support she gets from the United States. Under the Reagan administration, there is only one perception — the USSR as a constant enemy and Cuba as its instrument. The implications of such a policy for moving conflicts in Southern Africa nearer violence does not enter into US calculations. This case is an example of how events in the environment can move the compass needle towards violence in a conflict and towards breakdown in a negotiation.

Not every change in the incumbent of the presidency of the US affects international negotiations equally. The Third UN Conference on the Law of the Sea (UNCLOS) was thrown into total disarray by the demand of the United States, after Reagan's election, that the provisions of the treaty laboriously hammered out over many years should be reopened. Between 1973 when the conference began, and 1981 when Reagan was elected president, there were three presidents — Nixon, Ford and Carter — two Republicans and one Democrat. But the approach of the US in UNCLOS was significantly affected *only* when Reagan was elected.

Perception of Changes in Bargaining Power

All changes in bargaining power are not perceived with equal clarity. Sudden changes in the environment usually prompt negotiants to re-evaluate their bargaining power and bargaining strategy. Predictable changes are usually built into the strategy well in advance. Where the change in the environment is gradual, its effect on bargaining power goes unnoticed. Two examples will illustrate this point.

Throughout the 1950s and 1960s, a fundamental, though gradual, change was taking place in the relative bargaining power between the industrialised countries and the oil exporters. The post-war development of the major economies, based on mass consumption of automobiles and consumer durables, was built on the availability of cheap energy supplies. Without cheap oil, the car industry in the OECD countries would not have developed as it did, there would have been no mammoth tankers, the shipbuilding industry would have been smaller. Without the need for millions of cars and hundreds of supertankers, the steel industries would not have grown so big and later been faced with problems of contraction. The availability of oil and, for historical reasons, the cheapness with which it could be acquired, meant that countries gradually became more and more dependent on imports without realising the consequences in store for them. When, in 1973, the oil exporting countries perceived that bargaining power had shifted decidedly in their favour, the price rose sharply. There might have been a few who sounded the alarm against excessive import dependence; for the most part though, western countries chose to assume that cheap oil would continue to flow while, all the time, they were losing precisely that bargaining power that could ensure that oil would continue to be cheap.

The change in the power balance in the UN General Assembly provides another example of a gradual change going more or less unnoticed. In the early years of the UN, the power of the United States was almost total. The US controlled the entire agenda. It could decide which resolutions should be passed, which rejected and what should be the content and wording of the ones found acceptable; power was used to control the admission of new members and the US never had to exercise its veto since the membership of the UN was then more amenable to its wishes. Now, the US is as ready to use its veto as the USSR once was.

US bargaining power in the General Assembly began to decline in the 1960s. The decline was an inevitable consequence of the increase in UN membership, with most of the new members choosing to stay out of the Cold War power blocs. This decline can be traced using the example of the Chinese seat — whether the People's Republic of China should occupy it or whether it should continue to be held by the remnant of the Kuo Min Tang government in Taiwan.

In 1949, soon after the People's Republic came into being, India proposed that the Chinese seats in the Assembly and the Security Council should be occupied by mainland China. For many years, the US succeeded in getting a resolution passed deferring the consideration of the seating question (i.e. it was never brought to a vote). However, during this period, the majority in favour of deferral had gradually shrunk and, by 1960, the number of countries supporting the US had become less than the number which either voted against or abstained. When the US saw that there could soon be a majority in favour of seating the People's Republic, it proposed making the question subject to a two-thirds majority instead of a simple majority by introducing a resolution stating that the question was an 'important' one.

The US was then able to get an adequate majority each year for this apparently procedural vote. By 1970, this too became difficult; that year, the Assembly passed two contradictory resolutions. For the first time, the number of countries voting in favour of seating Peking was more than those voting against. However, the Assembly also passed the resolution making it an important one requiring two-thirds majority. Obviously, some countries voted one way on one resolution and the opposite way on the other. Though the US did not actually fail, the day when it might was not far off.

The United States did a complete about turn on its China policy when, on 15 July 1971, President Nixon made the announcement that the then Secretary of State had been to Peking and that he himself was going to China in early 1972. Having dramatically changed the 20-year-old policy of unremitting hostility to the People's Republic, the US could no longer oppose Peking's occupation of the Chinese seats in the UN. In November 1970, the White House Press Secretary had said: 'The United States is opposed to the admission of Communist China to the UN with a seat in the Security Council at the expense of the expulsion of Nationalist China.'[2] But, in less than a year, the US sanctioned exactly that. What had changed was only the acknowledgement of the common perception, by both mainland China and the US, of the Soviet Union as the common enemy.

Two more quotations aptly illustrate the magnitude of this change: 'The international conduct of the Peking Government is so low that it would take considerable improvement to raise it to the general level of barbarism' (Dean Acheson, 1951); 'The Chinese are a great people' (Nixon, 1972). Surely the Chinese people had not moved from the depths below barbarism to absolute greatness in just 20 years! Indeed, the reality was exactly the opposite. When Nixon indulged in his hyperbole, China was in the throes of the Cultural Revolution; friends of China, like Theodore White, have subsequently recorded many of its barbarities.

During the General Assembly session of 1971, the US changed the content of the two-thirds majority resolution making only the 'expulsion of the Republic of China' the important question. This resolution was defeated amidst prolonged cheers and thunderous applause, which astonished the United States. The presidential spokesman commented that President Nixon had been distressed at the 'shocking spectacle of personal animosity'. The 'animosity' was the result of the arm-twisting of the previous 20 years and the 'shocking spectacle' was the eruption of pent-up dissatisfactions. The US later avenged what it perceived as an insult by vetoing, in 1980, the election of the then Tanzanian Foreign Minister as the Secretary-General of the UN.

While the replacement of Taiwan by Peking was primarily due to the perception of the USSR as the common enemy by both the PRC and the US, the gradual decline in American bargaining power is also a relevant factor. The surprise that the decline was so steep is shown not only by Nixon's reported reaction quoted above, but also by the American representative to the UN, Daniel Patrick Moynihan, saying that the United States had few allies and that many members were 'slipping into almost irreversible patterns of appeasement based on the assumption that American power is irreversibly declining.' The interesting point about this reaction is that a decline in bargaining power by itself need not produce belligerency; the sudden realisation that power had declined probably does. It is the feeling of vulnerability that produces a violent reaction.

Increasing One's Bargaining Power

Bargaining power determines when a negotiation will begin. With his knowledge of the past history and the information acquired during a NAN, a disputant can perceive whether his bargaining power is commensurate with those of other potential negotiants. If, in his perception, his own bargaining power is so weak that the others will not be persuaded to agree on courses of action that will reduce his dissatisfaction, he has no incentive to enter a negotiation. He has to put up with his discontent until a more opportune time, while continuing to voice it.

A strong potential negotiant who sees no need to change his course of action will also refuse to negotiate even when faced with the dissatisfaction of another. We have already discussed refusal to recognise and refusal to negotiate. This, of course, is clearly the case with South Africa, whose intransigence is strengthened whenever an increase in bargaining power is perceived.

We have to conclude, therefore, that *no negotiation can commence if there is too great a disparity in the bargaining power of the potential negotiants.* The littoral states around the Indian Ocean, for example, have been asking for a conference of the super-powers over avoiding their rivalry in that ocean. Such a conference has not been, and is unlikely to be, held because of the very great disparity in the bargaining power between the super-powers on the one hand and the littoral states on the other.

A negotiant may rely on time to produce a favourable change in his bargaining power or he may create facts which will augment it. The policy of the Reagan administration regarding arms limitation talks with the USSR illustrates both tactics. The ratification of the

SALT II agreement, negotiated by the Carter administration, ran into difficulties in the US Senate because it was perceived by many as having been concluded when US bargaining power was weak. Two conclusions followed: (i) the agreement was detrimental to the US precisely because it was negotiated under conditions of imbalance in bargaining power; and (ii) without such a disparity a better agreement could be negotiated. In order to augment its bargaining power, the US needed time to realise a programme of increasing defence expenditure, producing B1 bombers and cruise missiles, stockpiling neutron warheads, chemical and biological weapons, and so on. We need not doubt that the USSR, threatened with a loss of bargaining power, also embarked on a programme for maintaining the differential by similar means.

Creating facts to increase one's bargaining power is also well known. We referred to two examples in Chapter 5 — Israel creating more settlements in occupied territories, and the European Community devoting enormous resources to producing sugar at very high cost and building up an export market for it by subsidising it. Those who have the power can utilise it to create facts which tilt bargaining power in their favour. This is why when Turkey invaded Cyprus, it seized 40 per cent of the island, even though the Turkish Cypriots number only 18 per cent of the population.

It may seem logical to assume that every negotiant starts a negotiation when his relative bargaining power is to his best advantage. But the 'best' time to start is a matter of judgement involving choosing between perceived immediate and perceived long-term gains. For example, in negotiations for concluding ICAs, the bargaining power of the exporting countries is at its maximum when there is a likelihood of shortage of supplies and the possibility of a rapid rise in prices. In these situations, the importing countries will be anxious to conclude stabilisation agreements so that they can be assured of supplies at reasonable prices. They might be more willing to accept higher floor and ceiling prices. But it is precisely at these times that the enthusiasm of the exporting countries for negotiating an ICA declines. The converse also happens; importing countries are reluctant to conclude ICAs when there is an excess of supply over demand and low prices prevail, though their bargaining power is highest then. While the phenomenon of preferring short-term gains is applicable to all countries, it is accentuated in democracies which have periodic elections. If there are elections every two years (as in the US with congressional and gubernatorial ones), the chances of long-term gains being taken into account become even less.

There are two aspects of the negotiating process — negotiating skills and secrecy — which are sometimes misunderstood in their effect on bargaining power. Changing a negotiator for a more skilled one enables a negotiant to make the best use of the available power, but this cannot produce *more* power if none exists or if the environment does not allow it. Negotiators are sometimes changed, not because they are incompetent, but because the institutional negotiant does not like the outcome. For example, one of the first acts of the Reagan administration was to change the entire sets of negotiators for the Madrid ECSC Conference and for UNCLOS. In the event, the new US negotiators only managed to delay the conclusion of the Law of the Sea Treaty, without changing it substantively; the US then decided to stay out of it. Changing negotiators is often a public relations exercise intended to affect the negotiations *within* the institution rather than the actual negotiation with other parties. Likewise, secrecy in negotiations is often maintained in order to forestall criticism from *within* the institution.

Bargaining power can also be lost. Generally speaking, it is lost when a country withdraws from the scene of action — the opting-out mentioned in Chapter 2. An example is the withdrawal of Greece, following the Turkish invasion of Cyprus, from the NATO military council. The consequence was that Greece lost bargaining power with the loss of military assistance to the level she thought she needed from her NATO allies, particularly the United States. A part of the NATO command structure was also shifted to Turkey and a great deal of negotiation had to be gone through before Greece could regain some of its lost power. The USSR left its Security Council seat unoccupied in the 1950s, and so was unable to influence other Council members and exercise its veto. This made it much easier for the US to intervene in Korea under the UN flag. Pakistan withdrew from the Commonwealth when the independence of Bangladesh was recognised by many in the group; it has found it quite difficult to get back in. We shall refer later to the one case where the vacant chair tactic was employed effectively — by France in the Community dispute in 1965.

Measuring Bargaining Power

The fact that people recognise disparities in bargaining power implies assessment, albeit of a subjective nature, since there are many negotiations where bargaining power cannot be measured or quantified. In inter-personal relationships, we can make general statements such as society places women in a weaker position than men or an earning husband is more powerful than his dependent wife. But these are true only in the statistical sense; an individual example will fall anywhere in a wide range.

We may be able to measure bargaining power in certain types of market situations; for example, the relative bargaining power of house buyers and sellers can be computed. A survey can be made on the number of enquiries each property gets, how long they remain unsold, the reduction, if any, the sellers have to make on their offer prices, the extent to which sellers renege on their promises after taking a deposit, and so on. This exercise can be done with a reasonable degree of accuracy over a period of time. But the interesting point is that most people do this automatically during the course of a negotiation on buying or selling a house.

An assessment of bargaining power is different from quantifying it. Every trade union makes an assessment of its bargaining power before tabling a demand for more wages or shorter working hours.

Throughout this book, we have made a distinction between two kinds of international negotiations — those conducted within an agreed framework of rules (a treaty) and those without any framework. Wherever there is an agreed framework, there is usually an attempt at quantifying the bargaining power of the participants during its implementation. The quantification in ICAs (1000 votes each to the group of exporters and the group of importers, further subdivided among the members in each group according to market shares) was referred to in Chapter 9. Three further examples — the European Community, the UN and the IMF — will help to clarify the distinction between the two types of international negotiations.

Bargaining power within the EEC is shown in two ways — by the votes which each country has in the Council of Ministers and by the number of persons each country can appoint to the Commission (the executive organ of the Community). Table 12.1 shows the number of Commissioners from each country at various stages in the evolution of the Community. For the most part, a clear distinction was made between the big three (or four) and the rest;

Table 12.1: Number of Commissioners in the Commission of the European Communities

	Initial (Economic Community only, 1957)	Increase (on merger of Economic, Steel and Atomic Communities)	Reduction in July 1970	First enlargement (UK, Ireland and Denmark)	Second enlargement (Greece)
Number of member countries	6	6	6	9	10
Number of Commissioners					
Total	9	14	9	13	14
from large countries					
France	2	3	2	2	2
Germany	2	3	2	2	2
Italy	2	3	2	2	2
United Kingdom	—	—	—	2	2
from medium countries					
Belgium	1	2	1	1	1
Netherlands	1	2	1	1	1
Denmark	—	—	—	1	1
Ireland	—	—	—	1	1
Greece	—	—	—	—	1
from small countries					
Luxembourg	1	1	1	1	1

for a short period, there was a further subdivision between the smaller countries and the smallest of them all, Luxembourg. The power balance in the Commission does not rest merely on the number from each country; with every recomposition of the Commission there is a struggle for portfolios, with each member country wanting for its nominee the most important departments (e.g. agriculture, industry, external relations or budget). Bargaining power really comes into play in the division of responsibilities.

The principle of dividing the member countries of the Community into large, medium and small is carried over into the power of the Council of Ministers, with one crucial difference. The votes are allocated in such a way that the big countries cannot overrule the smaller ones on important questions. The Community Treaties provide for safeguards in the form of three different kinds of majority. The simple and qualified majority systems are used when less or more important proposals are made to the Council by the Commission. The third system of voting, by special qualified majority, applies to cases where a proposal not emanating from the Commission is considered by the Council. In such cases, the requirement is not only for a specified percentage of votes but also for a specified *number of countries* agreeing to the proposal.

The original intention in providing a harder test for proposals which did not originate in the Commission was to strengthen it and make it a powerful body with a 'European' outlook. It was precisely the possibility of the Commission acquiring so much power that led to France adopting the 'policy of the vacant chair' in order to put pressure on other members to accept the French view that, if any country felt that an issue was of vital importance to it, the majority vote should not be used. The question of 'vital interests', as defined by the countries themselves, is an important one for international rule of law and for limitation of conflict; this will be considered again in Chapters 14 and 15. Since 1966, the question of whether majority voting is possible in politically troublesome cases has been avoided. Though this is clearly against the letter and the spirit of the Rome Treaty, it has the merit of pragmatism, recognising that no country should be left so dissatisfied that it is provoked into questioning its very membership of the Community.

Table 12.2 shows the delicate power balance in the Council. In the Community of the Six, the three big countries could muster 12 votes among themselves and outvote the smaller three on all issues except the ones requiring special qualified majority. In such cases, they needed the support of at least one smaller country. The interesting point about this distribution is that five of the countries acting together could outvote any *one* of the big three. It was this prospect that alarmed France and led to the crisis of 1965-66. After the first enlargement it was never possible for the big four countries acting together to outvote the rest. For a qualified majority the big four needed the support of one of the smaller countries and for a special qualified majority, at least two. At the same time, the smaller countries required the support of at least three of the big four to pass any important proposal. The second enlargement with the accession of Greece did not affect these basic principles.

The distribution of voting power in the UN satisfies no one. In the Security Council, the most important organ for peace-keeping purposes, the five so-called Permanent Members (the United

Table 12.2: Voting Power in the Council of Ministers of the European Communities

	from 1 January 1958	First enlargement with Norway	First enlargement without Norway	Second enlargement
Initial Six				
France	4	10	10	10
Germany	4	10	10	10
Italy	4	10	10	10
Belgium	2	5	5	5
Netherlands	2	5	5	5
Luxembourg	1	2	2	2
First enlargement				
Great Britain	—	10	10	10
Denmark	—	3	3	3
Ireland	—	3	3	3
(Norway — did not accede)	—	(2)	—	—
Second enlargement				
Greece	—	—	—	5
Total number of votes	17	60	58	63
Votes for qualified majority	12	41	41	45
(% of total)	(70.6%)	(68.3%)	(70.7%)	(71.4%)
Special qualified majority — minimum number of countries voting in favour	4	6	6	6

States, the USSR, Britain, France and China) have the power to veto any resolution. Of the five, one was for a long time held by the Republic of China (Taiwan) which was quite unrepresentative of mainland China. While the number of elected members of the Council has been expanded once, from 6 to 10 in 1966, the power of veto has remained in the hands of the original five. Even the expansion of the strength of the Council was at first resisted by the US, France, Britain and the USSR (General Assembly session of 1963). This only proves the point that those who have power are reluctant to let it go. Even though now there are a number of countries (Japan, West Germany, India, Brazil) which have political or economic power equal to that of France or Britain, it is unlikely that the original five will contemplate sharing their veto power with others. The fact the countries with veto power are also the countries with nuclear weapons may well have a bearing on the perceptions of near-nuclear countries about their place in the world.

In contrast to the Security Council, every country has only one vote in the General Assembly. In this case, equality is resented by the big countries, especially those who contribute most to the budget. The United States has always made the largest contribution, with a share of nearly 40 per cent in the early years, reduced to a maximum of 25 per cent in 1974.[3] Compared to the US, there are 70 members each paying just 0.01 per cent of the regular budget. There is a natural resentment on the part of the US which explains the reaction of Nixon and Moynihan referred to earlier, on the expulsion of Taiwan.

The decline in the economic power of the US is best seen in the votes it holds in the International Monetary Fund (IMF). The IMF is one of a small number of organisations that operates on the basis of weighted voting.[4] The actual voting system is quite complex and the votes which a country can cast at a given time are also affected by whether it is a debtor or creditor to the Fund. In the discussion which follows the more abstruse details of changes in voting power have been omitted. A factor which influenced the steady decline of US voting power is the continuous and substantial increase in the membership of the Fund (39 in 1946 to 146 in 1983). Decolonisation and increase in the number of sovereign states affects the power balance in all international organisations. This too has implications for the limitation of conflict among nations.

Voting power in the Fund is determined by two principles.

204 *Bargaining Power*

Figure 12.1: Voting Power in the International Monetary Fund

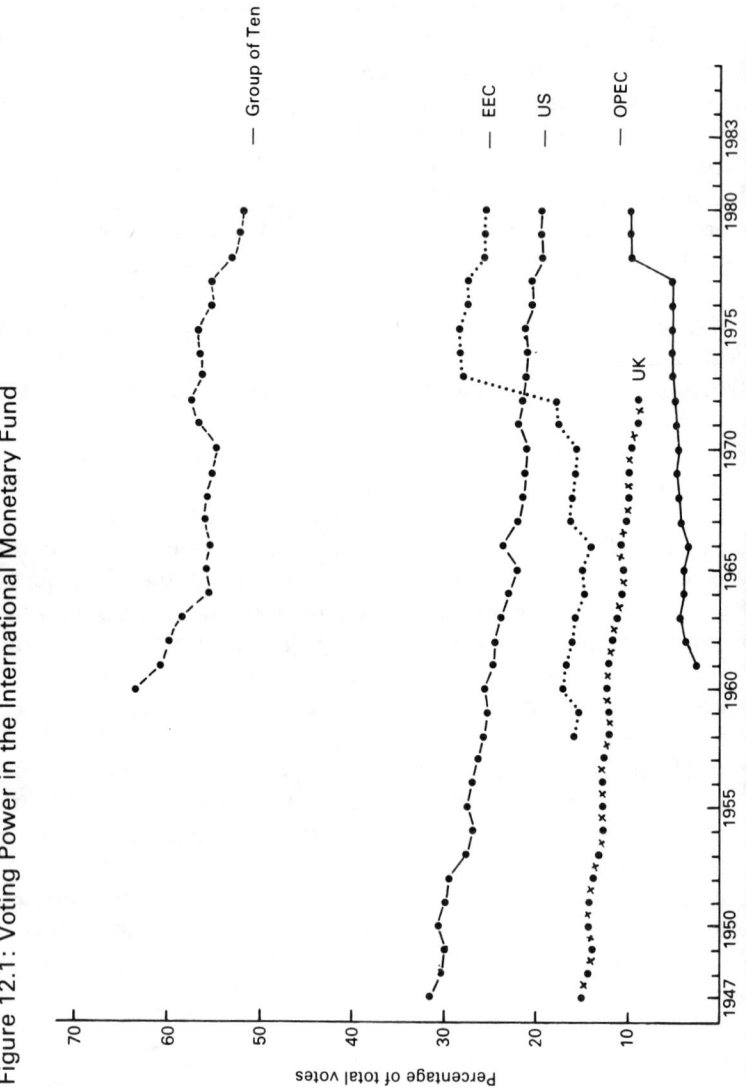

Every member gets a 'basic' 250 votes (thus preserving the doctrine of equality of states) and an additional one vote for each 100,000 units (first dollars and later Special Drawing Rights) of its quota. The latter, reflecting economic power, is the real determinant. For example, in 1983 the US had 126,325 votes of which the basic was only 250.

We must note that the increase or decline in the economic power of a country is reflected in the IMF voting power with a time lag, countries in decline resisting changes for as long as they can. Actual bargaining power is also maintained by changing the rules regarding special majority requirements.

The voting power of the US and some other important economic groups is shown in Figure 12.1. This shows two things: (i) the undisputed supremacy of the United States in the early years of the Fund, and (ii) the steady decline in its bargaining power since then. In December 1945, the US had nearly 38 per cent of the total votes; this power had declined by half, to 19.5 per cent by 1983. The power of the European Community has steadily increased to nearly 25 per cent of the total; this is the result of the rise in economic strength of countries like West Germany as well as the expansion of the Community to 10 members. However, the power of the major industrialised countries has not declined by very much (from about two-thirds to just over half). One can even see why the Group of Ten was formed around 1960; the demand of the poor countries for a greater say in the international economic order was becoming more vocal throughout the late 1950s and eventually culminated in the holding of the first UN Conference on Trade and Development (UNCTAD I) in 1964. Anticipating this threat to their power, the rich countries formed a coalition in the form of the Group of Ten. The only significant threat to the power of the developed countries is the rise in the economic power of the OPEC countries after the oil price rises. By 1983, this group had over 10 per cent of the total votes.

Notes

1. For a detailed account of South Africa's aggressions against its neighbours, see the special report, 'Destabilisation in Southern Africa', *The Economist*, 16 July 1983.
2. All quotations (Nixon, Moynihan and others) from the relevant issues of *Keesing's Contemporary Archives.*

3. The US contributions referred to are those made to the regular UN budget; they do not include other contributions which the US makes to special programmes such as the Special Fund, in which its share was 40 per cent. International agencies which have their own budgets (FAO, UNESCO, etc.) may have different percentage contributions, depending on membership. Many contributions are voluntary, e.g. UN High Commissioner for Refugees, the International Fund for Agricultural Development.

4. A consolidated table for all members of the IMF for the years 1946 to 1971 is available in Joseph Gold, *Voting Decisions in the International Monetary Fund: An Essay on the Law and Practice of the Fund* (Washington, D.C., IMF, 1972), Appendix III, pp. 227-39. For the years after 1971, the votes of each member are available in the Annual Reports of the Fund; the totalling for different groups is mine.

13 POLITICAL WILL

> The persistent lack of agreement on procedures, agenda and time frame betrayed an absence of requisite political will on the part of some developed countries.
> Chairman's summing-up of the
> New Delhi Consultations of 44 countries,
> 24 February 1982

At the beginning of Part Three there is a quotation from Winston Churchill's speech in Zurich on the unity of Europe. Many people have argued that such a United States of Europe was perfectly feasible, if only there was the requisite 'political will'.[1]

'Political will' is a catch-all phrase which everyone uses but few can define. 'If the British government had the will, it could solve the Northern Ireland problem'; 'If the management had the will, the strike would not be necessary'; 'The rich countries lack the political will in the North/South dialogue.' In all these instances, the blame for failure is laid at the door of an inchoate concept, when in reality failure is due to an intricate mixture of interests, attitudes and perceptions. Why did a negotiation fail? Because there was a lack of will. How do we know that there was a lack of will? Because the negotiations failed.

Discussing negotiations for settling international disputes, Northedge and Donelan have stated that 'negotiation can only hope to be successful where there already exists *enough common ground* between the disputing states for the diplomatic process to throw a bridge between their respective positions'[2] (emphasis added). What 'enough' and 'common ground' are is not explained. It seems that we know there is enough common ground only when we see that a bridge has been thrown. This is no help if we want to find out in advance whether a negotiation is likely to succeed.

We argued earlier that negotiation was a rational process indulged in by people who often behave irrationally. The total concept called political will is therefore bound to be a mixture of the logical and the psychological. Political will is a special case of the will to negotiate and the will to conclude an agreement, irrespective of whether the negotiants are governments, management and labour, or individuals. For want of a better word, we shall use 'political will' to cover all bargaining situations.

Political will can be defined as a factor in negotiations, based on the negotiants' perceptions of the environment, their relative bargaining power, and their expectation of the value of the agreement that may be reached.

Causes of Breakdown

In the preceding chapters we have identified a number of phases of the negotiating process and pinpointed the situations which could result in a breakdown. The more important ones are shown in Figure 13.1. The number of events which can cause a breakdown are clearly seen. Of course, many negotiations do end in agreement, the vertical path showing this clearly. The fact that changes in the environment can take a negotiation back to any prior stage is also indicated. In order to assist in understanding the figure, real-life examples for each of the different causes of breakdown are briefly given below.

The earliest stage at which prior negotiations about negotiations (NANs) can break down is when one party to a conflict refuses to recognise the existence of another, let alone recognise the validity of the dissatisfaction or vulnerability. Non-recognition of the PLO by the United States and Israel, Morocco's non-recognition of Polisario and South Africa's of SWAPO can all be cited as examples.

Many negotiations are not really negotiations in substance. Sometimes this is due to one negotiant deliberately setting prior conditions which the others cannot accept: Argentina insisting on recognition of sovereignty over Malvinas as a prior condition to any negotiation is one example; Iran's demand that Saddam Hussain should be removed from the Presidency of Iraq before beginning negotiations about ending the war is another. Sometimes negotiations seem to get bogged down on procedural questions but these really mask substantive preconditions. The notorious case of the shape of the table in the Paris talks on Vietnam, cited in Chapter 9, provides an example.

Other parties who are called upon to ameliorate a dissatisfaction or assuage a fear can refuse to negotiate, even if they recognise that such problems exist. In some cases this is due to

Political Will 209

Figure 13.1: Causes of Breakdowns in Negotiations

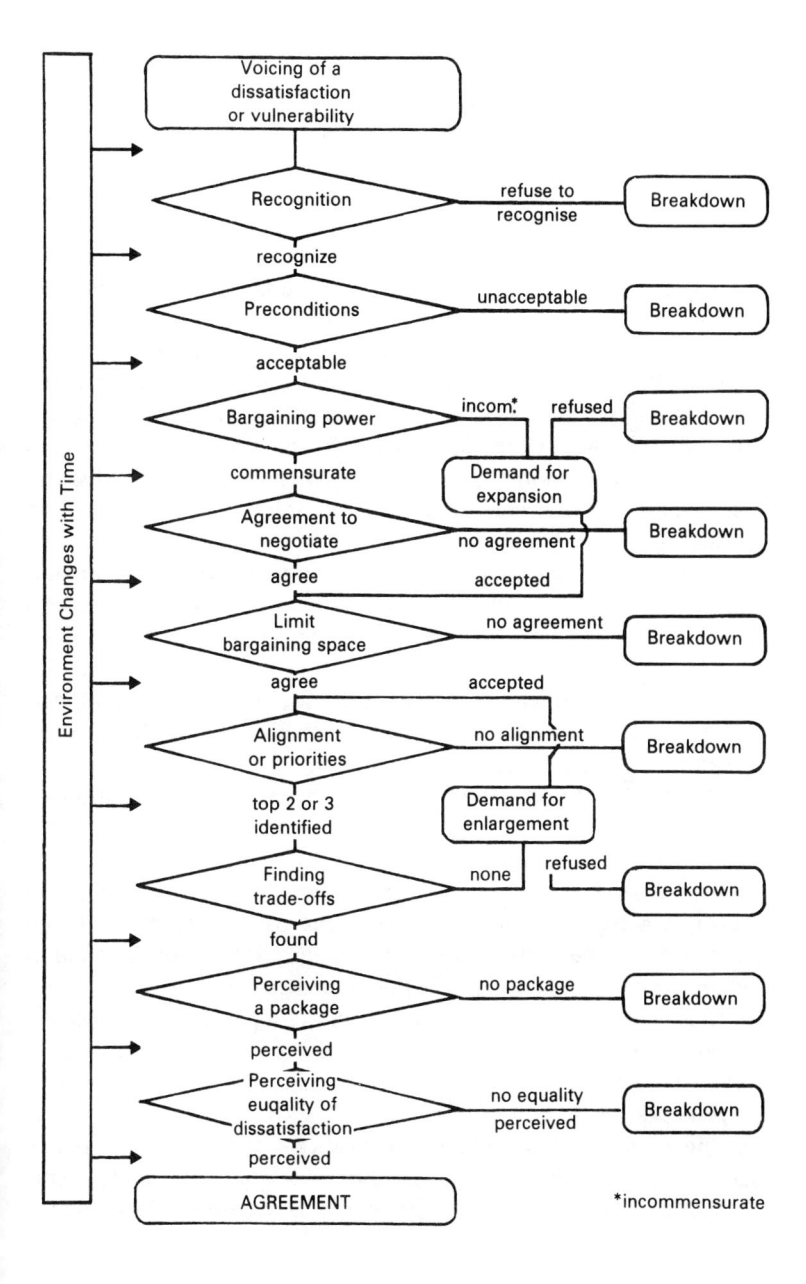

*incommensurate

their having considerably superior bargaining power. The refusal of the rich countries to negotiate on the NIEO is due, in part, to the disparity in bargaining power and, in part, to the reluctance of the 'haves' to make sacrifices.

Where a dissatisfied or vulnerable party feels that it has inadequate bargaining power it can seek to expand it by adding new negotiants; this demand can be refused by others (e.g. the attempt of Bangladesh to expand the river water dispute with India by the addition of Nepal).

In some cases, refusal to negotiate is a time-buying exercise. The initial reaction of some members of the European Community to Britain's demand for substantial refunds from the European Budget is an example.

Even after agreeing to negotiate, there may be no real negotiations because of disagreement on what to include in the bargaining space. The START II negotiations, though they look like real negotiations, were, in mid-1984, still only at the stage of identifying dimensions; there was no agreement on whether British and French missiles were to be included or left out of the reduction process.

After identifying the dimensions to be included in the bargaining space, the negotiants may fail to agree on which are the most important dimensions. The case of the Screen Actors' Guild, cited in Chapter 8, is a real-life illustration.

If an adequate trade-off cannot be found to compensate differing dissatisfactions in different dimensions, negotations break down. Any labour dispute which ends in a strike is an example.

Where a trade-off cannot be found from among the important dimensions in the bargaining space, one negotiant can demand the inclusion of a new dimension from the immediate environment. If enlargement is refused, the negotiation may break down; an example is Syria refusing to agree to the withdrawal of all troops from Lebanon unless the question of the Golan Heights was, at least implicitly, included in the bargaining space.

Eventually, the negotiants must perceive a package. In the interminable talks between the Greek- and the Turkish-Cypriots, no such package is visible.

A breakdown can occur at the final stage of the negotiation if the negotiants fail to perceive a totality of equality of dissatisfaction in the dimensions of the bargaining space as a whole. Even at this stage, one or the other party can be accused of exhibiting a lack of political will. The failure, in March 1984, of the European Community Summit on the package of reforms of the CAP and Britain's rebate is an example.

Enough examples have been cited in the previous chapters to show that changes in the environment affect negotiations and can often move them back a few stages. If the changes are substantial, the negotiation which follows is, for all practical purposes, a new negotiation, with the previous one becoming a part of the past history.

Any one of the various causes for the breakdown in negotiations can be attributed to a lack of political will on the part of a negotiant. But with such a variety of reasons, it is unsatisfactory to blame it *all* on will.

Elements of Political Will

In every negotiation, the negotiants have certain logical interests to protect and some objectives to attain. For example, in an industrial negotiation the employer has to protect his profits while labour's interest lies in improving the standard of living of the specific workforce as compared to the rest of the community. In negotiations under GATT for tariff reductions, some countries seek to protect their domestic industries from external competition while others want new or increased export outlets. In every river water dispute countries seek to protect their share of a fixed total.

Logical, objective interests are identifiable and even quantifiable. If Brazil wants to preserve its share of the world export market for coffee, it can set a precise percentage. The minimum profit that an employer expects to make can also be precisely defined. In many negotiations, the cost of making a concession can also be estimated fairly accurately. Where it is a constant sum quantity, as in the total quantity of water in a river system, one negotiant's gain is another's loss.

Many times in this book we have referred to the 'vital interests' of a country. How much importance is to be accorded to an interest is purely a matter of perception, not capable of measurement. Throwing 2000 Diego Garcians off their island was not 'vital' to Britain; 1800 Falkland Islanders being placed under Argentine sovereignty was.

Interests are least quantifiable when emotions are involved, especially when the root cause is fear or vulnerability. 'Security' is clearly a fundamental interest in many international negotiations; but how secure a country feels is a matter of perception. While arms reduction talks have to be conducted in terms of actual numbers of missiles or warheads, the exact number which is seen as guaranteeing a perception of safety is purely subjective. Even within a country there can be a variety of perceptions. Is unacceptable damage enough or should one aim at assured destruction? Caspar Weinberger has said that it was his duty, as the US Secretary of Defense, to plan for a 'winnable nuclear war'. This is quite different from deterrence, which is supposed to *prevent* a nuclear war.

The concept of safety is not confined to arms limitation negotiations. In any bargaining situation, negotiants like to keep a safety margin. This is generally thought of as a measure of security in case unpredicted changes in the environment happen. No exporting country in an ICA negotiation is satisfied with a quota of the exact tonnage equal to its actual exportable surplus; a little more is considered necessary, in case there is a bumper crop. We should make a distinction between this safety margin and the water in the quota referred to in Chapter 7. The latter is a negotiating tactic intended as a move in exchanging information on expectations. The safety margin is built into the limit position and is intended to allay psychological apprehensions.

If every negotiant wants a liberal safety margin, the total may well exceed the available quantity. In river water disputes, if every country wants to have what it can use, what it hopes to use, what it potentially can use and then have a safety margin on top of it all, there will never be enough water. One can only reduce safety margins by psychological means, by increasing trust and minimising fears. The psychological aspect of political will is therefore vitally important to attempts at limiting conflicts.

All negotiations are conducted under an umbrella of overall systemic perceptions and ideologies. An employer who hates trade unions is bound to have a different 'political will', compared with an employer who is used to negotiating with unions. The notorious conflict in England, the so-called 'Grunwick dispute', is one example; J.P. Stevens in the United States is another; one can find similar examples in any country. Any international negotiation in which the US is involved is conducted under the overall systemic perceptions produced by super-power rivalry. The negotiations for the independence of Namibia have become immensely more complicated by the introduction of the question of withdrawal of Cuban troops from Angola.

Political Will and Bargaining Power

Were it not for the complications introduced by perceptions, particularly systemic perceptions, we could say that political will bore a direct relationship to bargaining power. Suppose in one bargaining situation we are able to measure bargaining power, then a negotiant could make an estimate of the probable outcome and calculate the benefits and losses that would result from it. The balance of advantage would then represent a measure of political will. Because perceptions affect judgements, the relationship between bargaining power and political will is not so straightforward.

The existence of dissatisfaction itself affects the perceptions of the negotiant voicing it. While such a negotiant perceives the benefits that would reduce his dissatisfaction, he may not perceive equally clearly the costs associated with it. Because unrelieved dissatisfactions turn into frustrations, stronger emotions are vested in it and will become dissociated from rational calculations of bargaining power. The dissatisfaction loudly voiced by the developing countries about the international economic order is an expression of this vulnerability and has little to do with their power to change things.

Possession is usually an identifiable, even measurable, interest. But possession modifies perceptions. 'A bird in the hand ...' is an argument usually advanced by anyone who fears a change in the *status quo*. It is easier not to give up something which one has for the sake of a potential gain which is almost always perceived as unpredictable. In the last chapter, we cited the example of exporters and importers in a negotiation for an ICA behaving irrationally in the sense of not engaging in negotiations when relative bargaining power was in their favour. This comes about because short-term gains are perceived as being more valuable than long-term ones. Even when gains and losses can be calculated, the weight attached to them can only be based on subjective judgements.

In Chapter 8, we briefly mentioned the case of countries entering into negotiations for concluding somewhat utopian economic integration schemes when an objective appraisal of facts would have pointed to more caution. Economic integration among the countries of Western Europe is the only success story in a long list of attempts made in various parts of the world. The East African Community, on which great hopes were placed as one of the earliest of such attempts among developing countries, ended in acrimony and disarray. The Andean Pact, the Central American Common Market, the Economic and Customs Union of Central Africa, the Economic Community of Western African States, ASEAN, progress in all these schemes is either painfully slow or non-existent. The countries involved in these schemes are, no doubt, sincere and have the requisite political will to aim for integration. It is when the realities of integration (e.g. sharing of industries) come to be worked out that size and bargaining power come into play. If, on top of this, the benefits accruing from integration are seen as being divided inequitably, disillusionment sets in. The interesting point is that the political will for integration is there; what is lacking is the ability to make it work.

If bargaining power cannot be converted into political will, neither can changes in it. It is not the magnitude or the direction of change in bargaining power that influences will but how these changes are perceived. A small loss of bargaining power may lead to a sudden change from being in favour of negotiation to a 'lack' of political will. The small margins by which treaties like the Panama Canal Treaty could be passed or defeated in the US Senate shows that small changes can have a significant impact by affecting marginal senators. The invasion of Afghanistan by Soviet troops had, by itself, no direct impact on the nuclear power balance; however, its impact on perceptions in the US and Europe on negotiating arms control agreements was traumatic.

Change of will during NANs is more directly important for limiting conflicts. We have seen that the usual reaction to the voicing of a dissatisfaction is a refusal by others in a position to do something about it to recognise the dissatisfaction. It is only when they find that the costs of doing nothing outweigh the current benefits they possess that a change of will occurs.

The will of potential negotiants can be changed by persuasion. While it is easy to find examples of negotiations failing for 'lack of political will', it is difficult to find examples where there was a will to succeed. This is not because such cases are few, but because successful negotiations are not newsworthy. Whether in industrial relations or international relations, whenever negotiations succeed it is rarely attributed to 'adequate political will'. It is odd that everyone is capable of recognising its absence but not its presence! In Chapters 1 and 2 we referred to the fact that, compared with the question of why people commit crimes, why people are in general law-abiding is rarely studied. Every negotiation which succeeds in producing an agreement is a successful example of enough will resulting in the limitation of conflict. A degree of trust between the negotiants is obviously an essential element in producing this will; the existence of linkages which can reinforce trust is another. An awareness of another party's dissatisfactions and fears and acceptance of the need to ameliorate them are also important.

What is Politics?

We cannot discuss political will in international conflicts without understanding that, in the 1980s, there is no clear-cut division between what is political and what is not. This, too, has become a matter of perception.

The world of sport provides the best illustration that politics is in the eye of the beholder. If the non-white countries refuse to have sporting events with South Africa, they are castigated for 'politicising' sport. But, when Mrs Thatcher or President Carter vociferously discouraged athletes from participating in the Moscow Olympics, it was paraded as a legitimate expression of disapproval of USSR action in Afghanistan. This only emphasises the point that to the United States and its allies communism is a greater evil than racism of the worst kind; it is natural that countries which sympathise with the non-white victims of South Africa have a different order of loathing. Which one is hated more is a matter of judgement and perception.

Until recently, political problems were considered the 'high road' of international relations and economic problems the 'low road'. This is no longer true. The heads of the seven most important countries in the American camp spend their time primarily discussing economic questions. Heads of governments make official visits for selling factories or, more often, arms. Sales of wheat are no longer a commercial deal but are a weapon in the interstate relations between the US and the USSR. Buying natural gas is political.

Culture is political; visits of ballet corps or orchestras are encouraged or cancelled depending on the political climate between the sending and recipient countries. We can now add ballet diplomacy to ping-pong diplomacy and megaphone diplomacy.

The saddest thing is that peace has now become a political word, a victim of bi-polar confrontation. If Lech Walesa is awarded the Nobel Peace Prize, it is acclaimed because it can be portrayed as a slap in the face for the Soviet Union. If Alva Myrdal and Robles are the recipients, it either passes unnoticed or is reported with snide remarks. *Time Magazine* accused these two Peace Prize winners of naiveté, and blamed them for not succeeding in achieving disarmament. This is a strange criticism; the failure to achieve any measure of nuclear arms control cannot be laid at the door of those like Myrdal but only at the doors of the superpowers and those who have a vested interest in perpetuating hostility, confrontation and nuclear terror.

There is no field of human activity which cannot now be raised to a political level by one country or another. All this only adds to the complexity of conflicts and makes their limitation more difficult. There is little point in accusing one or the other of politicising sport or culture: all nations are guilty.

Anatomy of Political Will

To illustrate the complex nature of political will, we can consider the example of international commodity negotiations. There have been innumerable negotiations covering mainly commodities such as coffee, tin, cocoa, sugar, wheat, rubber and tea. The Common Agricultural Policy (CAP) of the European Community is a special case of commodity negotiations under a framework treaty on economic integration. Leaving aside the CAP, the history of international negotiations for concluding ICAs shows that they sometimes succeed and sometimes fail. The Agreements themselves often collapse during implementation.[3] Any failure can be attributed to a collective lack of political will. Individual countries may, of course, accuse one or the other of engineering a breakdown. Whether there was a collective lack or an individual lack, we have to start first by assessing the political will of the countries most important for the success of the negotiation.

Since politics is an amalgam of interests, attitudes and perceptions, we start by asking a series of questions. These should cover systemic and ideological perceptions, the general characteristics of the country, the special interests it may have in the commodity, and its bargaining power. Since time is an important factor, we also have to consider the state of the environment at the time will is assessed.

Systemic Perceptions

(1) Is the country developed or developing? The two groups differ fundamentally on the analysis of the problems of commodity trade, especially on whether the terms of trade of developing countries show continuous deterioration or not. They also differ on what should be the 'equitable' price that an ICA should aim for (whether the price should be the so-called long-term equilibrium price, or whether it should take into account the developmental needs of the poor countries).

(2) What is the attitude of the country to commodity agreements? Some, like the US, believe in the efficacy of the market mechanism; others believe in an indicative price range within which the ICA should operate; yet others believe in a market regulatory mechanism with quotas and buffer stocks.

General Characteristics

(1) Is the country an exporter or an importer? In general, importing countries are more interested in assured supplies somewhat in excess of demand in order to keep prices low. Exporting countries, as a whole, are more interested in higher prices, increasing outlets and co-operation from the importing countries in maintaining discipline by not importing from non-members of the ICA.

(2) What is the degree of dependence on the commodity in the export or import trade of the country? A country dependent on a single commodity for a significant share of its export earnings will have a greater interest in the success of the negotiations, even if it is not a large producer. Likewise, an importing country with no domestic source of supply will have a greater interest in the outcome.

(3) What is the economic interest of the country in that commodity? Even if a country is not significantly dependent it may have an economic interest. An importing country may have a processing industry (e.g. chocolate-making in the case of cocoa) providing substantial employment. In an exporting country, the

commodity may be of social importance to one region (e.g. jute in Bengal) which could be devastated by loss of markets.

Specific Characteristics

(1) Is the country a large, medium or small exporter or importer? Countries with a large share of the export or import market are more important in any negotiation. Large exporters are usually more interested in maintaining their dominant position while medium exporters are usually more interested in their quotas, often seeking increases to enable them to increase their production. Small exporters often seek exemptions from the rigours of an ICA and also have the power to disrupt.

(2) Is the country an established exporter or a new entrant? An established exporter has both a market share and actual markets to protect. A new exporter lays claim to both, leading to a conflict between the 'haves' and 'have-nots'.

(3) For an importing country, is there a domestic production and, if so, what is the degree of protection afforded to it? An example of this factor is the complex relationship between domestic beet producers, domestic cane producers and importers and refiners of sugar in the United States.

(4) Among exporters, what are the characteristics of production and marketing? Whether production of rubber is organised in large plantations or in a large number of small holdings affects the judgement. If production and marketing are controlled by one or two large multinational corporations (e.g. copper, aluminium, bananas), that also affects the judgement.

Bargaining Power

(1) What are the relative strengths of different domestic pressure and power groups connected with the commodity? The negotiating stance and, therefore, the political will, of the country will be the result of negotiations *within* the country.

(2) Who are the country's political or cultural allies? With whom can it form coalitions? Who are its adversaries?

Prevailing Conditions

(1) What is the level of prices — high or low? Which way are prices expected to move in the immediate future? The level of prices and an anticipated rise or fall have a direct impact on the

attitudes of countries towards crucial aspects of any ICA, such as quotas and prices.

(2) What are the total stocks of the commodity? Are they adequate, overhanging or insufficient? If the stocks are high, what is the holding power of any exporting country? These questions are not only relevant to the price levels but also for maintenance of discipline in an ICA. If there are large overhanging stocks and countries do not have the financial power to hold them, then export quotas are likely to be breached.

(3) Is there a prospect of a downturn in production due to natural calamities, production cycles or strikes?

(4) Is there a likelihood of political turmoil in a major producing or consuming country?

These questions are meant only to illustrate; for a specific commodity, one needs to add more particular ones. For rubber, we have to ask questions about the state of synthetic rubber production, the price of crude oil, the degree of excess capacity in consuming countries, and so on. For tin, we have to study the political situation in the USA about the release from the strategic stockpiles. The purpose of listing the questions is only to indicate that the constituents of political will of a country towards an ICA can be assessed as obtaining at a particular time. In doing so, we have to apply some psychological factors on the thinking of the leadership of the country and on the way the country had behaved in the past. One could grade each country, say, from 1 to 5 on each of the questions, and then assign weights to answers, using the psychological factors and interest factors. For example, the level of stocks could be assigned a higher weight than expectations of natural calamities or political turmoil. For a small exporter, dependence could be accorded a low weight and the political influence of a mighty neighbour a higher one. A leadership out to make its mark in the international arena could have its total marks increased by an arbitrary percentage. We could then arrive at a composite number that would roughly indicate the political will of the country. This would help us to rank the countries participating in a negotiation with reasonable accuracy.

When, as in an ICA, we are dealing with a large number of countries with widely varying wills, we cannot predict whether the negotiation will succeed unless we are able to claculate the 'collective will'. For this, we have to assign weights to their different wills. Countries without which an ICA could not function have to be assigned high weights; those who have the power to disrupt also have to be given importance. Only then can we get at least a range of figures for the collective will of all negotiants. Negotiations for concluding ICAs have, in the past, failed often and succeeded sometimes. By analysing past negotiations empirically, we may arrive at an approximation of the weights to be used for calculating both the individual and the collective will. The importance of analysing both successes and failures cannot be overemphasised. If we know why some negotiations fail while others succeed, we may then begin to understand what is often loosely called 'political will'.

Notes

1. The quotation is from an article in *The Times*, 12 Sept. 1983. The writer comments further: 'But, as Frederick the Second of Prussia wrote to his friend, the philosopher Voltair, "The plan is perfectly feasible. The only thing it lacks for success is the agreement of Europe and a few other minor details" ... Until there is political will, the idea of unity will remain in the doldrums.

2. F.S. Northedge and M.D. Donelan, *International Disputes: The Political Aspects* (London, Europa Publications for the David Davies Memorial Institute, 1971) p. 282.

3. L.N. Rangarajan, *Commodity Conflict: The Political Economy of International Commodity Negotiations* (London, Croom Helm, 1978). See Chapter 2, 'More Disagreements than Agreements', pp. 35-52; Chapter 10, 'The Politics of Commodity Negotiations', pp. 250-66; and Chapter 11, 'Political Will', pp. 267-72.

PART FOUR

ON PEACEFUL CHANGE

All members shall settle their international disputes by peaceful means in such a manner that international peace and security, and justice, are not endangered. All members shall refrain in their international relations from the threat or use of force against the territorial integrity or political independence of any states, or in any other manner inconsistent with the Purposes of the United Nations.
    The Charter of the United Nations

A Party cannot invoke the provisions of internal law as justification for the failure to perform a Treaty.
    Article 27, The Vienna Convention of the
    Law of Treaties

Mediators goynge betwixte, pees was made.
    Trevisa, translation of
    Higden's *Polychronion* (1357)

14 THE RULE OF INTERNATIONAL LAW

> But if thou will not carry on this righteous warfare, then by casting away thine own duty and thine own honour, thou wilt incur sin.
>
> The Lord Krishna exhorting Arjuna
> to fight his cousins, *The Bhagvad Gita*, 2: 33

> Kings and persons of sovereign authority, because of their independency, are in continual jealousies, and in the state of posture of gladiators; their forts, and garrisons, and guns upon the frontiers of their kingdoms, and continual spies upon their neighbours; which is a posture of war.
>
> Hobbes, *Leviathan*, Chapter 13

A well-known columnist has written that international law must be understood on the analogy of municipal law, 'for we have no other model for it'.[1] This is nonsense. A reference to any textbook on the subject would have taught him how international law differs from the internal laws of states — municipal law in legal terminology. For instance, Oppenheim defines international law as 'law *between* states, *not above* states'. The columnist has argued that an international rule of law can only exist if there is a power to enforce it and a general readiness to obey it. This is true only if the international law we are looking for is to be exactly like the rule of law within states. In the same article, the journalist advocates a policy of Western Europe and the United States confronting the USSR at 'the deeper level of genuine enmity'. To fan the flames of hostility and, at the same time, to blame international law for failing to enforce peace, shows a confused mind. There are so many people talking loosely about international law that we have to understand what it means in today's world if we are to approach the limitation of conflict between states on a realistic basis.

International law has evolved with the historical experience, since the Middle Ages, of the states in Europe. Until the first world war, two principles dominated international relations — the concept of *exclusive nationalism* and the theory of *national sovereignty*. The carnage of the war was followed by an attempt made in the Covenant of the League of Nations to prevent the recurrence of wars on such scale; but the great powers of the 1920s and 1930s were unwilling to implement it and this failure led to an even more devastating war. The Charter of the United Nations, drawn up after the second world war, was a renewed attempt to maintain peace, and tried to take into account the supposed reasons for the failure of the League. However, the dominant characteristic of international relations since 1945 has not been rivalry between a number of approximately equally powerful states but the ever-increasing destructive power of the two super-powers, who maintain a state of more or less permanent and vociferous hostility.

But while power was being concentrated in the super-powers, it was also being diffused in the increasing number of sovereign states. The 158th member was admitted to the United Nations in September 1983 — an addition of 127 new states in less than 40 years! All the new states adopted unquestioningly the concepts of exclusive nationalism and absolute sovereignty within their boundaries. Unfortunately they did not reject them as emanating from an alien, colonising civilisation. On the contrary, they enshrined them along with the inviolability of inherited colonial boundaries.

The newspaper article referred to earlier was written in justification of the US invasion of Grenada, and began with the rhetorical question: 'Should the United States be prepared to act in defiance of international law when its long-term interests are threatened by obeying it?' The answer given to this question is at least an honest recognition of a fact of life — that states go to war when they feel threatened. The problem of subjecting sovereign states to the rule of law is a very difficult one because war is an instrument of policy and not of law. The maintenance of peace by international law is an ideal which many share; but the expectations aroused that the United Nations would somehow become a potent force for the maintenance of international peace since the second world war have been belied.

We are, however, apt to forget that the international community has also succeeded in reducing uncertainty and creating order in many areas of activity. An important development throughout the twentieth century has been the growing interdependence of the world, brought about by rapid technological progress. Starting from the International Telegraphic Union in 1865 and the Universal Postal Union in 1874, a need for more organisation of international activities has arisen. With every new organisation, a new set of rules has been created and a new international law has been made. The Law of the Sea, finally agreed to by a large number of states after 10 years of negotiation, is an example of wholly new principles of international law being created.

We shall, therefore, examine in this chapter the inherent contradiction between absolute sovereignty and international law, the impossibility of treating international law as an extension of municipal law, and the reasons why states go to war. The contradictory tendencies of failure to maintain peace and security while, at the same time, striving for greater order in many areas of international activity are covered in the later sections. This chapter borrows heavily from Brierley's excellent book, *The Law of Nations*, which will be quoted often[2]; nevertheless, the responsibility for the views expressed herein is mine.

Sovereignty

The quotation from Hobbes at the head of this chapter is probably even more true today than it was in 1651 when it was written. The doctrine of sovereignty has undergone many changes as the political facts (or the understanding of these facts) changed in the countries where people thought about such things. When nationalism gained strength in nineteenth-century Europe, nations claimed absolute sovereignty. There is a fundamental contradiction between the concept of absolute sovereignty and the idea of an international rule of law: 'If sovereignty means absolute power, and if states are sovereign in that sense, they cannot at the same time be subject to law.' The belief that accepting international obligations is a surrender of sovereignty is still very strong. An argument that is often put forward against Britain's membership of the European Community is that this diminishes the 'absolute sovereignty of the British Parliament'. An American court has pronounced that 'international practice is law only in so far as we adopt it; and like all common or statute law, it bends to the will of Congress.'

The following quotation from the report of an American Commission set up during the second world war to study the organisation of peace sums up what states mean when they claim to be sovereign:

> A sovereign state ... at the present time claims the power to judge its own controversies, to enforce its conception of rights, to increase armaments without limit, to treat its own nationals as it sees fit, and to regulate its economic life without regard to the effect of such regulations upon its neighbours. *These attributes must be limited.* (Emphasis added.)

The call for limitation of sovereignty was a consequence of experiencing two horrific world wars within 40 years of each other. Since then some attempts have been made to regulate economic behaviour to take into account adverse effects on other states. Some progress has been made in the general acceptance of the principles of human rights, but this has not limited significantly the power of states to 'treat its nationals as it sees fit'.

The adoption of the concepts of sovereignty and territorial integrity by newly-independent states has given rise to many conflicts when confronted by the spirit of exclusive nationalism. When a people feel themselves to be a separate 'nation', they want to display this by having sovereignty over their own affairs. Bangladeshis, Basques, Biafrans, Catholics in Ulster, Eritreans in Ethiopia, Turkish-Cypriots, Sri Lankan Tamils are all examples of peoples who have made (except in one case) unsuccessful attempts to equate nationalism with sovereignty. The same principle of sovereignty is used both by the group which wants to secede and the state which wants to prevent this from happening.

With an ever-increasing number of sovereign states, the doctrine of equality of states has also gained ascendancy. This is an anomalous doctrine, considering real-life experience. All states are not equal, whether in terms of geographical extent, population, wealth or any other criteria one chooses. If, according to the doctrine of sovereignty, every state is free to do what it likes within its territory, then each is equal only in possessing that quality. But then, there can be no such thing as international law. However, the existence of power is recognised in many international rule-systems such as the IMF, the IBRD and ICAs. Further, the Security Council recognises two classes of states — those with the power of a veto and those without.

International Law and Municipal Law

Unlike the American or the Indian Constitutions, there is no such thing as *the* international law. Article 38 of the Statute of the International Court of Justice lists the sources which the Court should use for determining the law in any particular case. Of these, the most important are treaties, followed by international custom and the general principles of law 'recognised by civilised nations'. The Court may also refer to past judicial decisions, and the writings of recognised experts.

Treaties are agreements voluntarily entered into by states. They may be bilateral or multilateral and may be of general or particular application. Where two states enter into a treaty regulating a particular activity, any dispute concerning that activity will be judged strictly within the terms of that treaty. Only if there is a judicial doubt will other things like custom and principles be called upon to assist in decision-making. Examples of multilateral treaties covering specific areas of activity are the GATT on regulating international trade in manufactured goods, treaties on the use of specific rivers like the Danube and the Rhine and the Law of the Sea. Such treaties usually have their own dispute-settlement procedures. General treaties, like those on maritime warfare, treatment of prisoners of war, chemical warfare, or on diplomatic immunities and privileges prescribe codes of conduct in particular situations.

An important point concerning all treaties is that they bind only those states which are parties to them, thus emphasising the voluntary nature of the commitment. Since states can also contract out of treaties, the optional nature is further reinforced.

As regards international custom as a source of international law, the following observation by Brierly may be noted:

> Custom in its legal sense means something more than mere habit or usage; it is a usage felt by those who follow it to be an obligatory one. There must be present a feeling that if the usage is departed from some sort of evil consequence will probably, or at any rate ought to, fall on the transgressor; in technical language there must be a 'sanction', though the exact nature of this need not be very distinctly envisaged.

What the International Court of Justice means by 'principles of law recognised by civilised nations' is not at all clear. Which states are to be construed as 'civilised nations', and what principles they recognise are more difficult questions, because the judgement on civilised behaviour changes with time. Until the Congress of Vienna (1815) declared slave trade illegal it was 'civilised' to own slaves. After the experience of the first world war, it began to be considered 'uncivilised' to use chemicals in warfare. The Permanent Court of Justice under the League of Nations would, no doubt, have considered Germany under the Third Reich a 'civilised' nation, in spite of the Holocaust. Civilisation, as much as fairness and equity, is a concept which changes as perceptions change.

In contrast to international law, acceptance of municipal law has elements of both rule-obedience and coercion. Rule-obedience is encouraged because municipal law gives protection to the juridical persons within a state. The judicial organs of the state are part of the whole complicated machinery of a state's govenment, which upholds the system and which, in turn, protects those persons. A national court functions in an environment in which the judiciary and most citizens share the same values, traditions and sentiments. More often than not, what is considered 'fair' is the same for all. Further, municipal law has a regular system of appeals, and a hierarchy of courts. International law has no such safeguards.

While promoting obedience, municipal law also has powers of enforcement and punishments for transgressors. The coercion that exists in international law is arbitrary, and depends largely on which state is more powerful.

It is a misunderstanding to think that the police enforce the law. To quote Brierly again:

> It is not the existence of a police force that makes a system of law strong and respected, but the strength of the law that makes it possible for a police force to be effectively organised ... national law has developed a machinery of enforcement that generally works smoothly because the imperative character of law is felt so strongly and the obedience to it has become so much a matter of habit.

This, of course, does not apply to states in which the police set themselves above the law and procure obedience by coercion and intimidation.

The way municipal law tackles dissatisfactions and grievances in the population is different from the handling of dissatisfaction of states in international law. When large groups within a state become dissatisfied with the state's legal power, a wise government does not prosecute them; it considers *changing* the law. Whether it be civil rights for blacks in the US, divorce in Italy or the dowry system in India, changes in the law are often brought about by the voicing of a dissatisfaction by significant groups of people. On the other hand, dissatisfied states, if they cannot obtain redress by negotiation, resort to war.

A fundamental distinction between international and municipal law is that the latter differentiates between the just and unjust use of force. In municipal law, a contract between two parties obtained by one coercing the other is, *ab initio*, invalid. In international law a dictated treaty is as valid legally as one freely entered into on both sides. This is generally called the 'sanctity of treaties'. International law has not been — and is not now — strong enough to prevent states from settling disputes by force. A dictated treaty following victory in war is an accomplished fact and other states have to recognise its validity. What cannot be cured has to be endured, and is then enshrined as a principle of international law.

The principle of sanctity of treaties has been questioned by the People's Republic of China, which has coined the term 'unequal treaties' for those signed under duress. Some treaties are considered by China to be unfair because they were concluded at a time when the then government was weak and had no option but to sign. What this challenge to the principle of sanctity of treaties really means is that now that China has again become powerful, it is exercising the right to demand a revision of the treaties to correspond with the current power balance. Both the dictation of a treaty and the call for its revision, backed by the threat of repudiation, are expressions of power.

Just and Unjust Wars

Grotius (1583-1645), credited with writing one of the earliest authoritative works on international law, made a distinction between just and unjust wars. In his view, war was just if it was undertaken by a sovereign either to protect the state (its people or its possessions) or to punish another offending state. Whether it be the Crusades, Lord Krishna persuading Arjuna to fight a righteous war, or the Jihad of Islam, the concept of a just war is common to all religions. However, sovereign states have never limited themselves to fighting only 'just' wars: states go to war to achieve aims which they believe to be in their interest — concepts of justice rarely enter into it. It is also naive to think that states go to war only to obtain redress for their grievances. If this were true, there would be no wars of aggrandisement, revanchism or territorial expansion.

States also seek to conquer because of fear; we have quoted examples from ancient to current history to show that countries go to war to protect supply sources and to relieve themselves of dependence and vulnerability. The all but open war waged by the United States against Nicaragua and the invasion of Grenada in 1983 were prompted by fear of a threat to its 'way of life'. The invasion of Afghanistan by the USSR was prompted by a fear of an unstable or unfriendly regime in a state on its borders. The fact that the United States is a democracy is often adduced by its apologists as somehow a justification for its armed intervention. But in international law there is no difference between an attack by a democratic state or a socialist one.

Some conflicts end in war because of the intransigence of one party in denying a just grievance. Few will deny that the war of independence in Algeria against France was a 'just' one.[3] But protracted French intransigence led to carnage on a large scale before independence could become a reality. The continued oppression of the black majority by the whites in South Africa makes most observers despair of a peaceful outcome to this conflict.

Though the amelioration of dissatisfaction has been emphasised a great deal in this book, I would not claim that this alone will stop all conflicts and make wars unnecessary. It is easy to say that international law should only make 'just' changes and not 'expedient' ones. But no two persons and no two states need agree on what is 'just'. We have to admit that changes are made because they are demanded by those who have the power to make their demands prevail. When Italy invaded Abyssinia in 1935-36, the members of the League of Nations could have used the procedure in the Covenant for applying sanctions against Italy, but because it was not politically expedient to do so, Italy was allowed to prevail.

Self-defence, reprisals and the exercise of a treaty right are the most common reasons given for going to war. An example of reprisals was the so-called 'police action' in February 1979 of China against Viet Nam 'to teach them a lesson'. That such an action is no longer a respectable cause for aggression is shown by the *New York Times* characterising it as 'vigilantism' and 'lynch law logic'.[4]

Self-defence is a right clearly recognised by Article 51 of the UN Charter, but it has now been widened so much that it is used to justify any act of aggression. When Israel destroyed an Iraqi nuclear reactor under construction, it was called a 'pre-emptive strike'; when South Africa attacks its neighbours it is called 'self-defence'; the Soviet Union's invasion of Afghanistan and the US invasion of Grenada were both 'by invitation'. Protecting an ideology is now considered adequate justification for aggression. As an extension of the doctrine of self-defence, we now have something called 'self-preservation'. 'The truth is that self-preservation is not a legal right but an instinct.'

The doctrine of collective self-defence, another extension of the principle, is now firmly established in such treaties as NATO and the Warsaw Pact. Any collective self-defence treaty cannot but entrench conflicts, since the motivation is primarily against another group of countries.

War is no longer the only method of aggression. Powerful states intervene in the affairs of other countries by propounding the Nixon or the Brezhnev doctrines. Covert action to destabilise other countries is now so common that it needs no elaboration. This is no more justified in international law than naked aggression.

Even when actual war is taking place, it goes by another name. The war between Britain and Argentina on the Falkland Islands/Malvinas was never called a war; the formality of a declaration of war was also dispensed with. An entertaining article in the *Washington Post* has described how words are used to conceal the activity of armed conflict.

> 'Protective reaction' is what Richard Nixon called the invasion of Cambodia, where they did not drop bombs but instead engaged in 'air support' ... War itself is now a 'nuclear exchange' which sounds like high-technology gift-giving ... 'Counter-value attack' means that one side in a nuclear war retaliates by bombing things of value — i.e. people and cities.[5]

Power and the Maintenance of Peace

The League of Nations did not prevent war because when member states decided to achieve their aims by war, they did so irrespective of the Covenant. From this experience, the United Nations Charter created a Security Council, giving it the 'primary responsibility for the maintenance of international peace and security'. By Article 24 of the Charter all the members of the UN granted the Council the power to act for them *all* and, by Article 25, agreed to 'accept and carry out the decisions' of the Council. These are the most wide-ranging powers ever given to an international body for maintaining peace.

Whenever there is a conflict, the question is asked, 'What has the UN done?' because the UN Charter has aroused expectations that somehow peace will be maintained. In spite of its wide-ranging powers, the Security Council has been ineffective because the super-powers wrote into the Charter the power of veto for themselves. On questions of war and peace, the Council can only act if the permanent members agree among themselves.

The reason for inscribing the veto was the fear that a large number of smaller states might form a coalition to force the great powers to take actions against their interests. It is significant that the great powers have never bound themselves to take any action which would primarily have been for the maintenance of peace. For example, there is a provision that, when a Security Council member is a party to a dispute which the Council is investigating, that member must abstain from voting. It is difficult to imagine any dispute or conflict in which the super-powers are *not* interested, but they have never abstained from casting their vote. The members of the Council either stop short of taking any decision which could bind all the members of the UN, or call the dispute by some other name. The Falklands War was never a war, nor even a dispute; it was a 'situation'.

In the Charter, there are provisions for creating a UN force by special agreement. Since the permanent members have never been able to agree on the kind of special agreements that would create an independent UN force, no such permanent force exists. In any of the conflicts in which the UN has been involved militarily (e.g. Korea, Congo) the forces have been sent voluntarily.

Nor has the Council been successful in promoting pacific settlements of disputes. Since the veto has made collective enforcement impossible, the Council can only make recommendations. Even small countries accept these recommendations only when it suits them. In some cases, a Council recommendation might have been helpful in curtailing hostilities by promoting a ceasefire. But the example of the Iran–Iraq War can lead only to the conclusion that the five permanent members — especially the two super-powers — will let the war go on, so long as it does not affect what they perceive as their 'vital interests'.

What Brierly wrote in 1954 is still valid:

> The result of insisting that only a body that had the power to make binding decisions could act effectively has been to give us a body that can neither decide nor act. ... Small power aggression never has been and never can be a serious problem to the peace of the world if the Great Powers are agreed among themselves. ... The only event today which can seriously endanger the peace of the world is aggression by a Great Power, and a system which solemnly declares ... that its purpose is to 'take effective collective measures for the prevention and removal of threats to peace and for the suppression of aggression' and yet does not propose to deal with the aggression of a Great Power is little better than a sham.

The UN Charter repeatedly refers to the maintenance of peace and peaceful settlement of disputes through regional organisations. The most important of these are: the Organisation of American States (OAS), the Organisation of African Unity (OAU) and the League of Arab States (Arab League).[6] None can be said to have had any conspicuous success in limiting conflict. The OAS suffers from a gross disparity in power between the United States and the other members, which have a well-founded suspicion that the 'United States is apt to use the system as a rubber stamp for intervention in their affairs in the service of its own national purpose.' An example is the way the US intervened in 1954 in Guatemala to overthrow Colonel Arbenz because his reformist government threatened the interests of the United Fruit Company, the largest landowner and effective controller of the Guatemalan economy. The then Secretary of State, John Foster Dulles, succeeded in transferring the case from the UN Security Council to the OAS so that the Guatemalan government could commit 'suicide' by giving some kind of cover for US military intervention.[7] Guatemala in 1954,

Cuba since 1959, the Dominican Republic in 1963, Chile in 1973, El Salvador and Nicaragua in 1984 — the memories of the countries in Central and South America are so etched with the history of the United States pursuing its own interests that one can no longer expect the OAS to be credible as an independent peace-making or conflict-limiting body.

The OAU, too, has had little success in limiting the many conflicts in Africa. Morocco, Algeria, Libya, Chad, Somalia, Ethiopia, Kenya and Uganda have all been involved in conflicts with neighbouring states. In addition, many countries in Africa have had secessionary conflicts (Biafra, Eritrea, Tigré, Katanga, Buganda, Matabeleland, Southern Sudan). Though inheriting totally illogical boundaries cutting across tribal, ethnic, linguistic and cultural entities, the OAU decided, from the beginning, not to open the Pandora's box of redrawing boundaries and thus bound itself not to intervene in the inevitable conflicts which followed.

The disunity among the members of the Arab League, though they all perceive Israel as the collective common enemy, has made it a body which has proved powerless in limiting conflicts among its members. Until recently, one had to look hard to find at least one or two Arab countries which were not at odds with their neighbour. In fact, the Arab League has exported its internal conflicts into other organisations; the Morocco/Algeria/Polisario conflict was used by the Arab states to disrupt the OAU, not their own League. Egyptian intervention in the Yemen, Libyan intervention in Chad, Syrian support for Iran in the Iran—Iraq War — Arab disunity and rivalry has consistently enlarged the theatre of conflicts.

Rule-systems and International Order

The problem of trying to limit conflicts between states is how to deal with the readiness of all types of government to act to protect their interests by force, even if it involves a violation of international law. Exercise of power, insistence on sovereignty, the powerful hold of nationalism, the perception of vital interests, these are the realities. Since we cannot subordinate the use of force by states to international law, we have to deal with conflicts between states in the situation we find them.

The growing interdependence of the world, fostered by technological progress, has pushed states, willy-nilly, into creating a large number of rule-systems. We now take for granted that letters posted in one country will be delivered in another, but this requires Postal Conventions, an example of an international rule-system working unobtrusively. A list of just the major treaty-made rule-systems covers the following subjects: trade in some primary commodities, trade in manufactures, balance of payments and exchange rates, postal agreements, allocation of radio frequencies, positioning of geostationary satellites, merchant shipping, air traffic control, nuclear power generation, control of epidemic diseases, pollution, slavery, and safety in the workplace.

We should also note the need for extensive rule-systems when a group of countries, like members of the European Community, embark on a process of integration. The harmonisation proposals of the Commission in Brussels sometimes provoke laughter and sometimes anger; but such details are a necessary part of elaborating rule-systems.

Many non-governmental rule-systems have also been created. There is a well-established international commercial arbitration procedure; agreements between banks on syndicated loans are big business; liner conferences are rule-systems governing merchant shipping on regular services; airlines have IATA.

An essential characteristic of any rule is that it has to be *explicit* if it is to succeed in reducing uncertainty and increasing predictability. This is especially so in the case of rules negotiated between institutions, including states. The actual negotiators representing institutions do change frequently and any rule formulated by one set of negotiators must mean the same to any other set.

A rule-system can be defined as a framework of rules agreed to by the parties after a negotiation covering a specified area of activity. This definition covers any activity in which some future action is made contingent on some other event. A rule-system can govern transactions between individuals like traders, relations between labour and management or conduct between governments. A Charter Party, a Bill of Lading or a standard contract (like contract terms for civil engineering construction with a builder) are also rule-systems. In such standard contracts, the negotiants do not actually bargain over each clause; the forms have become standardised by previous negotiations, arbitrated decisions and judicial pronouncements. Nevertheless, they are agreements by negotiation, the bargainers deciding to take them as read and agreed to.

Rule-systems differ widely in the extent of their elaboration. Some may try to anticipate every possible contingency and provide an appropriate rule for each one; others may deal only with broad elements, leaving much to be decided as time and circumstances change. An example of an elaborate rule-system is the type of agreement between workers and management in a factory, specifying work norms, classification of jobs, night-duty rotas, tea-breaks, washing-up times, safety precautions, and so on. On the other hand, some provisions of the Rome Treaty, such as those on the free movement of people, contain only broad provisions; the details of whether a doctor or an accountant qualifying in one country can practise his profession in another Community country are still to be elaborated.

Generally speaking, international agreements on economic matters tend to be more structured than agreements on political matters. GATT, for example, is comprehensive in its coverage of the different aspects of international trade in manufactures. It has clearly defined objectives, a set of rules for achieving them, a set of criteria for suspension of the rules, and a procedure for resolving any conflicts that may arise during its implementation. Of the international systems which cover political, strategic and economic questions, the most elaborate is the Law of the Sea.

Though every voluntarily negotiated rule-system starts with high expectations of discipline and obedience, enforceability depends on the backing behind the system. Where a rule-system operates entirely within the boundaries of a state, then the laws of the state provide the necessary backing. In trans-national contracts between non-governmental parties, provision can be made for disputes to be resolved by the laws and in the courts of the state of one of the parties. In commercial contracts and Charter parties, there is usually a provision for binding arbitration.

An exceptional multinational system which has its own court and adjudication system is the set of treaties comprising the European Communities (Coal and Steel, Euratom and the Common Market). Under the Common Market, there are elaborate rule-systems such as those governing the CAP for different products (cereals, dairy products, meat, poultry, wine, olive oil, etc.). The structure is remarkable — rule-systems functioning under a treaty which, in turn, is backed by the adjudication procedure of the European Court of Justice. As an example of international law-creation, it is unique.

If more rules can be created and if these can be made to function effectively, greater order will prevail, vulnerability will be reduced and security strengthened. Rule-making and rule-obedience are, therefore, essential for limiting conflicts. Conversely, rule-disobedience decreases faith in the system thereby making conflict limitation more difficult. Making, obeying and disobeying rules are the subjects of the next chapter.

Notes

1. Roger Scruton, 'When the Writ of Law Stops Running', *The Times*, 15 Nov. 1983.
2. J.L. Brierly, *The Law of Nations: An Introduction to the International Law of Peace* (Oxford, Clarendon Press, 5th edn, 1953). Quotations without note numbers are as follows: Oppenheim (p. 47); Hobbes (p. 43); sovereignty and international law (pp. 16, 46); American Commission (p. 48); custom (p. 60); self-preservation (pp. 318-19); Security Council (pp. 112, 305, 306).
3. According to newspaper reports, Caspar Weinberger, the US Secretary of Defense, offered this as the main justification for US armed intervention, in an Oxford Union debate in 1984.
4. *New York Times*, 28 Feb. 1979. The paper also added: 'One fellow's police action tends to be another's imperialism. ... Whoever invokes the code of the vigilante is also likely to have it invoked against him. ... By emulating those whom he would instruct, Mr Teng fails all the world.'
5. Elisabeth Bumiller, 'Newspeak — Washington Version', *Washington Post*, reproduced in *Guardian Weekly*, 18 Sept. 1983.
6. F.S. Northedge and M.D. Donelan, *International Disputes: The Political Aspects* (London, Europa Publications for the David Davies Memorial Institute of International Studies, 1971), p. 260. Chapter 11, pp. 243-76, 'The Work of Regional Organizations', has a detailed description of all types of regional arrangements, including NATO and the Warsaw Pact.
7. ibid., p. 261. The authors sum up the episode by quoting Inis Claude, *International Organization*, March 1964, p. 30: 'In insisting that the Government of Guatemala should resort to the OAS, the United States was recommending what it hoped and intended would prove a suicidal act.'

15 MAKING, OBEYING AND DISOBEYING RULES

> The Court has committed an abuse of law. ... Faced with an abuse of law, a sovereign state has a right to observe only the law which it finds legitimate.
> Michel Debré, former Prime Minister of France

> If it is in the rules of the game, it is fair play.
> Greg Chappell, captain, Australian cricket team

Making rules satisfies the desire for greater order. Obeying the rules assuages vulnerabilities because the psychological satisfaction accruing from predictability is also desired. But the mere creation of a rule-system does not eliminate dissatisfaction or vulnerability. Perceptions of fairness and equity continue to affect the actions of signatory parties to a rule-system while it is being implemented. There are many methods, acts of omission and commission, by which contracting parties express their dissatisfaction or vulnerability. Governments also display great ingenuity in circumventing rules instead of disobeying them openly. The concepts often stressed in this book — vital interests, vulnerability, dissatisfaction, perception of fairness — are all relevant to the examination of the making and obeying or repudiating and circumventing of rules. From this analysis, we can draw up a set of guidelines for creating more effective rule-systems, promoting discipline and encouraging rule-obedience.

Making Rules Internationally

Since all human activity *inside* states is governed either by statute law or by customary law, making a new rule invariably means changing an old one. Some changes, like the abolition of the death penalty, homosexual relations, abortion or divorce, involve moral or ethical questions and arouse deep emotions. Nevertheless, such changes are constantly being made. India has made discrimination against the *harijan* (the untouchables) and Sudan female circumcision crimes. Age old practices do not disappear by bringing them within the ambit of the law, but these are essential first steps in societal changes.

One should not assume that there is difficulty only in changing rules which touch on fundamental moral questions. A set of rules governs the organisation in divisions of professional football clubs in Britain. Almost everyone is agreed that there are too many divisions for the declining number of spectators, too many clubs, too many matches, and too little money to go around, but changing the system has proved very difficult.

Making international rules is bound to be a far more difficult undertaking. But, as mentioned before, interdependence and the increase in the number of linkages have evoked an acute need for rules in different areas of activity. The proliferation, since 1945, of international organisations, such as the specialised agencies of the UN, is a reflection of rule-making on a vastly expanded scale. Such rule-making has not been achieved by glamorous head-line-catching negotiations but the bargaining in these is as arduous and time-consuming as in any international rule-making endeavour.

An important function of international rule-making is codification. By custom and experience different rules governing an activity develop; at some point it becomes necessary to put them together, in order to make them more explicit and precise, thereby improving predictability. A large part of the work of the 11 sessions between 1973 and 1982 of the Third UN Conference on the Law of the Sea, was concerned with codification of the law as already accepted. The remarkable work done by the Third Conference can be gauged by just a glance at the subjects covered by the Treaty.[1] There had been two previous attempts at codification. In the 1958 and 1960 Conferences some problems, such as the precise extent of the territorial sea and jurisdiction over fisheries, proved incapable of agreement; these were successfully codified in the Third.

The importance of the Law of the Sea, as agreed to by 131 countries in 1982, lies in the fact that, in addition to the massive work of codification, it created the largest set of new laws. Between 1960 and the time the Third Conference was convened, totally new subjects had emerged due to technological progress; resources such as offshore oil and gas became economically important and their extraction feasible. Mining the deep sea for minerals has become a possibility. One of the most important of the new laws is the concept of *common heritage*, a principle which transcends the concept of national sovereignty — states grabbing whatever they can lay their hands on. The common heritage principle may well become accepted for the Antarctic and for outer space. The Law of the Sea has also created for the first time a public international institution, the Seabed Authority, that can generate revenue on an international basis, co-operate with multinational companies, plan global resources and protect and conserve the marine environment. Other innovations include the concepts of economic zones, of an international environmental law, and of archipelagic states.[2]

The Law of the Sea is the latest and most ambitious example of law-creation. But this is not a new activity. When the Congress of Vienna declared the slave trade illegal in 1815, this was a totally new law. As circumstances change, and new needs arise, new laws are needed. When it was found that only a limited number of geostationary satellites could be put into orbit, the international community needed a new law to decide how the available slots could be divided up equitably.

There are a number of areas until now thought to be within the exclusive jurisdiction of states which may need new rules. For example, immigration is a subject over which all states have exclusive sovereignty. But changes in the laws in Germany affect Turkey, those in France affect Algeria and the question of 'illegal aliens' in the United States is a matter of interest to Mexico. Whether they like it or not, states are forced to take into account the repercussions of their actions on the emigrant states. Another example is the international law relating to civil aviation. The Chicago Conference of 1944 led to the creation of the International Civil Aviation Organisation and the enunciation of a number of principles. Forty years later, the civil aviation industry is still governed by a forest of bilateral agreements. This has given rise to gross anomalies in all areas: fare structures, number of flights, which airlines can fly to which cities, and how often, and who can travel in them.

Yet another area in which there is no agreed international rule-system is the use of the great river systems. There are precedents for the creation of an international set of rules for rivers passing through many countries (e.g. the second Treaty of Paris (1856) which created the Danube Commission, and the Convention of Mannheim (1868) which provided for freedom of traffic on the Rhine). In this century rivers have become important not so much for navigation as for irrigation and the generation of electricity. In many parts of the world, river pollution is also causing concern. The sharing of river waters is always a source of conflict. Little attention has been paid to evolving international rules on this subject.

We need more rule-systems. The advantage of having a number of systems is that each one delimits a specific area of operation and, to that extent, isolates it from others. Conflicts in one rule-system need not spill over into another and limitation can then become possible. Separate rule-systems also compartmentalise interest groups within states. Many of the member countries of GATT are also signatories to the Law of the Sea; but the domestic constituents influencing a government's role in the two multilateral treaties are quite different. The negotiators are selected from different departments and have different orders of priority among the national interests which they seek to protect and advance. Since a single comprehensive order covering all international activity is impossible, it is a definite advantage for limitation of conflict to break up different activities into different rule-systems.

Though the need for more rule-systems is obvious, negotiating workable ones has not been easy. There are two reasons for this. First, acceptance of any treaty is voluntary; states often negotiate an instrument and then fail to adhere to it. Second, the negotiating process has been made more complicated by becoming more open and more susceptible to public pressure. Four important maritime countries, including the United States, voting against the final draft of the Law of the Sea is an example of the first kind of difficulty. During the nine years it took to negotiate the Convention, these states participated fully and made sure that their interests were fully protected. Even during the closing session of the Conference, the United States extracted concessions from other negotiants. The dissatisfaction of the United States and its close allies was only about a small part of the whole treaty — the mining for minerals from the deep seabed. For all one knows, such mining may never become a practical proposition because of the huge expenditure required.

We have to note the special role of the United States in ratifying negotiated agreements, because of its importance in maintaining world order, particularly the world economic order. The earliest post-second world war example of the United States *not* ratifying an agreement after negotiating a final text is the scuttling of the

International Trade Organisation (ITO) which was to have been created under the Havana Charter (1948). The US also refused to sign the International Sugar Agreement after getting all its points included in the negotiating conference; it failed to implement the modification of the American Selling Price System for levying customs duties on imported chemicals, after promising to do so in the Kennedy Round of GATT negotiations as part of a set of reciprocal concessions; and it abruptly and unilaterally cancelled the Memorandum of Understanding for a joint European–American solar mission.[3] Neither did it ratify SALT II.

The usual reason given for all the failures of the United States to ratify the agreements it has signed is that Congress would not have approved. Some experts have argued that 'there is no legal or moral duty on a state to ratify a treaty signed by its own plenipotentiaries; it can only be said that refusal is a serious step which ought not to be taken lightly.'[4] Even so, repeated repudiations make it difficult for other states to consider the US as a serious partner in creating and maintaining international law. The most powerful country bears a greater responsibility for maintaining order than 100 small ones.

This brings us to the question of how public many sensitive international negotiations have become. States can no longer indulge in totally secret negotiations like absolute monarchs. Public opinion now plays an important part in the making of treaties, especially where fears of survival are involved. The task of plenipotentiaries is now even more difficult than it used to be. In the case of the celebrated 'walk in the woods' the US and USSR negotiators were repudiated by their respective governments even before anyone knew what they had actually said![5]

Rule-obedience

Law violations are rare in all customary systems and international law is no exception. We saw in the last chapter that there are many reasons why municipal law is obeyed — the homogeneity of society, the complex structure of the state involving the judiciary and the police, a well-organised hierarchical judicial system, all combine to make the majority of people obey the law most of the time. But not all laws are obeyed by all of the people all of the time. Even in democratic societies obedience to the law varies with the individual laws. Most people are prepared to exceed the speed limit, smuggle something through customs without paying duty, or not declare all income for tax purposes even though these actions are illegal. Such transgressions are considered minor; despite this, there is a considerable degree of propensity to obey.

States normally observe international law because they find it convenient, expedient or prudent to do so. It is convenient to obey the international rules on air traffic control, since there is little to be gained by being a maverick. Even if a state finds a particular international law irksome, it may find it expedient to obey it: ICA members may obey export restrictions even though sorely tempted to export all the surplus they have. Prudence is a motivating factor when a state confronts a more powerful state or international organisation. Acceptance of stringent conditions imposed by the IMF is prudent if a state needs the money which only the IMF can provide.

The reason why rule-obedience by states passes unnoticed is that it is unexciting; whereas the occasions when international law is broken are sensational. But the media emphasis on violations and circumventions should not make us forget that international law and the great majority of treaties are on the whole regularly observed. International law, in fact, performs a useful and necessary function in enabling states to carry on their day-to-day activities along orderly and predictable lines. Obedience to international law is as much a matter of expedience and custom as obedience to municipal law.

To see why some rule-systems are more readily obeyed than others, we can compare two systems — GATT and ICAs — both concerned with international trade. Notwithstanding the circumventing of its principles by many countries, GATT has had considerable success in liberalising trade in manufactures. Tariffs have been brought down to low levels in products of interest to the rich countries. Import duties on similar products in different countries have been harmonised to approximately similar levels. Non-tariff barriers are at last being tackled. On the whole, obedience to the detailed rule structure of GATT is reasonably satisfactory.

The experience of ICAs on rule-making and rule-obedience is quite unsatisfactory. Commodity Agreements depend for their success on compliance with specific provisions such as export quotas and maintenance of the price within the specified range. Yet exporting countries with a surplus over their authorised quota often try to export the surplus all the same. In times of shortage, there is less self-discipline in maintaining the price below or at the agreed ceiling. In most ICAs compliance is effectively voluntary since no adequate monitoring arrangements are inscribed in them. Importing countries rarely help in promoting compliance. In most ICAs, the dispute settlement procedure is sketchy and there are usually no clearly defined procedures for consultation, conciliation or arbitration. The history of the ICAs shows that member countries tend to join or leave them, as it suits them. In short, there is a much more cavalier attitude to rule-making and rule-obedience.[6]

GATT has been comparatively more successful because it is run by a group of like-minded countries with preponderant power in international trade in manufactures. By contrast, the powerful countries have a pronounced antipathy to ICAs. Equally, there is very little unity among the producing countries. For these reasons, the number of commodities for which ICAs have been negotiated are very few, and even these have had short or intermittent lives.

If a rule-system is to have a high degree of discipline, its powerful members must have a 'propensity to obey'. This will be severely tested in times of crisis. So long as there was an increasing need in the industrialised countries for oil imports, OPEC was successful. When the demand for OPEC oil fell sharply — mainly as a reaction to the high prices which promoted conservation and encouraged new oilfields exploration — OPEC was threatened with disintegration. OPEC survived only when Saudi Arabia agreed to become a 'swing producer' so that the other members could export at least a large part of what they wanted to export. (The more powerful members of any rule-system are often called upon to make disproportionate sacrifices in the interests of maintaining it.)

Vital Interests, Dissatisfaction and Disobedience

Violations of international law happen when states exercise their power, reasonably or unreasonably, and, sometimes, when they have a genuine grievance. In both cases, states perceive a 'vital interest'.

The following is a revealing example of how a powerful country violated a treaty it had promoted, signed and ratified voluntarily. During Alexander Haig's confirmation hearings in the US Senate,

Senator Tsongas questioned him about decisions made in the White House when Haig was deputy to Henry Kissinger, with the intention of preventing the accession of Salvador Allende to the Presidency of Chile. General Haig conceded that the decisions were 'in contrast to the spirit' of the Charter of the OAS, which prohibited interference in the internal affairs of other member-states and added: 'I don't think you, Senator, or anyone in this room would want a rigid, legalistic preoccupation which does not assess the exigencies of the moment.' When Senator Tsongas asked whether other member-states of the OAS could not legitimately expect the United States to live up to its Treaty commitments, General Haig replied: 'Yes, I think so, unless we were to withdraw or modify and, of course, the OAS Treaty was spawned and signed at a time when the basic issues — and I put ... I mentioned this in my formal statement yesterday — when the circumstances have changed, then these things have to be either adjusted or re-assessed.'[7] This is 'Haig-speak' showing that the United States will violate any treaty if it believes that compliance is against its interests.

Something similar was said by the British prime minister, Harold Macmillan, when he was questioned in the House of Commons about the legality of President Kennedy's blockade of Cuba in 1962. Macmillan did not think that 'this is the moment to go into the niceties of international law' and that 'in new situations ... we cannot rely on a pedantic review of precedents.'[8] What he chose to call 'a pedantic review of precedents' was, in fact, the second most important source of international law according to the Statute of the International Court of Justice.

The occasion when Michel Debré made the comment quoted at the head of this chapter was the ruling of the European Court of Justice that French regulations preventing the import of sheep meat from Britain were illegal. Debré propounded a new principle of international law, namely that a nation could pick and choose which laws it would obey. In the sheep meat case, it was not just a principle of international law that was violated, but the Rome Treaty itself. When presidents and prime ministers justify their violations, it is because they perceive their interests to be threatened. Yet again we can see the need to attach importance to perceptions of dissatisfaction and vulnerability of people and nations. We should also add that there are people who argue vigorously in favour of obeying international law. Senator Tsongas's questioning of Haig is an example. During a great debate which followed the agreement with Iran on the release of American hostages, a senior senator on the Foreign Relations Committee, Alan Cranston, did not want the US to honour any part of the agreement that was 'against our national interest'. His reason was that 'The word you give under duress when hostages are being held, when kidnappers are at work, is different from the word freely given.' On the other hand, former Secretary of State, Edmund Muskie, the former Deputy Secretary and chief hostage negotiator, Warren Christopher, former White House Counsel Lloyd Cutler, Senator Charles Percy and Senate Minority Leader Robert Byrd all agreed that the United States should honour any commitments it had made or risk losing its international credibility.[9] In this example, we see the conflict between those who wanted to transfer into international law a principle of municipal law (a contract extracted under duress is *ab initio* invalid) and those who believed in the principle of implementing agreements entered into.

We have drawn attention repeatedly to the residue of dissatisfaction left behind after any agreement. Clearly, the residue left after an agreement imposed by a superior power will be considerable. Dissatisfactions, such as the complaint about 'unequal treaties' by China, show that there is a need for rule-systems that can accommodate changing power patterns. In any ICA, some members are bound to feel that their quotas are unfair. When a country increases its production and hence generates a surplus, its dissatisfaction increases and it then demands an upward revision. Provisions in ICAs for periodic renegotiation of quotas are designed to accommodate such demands.

Even without a major shift in the power balance, a rule-system may be strained by the residue of dissatisfaction looming larger because of the passage of time. The often-quoted British dissatisfaction with its contribution to the Community Budget is a case in point. While the principle that Britain would not be a net payer might be acceptable, it becomes unacceptable when, over the course of time, the actual amounts of contribution are perceived as onerous. Rule-systems have to provide for this type of contingency also.

Some dissatisfactions surface subsequently because, in the negotiations preceding the conclusion of an agreement, a dimension had been pushed to one side. One can find many examples in industrial disputes. Once wages, productivity norms, overtime rates and pension contributions are satisfactorily settled, the negotiants will then raise such issues as health and safety regulations, or absenteeism.

Fairness and unfairness are vital perceptions which affect how contracting parties judge the operation of a rule-system. President Reagan has said that he believes in free trade 'but it must also be fair trade.'[10] This kind of political dictum is illogical but illuminating: illogical because it attempts to compare something objective and quantifiable (e.g. the existence or absence of barriers to trade) with something wholly subjective like 'fairness' — we do, however, learn that 'free', in President Reagan's view, is qualified by his perception of equity. One view of what is fair is Greg Chappell's, quoted at the head of this chapter. Having done something totally unexpected (bowling the last ball of a cricket match underarm, so that victory could be ensured) Chappell justified his tactic by pointing out that there was nothing in the rules against it! People often talk about the 'spirit' of a rule; this is the underlying concept of fairness.

How Rules are Disobeyed

There is a whole range of methods by which a party to a rule-system can convey its dissatisfaction. In labour disputes, this is first voiced by filing a grievance. If nothing is done to redress it, the workforce may resort to a work to rule, or refuse to work overtime; eventually they may go on strike. Among the graded set of measures available, the last — strike action — amounts to repudiation of the rule-system as a whole. After a strike, everything in the old agreement is subject to renegotiation though, in practice, many old rules will be incorporated. In the UK-EEC Budget dispute, the graded set of actions have been: blocking progress in other areas such as an agreement on the fisheries policy; refusing to agree to price increases in the CAP; and insisting on the wholesale reform of the CAP. Refusing actually to transfer the amounts due to be paid into Community coffers would be the next step. Leaving the Community is the step repudiating the whole rule-system of the Rome Treaty.

On failure to implement obligations, the Vienna Convention of the Law of Treaties states that a nation cannot use domestic law as an excuse for not obeying the provisions of a treaty. This is not as draconian as it sounds; after all, nobody compels a country to negotiate and sign a treaty, if it does not want to change its internal law. The commitment of signing implies a willingness to change incompatible domestic legislation.

Non-compliance with treaty obligations can be illustrated by an example from ICAs, which require exporting member countries to report periodically their actual exports to the Council. Failure to report is an infraction of the rules. But it is important to examine why a country fails to report. The reason could be inefficiency in administration; if the country is one which otherwise obeys the rules, then it probably needs help, not punishment. On the other hand, non-reporting may be a deliberate tactic to conceal exports in excess of the permitted quota. This is a major infringement of the rules adversely affecting the export markets and the price for all exporters.

Similar to non-reporting is the case of member countries of international organisations not paying their dues. This could be due to genuine financial difficulties or could be used as a means of expressing disagreement. For example, the USSR has not paid its share of the costs of some of the peace-keeping operations of the United Nations because it did not approve of the UN involvement in those conflicts. The United States withheld, for a while, its budget contribution to the ILO because the organisation collectively was perceived as adopting an anti-Israel stance.

An act of commission, violating the rules of GATT, is subsidising the export of any product. Almost every country subsidises some sector or another, sometimes openly, more often covertly. The enormous subsidies given to ship-building and steel by almost every industrialised country are well known. Some subsidies (such as helping industrialisation of underdeveloped regions, assisting modernisation of older industries, relocating industry, retraining redundant workers, sharing in research and development costs) have valid economic and social objectives. They only become contentious when they cause injury to others.

The ultimate violation of a rule-system is its wholesale repudiation by a contracting party. This is not an uncommon phenomenon. Every treaty has a withdrawal provision, whereby a contracting party can withdraw from it after giving the required notice. Repudiation can occur for both rational and psychological reasons. A country can decide, on mostly objective calculations, that the costs of continuing within a rule-system are not commensurate with its benefits and that its net profit benefit would increase if it ceased to be a party to the treaty. The decision to withdraw can also be out of pique or anger: an angry Pakistan withdrew from the Commonwealth after Bangladeshi independence was recognised; the United States has given notice to withdraw from UNESCO.

Circumventing Rules

Circumventing a rule by calling the violation something else is an often-used technique. The most glaring example is the use of the 'voluntary export quotas' used by the United States and many European countries to restrict imports (e.g. of cars, TVs and videos) from Japan. The rules of GATT, drafted by the United States and Britain in accordance with their proclaimed principles of free trade, specifically prohibit discriminatory import controls. If a country, in exceptional and clearly-defined circumstances, has to impose a quantitative restriction the total quota should be available for competition from all member countries. Non-discriminatory application of tariffs and quotas is, in fact, a cardinal principle of GATT. But when the so-called free-traders want to restrict imports from Japan and find that they cannot do so legitimately, they apply pressure on Japan to restrict exports 'voluntarily'. This is yet another example of the use of political and economic power in disregard of voluntarily agreed rules.

Restrictions on imports from Japan only might well have become necessary because of the significant changes in the international economic scene since GATT came into force. In this case, GATT should have been amended accordingly. But GATT cannot be amended without admitting that the principle of free trade has failed. The developed countries are caught in the dilemma of professing one doctrine and having to practise another. One of the main causes of rule-circumvention is the hypocrisy of governments.

Hypocrisy is endemic in international trade and economics. The European countries castigate the US for its protectionist policies in steel; at the same time, in its Common Agricultural Policy, the Community operates the biggest protection system of all! US and European commentators vehemently castigate OPEC, as an oil cartel, but Britain, Australia and Canada rushed to pass laws protecting their companies found to be running a uranium cartel! All the developed countries join together in erecting high trade barriers against the imports of textile products from the poor countries under the Multi-Fibre Agreement (MFA, negotiated under GATT) whose main objective was to provide for an *orderly increase* in the textile and apparel exports from the poor to the developed countries. The MFA is now used unashamedly as a protectionist device.

Many are the tactics adopted to circumvent the rules of GATT and the principles of free trade. The US used peculiar valuation methods to restrict import of chemicals. Creating impenetrable administrative barriers and technical certification methods was the technique used by Japan to keep imports of foreign cars down to 60,000 a year, at a time when Japan itself was exporting 500,000! More rules, therefore, had to be created to counter the ease with which countries were circumventing the principles of free trade. At the end of the Tokyo Round a whole new set of Codes was negotiated. Creating these new rules does not mean that countries have stopped these practices. The much-publicised example of France ordering that all imports of Japanese videos had to go through a single customs point, manned by as few inspectors as possible, happened *after* the Tokyo Round was signed.

Though the Rome Treaty is a highly structured rule-system governing the economic activities of the European Community, the member countries often thwart the fundamental principles of economic integration. The contortions which Britain went through to prevent imports of UHT long-life liquid milk is a recent example. In this case, the actions of the British government were not merely a contravention of the Rome Treaty and rules of the CAP, but were adjudged illegal by the European Court of Justice. Another technique often used is to 'buy time' by continuing to practise a violation until actually ordered by the Court to stop it. Discriminatory duties between wine and beer or between home-produced and imported spirits is common practice. Preventing imports of sheep and pig meat or wine is a recurrent violation. A reluctant signatory will always exercise the utmost ingenuity in circumventing rules.

Towards More Effective Rule-Systems

Once a rule-system has been agreed, three different kinds of dissatisfaction can arise during its implementation: (i) difficulties that existed even while the rule-system was being negotiated; (ii) difficulties that were anticipated to occur during the operation of the agreement; and (iii) unanticipated difficulties.

Escape Mechanisms

The first two kinds of dissatisfaction can both be dealt with by escape mechanisms. In each case there are two techniques. Facts which are perceived as not being capable of being fitted into the proposed rule-system can be accommodated by reservations and exceptions. Difficulties which can be anticipated can be tackled by safeguards and waivers.

Reservations

Reservations can be made to a treaty at the time of accession by a party agreeing to abide by all the rules with the exception of the 'reserved' ones. This mechanism encourages parties to join if they can accept most of the clauses but have difficulties with a few. The other parties also have to agree to have a new member with less than total commitment. They have to judge which is the lesser evil — a conditional member, or one who can disrupt the system from outside.

Exceptions

These are a means of taking into account particular cases which do not fit into the general formula. GATT, for example, exempts from the most-favoured-nation (mfn) principle all the preferential arrangements extant on the day it came into force. ICAs generally provide for exceptional treatment for countries with unique problems, and also exempt very small producers from some obligations (e.g. freedom to export up to a limit without attracting quota provisions).

Safeguards

Safeguards are a protective device. The GATT safeguard provision deals with measures for restricting imports that can be imposed for a period by a country faced with an acute balance of payments crisis. The MFA provides for safeguards if imports threaten a particular segment of the textile industry of an importing country.

Waivers

These can be sought by a party either to relieve it from an obligation or to provide it with a special benefit. ICAs generally have provisions enabling exporting members to declare a shortfall; conversely, they can also be permitted selectively to export more than the allotted quota. In GATT, if a contracting party contemplates a departure from the rules, it cannot do so unilaterally but must seek a waiver.

To minimise dissatisfaction and, at the same time, protect the system, escape mechanisms must have clearly defined procedures. In their comprehensive article, 'Management of Trade Relations in the GATT', Gerard and Victoria Curzon have described GATT as an agreement in which 'each rule was accompanied by an exception, and each exception was governed by a procedure, which was intended to prevent the exception from swallowing up the rule.'[11]

Disputes

However well-intentioned and well-structured an agreement may be, it can never be perfect. Unforeseen dissatisfactions can grow into disputes. The Curzons have identified three methods of dealing with disputes — evasion, avoidance and settlement. Nobody can write a rule for dispute evasion; it happens when all parties tacitly agree to condone a violation and prefer not to raise it to a dispute.

Dispute Avoidance

Discouraging parties from attempting to violate the letter or spirit of a rule is essential for limiting conflicts. Rule-obedience can be encouraged and disputes avoided by having recourse to openness, inspection and supervision.

Transparency means the acceptance by all parties of an obligation to take all actions under a system openly and to notify all other parties of any action they take that might affect the others adversely. Every rule-system should have provisions against refusal to disclose information, exceptions, if any, being precisely specified.

Inspection is the means of permitting other parties to scrutinise and verify a notified action. For example, in ICAs stocks notified as existing have to be verified for both quantity and quality. The need for inspection in arms control agreements is obvious.

Supervision and surveillance are essential to the successful operation of any international rule-system. This could be either by a supra-national body or by an organ of the system itself. An example of supervision by an outside body was the creation of the International Commissions for Supervision and Control in the Indo-Chinese states (three separate ones, with identical tripartite membership). The Commissions became victims of the Viet Nam War and United States hostility to them. The Textile Supervisory Body (TSB), created within the MFA rule-system itself, has also failed to stop its misuse by the developed countries who changed it from a gently liberalising agreement to a blatantly protectionist one. The past experience of supervision in international agreements is thus not encouraging. But these failures only emphasise the need for more effective supervision and surveillance. In a world where there is little trust and where violations by countries in their perceived national interest are always probable, no rule-system can hope to survive unless it includes credible provisions for supervision.

Encouraging rule-obedience need not be viewed negatively as a restriction on the freedom and an infringement of the sovereignty of nations. Restraints imposed by international obligations are sometimes welcomed by governments as a means of dealing with domestic pressure groups (e.g. resisting protectionist pressures on the grounds that these will result in violations of GATT rules). International obligations can also be used to justify marginally unwelcome measures to a state's own citizens.

Dispute settlement

GATT experience suggests that for tackling disputes effectively, two conditions are necessary. First, any party must have the right to raise any point which it perceives to be a violation of obligations adversely affecting its own interests. Second, the other parties, including the alleged violator, must consider the complaint. The *right to speak and the right to be listened to* are fundamental to the promotion of rule-obedience.

Once a complaint is heard, GATT allows a period of time for bilateral consultations, if the threatened dispute concerns only two parties. Other procedures are brought in only if the two fail to come to an agreement. The mechanism of a *cooling-off period* is also one which the President of the United States can impose in labour disputes when a strike is imminent.

The Covenant of the League of Nations also had in it a provision for a cooling-off period. Members undertook not to resort to war for at least three months after a dispute was referred to any of the League's organs. Though, in principle, this was a sound provision, the members of the League of Nations did not obey it often enough to prevent aggression.

Any rule-system must have adequate procedures to deal with disputes brought formally before all contracting parties. The aim must be to ensure that dissatisfaction after the dispute is settled is not greater than the dissatisfaction that gave rise to it. The components of a dispute settlement procedure are the following.

Investigation. This procedure should not be sketchy but provide for the taking of evidence and verification wherever necessary. The example, given earlier, of the need to verify that non-reporting by an exporting member in an ICA was not a means for covering up excess exports, is relevant. As in the case of inspection, there should be as few loopholes as possible for a party to refuse to disclose information.

Determination has the aim of establishing whether any rule has been violated, whether other parties are likely to suffer as a consequence and, if so, to what extent. From this must emerge sets of alternative courses of action. Political considerations and subjective perceptions will play a part in this phase. The experience of the tripartite International Commissions in Indo-China shows that, when political attitudes become predominant, determination is impossible.

Enforcement. A dissatisfied party can adopt a series of actions to express it — from voicing a grievance to opting out of the system altogether. Correspondingly the provisions for enforcement must also be numerous and graded. The reward for rule-obedience is the benefits which flow to a party. If the sanctions and punishments are not graduated, as they are not in ICAs, disputes either tend to become entangled with larger issues or are raised to the political level to be settled by exercise of voting power. Enlargement of the bargaining space and decision-making by power both carry the risk of total dissatisfaction increasing.

One cannot write out a single set of graded sanctions that could be applied to all rule-systems. In industrial disputes, the set to be used against employees might include reprimand, censure, loss of leave, loss of pay and, for repeated violations, the ultimate sanction of dismissal. The set to be used against the employer might include compelling withdrawal of offending action, cash compensation and, in the worst cases, prosecution in a Tribunal or a court of law.

In treaties between governments requiring removal of an injury-causing action, permitting others to take retaliatory or countervailing action, or providing compensation to the injured are some of the sanctions that can be used. There is really no equivalent to dismissal in multilateral treaties. The expulsion of a disobedient member merely encourages that member to continue with the violation outside the constraints of the system. In practice, a party likely to be expelled usually opts out first. One sanction usually provided in treaties is the denial of voting rights (i.e. taking away the right to participate in decision-making). This drastic measure is usually threatened only for non-payment of financial contributions.

Enforcement under international law will always be less satisfactory than enforcement under municipal law. Persuasion, threat of denial of some benefit, actual denial of benefit, threat of imposition of a special disadvantage, actual imposition of the disadvantage — a series of such sanctions, short of expulsion or ostracism, have to be inscribed in rule-systems.

An ever-shrinking world does not contain only disputing states; it has other states and institutions which may have an interest either in escalating the dispute or limiting it. How third-party intercession can help to limit conflicts is the subject of the next chapter.

Notes

1. The Convention consists of 17 parts with 320 Articles and nine Annexes with over 100 Articles. The major subjects covered in the main parts are: territorial sea including passage by merchant ships and warships, the zone contiguous to the territorial sea, straits used for international navigation, archipelagic states, the exclusive economic zone with special reference to fishing, the continental shelf, freedom of the high seas, piracy, submarine cables, the rights of landlocked states, the regime for mining the deep seabed, including setting up an authority and an

enterprise for this purpose, protection of the marine environment with particular reference to pollution, marine scientific research and development of marine technology.

2. For more information, see two articles in the *Third World Quarterly*, by Dr S.P. Jagota in the April 1981 issue, and by Elizabeth Mann Borgese in the October 1982 issue.

3. *The Economist*, 16 May 1981. The paper commented that the unilateral breach of the Memorandum of Understanding 'might result in a loss of confidence in the US as the major partner in international space research.'

4. J.M. Brierly, *The Law of Nations: An Introduction to the International Law of Peace* (Oxford, Clarendon Press, 5th edn., 1955), p. 246.

5. As soon as their 'walk in the woods' became public, both governments repudiated the unofficial arrangement worked out in private by the two chief negotiators (Paul Nitze for the US and Yuri Kitvinsky for the USSR) at the Geneva arms control talks to limit warheads to 225 each.

6. For more details, see L.N. Rangarajan, *Commodity Conflict: The Political Economy of International Commodity Negotiations* (London, Croom Helm, 1978), especially Chapter 2, 'More Disagreements than Agreements'.

7. The quotations are respectively from *International Herald Tribune*, 12 Jan. 1981, and *Guardian*, 12 Jan. 1981.

8. F.S. Northedge and M.D. Donelan, *International Disputes: The Political Aspects* (London, Europa Publications for The David Davies Memorial Institute for International Studies, 1971), p. 322. The source (House of Commons Debates) is given in the note thereto.

9. *International Herald Tribune*, 26 and 27 Jan. 1981.

10. President Reagan, addressing the American Legion Convention, pledged 'to foster the continued pattern of even freer trade which has served the world so well. It must also be fair trade.' (Official text distributed by US-ICA.)

11. Gerard and Victoria Curzon, 'The Management of Trade Relations in GATT', in Andrew Shonfield (ed.) with Hermia Oliver, *International Economic Relations of the Western World, 1959-71, Vol. I, Politics and Trade* (London, Oxford University Press for the Royal Institute of International Affairs, 1976).

16 CONCILIATION, MEDIATION, ARBITRATION AND ADJUDICATION

> Wherefore, brethren, look ye among you seven men of honest report, full of the Holy Ghost and wisdom, whom we may appoint over this business.
> *Acts* 6: 3

The four methods of third-party intercession in settling disputes fall into two distinct classes. In arbitration and adjudication the disputants agree to accept the terms of a settlement *dictated* to them by an arbitrator or judge. In mediation and conciliation, the disputants are *persuaded* to agree among themselves on the terms of a settlement. Within this broad classification, the methods differ considerably. In Table 16.1 the differences are summarised under 16 different headings.

The four methods of third-party intervention are important for limiting all types of conflicts. Their use in labour disputes is now recognised as so important that many countries have set up special bodies to promote peaceful settlement of disputes.[1]

We must note that, even when third-party assistance is invoked, negotiations are required to appoint mediators or conciliators, to choose arbitrators, or decide on the remit to be given to the arbitrator and to choose the presiding member of tribunals. Negotiation underlies all methods of dispute settlement.

Since this book is primarily about limitation of conflicts between states, this chapter is largely devoted to examining the four methods in relation to international disputes. It is a fact that governments are disinclined to accept impartial binding arbitration and prefer political methods of dispute settlement. For example, GATT offers a choice of two methods: a panel of conciliation and the somewhat larger working parties which include the disputing members. While panels can propose compromise solutions, working parties tend to produce majority and minority reports and no constructive solutions. Even so, there is more recourse in GATT to the latter.

I have to add the usual caution that this chapter is by no means comprehensive, either on the methods themselves or on dispute

Table 16.1: Third-party Intercession: the four techniques compared

Aspect	Conciliation	Methods of Persuasion — Mediation	Arbitration	Methods of Dictation — Adjudication
General				
1. When used	After dispute arises but before too much bitterness	Before, during and after violent action	Prior agreement before dispute arises; sometimes after	Generally after other methods fail
2. The technique and the law	If method fails may lead to adjudication	Avoids having to go to court	Has legal force	Recourse to law
Acceptance of method				
3. Acceptance by disputants	Voluntary attendance	Voluntary	Voluntary prior acceptance	No need for all disputants to agree
4. Aim of disputants in using technique	To avoid total breakdown	To avoid violent unilateral action	(i) in case of rights to avoid violent action (ii) in case of issues to create new rules	To establish rights by law
5. When rejected	When there is little goodwill	When acceptable mediator cannot be found	If half-way point between last positions unacceptable to one disputant	Cannot be rejected in domestic disputes; can be internationally
6. Emotional state of disputants	Enough goodwill to seek conciliation	Some goodwill helps	Objective	Goodwill unnecessary
7. Nature of decision expected	Harmonising	That which will prevent violent action	At least half-way between last positions	Unpredictable
Implementation				
8. Selection of person	Service may be taken advantage of	Mediator chosen by mutual consent	Arbitrator selected by mutual consent or equal number by each disputant with umpire	No choice

9. Qualification of person	More concerned with human relationships and psychology	Expert knowledge not essential but basic knowledge necessary	Has to have expertise	Legal background
10. Remit	Determined by conciliator and disputants	Within bargaining space	Strictly limited	Prescribed by legal system
11. Privacy	Strictly private	Mostly private	Hearings private; decisions public	Public
12. Time taken to reach decision	Uncertain	Uncertain	Quicker than adjudication	Long
13. Nature of decision	Reconciliation main aim not decision	Can only suggest	Binding award mostly judicially enforceable	Decision binding and non-compliance subject to penalties
14. Cost	Least expensive	More expensive than conciliation but less than the other two	Moderately expensive	Most expensive
Future				
15. Compliance after decision	High probability of compliance	Depends on residues of dissatisfaction	High in binding arbitration; repudiation rare	Backed by sanctions
16. Next step	Recourse to law	Strike or other disruptive action	None; in a few cases, courts	Hierarchy of courts

settlement in international treaties. The UN has published two surveys on Treaties and Treaty Provisions for the Pacific Settlement of Disputes, covering the periods 1928–1948 and 1949–1962. There are various regional treaties on pacific settlement of disputes. UNCITRAL has produced Rules on International Arbitration. International arbitrated awards are published in an authoritative series. There are many books on commercial arbitration and arbitration in labour disputes. My aim is limited to relating third party intercession to limitation of conflict.

Mediation and Conciliation

These two techniques, both depending on persuasion for achieving an agreed outcome, have many things in common, the difference between them being the psychological approach adopted by the disputants as well as by the person chosen to be third party. Conciliation has the underlying concept of harmonising different points of view. Mediation, displaying its obsolete meaning of 'to divide into two parts', implies a middle position between the disputants. The mediator plays a more active role and may even be expected to act as the guarantor of any settlement that might be reached.

Mediators and conciliators have to work with facts as well as emotions, because conflicts and negotiations are a mixture of rationality and irrationality. In disputes between husbands and wives, a Court of Conciliation, being a forum for composing differences, may sometimes be so successful that it even prevents the break-up of the marriage; in most cases it helps in settling contentious issues (such as custody of children and division of mutually-held property) with the least possible psychological damage to the disputants and especially the children. Any settlement is voluntary and the degree of compliance is usually very high. Clearly, a dispute settled by conciliation leaves behind a much smaller residue of dissatisfaction; the chances of further conflicts arising from this residue are therefore much less.

Conciliation has time and cost advantages; in fact, it is the cheapest of all four methods. The procedure is usually informal and the disputants speak for themselves and not through the mouths of advocates. They have the opportunity to vent their frustrations. If the party whose actions have given rise to the dissatisfactions takes them seriously and undertakes to ameliorate them, the dispute gets limited to a few dimensions, or even none at all.

Conciliation is a useful technique for all types of conflicts. The two prerequisites are (i) the disputants must have had a close and multi-linked relationship, and (ii) there must have been mutual trust, at least some time in the past. Conciliation is ineffective if a dispute has already reached the stage of bitterness, caused by dissatisfaction in at least one disputant turning into unrelievable frustration. Adopted in time, when there is still adequate goodwill, it is the best method for limiting conflicts.

A mediator also tries to reconcile, but both the technique and the role of the chosen mediator are more complex. Even the selection of a mediator sometimes becomes a dispute. In a dispute in the US between baseball players and club owners, the two sides had no difficulty in agreeing to have a Federal mediator who played an active role. On the other hand, when the players of the National Football League went on strike in 1982, they rejected the offer of help from the Federal Mediation and Conciliation Service. It was only in the fourth week of the strike that the two sides were able to agree to appoint a private mediator.

A mediator, unlike an arbitrator, cannot make an award but can only make recommendations. Unlike a conciliator, a mediator need not do all his work with both parties present; he can act as a communicator, meet the disputants individually and put forward different proposals. Though he may suggest splitting the difference, the disputants are under no compulsion to accept this. Mediation differs from conciliation and arbitration in being able to continue during and after a violent action, like a strike. If conciliation breaks down, the dispute ends up in the courts and the chances of it reverting back are remote.

Arbitration and Adjudication

Both arbitration and adjudication are legal processes; in fact, some writers on international disputes do not even make a distinction between them.[2] But there are some significant differences, the most important being that all the disputants have to agree to subject a dispute to arbitration. In disputes domiciled within a state, one party can go to court whether the others like it or not. Going to an international court in disputes between states has, until now, been more like arbitration than adjudication. With the coming into operation of the European Court of Justice, we now have to make the distinction between arbitration and adjudication in international disputes also.

There is a great deal of informal arbitration in everyday life. Parents arbitrate in disputes between children, and a superior does so in the office. That the person in authority has the power to guarantee its implementation is only one part of it; making the award in such a way that the least amount of dissatisfaction is left behind is the essence of a good arbitration award.

In all disputes which are confined within the boundaries of a state, arbitration has the backing of the law and the award of an arbitrator, if undertaken under the relevant Arbitration Acts, is enforceable through the courts. In transnational disputes, such as those between traders in different countries or between shipowners and charterers, the parties agree beforehand where and how arbitration is to be effected. The International Chamber of Commerce or well-established centres like London are normally used. In commercial disputes, it is usual for each party to nominate an arbitrator; these together then choose an umpire; decisions are by majority.

Arbitration as a dispute settlement mechanism is agreed to by the negotiants *prior* to the implementation of an agreement and before any dispute even arises because it is perceived to be more advantageous than adjudication. The expert knowledge which an arbitrator brings to bear helps in reducing the time taken to reach a decision. The proceedings are usually held in private, a consideration important for preserving commercial secrecy.

The selection of a qualified arbitrator or umpire in commercial disputes usually poses no problem. In labour disputes, the range of options is wider. In some cases (e.g. British Rail) the arbitration mechanism is part and parcel of the agreement between management and the unions and a permanent institution is set up. In others, recourse to arbitration is left as a possibility and the help of a governmental arbitration body may or may not be taken. The question of whether the arbitrator's award should be binding or not can also be left vague. This itself can become a point of conflict.

Whether the disputants agree to binding arbitration or not depends on what they expect the eventual award of the arbitrator to be. It is generally assumed that an arbitrator splits the difference, that is to say, the award is approximately midway between the last positions of the negotiants on the most important dimensions. If one of the disputants feels that the midpoint is beyond what he is prepared to agree to (his limit position) he will be reluctant to accept binding arbitration. In Britain, Mrs Thatcher's government became unhappy with arbitration in disputes involving the state sector, because it was felt that half-way awards were always in excess of the limits for pay increases it set.

Is an arbitrator, like a judge, a totally disinterested person? Where an arbitrator is not a single individual but a board of three or five (or any odd number), the arbitrator nominated by one of the disputants is expected, in part, to act as an advocate of the nominator. This does not seem to affect the acceptability of the outcome because an arbitrator can either stop pressing his nominator's case or can be outvoted. The arbitrator, though he can argue for a disputant, is not directly involved; unlike the disputants he does not carry the burden of emotional and psychological history. The fact that a small number of people work in private assists in building up personal relationships and linkages of trust. Two concepts referred to earlier — trust and reduction in numbers — are again seen to be relevant to limitation of conflict.

An important difference between arbitration and adjudication is that the jurisdiction of the former is strictly limited. That arbitrators should not 'introduce in their award questions which have not been left to them' is an accepted legal principle. A judge in a court of law, on the other hand, can range as widely as he likes and take into account in his judgement not only the law as it stands, but also case law, the principles of natural justice and pepper it with *obiter dicta*. Within the limit of his remit, an arbitrator can exercise his judgement subjectively, taking into account fairness and equity. He need not, unless he chooses to, give reasons for his award; every judge has to justify in detail his reasons for the judgement.

Arbitration in commercial disputes is invariably about money; the compensation for loss or damage can be computed in cash terms. Arbitration of labour disputes can be of two kinds — either to secure a right already believed to exist or to create a new right. In the first case, arbitration is a method of redressing a grievance (e.g. labour's complaint that adequate safety equipment or canteen facilities, previously agreed to, have not been provided; employer's complaint that the workforce is not permitting him to exercise his right to appoint supervisors or managers). Awards on rights should be fairly easy to arrive at, but are often made difficult by the expectations of the disputants on fairness and equity. Arbitration of rights disputes avoids the need for taking disruptive action every time a dispute arises.

While rights disputes are concerned with rule-obedience, disputes can also be about rule-creation. Manning levels are an obvious example. How many workers are required in a paint shop or how many are needed in a railway engine or aircraft cockpit are not immutable rights. Preservation of the total number of jobs in an industry or among the members of a union can be made a 'right' only if it is first negotiated as an issue and written down in an agreement. Though arbitration is possible in such cases, rule-creation by this method is more difficult.

Arbitration awards — even binding ones — can be repudiated by a disputant. The conflict then moves to a different level. A strike may ensue or enforcement may be sought in a law court.

Adjudication through the courts is time-consuming and expensive. In disputes confined within a state, the decision is made at the end of a hierarchy of courts, as high as the disputants can afford to go. The court procedure is made more objective by the disputants being represented by lawyers and decisions being made by judges with no personal interest in the dispute, not even arbitration fees.

As in other methods, the sense of fairness plays a major role in the judicial process. A dissatisfied employer can sack a worker; whether the dismissal was 'fair' or 'unfair' can, in Britain, be taken for adjudication by an industrial tribunal. Many countries provide for a variety of judicial bodies — family courts, labour tribunals, administrative courts like tax tribunals and immigration tribunals. The right to appeal is an integral part of the adjudication process.

Not all disputes are resolved by a court pronouncement: Brierly quotes two instances in which the decisions of courts have had exactly the reverse effect, and have been contributory causes to the outbreak of war. 'The Hampden case in Britain in 1637 in which the court declared on the question of ship money and the Dred Scot case in 1857 when the American Supreme Court declared on the law on slavery; both were followed by civil wars, fought, in part, to determine the very issues which the court had decided.'[3] Later in this chapter we shall note another example of a decision of the International Court of Justice which intensified the conflict in Southern Africa.

Conciliation and Mediation in International Conflicts

A great deal of conciliatory effort — often called 'good offices' — goes on in international disputes without ever coming into prominence. In the European Community, countries which do not perceive an issue as vital to them make efforts at conciliation because they have a stake in preventing these disputes from becoming more intractable. In the Disarmament Conference, non-aligned countries like India and Yugoslavia and neutral countries like Switzerland and Sweden constantly make efforts to bridge the gap between the super-power blocs. In the Law of the Sea Conference, a group of 11 medium and small industrialised countries formed themselves into a 'Friends of the Conference' and attempted conciliation between the United States and the developing countries.

It is not in the head-line-catching crises of the world that we should look for evidence of the success of conciliation. It is in small things like producing an acceptable division of quotas in ICAs that day-to-day conciliation succeeds. In these negotiations, a small group of respected figures (usually 'three wise men') are appointed to act as conciliators. They meet all the interested parties and suggest a solution which is an amalgam of what would be seen as fair and what would cause the least amount of dissatisfaction. The conciliators may be selected from the importers or the exporters groups, their main asset being the degree of trust the others place in them.

The mere fact of nominating three people is no guarantee that they will produce an acceptable solution. In the three-member ICSCs in the Indo-Chinese countries, with Canada and Poland advocating the points of view of the opposing sides and India in the uneasy middle, any unanimous decision was inconsequential and any majority decision was unacceptable to either North or South Viet Nam. The Soviet Union's proposal to appoint a 'troika' instead of a single Secretary-General of the UN did not find favour with anyone because three members who are unwise enough to quarrel among themselves, will be quite ineffective in limiting conflicts.

Conciliation has been written in as a procedure available for dispute settlement in many treaties. Under the 'Bryan Treaties', concluded after 1914, the United States and Britain agreed to refer all disputes between them to a standing Peace Commission of five members which was required to investigate and report on disputes within one year and the two countries undertook not to resort to war until the report was received. The Hague Convention for the Pacific Settlement of Disputes had a provision for 'Commissions of Inquiry', which were required to investigate the facts of a dispute and make a report without giving it the character of an award. The Locarno Pacts of 1925 had a similar mechanism. On the whole, such Commissions were not made much use of, probably because disputes which are purely political have little to do with facts but more to do with what states believe they want and deserve.[4]

An area well worth studying further is why conciliation sometimes succeeds and in dealing with what kinds of problems. It may then be possible to form some practical ideas about the stage when conciliation should be attempted in order to limit conflicts.

Successful examples of international mediation are easier to find. In 1965, India and Pakistan fought two wars — a small one in the Rann of Kutch in April, and a much bigger one all along the border in August and September. In the first conflict, a ceasefire was brought about and the parties persuaded to remit the question to arbitration with the mediatory help of Britain. After the second, the successful mediation of the USSR assisted India and Pakistan in reaching an agreement in Tashkent in January 1966. In the dispute between Argentina and Chile about the Beagle Channel islands, arbitration failed but mediation looks likely to succeed. The two countries almost came to the brink of war when Argentina rejected the arbitration tribunal's award. The Pope then intervened and the two countries accepted a papal representative as mediator. He was unsuccessful so long as a military government was in power in Argentina; after the return of civilian rule, the two countries announced the acceptance of the settlement proposed by the papal mediator in 1979.

There are examples of successful mediation by institutions other than governments. In 1961, the World Bank successfully mediated between India and Pakistan on the sharing of the waters of the Indus river system. In this case, the Bank acted as a guarantor, undertaking to provide the financial resources for the development of the rivers. In 1972, the World Council of Churches played a crucial role in helping to bring about an end to the civil war between the Government of Sudan and the Anya Nya movement of the peoples of Southern Sudan. Though only superficial details are available, it is clear that the Church in Poland plays an important role in conflict-limitation in that country.

The ability of the United States to act as a guarantor was not the only reason for President Carter's success as a mediator in negotiating the Camp David agreements between Israel and Egypt. Notwithstanding the superficial impressions of the quality of the Carter presidency, he undoubtedly exercised remarkable skill as a mediator. Contrary to what one would expect, Carter found that Sadat trusted him too much and Begin not enough! Begin's distrust appears to have been aroused by the amount of prestige that the President had invested in reaching a peaceful settlement. Correspondingly, Sadat appears to have been encouraged by the evident sincerity which Carter brought to his role. The skill and trustworthiness of an individual mediator play a significant part, even if he is known to be less than totally impartial.

That not all US mediation in the Middle East conflict has been successful is shown by the later failure of its efforts in Lebanon. A reason for this failure was that the United States ignored (or took for granted) a party with vital interests, namely, Syria. This failure has had the curious effect of bringing in another mediator, Saudi Arabia, to mediate between the first mediator and a disputant! At this stage, even mediation became complex, with the result we all know. Refusal to recognise, bad enough when it is practised by disputants, is worse when it is practised by a mediator. After all, the main role of a mediator is to talk to the disputants who may not want to talk to each other.

Successful mediation can be undone by changes in the environment. In 1975, Algeria successfully mediated between Iraq and Iran, then ruled by the Shah, on the Shatt-el-Arab dispute. When the Shah was overthrown, Iraq saw an opportunity to get what it wanted by recourse to war. In 1964, General Abboud, then President of Sudan, played a significant mediatory role in the conflict between Ethiopia and Somalia by not only helping to bring about a ceasefire, but also in getting the parties to agree to a more lasting solution. That conflict again erupted into violence mainly because glowing dissatisfaction was fanned into flames by super-power rivalry. Mediation should not always be expected to settle a conflict with peace ever after; even if it succeeds only in postponing violence, it achieves limitation for a period.

Though historically a mediator has been an individual, a recent tendency is for mediation to be undertaken by groups of countries. While the super-powers are powerful enough in themselves to take on this role, other countries find an institution a useful umbrella for mediation efforts. The Islamic Conference and the non-aligned nations have both tried group mediation in the Iran—Iraq War. The Contadora group of South American countries have tried the same in the dispute between the United States and Nicaragua. The evidence available so far does not indicate that group mediation is any more or any less successful than individual mediation. As in the case of conciliation, failure may well be due to their tackling the most difficult problems like disarmament, the Iran—Iraq War or conflicts with super-power involvement.

The last named conflict has also had UN mediation. The Secretary-General of the UN is often asked to mediate by the Security Council only because the Council itself is unable to decide what to do. The present Secretary-General, Mr Perez de Cuellar, was himself a mediator in the Cyprus conflict. It is no fault of his, or his successor, that a settlement is as remote as ever. Both Greece and Turkey are members of NATO and the one power which could mediate and be a guarantor of a settlement, the United States, has chosen not to play this role. By asking the Secretary-General to mediate the Security Council passes the buck; he is, after all, subject to the same political constraints as the great powers in the Council.

States often reject offers of mediation. Iran rejected mediation for bringing about an end to the Iran—Iraq War because no mediator can bring about the kind of preconditions (e.g. removal of President Saddam Hussain) that Iran sets. In the Falklands conflict, mediation could not succeed because handing over sovereignty was a precondition set by Argentina. A powerful country will reject mediation if it thinks that aggression will change the environment to its benefit. Mediation is also rejected on the grounds of sovereignty and nationalism if a country perceives a conflict to be an internal affair. A case in point is the report which a Committee of the European Parliament prepared on the Northern Ireland conflict. Though the report was well-intentioned and contained nothing against the vital interests of the UK, Mrs Thatcher's government rejected it as an unwarranted intrusion. Rejection of mediation is always a step moving a conflict towards violence.

Arbitration in International Disputes

International arbitration has a long history. It was common in Europe in the middle ages for the Pope to be called upon to act as sole arbitrator. In the eighteenth and nineteenth centuries some disputes between the United States and Great Britain were also settled by arbitration. The first and second international conferences to codify the procedures for international arbitration were held in The Hague in 1889 and 1907. The Hague Convention stated: 'International arbitration has for its object the settlement of disputes between states by Judges *of their own choice* and on the basis of respect for international law. Recourse to arbitration implies an engagement to submit in good faith to the award' (emphasis added). In 1902 a Permanent Court of Arbitration was set up, with each signatory country appointing four members to it. From the pool so formed, arbitrators could be selected by the disputants. After the League of Nations came into being, the Court became a Permanent Court of Justice and was renamed the International Court of Justice (ICJ) under the United Nations Charter. The ICJ now has 15 permanent judges.

The ICJ has retained two important characteristics derived from its history as a court of arbitration. First, recourse to it has to have the consent of all the disputants, and second, countries still have the right to nominate an *ad hoc* judge of their own nationality if one is not already on the bench. Article 36(2) of the Statute of the ICJ is the misleadingly named 'optional' clause under which states can accept beforehand the compulsory jurisdiction of the Court. Not many have made Declarations accepting this clause and those that do hedge it about with limitations, reservations and conditions. An example is the Connally Amendment to the Declaration of the United States accepting the optional clause. By this amendment, the United States reserved the right to define what were matters of domestic jurisdiction, in effect saying that it was up to the US to decide on what cases it would accept the compulsory jurisdiction of the ICJ. When Britain first accepted the clause in 1929, four classes of disputes were excepted from the purview of the Court, the practical effect of which was to remove most disputes from the ICJ's jurisdiction. In 1957, Britain amended its Declaration to remove jurisdiction on matters it judged to involve national security to prevent the question of the legality of its nuclear tests in the Pacific being brought before the ICJ. The

Soviet Union, though it has always had a judge on the Bench, has never taken much notice of the Court. When the United States rushed to remove from the jurisdiction of the ICJ the legality of its helping to mine the territorial waters of Nicaragua, it was only doing what any great power could be expected to do.

In theory, nominations to the judiciary of the ICJ are to be made by 'national groups' of legal personalities, giving the impression that these are independent choices. In practice, all candidates are nominated by governments and the election is by members of the General Assembly and the Security Council of the UN voting separately. The election of the judges is as much a political process as any issue before the UN.

The fact that disputants, even when they agree to the arbitration of the ICJ, can nominate an ad hoc judge of their own nationality shows that states want to have an advocate on the Bench. This distrust is not surprising in a world where exclusive nationalism reigns supreme.

Reserving the right to accept or reject the jurisdiction of the Court is an indication that states do not want impartial arbitration, even if it can be relied upon to produce 'fair' decisions. Unfortunately, there are good reasons for distrusting the ability of the Court to produce credible judgments. First, it takes many years to pronounce on any dispute; in a rapidly changing world, few states have the patience to wait on the Court and not be tempted to alter the *status quo*. Second, the Court has always been conservative (in the sense of cautious) and legalistic, and has never found a way of dealing with new problems which need a law-creating role.

Adjudicating by the ICJ is often rejected because the side proposing it is favoured by the existing legal situation while the other side is calling for a change in the law.

> In the South Tyrol question ... judicial settlement was proposed by Italy, the country benefiting from the *status quo*, while Austria, who wished a change in the *status quo*, was opposed to settlement by judges on the basis of existing law. ... In the Anglo-Icelandic fisheries question, it suited the United Kingdom that the dispute should go to the world court ... but the Icelandic government, which was arguing on behalf of a change in the law of the sea ... was naturally unwilling.[5]

In the dispute between Ethiopia and Somalia, the former was willing to submit the dispute to the ICJ, because the 1908 treaty between the two countries favoured its case. Somalia rejected this because a conservative Court could not be trusted to give the comparatively new principle of 'right of self-determination' greater importance than the principle of 'sanctity of treaties'.

Inordinate delays and the inability to deal with a changing world are shown by the Court's attitude to the question of independence for Namibia. The Court dealt with this question more or less continuously over a period of 21 years and gave six advisory opinions and two important judgments in 1962 and 1966, which contradicted each other. In the 1966 case the Court ruled that, though Ethiopia and Liberia had been members of the defunct League of Nations, they had no right to challenge before it the administration of the mandated territory by South Africa. This judgement has been criticised on legal grounds since all preliminary points were supposed to have been settled by the 1962 judgement, and the 1966 ruling was intended to be about the merits of the case. Credibility of the Court did not improve by its splitting 7-7, the decision being made by the Australian president casting his vote in favour of South Africa, having already used his own vote to bring about the tie; nor, when it turned out that the Pakistani judge had been made to withdraw by the President using unusual methods.[6] For 15 years, it was the newly-emergent states which placed faith in the Court and in the rule of international law in trying to secure independence for Namibia from an illegal annexation by South Africa; it was the judges from the European countries and the Australian president who undermined that faith. The Court's bare majority decision, far from limiting the conflict, only led to more violence and injustice, a state of affairs for which the end does not seem to be in sight.

The ineffectiveness of the ICJ is also due to the fact that it cannot escape the reality that international disputes are political in every sense of the word. In spite of the increase in the number of treaties regulating diverse international activities, few disputes within the specialised agencies of the UN system have been referred to the ICJ for advisory opinions. The states have always preferred to settle these by political negotiation. The decline of the Court parallels the increasing politicisation of all international activity.

Notwithstanding the failure of the ICJ, arbitration as a mechanism for the peaceful settlement of international disputes is not totally defunct. The Rann of Kutch conflict between India and Pakistan, which erupted into hostilities in April 1965, concerned the claim by both countries to 3500 square miles in the northern part of the marshy Rann. After a ceasefire was negotiated, the two countries agreed to refer the dispute to an international tribunal. India nominated a Yugoslav judge and Pakistan, an Iranian. Since the two countries were unable to agree on the chairman, the Secretary-General of the UN nominated a Swedish judge. In February 1968, the Court announced its majority award (Yugoslav judge dissenting) giving Pakistan approximately 350 square miles and the rest to India. The two governments accepted the award within days of each other, even though there was a public outcry and agitation against acceptance in India. The award was implemented in full by boundary demarcation and an exchange of maps in July 1969. Within a period of four years, a dispute which had erupted into a war was fully settled. The importance of this case lies in acknowledging that (i) the acceptance of the rule of international law by newly-independent states with a legacy of colonial boundary problems is just as good, if not better, than by the 'civilised' nations of Europe; (ii) it was necessary for the bigger country, India, which had reason to be dissatisfied with the award, to accept it and face its internal troubles; and (iii) the countries involved did not have the kind of cordial relationship which some writers see as essential for the settlement of disputes by arbitration.[7]

Unlike the Rann of Kutch dispute, the Beagle Channel islands dispute provides an example where the award of the arbitrators was repudiated by one disputant. The source of the dispute, ostensibly the ownership of three tiny islands in the Beagle Channel in the southernmost tip of the South American continent, was really about whether Chile was to have any foothold in the Atlantic Ocean or be only a Pacific Ocean state. Argentina claimed that the two-ocean principle was agreed to in a Protocol of 1893, whereas Chile claimed that, under a Treaty of 1881, it was assigned all islands west of Tierra del Fuego and south of the Beagle Channel down to Cape Horn, thus including the three islands. The dispute was not just about the islands but all the rights to the sea that might go with it — the exploitation of oil, minerals, fish and krill, and establishing Antarctic bases. The two countries agreed in July 1971 to submit the dispute to arbitration by the British Crown, as provided for in a Treaty of 1902 (on the expiry of this Treaty in 1972, this was changed to arbitration by the ICJ).

The Queen appointed five judges of the ICJ as the Arbitration Tribunal which produced an award in February 1978, giving the three islands to Chile. This was rejected in January 1978 by Argentina, which declared that 'nothing could oblige Argentina to accept a decision against its "vital interests".' As a result of this rejection, belligerency increased on both sides and the two countries almost came to war in April 1978.

There is a contradiction between the concept of 'vital interests' and the rule of law implied in accepting binding arbitration. In 1903, Great Britain and France entered into an arbitration treaty agreeing to refer matters to The Hague Court provided 'they do not affect the vital interests, the independence or the honour of the two states.' When the United States made an arbitration treaty, the Senate insisted that every special agreement on referring a dispute to arbitration had to be sent to it for advice and consent. Since a vital interest is what any country thinks it is, a world in which exclusive nationalism and absolute sovereignty dominate cannot also be a world of impartial arbitration.

Adjudication in International Disputes

So far as I know, the only example of states voluntarily submitting to rule of law by a supra-national court is the European Court of Justice, established by the Treaties of the European Communities. The earliest, the 1951 Treaty establishing the Coal and Steel Community, set the precedent for an independent court to judge disputes arising from the Treaty. The two Rome Treaties of 1957, establishing the Economic Community and Euratom, carried this principle over. The surrender of sovereignty to a court was one of the most important of the many far-reaching decisions taken by the founders of European integration. As the example of the United Nations has shown, even the horrifying experiences of the second world war have not been adequate to persuade states to surrender sovereignty; such decisions require vision and courage. Another far-reaching innovation was to make the Court open to anyone, individuals or juridical persons, and not merely the states. A similar right of individuals to approach the European Court of Human Rights is also a landmark in promoting the rule of law internationally.

The sheep meat case cited earlier is evidence that the road to full acceptance of the European Court's judgements is not an easy one. It should not surprise us if it takes many years before Britain harmonises the duties on beer and wine, or Italy the duties on whisky and locally-produced spirits. Acceptance of judgements given by a supra-national court is a new phenomenon in international politics. The sanctions which the European Court can impose are such that states can ignore them if they want to. Nevertheless, the Court has been successful in interpreting the Community Treaties in Community interest. With every obedience to the Court's judgement, the propensity to obey is strengthened and eventually obedience will become a matter of habit.

Peaceful Settlement of Disputes

The massive document of the Law of the Sea has the most comprehensive list of dispute settlement procedures ever to be inscribed in an international treaty. Apart from a separate Part (XV) on Settlement of Disputes, many special mechanisms are to be created for various issues likely to prove contentious. Article 279 imposes an obligation, piously accepted by all the signatories, to settle disputes by peaceful means. Article 283 provides for a mechanism called 'exchange of issues' (equivalent to settlement by bilateral negotiation in GATT) to enable the disputants to settle an issue among themselves. Article 284 provides for conciliation. If negotiation and conciliation fail, the Treaty envisages legal determination. The contracting parties are offered a choice of four methods in Article 287: (i) the International Tribunal of the Law of the Sea, (ii) the ICJ, (iii) the Arbitration Tribunal, or (iv) a Special Arbitration Tribunal. The last named is really more like a Commission of Inquiry. The special bodies for specific questions are the Commission on the Continental Shelf and the Sea Bed Disputes Chamber.

Notwithstanding such an array of measures, the Convention, as a whole, does not have a graded set of sanctions. A member state can be suspended for 'gross and persistent' violation (Article 185.1) and can have its voting rights suspended for not paying its dues. These are the usual two sanctions in many international agreements and are quite inadequate. Though member states are given a choice of four methods of arbitration and adjudication, they are also given the right to make reservations about not accepting the binding nature of awards in disputes on the territorial sea, economic zone and continental shelf. All military activities are excluded from the provisions of the Convention, even on issues like not polluting the sea. If two disputants do not agree on the method of dispute settlement, they are urged to resort to conciliation as the least offensive of all the methods. Whether the 'supermarket' approach and reliance on conciliation will enable conflicts on the great carve-up of the oceans to be limited to peaceful settlement, only time will tell.

Both conciliation and mediation have been successful in limiting international conflicts but these are not widely known precisely because of their success. They are important because they take care of the problem of 'saving face' (i.e. national honour). Arbitration and adjudication are both basically more confrontationist.

The decline of the ICJ parallels the increasing politicisation of all disputes. Only in the case of the European Community can we discern an acceptance of supra-national jurisdiction and an increasing propensity to obey. The day when most states will follow suit is still far off.

One myth which can be laid to rest is that the countries of the so-called 'free world' are more law-abiding than others. In the post-war world, the newly independent countries have been as concerned about obeying the principle of international law as the older states. The existence of one or two maverick states does not invalidate the truth of this settlement.

Though peaceful methods of dispute settlement are important, we should not fall into the trap of thinking they resolve conflicts. The four methods come to an end at some point; whether the solutions reached survive is a different matter. Arbitrated awards can be repudiated; court judgements can be ignored. When states commit such violations, there is little that can be done except to push the conflict into the next round of negotiations. If the repudiation is not due simply to intransigence but to a deep-seated frustration, the lessons learnt from the previous failure may be usefully employed in the next round. Sometimes the conflicts will erupt into violence, perhaps due to changes in the environment and bargaining power.

Notes

1. The Federal Mediation and Conciliation Service in the United States and the Advisory, Conciliation and Arbitration Service (ACAS) in the UK both provide mediators and conciliators. On the other hand, the Australian Conciliation and Arbitration Commission is a quasi-judicial tribunal determining wage awards.
2. F.S. Northedge and M.D. Donelan, *International Disputes: The Political Aspects* (London, Europa Publications for the David Davies Memorial Institute of International Studies, 1971), p. 314. See, particularly, note 6.
3. J.M. Brierly, *The Law of Nations: An Introduction to the International Law of Peace* (Oxford, Clarendon Press, 5th edn., 1955), p. 289.
4. ibid., pp. 293-5.
5. Northedge and Donelan, *International Disputes*, pp. 320-1.
6. A.U. Obozuwa, *The Namibian Question: Legal and Political Aspects* (Benin City, Ethiope Publishing Corporation, 1973). For a detailed examination of the question of the 'withdrawal' by Judge Sir Muhammad Zafrulla Khan, see pp. 106-13.
7. Northedge and Donelan, *International Disputes*, particularly note, p. 324. The authors, somewhat strangely, conclude that international arbitration to be an ineffective mechanism but omit to mention the Rann of Kutch settlement, though they have included other India—Pakistan disputes.

PART FIVE

THE LIMITATION OF CONFLICT

> Gladly would the prophet prophesy pleasant things. But his duty is to tell what he sees. He sees a world still firmly controlled by soldiers, patriots, usurers and financial adventurers; a world surrendered to suspicion and hatred, losing what is left of its private liberties very rapidly, blundering toward bitter class conflicts and preparing for new wars.
>
>   H.G. Wells,
>   *What Will This World Be Like
>   Fifty Years From Now?* (1931)

> Disarmament with mutual honor and confidence is a continuing imperative. Together we must learn how to compose differences, not with arms but with intellect and decent purpose. Because this need is so sharp and apparent I confess that I lay down my official responsibilities in this field with a definite sense of disappointment.
>
>   President Eisenhower, farewell speech, 1961.

17 CONFLICT-LIMITATION: A SUMMARY

> But we are not spectators at the last stages of the world's death. In fact, these last stages can have no spectators. Therefore, in the world with which we are immediately concerned there are stages which, though they occupy an insignificant fraction of eternity, are of great significance for our purposes, for in them entropy does not increase and organization and its correlative, information are being built up.
> Norbert Wiener,
> *The Human Use of Human Beings*

This book began with the statement that conflicts and negotiations were two rails of a track leading to an understanding of how to limit conflicts, especially conflicts between states. We have used the analogy of a compass bearing for conflict situations as well as negotiating situations. Any event can bring a conflict nearer to violence or move it away; likewise, in any negotiation, an event can move it towards agreement or towards breakdown. We have also emphasised that any conflict has a much longer history than the negotiations on it which may take place from time to time. A breakdown of a negotiation about a conflict arising from one party's dissatisfaction or fear will have the effect of increasing the level of dissatisfaction or feeling of vulnerability in at least one of the negotiants. The conflict then escalates, moving it towards disorder and violence.

Mao Tse-Tung's dictum, 'Political power grows out of a barrel of a gun', is not wholly true: it is valid only if we define political power narrowly as the power to compel obedience by force, or threat of force. There are other kinds of power — the power to persuade, the power to reason and the power to negotiate as well as moral power: none requires the gun. Anyone who believes in evolutionary change cannot subscribe to the thesis that all change derives from the threat of the use of force. The possibility of peaceful change presupposes a belief in the efficacy of negotiation as a means of limiting conflicts. This belief is not an axiomatic assumption of mine, but one borne out by the detailed analysis of conflicts and negotiations in Chapter 2.

Once again, we repeat our two caveats. A negotiation, if successful, can help to limit a conflict only if the aims of the negotiation are to redress a grievance, assuage a vulnerability and promote order. Since the negotiating process itself is neutral, any bargaining for increasing disorder will, if successful, only bring violence nearer. For example, international order may well be improved by a collapse of a collusive negotiation between two countries for waging war on a third. Secondly, we have only been talking about limiting conflicts, and not about resolving them.

Our approach to the study of bargaining and conflicts has been based on the crucial assumption that the participants do not always behave in a totally rational manner. That is why we examined the bargaining process from the subjective point of view of the different negotiants. Nor can we ignore the fact that, while the process of negotiation is itself neutral, negotiants are not. We have, therefore, stressed the important role that individuals play in determining whether a conflict moves towards violence and whether a system moves towards greater order. While de Gaulle was President of France, the chances of Britain being admitted as a member of the European Community were slim. His defeat in 1969, purely for reasons of internal politics, changed significantly the evolution of the Community. While the death of Salazar affected all conflicts in Southern Africa, the life and death of Mao Tse-Tung affected the whole of the international order. There is little point in devising theoretical models which ignore the importance of individuals.

Some Lessons from the Study of Negotiations

With the important qualification that not all conflicts can be neatly categorised, we identified two sequences that could end in violence. Individuals, groups or nations feel vulnerable either because they perceive their excessive dependence on others or because a perceived threat makes them feel insecure. Prolonged vulnerability degenerates into fear, leading to desperation. Feelings of dissatisfaction are aroused in an individual, group or nation when unfairness or inequity is perceived; sometimes failure to get what is seen to be attainable also produces dissatisfaction. A grievance nurtured leads to frustration: aggressive behaviour is one of the outlets for frustration which turns into desperation. Grievances and feelings of insecurity often go together.

An insecure or a dissatisfied person (group or nation) may voice his grievance as a demand for redress. The demand is addressed to those in the environment in a position to ameliorate the situation or remove the perceived threat. But these individuals (groups or nations) may then feel that they have to make a sacrifice, and feelings of dissatisfaction are seeded in them. When such a conflict of interest is perceived, all concerned can either negotiate about it or do nothing.

The presence of insecurity gives rise to a desire for order. Most laws, whether customary or statutory, are obeyed most of the time because people have a propensity to obey. An emphasis on deterrence and punishment is as misplaced in understanding order within nations as it is when considering conflicts among nations. When a conflict is perceived, the desire for order motivates people to negotiate about it. Simultaneously, people are reluctant to forgo what they already possess; giving up entails a reduction in power. This fundamental conflict between the desire to reduce insecurity and the desire to maintain power and possessions is ever-present. Though it may be rational to negotiate, say, about the conservation of human and material resources that could be irrevocably destroyed in a violent conflict, people (and states) also fear that the outcome may be disadvantageous to them. The feedback from other negotiants can reinforce, either positively or negatively, these apprehensions. The contradiction between wanting an agreement and fearing its outcome is also ever-present.

The desire for order is also prompted by a need to reduce uncertainty in one's life. To the extent that uncertainty is reduced, predictability is increased. Complete predictability, however, is not attainable. No one places absolute trust in another. Uncertainty thus affects every aspect of the negotiating process, particularly the perception of communications from others.

The attention paid to the past history of conflicts and negotiations, and the traces they leave on the memories of the participants, led us to stress the importance of trust and credibility. Reduction in uncertainty and increase in predictability depend crucially on trust, which is built up as a perception of past actions. This is especially true of conflicts between states, because there is no judicial enforceability of agreements: states which are parties to an agreement have to take on trust the word of the others. The tightness of coalitions also depends on trust. Even the credibility of threats depends on how the threatener has behaved on past occasions.

We have extracted lessons by studying negotiation as a process which takes place in real time, because as the environment changes, changes are induced in relative bargaining power. The expectations of the negotants are altered and the character of a negotiation can change by enlargement or expansion. Coalitions are formed or collapse; the will to negotiate and conclude agreements increases or declines. From this we concluded that *the* Middle East conflict or *the* Ulster conflict do not exist. All conflicts, and the negotiations associated with them, have to be understood by taking 'snapshots' of the perceptions of the disputants and negotiators at different points in time. In this way, we can see that what could have limited a conflict at one time may not suffice at a later time. In general, we could say that a later agreement has to contend with a higher degree of dissatisfaction or deeper fears.[1]

We have analysed the close interaction between a bargaining space and its immediate environment and noted that additional issues and additional negotiators can be drawn in from the environment to make the negotiation more complex. Because the environment is the source of disparities in bargaining power, the nature of the agreement is influenced by it. Further, no negotiation can commence if there is too great a disparity in bargaining power between those who demand a change and those who have to act to satisfy the demand.

Even after an agreement is arrived at, residues of dissatisfaction will remain. These may give rise to new conflicts and new negotiations. Even if a conflict ends in violence, negotiations will still have to take place after the violent action has brought about a change in relative bargaining power. Trade unions and employers have to negotiate after a strike; states have to coexist after a war. The process of negotiation never stops; the aim of limiting conflicts too can never stop.

An important conclusion, derived from studying enlargement and expansion, is that we can understand negotiations better if we break them up into smaller components. This follows from two empirical observations: (i) The human mind cannot deal effectively with more than two (at most, three) interrelated issues simultaneously. Any further increase in complexity inevitably leads to failure; (ii) A decision cannot be reached by a large number of people negotiating together. The analogy of a set of nesting Russian dolls has been used: inside every complex negotiation there are other smaller, more compact negotiations. We can understand how large institutions like governments arrive at negotiating positions or how coalitions form only by looking at the subsidiary negotiations.

Unlike other theories of bargaining, we have paid special attention to finding out why negotiations break down. In the evolution of a conflict, a breakdown has serious repercussions, particularly on the level of dissatisfaction of the negotiant who voiced the initial grievance or vulnerability. The failure of a negotiation not only leaves the original complainant uncompensated but his bitterness is increased by failure.

Some negotiations do not start in any real sense. A disputant in a conflict can indicate refusal to negotiate by a variety of tactics, such as the refusal to recognise an essential participant. Among the numerous examples of this problem we cited: the refusal of Israel and the US to recognise the PLO; of South Africa to recognise SWAPO; and of Morocco, the Polisario. Refusal to recognise may be masked by tactics about procedure and status. The ludicrous wrangle between the US and North Viet Nam on the shape of the table at the Paris peace talks and the use of procedural voting by the United States to keep the People's Republic of China out of the UN, were described in Chapters 11 and 12. In some cases, negotiations ostensibly commence but are destined to fail because one of the negotiants has no intention of negotiating seriously on the issue which is considered to be the most important by another. Whether it be the film producers or the owners of baseball clubs, a disputant prepared to have a show-down will do so by ignoring the vital interests of others. Such instances are preludes to trials of strength and any negotiation which takes place is purely for tactical purposes, usually to gain time so that the strike or war happens at a time best suited to the negotiant intent on a show-down. Imposing unacceptable preconditions is another tactic used in refusing to negotiate. All these tactics can be understood only by placing them in the phase of negotiations about negotiations (NANs) which take place before negotiations on the substantive issues.

During a NAN, the negotiants attempt to delimit the bargaining space by deciding which issues they will *not* negotiate about. The failure to delimit the bargaining space with a minimum of uncertainty can also result in negotiations about substantive issues not commencing. If all these hurdles are crossed and a negotiation begins, it can still break down at a number of points which are summarised in Figure 13.1.

A negotiation will end in a breakdown if there is no perception of equality of dissatisfaction among all the negotiants. An agreement is possible only when two conditions are satisfied: (i) every negotiant perceives that he has gained something from the agreement; and (ii) that that gain is extracted from the *other negotiants*. 'Utility', as normally understood, is implied in the first condition; the concept of dissatisfaction is implied in the second.

While there is an apparent coherence in the way I have set out the causes of breakdowns, negotiations in real life, which must take into account the negotiants' rationality and emotion, do not fall into such neat theoretical patterns. Phases merge into one another, they may occur out of sequence, and the negotiants themselves may behave unpredictably. For example, a negotiant may express unrealistic expectations. If these are genuine others may be able to negotiate with him to moderate them; on the other hand, they may be a tactic concealing a refusal to negotiate. They may even be a mixture of both, as when President Reagan proposed his 'zero option'.

On Limiting Conflicts

Any attempt at limiting conflicts, whatever their nature, must address the disputants' feelings of insecurity. We have looked at insecurity from different angles. Sometimes it is induced by a sense of powerlessness; sometimes it is due to a nurtured grievance or perception of threat. Above all, uncertainty breeds insecurity. Uncertainty causes people to view the future with apprehension whereas greater predictability gives a sense of greater confidence. There can be no other reason for the popularity of horoscopes and other methods of prediction, even though the people consulting them may deny any belief in astrology, numerology or palmistry!

The earliest stage at which a conflict can be limited is by ameliorating a dissatisfaction or grievance as soon as it is voiced. The longer it is left, the greater the compensation required. If it turns into frustration, ways will have to be found for neutralising not only the original grievance but also the subsequent psychological additions.

Since dependence produces insecurity, its alleviation can only come from promoting feelings of interdependence. Display of power emphasises the powerlessness and subordinate position of others; showing that dependence is matched by counter-dependence neutralises that feeling. In this sense, there is a similarity with animal behaviour where conflict is avoided by submissive or non-aggressive behaviour signals. Showing willingness to negotiate about reducing dependence is non-aggressive behaviour. Acute insecurity leads to feelings of vulnerability, accompanied by a lack of confidence and trust. Building up trust is essential for limiting conflicts, whatever the stage they might have reached.

Prolonged vulnerability degenerates into fear. If this stage is reached a conflict is very close to violence. There are few ready prescriptions for assuaging fears, whether it is the fear of individuals, of groups or of nations. This requires consistent and systematic efforts over long periods of time. When frustration and fear degenerate into desperation, violence can break out suddenly.

The prescriptions in the previous paragraphs may look either unduly didactic or idealistically prescriptive. I must emphasise that the suggestions for action are practicable. Perceiving a dissatisfaction early on is practised by most of us in everyday life. A good manager is one who keeps his 'ear to the ground' and does something about complaints before they become grievances. Governments often change their internal laws to ameliorate dissatisfaction that threatens to become widespread. Only in international disputes do nation states, bedevilled by exclusive nationalism and perceived animosity, seem to have lost the capacity to listen to the dissatisfactions of other nations.

Conflict-limitation is possible only if we reduce the number of issues and the number of people (negotiants and mediators) to the minimum. Every conflict has to be tackled first by attempting to contract the bargaining space and by reducing the number of negotiants. International practice is often the opposite. In demanding a new international economic order, the developing countries have put into the bargaining space everything they can possibly think of — commodity trade, trade in manufactured goods, transfer of technology, aid, international monetary reform, shipping, patents, and so on. Since no one can negotiate on all these as a single package, no negotiations take place and rhetoric takes over.

We constantly underestimate the importance of conciliation and mediation by third parties. A great deal of conciliatory effort goes on, even in inter-state disputes. Compromise solutions are often found, which go unremarked and unreported precisely because they succeed in preventing the escalation of a conflict. Compared to the theories of terror and strategic deterrence, far too little attention has been paid to the study of effective methods of conciliation.

Mediation works quite effectively in a large number of labour disputes; so does conciliation in highly-charged disputes like divorces. There is a great deal that one can learn from these experiences for limiting international conflicts. Perhaps a good industrial mediator or a family court judge would be a better choice for tackling international disputes than the politician and the diplomat!

We have described some examples (the Camp David agreement, World Bank mediation in the Indus waters dispute) in which mediation succeeded because the mediator was also prepared to act as the guarantor of the agreement. I stress the need for studying *successful* efforts at international mediation and conciliation because current efforts are often *ad hoc*, and sometimes are even counter-productive, because there are too many mediators. Five-nation contact groups and seven-nation mediation teams abound. Too many mediators may end up arguing among themselves thus mirroring the conflict outside in their own discussions. Acting out a conflict by proxy among the mediators is only an illusion of mediation.

Leaders who take absolutist positions by insisting on exclusive national sovereignty wreck even the most well-intentioned mediatory efforts. Iran under Ayatollah Khomeini is not the only example. The hostility of Mrs Thatcher's government to the well-meant effort by a committee of the European Parliament and the subsequent rejection of the few modest proposals in the report were no help in limiting the conflict in Ulster.

How can we limit international conflicts whose causes lie in dissatisfaction and insecurity? One possibility is early identification. The UN Secretary-General, Javier Perez de Cuellar, has proposed the setting-up of an 'early warning system', which would identify conflicts that have the potential for escalation into violence. The parties could then be brought together to negotiate before they have taken too many public positions from which they cannot withdraw. There are many conflicts (river water disputes, sea boundary disputes and nationality conflicts) which may be dormant but could erupt into violence. Among territorial disputes the best-known ones are: Guatemala/Belize, Venezuela/Guyana,

Chad/Libya, the Horn of Africa (Ethiopia, Somalia and Kenya), India/China, India/Pakistan, South-East Asia (Viet Nam, Thailand and Kampuchea) and Cyprus. If identification, conciliation and mediation could be brought to bear at an early enough stage, some of these conflicts could be limited.

Insecurity can also be tackled by negotiation. The reason why the Camp David negotiation succeeded in reducing, at least in part, the level of conflict was that it concentrated on the mutual insecurity between Israel and Egypt. There is a mistaken belief that acquisition of territory or weapons enhances security. If anything, the Camp David agreement proves that Israel's security was enhanced by divestment of territory acquired by force earlier. Amassing nuclear weapons and increasing their capacity for mass destruction has only resulted in increasing the insecurity of the super-powers.

We should not place too high an expectation on any negotiation. A common way of avoiding a breakdown, particularly in international conferences, is by 'finding a form of words', in such a way that each negotiant can read what he likes into the agreement. This tactic is frowned on by negotiators like Henry Kissinger who believe that this only leads to inconsequential agreements and an illusion of progress.[2] To insist that there should be an agreement on the most important issues or none at all is too extreme a position to take. The second round of talks in Lausanne in March 1984 among the leaders of various Lebanese factions was dubbed a 'failure' because no agreement was reached on a new constitution and only a statement prolonging the ceasefire was issued. Given the complexity of the Lebanese conflict, and the history of violence behind it, it would have been a miracle if agreement on a new constitution had been reached in just two meetings. The fact that a total breakdown was avoided and some agreement, however fragile, on continuing the ceasefire was reached was a step towards preventing further escalation. There is a value for limitation of conflict in inconsequential agreements provided they assist in building trust and confidence.

Articles and books on international conflicts and intractable national conflicts invariably include the phrase 'given the political will ...'. Even Lord Zuckerman's eminently sensible and down-to-earth book on nuclear war states: 'Given the political will, a comprehensive [nuclear test] ban should not be a difficult treaty to agree.'[3] A comprehensive test ban treaty has not been agreed upon all these years because there are too many people in both the United States and the USSR with a vested interest in nuclear proliferation. Those who believe that a ban on further tests may well increase rather than decrease security have not been successful in convincing their political leaders of this.

A lack of political will may be due to a rational analysis of the costs and benefits of reaching a particular agreement, or it may be due to psychological causes. The European Community countries and Japan oppose free trade in primary commodities, particularly food, because they calculate the high cost of protecting agriculture to be worth the benefits accruing from increasing the incomes of their farmers and thereby securing their votes. A comprehensive test ban treaty cannot be concluded because it is easier to evoke fear than it is to convince people that they are secure. Instead of blaming political will, we have to look further and see which interests are perceived as vital and which fears are most potent.

Political will can be created and modified. Attitudes to slavery have changed; so have attitudes to centuries-old practices, like untouchability in India. World-wide, attitudes to the status of women or towards people of different colour have changed. There ought to be more studies on agreements successfully concluded to show that political will was not lacking in these negotiations. Then we may be able to alter the existing will instead of optimistically hoping that it will change of its own accord.

On International Order

It is worth emphasising that more international rule-systems have been created in the last 70 years than ever before. In spite of the large increase in the number of sovereign states, the propensity to obey the law is increasing, even if the reasons for doing so are convenience, prudence or expediency. I have drawn particular attention to the treaties establishing the three European Communities as pioneering examples of states voluntarily sacrificing their sovereignty to an international rule-system, backed by adjudicated rule of law.

Political and economic power can be used either to promote order or to dominate the world system irrespective of rules. There is nothing to choose between governments, rich or poor, of any ideological persuasion, in their readiness to break agreed rule-systems for political gains. Experience also shows that governments violate or circumvent the principles of international law when they feel threatened. Acceptance of a rule-system for promoting international order remains voluntary. The fact that most treaties are either time-bound or have provisions for withdrawal emphasises this voluntary character.

Why do governments negotiate and sign agreements only to violate them when it suits them? One reason is that governments still aspire to order but fail due to human frailty. Sometimes, of course, governments sign agreements because they perceive that they have to pay a higher political price for intransigence than for being subsequently accused of bad faith in implementation. There are no methods, short of war, of enforcing compliance. It is in this context that we have to see the role of rule-systems in promoting order.

In prescribing the norms for an effective international rule-system, we have to be realistic about what can and what cannot be achieved. Power counts. Therefore, any realistic negotiation for creating new rule-systems must take into account existing disparities in bargaining power, and any rule-system must be capable of renegotiation as the environment changes and as the power balance shifts.

If the powerful parties in a rule-system have a propensity to obey, then the system has a better chance of succeeding. But the powerful need to pay due regard to the dissatisfactions and vulnerabilities of the less powerful.

Rule-obedience must be encouraged. Systems, therefore, have to include procedures for transparency in action, inspection of facts and supervision of observance. Verification procedures are all the more necessary in areas where countries feel most vulnerable; arms control is the prime example. Though past experience is discouraging, we have to persevere in promoting supervision.

Rule-systems that have nation states as parties operating in real time cannot be so rigid that no deviation is permitted. Some escape mechanisms (reservations, exceptions, safeguards and waivers) have to be provided for. It is important to keep these within bounds so that the exceptions do not swallow up the rule.

The right to speak and the right to be listened to are important for containing dissatisfaction. Appropriate mechanisms, such as cooling-off periods, are needed to enable disputing parties to arrive at a settlement instead of raising them to higher political levels. Mediation and conciliation should be resorted to more often than they are now.

Even if there is enough propensity to obey and enough encouragement to continue obedience, sanctions and penalties will still be needed. Every rule-system has to have a graded set of sanctions so that the penalty can be made commensurate with the violation. Lack of a graded set of sanctions is a shortcoming common to many treaties creating rule-systems. At all times, the guiding principle must be that total dissatisfaction within a system should not increase.

There is a need to create more rule-systems in order to break up the complexity of international relations into more manageable segments. The Law of the Sea, however imperfect it may be, is a magnificent achievement. Powerful countries like the United States and Britain, in keeping out of it, do not promote international order. We need systems to tackle problems of river basins, greater equity in trade, more predictability in the international monetary system and many others made necessary by increasing interdependence. Every additional rule-system, however small an area it may deal with, strengthens order and security.

None of this is idealistic or visionary. There are no miraculous single-step solutions to the problems of international order. Understanding the many small steps that can be taken is a prerequisite for limiting conflicts.

Notes

1. See, for example, Solly Zuckerman, *Nuclear Illusion and Reality* (London, Collins, 1982) p. 134. 'With every delay in reaching an agreement on the control of nuclear arms, nuclear weapons change and build up so fast that the best that could be achieved later is worse than the worst that might have been concluded a year or two before.'

2. Fred Charles Iklé, *How Nations Negotiate* (New York, Harper & Row, 1964), pp. 21-2, has the following quotation from Henry Kissinger, *The Necessity for Choice* (New York, Harper, 1961), pp. 189-90. 'The inevitable consequence of such a conviction [that any agreement will act as a catalyst for worthwhile settlements later] is that more ingenuity is expended in finding things to agree on, no matter how trivial, than in coming to grips with the issues that have caused the tensions. In the process, a curious distortion takes place. The difficulties which are "ironed out" are often soluble only because they are inconsequential. But the mere fact that they are settled is taken as proof of "progress".'

3. Zuckerman, *Nuclear Illusion*, pp. 133-4.

18 WORLD ORDER AND CONFLICTS — THE NEXT FIFTEEN YEARS

Jataré Agnis thishtathu| Hridayé Sivas thishtathu|
[Let there be fire in my belly. Let there be peace in my heart.]
   Laghunyasa, The short invocation

Ich lebe in den Untergang
und wohne in bedrohten Raumen.
(I am heading for destruction/
and living in threatened surroundings)
   Karl Kraus

A book concerned with real conflicts in the real world cannot end with a theoretical discussion on how to limit them. In this final chapter, I shall examine the conflicts that currently beset this world, starting with a description of the environment.

The Twentieth-century Environment

All conflicts and all negotiations between states in the last 15 years of this century will take place in an environment with the following three major characteristics: (i) The most important is that this is basically a *bipolar* world of two super-powers with the capacity to destroy the world many times over.[1] (ii) At the same time, due to decolonisation, the *number of independent states has trebled* in the last 40 years. We have to add to the set of independent actors non-statal entities which exercise power (e.g. multinational corporations and international agencies). (iii) An often neglected characteristic is the astounding *progress in technology* made, of which space walks and moon landings are only the most dramatically visible part; the development of communications and the rapid dissemination of words and pictures around the globe influence conflicts more directly.

There are three psychological perceptions which affect how nations view their place in this environment. (i) *Exclusive nationalism* is still the most powerful motivating factor. (ii) Technological progress has made *interdependence* inevitable, though this often clashes with assumptions about sovereignty. Because interdependence is often perceived as dependence, feelings of insecurity are induced. This is made worse by the imminent threat of a nuclear holocaust. (iii) The result is that there is more *fear* than ever before.

Fear is the basic reason for the super-powers piling up ever more lethal weapons of mass destruction. Because their leaders talk belligerently about negotiating from positions of strength, we are misled into thinking that what we are witnessing is a power struggle between nations confident of themselves. In spite of the constant additions to their power to inflict death on many millions of people, the two super-powers are insecure and afraid. What are they afraid of? Strange as it may seem, the leaders of the two countries, and the groups that support them for a variety of reasons, do not seem to be afraid of obliteration. Indeed, to some of them Armageddon is inevitable.

In a bizarre extension of the 'better dead than red' or 'let us bury capitalism' philosophies, both sides are prepared for total annihilation in order to save what they perceive as their 'way of life'. In a series of editorials, *The Economist* justified the policy of confrontation and the amassing of nuclear weapons, arguing that these were necessary to guard against 'the danger of *being overawed by Mr Brezhnev's tanks not just being overrun by them*'[2] (emphasis added). In this view, the Soviet leaders would prefer to cow Western Europe into docility rather than conquer it militarily, by mixing threats and blandishments judiciously. A similar argument has been put forward in Uwe Nerlich's massive tome *Soviet Might and Western Negotiating Policy*.[3] 'Western Europe could become *increasingly dependent* on the Soviet Union. The role of military force ... would increasingly be limited to that of promoting political change in the Soviet interest in Europe while providing an umbrella for Soviet interests outside Europe' (emphasis added). Why do Soviet interests outside Europe come into the argument? Because in this atmosphere of fear of Soviet might and fear of becoming excessively dependent on it, everybody is seen as a potential, if not an actual, enemy. Conor Cruise O'Brien has warned the rest of the world that 'Non-westerners should see that it is in their own vital interest neither to strive to accelerate the West's decline nor to crow about it too much. A West in accelerated, humiliated decline could turn into a very dangerous animal, to others as well as itself.'[4] In other words, don't push us, or we will hit back violently!

These three quotations are not the words of people confident of their power; they come from scared minds. The usual reason given for producing more arms is to defend oneself when attacked. But if the Russians say that they will never use nuclear weapons first, why does one still need to proliferate? The reply is: 'We need more weapons because we are frightened of the Russian bear!' From a position based on the actual needs of defence, the argument has been shifted to the psychological plane of playing on fears. It is an adroit use of the perceptions of many in Europe and America to see the USSR as the total enemy. (I have no doubt that there is an identical camp in the USSR perceiving the United States as the total enemy and employing identical arguments for vertical proliferation and amassing overkill capacity, but quotations to justify this statement are not as easily available.)

The fear of the countries in Western Europe is understandable. Most have gone through two destructive wars, even if they started them themselves; they suffered a severe depression in the 1930s, and almost all have been defeated at one time or another. They once ruled the world but their power has been eroded by decolonisation and by the two super-powers becoming incomparably more powerful. They have seen the US dollar take over the financial world and resent their dependence on the United States for their own survival. They feel threatened economically by newly-powerful states like Japan; while newly-industrialised countries like Taiwan, Korea and Singapore compete with their old industries like textiles, and have forced their coal, steel and shipbuilding industries into steady decline. There is a lot in what O'Brien said. It is no use telling the Europeans that the emergence of new nations and new industrial centres are the inevitable consequences of change in the world. They may accept it rationally, but they can also feel resentful and embittered.

The fear of the United States is less understandable. It is still the most powerful country in the world; it holds almost undisputed sway in the American hemisphere and two oceans; it has military allies and bases all over the globe from Turkey to the Philippines, Greece to South Africa, Guam to Diego Garcia; in Cuba, which it perceives as an enemy, the US still has its base in Guantanamo Bay. The United States controls the world's economy through the strength of the dollar, and its power in the IMF, the World Bank and GATT. There is scarcely a country in the world which does not have an American multinational company operating in it; the list includes the USSR, China and all but one country in Eastern Europe. The commercial banks in the US were the ones to provide a haven when the OPEC countries amassed hundreds of billions of dollars in the 1970s. Its news magazines are read all over the world. Above all, the American mainland has never been attacked in a modern war so that the United States has never had to suffer a large-scale, destructive war on its own soil. Yet American leaders talk about the expanding *Soviet* influence! The facts do not support their argument. A nibbling at American power in three countries (Ethiopia, Angola and Nicaragua) does not justify the US response. The independence displayed by over 100 newly-independent countries, in their desire to be free of the power blocs, is mistaken for hostility — 'If you are not with us, you must be against us.'

One reason for the US feeling so afraid may be that it is no longer absolutely pre-eminent. The mere existence of an almost equal nuclear power generates fear. In spite of the all-pervasiveness of its power, the US also perceives that it is gradually declining: Japan, West Germany and Saudi Arabia have acquired significant measures of economic power. The realisation that even the US could become dependent on foreign sources for energy accentuated this fear. The United States also had to concede, in its involvement in Viet Nam, that there were limits to the exercise of even its massive military power. Insecurity results when a great power has to witness an erosion of its formerly undisputed authority; fear is the result. The all-pervasiveness of US power also has another consequence: others resent it. But this resentment surprises and angers Americans, with the result that some show signs of paranoia.

Just as the West perceives a threat to its way of life, so does the Soviet Union. In an attacking speech at the closing session of the ECSC Conference in Madrid, Andrei Gromyko, the Soviet Foreign Minister, said: 'The Soviet people feel legitimate indignation at attempts to slander their way of life and socialist system. They reject unasked-for advice as to how they should go about their business and what procedures must be established in their own home.'[5] The feeling of being besieged, encircled and ostracised is a part of the consciousness of the Russian people. Whenever any country in Europe has become powerful (France under

Napoleon, Germany under Hitler), Russia has been attacked. When the Russian Revolution succeeded in overthrowing the Tsarist regime, it was ostracised by the powerful European countries. In the second world war they suffered massive devastation and the death of 20 million people, a very large number of them civilians. Since 1945, they have been encircled by military bases and spied on continuously by U-2s and satellites. China, a country whose revolution they helped and to whom they gave nuclear weapons technology, turned against them and made an alliance with the USSR's perceived enemy. Today there are five nuclear entities notionally and independently poised against the USSR — the US, NATO, UK and France from the west, and China from the south.[6]

The super-powers, glaring fearfully at each other, have turned their conflict into an ideological one. Worse still, the conflict has increasingly been articulated in more and more absolutist terms. Nikita Khruschev threatened to 'bury capitalism'; Ronald Reagan talks of 'evil empires'. The ideological underpinning is superfluous and irrelevant. There is no such thing as *the* communist philosophy which threatens to conquer the world. Russian communism is different from Chinese, Yugoslav or Romanian communism. The number of communist parties in India sometimes seems as numerous as the number of people in that country! Likewise, there is no pre-planned capitalist conspiracy designed to convert the nations of the world into replicas of the United States. The superpower conflict is a conflict between two nations each seeking to preserve and expand its power and influence. A power struggle between two nations, conducted as between nations, is bad enough; when it is a struggle between super-powers, it becomes worse; if it is then couched in ideologically absolutist terms, it is a struggle to the death. And that death would encompass the whole world.

We have dealt at length on the consequence of nationalistic ideology and fear on the super-power conflict because it poses the greatest danger to human survival. Assuming that the world survives, we have to examine other conflicts for their adverse impact on world order. The same forces that affect the super-power conflict also operate in these. For example, the Iran—Iraq War continues because Iran has taken an ideological and absolutist position. The Middle East conflict cannot be limited because some Arab countries take an absolutist position on the existence of

Israel. In Ulster, the majority of both Catholics and Protestants seem to take only absolutist positions. There is a correlation between increasing uncertainty and insecurity in the world and increasing numbers of people taking absolutist stances. The rise of Islamic fundamentalism is an obvious example. The number of Christian fundamentalists, like those of the so-called moral majority, is also on the increase. The characteristics common to all fundamentalists are their conviction that they alone have all the right answers, and their intolerance of points of view different from their own. Those who call themselves the moral majority imply that those of us who do not agree with them are immoral; the Islamic fundamentalists would have us all follow their dicta on the status of women, drinking alcohol or even how to conduct business. Taking refuge in absolutist ideology may provide psychological certainty, but the more absolute the statement of an ideological position the less amenable is a conflict to any kind of limitation.

While not posing as great a threat to human survival as the super-power conflict, the widening gap between the rich and poor nations also has a potential for violence. The insecurity of the very large number of poor countries is due to their perception of excessive dependence on the few rich ones. There is a fundamental asymmetry in the relations between the rich and the poor, which is reflected in the great disparity in bargaining power between them. The poor nations being recipients (of aid from the governments of the rich nations and loans from their banks) are inherently less powerful than the donors and the lenders. The developed countries, being the 'haves', have no desire to part with their power by creating the so-called new international economic order or new international information order. The United States, for instance, proclaims the virtue of free trade, and actively promotes it in high technology goods. It has now asked GATT to promote freedom in services, particularly financial services. What it will *not* do is to open its market for imports of sugar and textiles, shoes and steel from the developing countries. Convincing the rich countries that they should divest themselves of some of their power requires something more than appeals to altruism.

This is not peculiar to the rich countries even though they have more of everything. In the Third UN Conference on the Law of the Sea, the coastal states formed a coalition to ensure that they gained large areas of the oceans. The land-locked and geographically disadvantaged, with inherently less bargaining power, could not prevent this from happening. In this case, exclusive nationalism and possessiveness marched hand-in-hand.

Of the three factors mentioned earlier in this section, interdependence is the only one which helps to promote international order. Unfortunately, people and nations seem to find it hard to perceive interdependence. While the developing countries are dependent on the rich, the latter are also dependent on the former for raw materials, for markets for their industrial products, and as countries to whom OPEC surpluses can be lent. One can argue that there is no strict one-way dependence in international relations. If the USSR is a hostage to the US for grain supplies, the American farmers are a hostage to the USSR as a market. If many developed countries are dependent on the OPEC countries for oil, these in turn need western manufactures, western arms and western banks in which to deposit their money.

International Order and War

Every violation of international law disturbs the international order. Some, like a country exporting more coffee than its quota under the International Coffee Agreement, have repercussions first on that Agreement and then on other commodity agreements. If the Coffee Agreement breaks down, it affects international order in trade. Which country commits the violation affects its importance. If a tiny country with little interest in international shipping registers an unsafe vessel, this is not as significant as Greece or Liberia doing so. If the United States condones a violation of GATT by calling a discriminatory import restriction a 'voluntary' export restraint, it is a grave threat to international order in trade.

That the powerful have a greater responsibility for maintaining the system than the weak is often forgotten. Jeanne Kirkpatrick, former US permanent representative to the UN, is only one among many Americans who complain of 'double standards', believing the Soviet Union to be judged less harshly in the UN Assembly by other countries compared with the US. I do not understand why she should complain. It is not in the Soviet Union's interest to maintain the international economic and financial order under which almost *all* the countries in the world conduct their business. Having created the rules of the order, and having predominant power within it, it is in America's own interest to maintain it. They are the custodians of the order.

Parts of the international order can break down without the whole collapsing: a commodity agreement can cease to exist; the Bretton Woods system of fixed exchange rates collapsed completely. While restoring order in these segments is desirable, there is a more serious threat to world order when countries actually fight a war. Preventing at least some conflicts between states from degenerating into violence is an essential aspect of studying conflict-limitation.

Large groups of people within a country — sometimes whole nations — react with high emotion to certain situations. The massacre of Tamils and the wholesale destruction of their property in Sri Lanka in 1983 is an example of not quite predictable violence on a large scale. The Cultural Revolution in China was a form of mass hysteria, sustained over many years with official encouragement. The high levels of emotion in the United States when Americans were taken hostage in Iran was sustained by daily reminders in the media (e.g. Walter Cronkite closing his news bulletin with the reminder of the number of days since the hostages were taken). In times of war, apart from the predictable 'my country right or wrong' attitude, suspicion and hatred of foreigners are raised to irrational levels. The internment of second-generation American-born Japanese during the second world war has now, to the credit of the American people, been recognised as an injustice. There are always *a posteriori* explanations for why mass hysteria or mob violence broke out. It is necessary to know more about the the causes before such collective violence happens, so that we can try to limit it. There is some indication that recent developments in the theory of chaotic behaviour may be of some assistance.

In George F. Kennan's opinion, 'Democracy fights in anger — it fights for the very reason that it was forced to go to war; it fights to punish the power that was rash enough to provoke it — to teach that power a lesson it will not forget.'[7] While this has a certain *prima facie* plausibility, (e.g. the United States and Pearl Harbor, India when inundated with millions of refugees from the then East Pakistan, Britain after the attack on Falkland Islands), it conveys the misleading impression that democracies are somehow more virtuous than nations with other forms of government. Democracies also go to war for ignoble motives — for conquest, or to retain their power and influence. There was no direct threat to the territory of the United States which made it fight a long and costly war in Viet Nam.

Among the many interventions by the United States in Central America, the overthrow of the government of Colonel Arbenz in Guatemala in 1954 was provoked by nothing more than the threatened nationalisation of the United Fruit Company. In this case, protection of a company's interests was elevated to a 'vital interest' of the nation. The Russian invasion of Afghanistan was provoked by the fear that it might slip out of the sphere of influence of the USSR. 'Teaching a lesson' was what China called its attack on Viet Nam. When it comes to fighting to protect one's sphere of influence, there is nothing to choose between democracies and other forms of government.

Possessions are always seen as a vital interest. The independence of Algeria was won after a great deal of bloodshed, because France was reluctant to part with a colony, especially one which had a large number of French settlers. The white minority in Southern Rhodesia fought for many years to hold on to their power, as does the South African white minority today. Nations also fight to acquire possessions. Iraq attacked Iran because it wanted to regain half the Shatt-el-Arab river. The war in Western Sahara started because Morocco annexed the former Spanish Sahara, claiming that it had previously been Moroccan. The whole of the nineteenth century was a period of wars for acquiring and retaining colonies with European countries, obsessed with empire-building, fighting all over the world. Which of the countries fighting colonial wars was a democracy and which was not is quite irrelevant. The promotion of democratic values is, of course, a matter of vital concern to those of us who are fortunate enough to live in such societies; but this has nothing to do with why nations go to war.

War is no longer even declared — whether the theatre of operations is the Falklands, Viet Nam, Afghanistan or Lebanon. The sharp distinction — if it ever existed — between a state of war and a state of peace is now lost. Covert operations involving armed action are indulged in by many countries; opposition personalities are assassinated, insurgent groups are armed and harbours are mined; borders are crossed with impunity in so-called 'hot pursuit', or 'to protect one's citizens'; nuclear reactors under construction in far-off countries are demolished because, one day, they may produce a fission product, which may become a nuclear weapon.

Let us not moralise about some nations being more virtuous than others in international law, but accept the fact that *any* country will go to war to protect what it has, to acquire what it wants, because it believes its way of life is threatened, to divert attention away from internal troubles, even out of boredom or accident.

Nuclear War and Theories of Deterrence

Much has been, and will continue to be, written about nuclear war and the imminent threat of a world-destroying holocaust. It is neither practicable nor necessary to deal at length in this book with the horrors that will be visited on this planet by such a war and the imperative need to limit the super-power conflict that might cause it. I can only commend Solly Zuckerman's *Nuclear Illusion and Reality* to which I am indebted for much of what follows in this section.[8] He has pointed out three central facts: (i) a nuclear exchange could destroy civilisation in both the Eurasiatic and North American continents; (ii) nuclear warheads are too dangerous to use in war; and (iii) while nuclear weapon states might be deterred from firing their weapons at each other, the existence of such weapons can neither prevent war nor defend in war.

The justifications usually given for the qualitative development and quantitative amassing of nuclear weapons are false. No anti-ballistic missile (ABM) defence system can ever be devised that will provide either side with a guarantee that it will escape disaster in a nuclear exchange. There are no means of containing a nuclear war at a predetermined level by propounding concepts of fighting with 'tactical' or 'theatre' weapons. We have been brought to this state of madness, not by military men planning for what they need for a war, but by enthusiastic scientists, armchair strategists and politicians who, for the most part, are without the scientific background necessary to understand the consequences. Weapons now being deployed, like the SS-20 or cruise missiles, began life on the drawing-boards at least a decade ago when there was no conceivable military threat for which they were needed. Once under construction, they created a threat which the other side then felt obliged to counter.

The role of the armchair strategist is even more curious and horrifying. Barbara Tuchman, the eminent historian, after attending a conference on US security and spending three days listening to the other participants talking of nuclear options, came away appalled:

> It was deeply impressive, the people were highly sophisticated, studious and hard-working. But the subject they were discussing was always death. It was an eerie experience.[9]

It is only realistic to recognise that there are some, in both camps, who have a vested interest in unabated vertical proliferation, however useless this may be for military strategy and for security.

A point which many scientists and experts on military strategy (the late Basil Liddell Hart, Jerome Weisner, Herbert York, Solly Zuckerman) stress is that the continued growth of nuclear arsenals not only fails to increase, but actually decreases, national security.[10] As Liddell Hart said: 'Nuclear parity leads to nuclear nullity — because the suicidal boomerang result of using such weapons induces strategic sterility.' In Chapter 1, I referred to Kolkowicz's pertinent conclusion that concentrating on bipolar mutual destruction strategies has resulted in a poverty of theoretical development of how to deal with conflicts lower on the threat scale. This decrease in security has been bought, and continues to be bought, at a higher and higher financial cost. Adding to defence expenditure in order to have more 'bargaining chips' that can be 'traded' in future negotiations has proved a worthless enterprise.

The vested interests have either prevented the conclusion of arms control agreements or have emasculated them. For example, no comprehensive test ban treaty has been concluded; exempting underground tests from the ban and pitching the yield-level high have resulted in the super-powers continuing unchecked in the escalation of weaponry.

Theories of deterrence are not only illogical (because more deterrence means less security) but also rest on fallacious foundations. If everyone believed that weapons of mass destruction were not meant to be used, they would at once lose their value as a deterrent! For this reason, NATO refuses to forgo the 'first-use' option, as the Soviet Union has done. If both sides declared that they would not use nuclear weapons first, there would be no need for these weapons. NATO has resorted to the pretence that first-use will be confined to 'tactical' or 'theatre' weapons, though everyone is aware that the use of *any* nuclear weapon can only mean all-out nuclear war. These so-called 'limited' weapons have the objective of 'taking out' (a euphemism for totally obliterating) *only* whole towns or cities! Strategic deterrence theory has nothing to do with military strategy; it is a strategy of terror, subjecting populations of millions to the threat of obliteration. This is, indeed, the cult of violence carried to its extreme.

Some Current Myths

A myth assiduously propagated by some of the vested interests (a notable advocate being the magazine, *The Economist*) is that deterrence has brought peace to the world for the last 40 years. We can always prove that there has been a period of peace by choosing as a starting point the end of the last war. Shifting one's base year to prove what one wants is a well-known technique. Economists of different persuasions use it either to 'prove' that the terms of trade of developing countries are declining or to 'prove' the exact opposite. To say that there has been no war between the two military alliances only because they have been terrorising each other with instant oblivion is a grotesque simplification. First an intention is attributed to the perceived enemy. Then, when it does not behave as imagined, this is promptly attributed to the enemy having been deterred: 'As the years pass we run the risk of not asking ourselves whether some presumed hostile intention really existed in the form we supposed.' From this self-delusion, attributing miraculous peace-making powers to nuclear weapons is only a short step.

Another myth propagated by vested interests is that horizontal proliferation (i.e. more countries acquiring nuclear weapons) is a greater threat to world peace than the unchecked vertical proliferation of the nuclear weapon powers. Any new nation acquiring nuclear weapons is presumed to be less responsible (or less moral) than the ones who already have them, especially if the new entrant happens to be a developing country. The fact that Israel may have stockpiled a nuclear arsenal and, given its history of aggressiveness, might actually use it, is rarely mentioned.[11] In Chapter 3, I pointed out that the acquisition of nuclear weapons is an example of 'keeping up with the Joneses'. Each country which has acquired them has done so because another country either already had them or was thought to be capable of making them.

The best figure for non-proliferation is not five or six or any real number; it is *zero*. The moment I say this, we see how unrealistic it is to expect that no new members will be added to the club. Is any current member of the club willing to give up its nuclear weapons? Even if we say that only the two super-powers should have them, will France give them up? Will China? If we cannot roll back, we cannot stop the roll forwards.

There can be no categorical answer to the question whether any new member of the nuclear 'club' is likely to be less responsible than existing members. History suggests that countries acquiring the capability have been extremely reluctant to share it with others. Some might argue that the use of chemical weapons by Iraq would indicate that a similar thing might happen with nuclear weapons also. Those who condemn Iraq conveniently forget that the United States caused environmental destruction on a massive scale by defoliation in Viet Nam and Cambodia with *chemical weapons*. That it affected not only trees, birds and animals but also people is proved by compensation being awarded to those Americans who came into contact with the chemical.

The reason why Iraq and the United States used chemical weapons was inexorable military strategic requirement. In a war, if any military commander from any country had nuclear weapons and felt that his operational strategy required their use, he would use them. As Field Marshal Montgomery, then Deputy to the Supreme Commander of NATO, put it: 'I want to make it absolutely clear that we at SHAPE are basing all our operational planning on using atomic and thermonuclear weapons in our defence. With us it is no longer: "They may possibly be used." It is very definitely: "They will be used, if we are attacked."'[12] It is hypocritical for any supporter of NATO, which bases its policy on the option of using nuclear weapons first, to wonder whether others will be more or less responsible.

Yet another myth is that the poor nations (the so-called Third World) are somehow more belligerent than the rich. Not only is there no proof for this assertion, the statistical evidence is probably to the contrary. No one has done the kind of thorough-going exercise that Richardson did in his *Statistics of Deadly Quarrels*. If there are 150 independent nations instead of 45, what is the probability of the number of wars in a given period? Have there been more or less since 1945? In any case, why take 1945 as the base year? If we take 1900 instead, the truth is that European countries have started more wars in which more people were killed than during any other period in human history. Even if we take 1945 as the base, and we count all the wars — overt and covert — in which the major powers have been involved — Aden, Afghanistan, Algeria, Cambodia, Czechoslovakia, the Dominican Republic, Guatemala, Grenada, the Falklands, Hungary, Iran, Korea, Lebanon, Suez, Viet Nam repeatedly — the litany of armed intervention by the United States, USSR, Britain and France is a very long one.

The pace of the arms race is set by the super-powers; others follow. If the casualties in many local wars are more now than ever before, it is because the arms-makers are also enthusiastic arms-sellers. The 'keeping up with the Joneses' attitude affects conventional arms even as it promotes both kinds of proliferation. The first reaction of all the major arms-producing countries (the United States, the USSR, France and Britain) to the sudden amassing of wealth by OPEC countries was to sell them expensive weaponry. It was a very cynical equation; if their oil is consumed in our cars, let us sell them weapons which will soon become obsolete, ammunition which will be consumed, and sophisticated planes which will crash. It was recently reported that as many as 17 countries (all the major arms-suppliers as well as Israel, Brazil and China) had supplied billions of dollars worth of arms to *both* Iran and Iraq.[13] After fuelling the war for five years, the same countries wring their hands in cynical horror at the use of chemical weapons or sending children to the front. The governments which provided the weaponry for the war for crass commercial considerations bear responsibility for its continuing.

A corollary to the myth of an enforceable international law is the tendency to blame *the* United Nations for not preventing or not stopping wars. There is no such thing as *the* UN; it is composed of over 150 nations, amongst whom the UN Charter specifically places responsibility for maintenance of international peace and security on the 15 members of the Security Council. Five of these, the permanent members, have the power of veto. It is on these five, particularly the two super-powers, that the peace-keeping responsibility squarely falls. A bipolar world in a state of constant confrontation is, by definition, a world in conflict. There is no use blaming the United Nations, or its Secretary-General, for failing to do what only the super-powers can do.

The Next Fifteen Years

A pragmatic book on the limitation of conflict between nations has to take into account the realities of the world today. For the forseeable future, this world will be dominated by the two super-powers, unless they choose to destroy themselves and others. Below them, power disparities will persist, and there will always be a spectrum among nations ranging from the most to the least powerful. All will be motivated by exclusive nationalism, insecurity and a desire to retain their possessions. The major problems facing the world are — in decreasing order of importance — super-power insecurity, current active wars and dormant conflicts, the North–South conflict and the maintenance of international order in the various sectors of activity.

Clearly, the most urgent requirement is to convince the vested interest groups within the two super-powers that they are not buying more security by spending ever-increasing amounts of money on nuclear weapons. Though this is a daunting task, Lord Zuckerman has suggested a number of practical steps that might be taken: (i) Reduce research and development work on new warheads and delivery systems; (ii) stop work on ABM defence systems; (iii) conclude a comprehensive test ban treaty; and (iv) convert the Strategic Arms Limitation Talks (SALT) into Nuclear Arms Limitation Talks (NALT), to cover *all* nuclear weapons.

All these are different aspects of the principle of containment advocated in this book. Only after the escalation is contained can we think of addressing the next important question. This is to convince the super-powers that, from the point of view of deterrence, nothing would be lost if the size of the nuclear arsenals of both sides were reduced. While containment and reduction are being attempted, mutual trust should be promoted and insecurity reduced by confidence-building measures. There is no other way of doing this but promoting interdependence between the two, especially in the maintenance of world order. The fact that promoting trust between the two super-powers looks a fruitless endeavour is no reason for not attempting it.

The principles of freeze, containment and reduction apply to all current violent conflicts. The practical steps that need to be taken are: (i) contracting the number of issues; and (ii) reducing the number of participants. The way to limit dormant conflicts which have the potential for becoming violent is to have an early warning system which will enable us to try for a negotiated settlement, however imperfect, before positions become publicly entrenched.

As in the case of the super-powers, this approach involves tackling the insecurity of potential belligerents. Whether it be India and Pakistan, China and Viet Nam, the two Koreas or the countries of the Middle East and Southern Africa, far too little attention has so far been paid to reducing mutual insecurity and increasing trust. Mediation and conciliation can be used much more effectively in the early stages than when the conflict moves to the brink of war.

An important element in increasing security is the reduction in the arms build-up by any country; the major arms-suppliers bear a particular responsibility for this. However difficult it may be to negotiate, we must strive for an international convention that no country will sell any kind of lethal equipment or spare parts to a country at war. The next step would be to contain the quantity and sophistication of the arms sold to countries in conflicts which threaten to escalate. The sad fact is that it may be easier to persuade rich countries not to sell arms than to persuade the poor ones not to buy them.

The maintenance of international order in the economic field is the special responsibility of those countries which wield economic power. In practice, this means the countries of the OECD. The emphasis of the developing countries on creating a new international economic or information order is quite misplaced. Nobody can evolve a new order by fiat. It is far more practicable to create a new order by changing bits and pieces of the old order and by removing the uncertainty in the operation of the segments so far untouched. A planned change in the order, to take into account the dissatisfactions and vulnerabilities of the poor countries, is better than the present haphazard and ad hoc way of changing systems.

Correcting these inequities requires an effort by both North and South. While the South can give up demanding wholesale change, the rich countries have to make actual sacrifices. States are not swayed by appeals to altruism, or by the prospect of long-term gains or even by the possibility of outbreaks of violence. People are quite happy buying time, even if it is only five or ten years, because they hope that 'something' will happen in the meanwhile to let them continue to enjoy what they have. Fear of the unknown is also a reason for intransigent behaviour. A practical alternative to altruism is to make a conscious and deliberate attempt at finding trade-offs. For the fearful we must provide something which enhances psychological security in exchange for their giving up something tangible in favour of the dissatisfied.

Ultimately, limiting conflicts depends on the approach. If it is confrontationist and adversarial, the conflict escalates. Everything the other party does is viewed with suspicion and imagined threats acquire alarming perceptional reality. If the approach is motivated by a desire to limit conflicts, then the suggestions made in this book will be seen to be eminently sensible. They are not pro or anti any ideology but only pro-humanity. This is not a book which has preached any philosophy of non-violence. This is a book against violence and against absolutist ideologies. Not that this approach will miraculously eliminate all conflicts and all violence. I have addressed myself only to those conflicts that are capable of limitation by negotiation. I am not so naive as to think that limitation of conflict is easy; it not only requires changes in attitude but also a great deal of hard work to make it happen. A world which devotes so much of its time and resources to creating weapons of mass destruction can surely afford to devote some of its labours to avoiding the need for violent action.

What we cannot afford to do is to despair. So long as there is human life left on this small planet, we have to strive to limit conflicts, enhance security and create order. I, therefore, commend the epilogue to the reader to ponder over.

Notes

1. I am aware of the existence of theories of multi-polarity. But the crucial fact is that the destructive capacities of the United States and the USSR are of a different order compared with those of the powers on the next rung of the ladder; that is why the two are called 'super'-powers. We must also note that the East—West conflict has a greater potential for mass violence than the North—South conflict.
2. *The Economist*, 22 Aug. 1981.
3. Karl Kaiser, *Die Zeit*, 29 July 1983; reproduced in the *German Tribune*, 7 Aug. 1983. The books referred to in it are: Uwe Nerlich, *Soviet Might and Western Negotiating Policy in the Light of the Changes in Military Power Relations* and *Containment of Soviet Power* (Baden Baden, Nomos Verlag, 1983).
4. Conor Cruise O'Brien, *Observer*, 6 Jan. 1980.
5. Andrei Gromyko, official text distributed by Tass, 8 Sept. 1983.

6. The count of five separate nuclear threats to the USSR is given by Solly Zuckerman, *Nuclear Illusion and Reality* (London, Collins, 1982), p. 68.

7. George F. Kennan, *American Diplomacy, 1900-1950* (New York, Mentor, 1951), p. 59, quoted in Roman Kolkowicz, US and Soviet Approaches to Military Strategy: Theory vs. Experience, *Foreign Affairs*, Summer 1981.

8. Zuckerman, *Nuclear Illusion*. The three conclusions in the paragraph are p. xiv; other quotations are: ABM systems, p. 51; on theatre and tactical nuclear weapons, p. 67; on the people responsible for proliferation, pp. 103, 105-8; and the theory of deterrence, p. 48.

9. Report of an interview with Barbara Tuchman in the *International Herald Tribune*, 14 Sept. 1982.

10. Zuckerman, *Nuclear Illusion*, pp. 61, 78.

11. In a report to a congressional committee, a number of countries said to have the technological capability for making nuclear weapons were listed; Israel's name was deleted when the report was made public. It is generally acknowledged that Israel is the only country to have stockpiled nuclear warheads without ever testing them itself.

12. Zuckerman, *Nuclear Illusion*, p. 62.

13. Stockholm International Peace Research Institute, *SIPRI Yearbook*, 1984.

EPILOGUE

With one part of our minds we know that statistically it becomes more and more probable every year that there will be a nuclear disaster, either through war or accident. Yet we have to go on podding beans, falling in love, planning next summer's holiday, worrying about our children's education, starting a piece of research that can't possibly show any results for a couple of years, considering which recipe it would be fun to try, and most of the time ignoring the deep nightmare, the total wiping out of our future. What then?
        Lady Naomi Mitchison,
        Guardian, 31 Aug. 1981

APPENDIX: ADDITIONAL MATERIAL ON THE THEORY OF NEGOTIATION

Mathematical Representation

The following symbols will be used:

  Negotiants: N1, N2, N3, etc.
  Dimensions: d1, d2, d3, etc.
  The expectation of N1: E_{N1}
  The expectation of N1 at time T_x: E_{N1}^x
  The expectation of N1 at time T_x in dimension d: $E_{N1,d}^x$
  When N1's expectation is perceived by, say N2, it will be shown as: $N2[E_{N1,d}^x]$. The negotiant outside the square brackets is the perceiver of the expectation of the negotiant inside the square brackets.

Reaching an Agreement in a Two-negotiant/One-dimension Short-Duration Negotiation

In a short-duration negotiation, the dissatisfaction of each negotiant is a function of the difference between his expectation at time T_1 and the agreement eventually reached at time T_0. The functions need not be the same.

Let the value of the agreeement at T_0 be A and let f_{N1} and f_{N2} represent the dissatisfaction functions of N1 and N2 respectively. Then, N1's dissatisfaction is:

$$D_{N1} = f_{N1}(\overline{E_{N1}^1 - A}) \qquad (1)$$

and N2's dissatisfaction is:

$$D_{N2} = f_{N2}(\overline{E_{N2}^1 - A}) \qquad (2)$$

N1 perceives N2's dissatisfaction as $N1[D_{N2}]$

and N2 perceives N1's dissatisfaction as $N2[D_{N1}]$. The perception of equality of dissatisfaction can, therefore, be represented by the equations:

$$D_{N1} \simeq N1[D_{N2}] \qquad (3)$$

$$\text{and } D_{N2} \simeq N2[D_{N1}] \qquad (4)$$

Duration of the Negotiation

Changes in perceptions and judgements may occur because of the dissatisfaction arising from time spent negotiating. Does this represent an independent set of dissatisfaction equations? No, because A, the value of the agreement, is itself time-dependent. If either N1 or N2 grows more dissatisfied with spending further time negotiating, he will change his expectations more rapidly to bring the negotiation to A, so long as it was within his limit position. The fact that agreement is reached at time T_o and not later, subsumes within itself the idea of growing impatience. A is a function of the total time spent negotiating, that is, the duration of the negotiation from T_B to T_o, call it T_T. The impatience functions of N1 and N2 can be shown as:

$$A = I_{N1}(T_T) = I_{N2}(T_T) \qquad (5)$$

The equations numbered 1 to 5 collectively represent the perception of equality of dissatisfaction which results in an agreement.

Residue of Dissatisfaction

While A is a precise point, N1 and N2 believe that it could have been any one in a range of points. This arises from two uncertainties — perception of E^1 and perception of E^o. This is why D_{N1} is not equal to $N1[D_{N2}]$ but only approximately equal.

N1's uncertain perception of N2's expectations at times T_1 and T_o gives rise to the uncertainty function:

$$U_{N1} = N1[E^1_{N2} + E^o_{N2}] \qquad (6)$$

$$U_{N2} = N2[E^1_{N1} + E^o_{N1}] \qquad (7)$$

In N1's perception, the agreement point could have fallen anywhere between $A + U_{N1}$ and $A - U_{N1}$. One of these will be furthest from his limit position and will represent the best agreement he thinks he could have got. Let us call this point A_{N1}. There will be a similar point, A_{N2}, for N2.

Since the residues of dissatisfaction for N1 and N2 are what they believe they could have got and what they actually got, the equations for residues of dissatisfactions are:

$$\text{Residue for N1: } N1[R(D)] = \overline{(A - A_{N1})} \tag{8}$$

$$\text{and residue for N2: } N2[R(D)] = \overline{(A - A_{N2})} \tag{9}$$

Splitting the Difference

In game theory, the point at which agreement is reached is an optimum point for all negotiants and is one which is invariant with time. In this theory, the point of agreement is arrived at by computation of dissatisfactions compared to earlier expectations and the perception of their equality. Further, the point of agreement is *dependent* on the duration of the negotiation.

At time T_{o-1}, the expectations of the two negotiants are E_{N1}^{o-1} and E_{N2}^{o-1} and the impatience functions are $I_{N1}(T-1)$ and $I_{N2}(T-1)$.

The general proposition is $A = I_{N1}(T) = I_{N2}(T)$ where T is the total time spent negotiating. Supposing the impatience functions are equal even at time o−1.

$$I_{N1}(T-1) = I_{N2}(T-1)$$

Any difference in the value of the impatience functions is eliminated by T−1. The perceived dissatisfactions are only due to the differences between E_{N1}^{o-1} and E_{N2}^{o-1}. This difference can be equalised only by splitting the difference. Therefore,

$$A = \frac{E_{N1}^{o-1} - E_{N2}^{o-1}}{2}$$

and is the outcome at time T_A.

A Comment on Nash's Theory of Bargaining

Nash's theory of bargaining (J.F. Nash, 'The Bargaining Problem', *Econometrica* (1950), 18: 155-62) has been extensively commented upon by Nicholson (Michael Nicholson, *Conflict Analysis*, London, The English Universities Press, 1970, pp. 71-3).

> Nash's rule for a fair bargain ... [is] that we should take the set of utilities of the two parties, multiply the members of each pair together, and then select that outcome as best which gives the highest number. ... Whether one is willing to adopt Nash's scheme or not depends on the extent to which one is willing to accept Nash's 'rules for negotiators'; it has no absolute validity as a prescription for the 'proper' solution of bargaining problems.

Nash's conclusions follow as a logical consequence of assuming that an agreement should possess four characteristics. These have been summarised by Nicholson as follows: (i) any bargain should be independent of the utility scales adopted for the participants; (ii) the solution of the bargain should not be affected by the zero point of the utility measure; (iii) if the alternatives and their pay-offs are symmetrical for both parties, the rule adopted should give an equal division to each party; and (iv) the solution should be on the boundary of the bargaining set.

In our theory, there is no common scale of dissatisfaction; the question of the zero point does not arise because each negotiant compares his expectation at a later time with his earlier expectation. The condition that the solution should lie on the boundary of the bargaining set assumes a finite and clear-cut boundary; in our theory, the bargaining space is finite but its boundaries are perceived differently by different negotiants. The condition based on symmetry is a further simplifying assumption.

Nash's theory becomes a special case of our theory if we assume that the two negotiants do not have different dissatisfaction functions. Supposing both N1 and N2 have the identical dissatisfaction function f. Then,

$$D_{N1} = f(\overline{E^1_{N1} - A})$$

$$D_{N2} = f(\overline{E^1_{N2} - A})$$

For both negotiants, dissatisfaction bears the same direct and proportionate relationship to expectations. Therefore, in order to reach agreement, they have to make equal concessions. Nicholson puts this as follows: 'Nash's solution is reached if the following general rule of concession is adopted — concede if, and only if, your opponent's relative utility loss is not less than your own.' In other words, equalise your dissatisfactions!

I think it is reasonable to say that Nash's theory is not a separate theory but only a special case of the theory advanced in this book, arrived at by ignoring irrationality, perceptional uncertainty and asymmetry.

Reaching Agreement in Multidimensional Negotiations

It was shown in Chapter 8 that in a multidimensional negotiation, the expectations of the negotiants are to be computed from time T_x, when alignment of priorities has been completed.

Let N1's expectations at time T_x be: $E^x_{N1,1}, E^x_{N1,2}, E^x_{N1,3}$ ... Likewise for N2: $E^x_{N2,1}, E^x_{N2,2}, E^x_{N2,3}$ ... Let the value of the agreement in the different dimensions be: A_1, A_2, A_3 ... Let N1's dissatisfaction functions be: $f_{N1,1}, f_{N1,2}$ ... and N2's dissatisfaction functions be: $f_{N2,1}, f_{N2,2}$ ... Let the two dimensions accorded highest priority by N1 and N2 after alignment be d1 and d2. Let the functional relationship between d1 and d2 for N1 be $F_{N1(1,2)}$. Likewise for N2 $F_{N2(1,2)}$.

If there are only two dimensions in the bargaining space, then N1's dissatisfaction at the time of outcome T_o, will be:

$$D_{N1} = F_{N1(1,2)} \left\{ f_{N1,1}(\overline{E^x_{N1,1} - A}), f_{N1,2}(\overline{E^x_{N1,2} - A}) \right\} \quad (1)$$

$$D_{N2} = F_{N2(1,2)} \left\{ f_{N2,1}(\overline{E^x_{N2,1} - A}), f_{N2,2}(\overline{E^x_{N2,2} - A}) \right\} \quad (2)$$

The equality of dissatisfaction equations are, as before,

$$D_{N1} \simeq N1[D_{N2}] \quad (3)$$

$$D_{N2} \simeq N2[D_{N1}] \quad (4)$$

and the time equation:

$$A = I_{N1}(T) = I_{N2}(T) \quad (5)$$

When there are more than two dimensions, the agreement reached at time T_o is tentative. The third highest priority dimension is now taken in hand. Then, D^o_{N1} is equation (1) above and D^o_{N2} is equation (2) above.

At time T_{o1} the dissatisfaction equation will be:

$$D^{o1}_{N1} = F_{N1(1,2,3)} \left\{ D^o_{N1,1}, f_{N1,3}(\overline{E^x_{N1,3} - A}) \right\}$$

$$D^{o1}_{N2} = F_{N2(1,2,3)} \left\{ D^o_{N2,1}, f_{N2,3}(\overline{E^x_{N2,3} - A}) \right\}$$

and so on, as more dimensions are added.

INDEX OF EXAMPLES

acts of violence 1, 2, 26
Anglo–Icelandic Fisheries dispute 270
arms control: arms race 40-1, 301; arms sellers 304; containment 305; SALT negotiations 49-50, 73-4, 142, 196, 198; START 18n13, 210; test-ban treaty 287-8; walk in the woods 242, 256n5; *see also* deterrence, nuclear proliferation
Assam agitation 32-3, 35
Beagle Channel dispute 266, 272-3
Board of Directors 40, 140-1, 147-8
buying chicken or turkey 92-4
buying potatoes 96-105
Cyprus conflict: bargaining power 185, 197; breakdown 136, 177, 210; containment 170, 181-3; mediation 268; serial solution 124, 183
dividing up 144-5
Ethiopia–Somalia conflict 234, 267, 270
Falklands conflict: perceptions 57-8, 211; rationality 17, 45, 298; reaction to threat 63; unacceptable preconditions 25, 83, 208, 268; war: and negotiations 24, calling by another name 19, 231
going on holiday: couple 13, 38-9, 94; family of three 145-6
husband and wife: arguing about mother 167-8; choosing holiday site 13, 38-9, 94; obedience 26, 36n11
International Commodity Agreements (ICAs): bargaining power 199; chance events 79; collusion 157-8; compliance 243-4, 248; conciliation in 265; conflicts of interest 55; environment 46; exceptions 251; expansion 177; exporters coalitions 145, 148, 155; functional relationships 126-7, 138n3; hierarchy 153; inspection 252, 254; International Coffee Agreements 131, 151, 153, 157-8, 297; International Sugar Agreements 148, 242, *see also* European Community, protectionism; International Wheat Agreements 148; negotiations 12, 58, 131, beginning of 197, 213, limits 71-4; political will 216-20; power to disrupt 189; residue of dissatisfaction 246; safety margins 212, water in the quota 96; sanctions 255; voting power 153, 199; waivers 252
Iran–Iraq war 84, 267-8, 295, 299, 304; unacceptable preconditions 24, 82-3, 208
labour disputes: arbitration 262, 263-4; cooling-off period 254; disobedience 247; environment 75-7, 185; escalation 24, 33, 175; negotiations 13, 40; particular disputes 175, 212, *The Times* 40, 131; priority among dimensions 120-1; reduction in uncertainty 68; residue of dissatisfaction 49; sanctions 255; trade-offs 129; *see also* Screen Actors Guild
laggers dispute 175
Law of the Sea: American policy 193, 198, 241, 290; coalitions in 150-1, 155, 296-7; conciliation in 265; Conferences 5, 153, 239; law creation 239-40; possessiveness 296-7; provisions of treaty 255n1, 274-5
Middle East conflict 170, 295; *see also* Carter, Camp David negotiations, Israel, Lebanon
Northern Ireland conflict: absolutism 296; changes in conflict 170, 179; containment 181; rejection of mediation 268, 286; special vocabulary 65; violence 31, 34
North–South conflict: Cancun summit 154-5; commodity trade 217, terms of trade controversy 55, 302; developed countries 187, 193-4, 205, 275, 306; developing countries 34, 41, 156, 185-6, 296, 303; new international economic order 188, 210, 285, 296, 306;

Index of Examples

new international information order 57, 296, 306
oriental market: expansion 174-5; process of bargaining 10, 12-13, 39, 81; reducing uncertainty 67; residue of dissatisfaction 48; trade-off 128; *see also* buying potatoes
parent and child 61-2, 128-9
Prisoner's Dilemma 60-1
river water disputes: and international law 240; India–Bangladesh disputes 115, 175-6, 210; institutional negotiants 141-2; perception of facts 55; protecting interests 211-12
Screen Actors' Guild 122-3, 210, 283

selling a house 50-1, 112-16, 125-6
sharing a flat 44-5
Southern Africa conflicts: *see* Namibia, Rhodesia, Salazar, South Africa
South Tirol conflict 270
United States–Mexico conflicts *see* United States
UK–EEC Budget dispute: dissatisfaction 7, 39, 246, 247; enlargement 169-71; environment 80; negotiations 82, 122, 211; perceptions 53; refusal to negotiate 42, 210
uranium cartel 56-7, 249

NAME INDEX

Abboud, General 267
Afghanistan 186; *see also* Union of Soviet Socialist Republics, invasion of Africa 234, 292; *see also* Algeria, Egypt, Ethiopia, Morocco, Namibia, Rhodesia, Somalia, South Africa, Sudan
Algeria 189, 234, 240, 267; independence of 230, 299
Arab League *see* League of Arab States
Ardrey, Robert 29
Argentina: *see examples*, Beagle Channel dispute, Falklands conflict
Aristophanes 189
Australia 56-7, 148, 152, 249
Austria 156, 270

Bangladesh 115, 175-6, 210
Begin, Prime Minister Menachem 56, 127, 267; *see also* Israel
Brazil 79, 153, 187, 203, 211, 304
Brierly, J.L. 225, 227, 228, 233, 264
Britain: arbitration 263, 265, 273; Diego Garcia 57, 211; domestic policies 46, 239; European Community 94, 151, 173, 225, 250, 280; International Court of Justice 269; International Wheat Agreement 148; mediator 266; Namibia 192; power of 186; uranium cartel 56-7, 249; wars 304; *see also examples*: Anglo–Icelandic Fisheries dispute, Cyprus conflict, containment, Falklands conflict, laggers dispute, Northern Ireland conflict; UK–EEC Budget dispute; Thatcher

Canada 56-7, 148, 176, 192, 249; *see also* International Commission for Supervision
Carter, President Jimmy: Camp David negotiations 56, 65-6, 130, 287, mediator 267, 286; commitment to Pakistan 62, 64; crisis in Iran 59, 66-7; other policies 142, 192, 215

Central America 157, 176; *see also* Guatemala, Mexico, Nicaragua
Chappell, Greg 238, 247
Chile 234, 235; *see also examples*: Beagle Channel dispute
China: arms sales 304; attack on Viet Nam 231, 299; language problems 64; perception of 14, 186, 187; seat in the United Nations 194-6, 283; unequal treaties 229, 246; *see also* Mao Tse-tung
Churchill, Sir Winston 114, 165, 207
Clausewitz 19
Cross, J.G. 22
Curzon, Gerard and Victoria 252

Debré, Michel 238, 245
De Gaulle, President Charles 280
Diego Garcia *see* Britain
Donelan, M.D. *see* Northedge
Dorfman, Robert 45

Economist, The 84, 292, 302
Eek, Hilding 3, 35n9
Egypt 234; *see also* Carter, Camp David negotiations
Ethiopia 234, 267, 270-1, 297
European Community: bargaining power in 199-202; coalitions 151, 155; Commission 39, 200-1; Common Agricultural Policy 173-4, 211; conciliation in 265; expansion 180; negotiants in 139; protectionism 249, 288; rule-system 236, 250, 275, 288; sugar exports 80, 197; *see also* De Gaulle, examples: UK–EEC Budget dispute, European Court of Human Rights, European Court of Justice
European Conference on Security and Co-operation (ECSC): confidence building 60; Madrid Conference 83, 124, 156, 190, 198, 294
European Court of Human Rights 273
European Court of Justice 236, 262, 273-4

Name Index

Fisk, Robert 31
Fleet Street: *see* differentials, examples: labour disputes, *The Times*
France: Algerian independence 230, 299; arbitration 273; Common Agricultural Policy 173; immigration 240; Namibia 192; negotiations with Britain 94; perceptions 70n6; UK–EEC Budget dispute 39, 42, 53, 122; vacant chair 198, 201; video imports 250; wars 304; *see also* Debré, De Gaulle, Giscard d'Estaing, *Le Monde*, Le Pen, Mitterand

General Agreement on Tariffs and Trade (GATT): as a rule system 211, 236, 251, 252; circumvention 249; compliance 243-4; dispute settlement 253-4, 257; Kennedy Round 242; subsidies 248; *see also* free trade, Multi-Fibre Agreement, voluntary restraint
Germany, Federal Republic: Common Agricultural Policy 226; immigration 240; minority party in coalition 190; Namibia 192; natural gas purchase 152, 189; power of 186, 203; UK–EEC Budget dispute 42, 122
Giscard d'Estaing 57
Gorovitz, Samuel 5
Greece 150, 180, 198: *see also examples*: Cyprus conflict
Grenada 15, 17, 224, 230, 231
Gromyko, Andrei 294
Grotius 229
Guardian 58
Guatemala 233, 299
Gulf Co-operation Council (GCC) 152

Haig, Alexander 142, 244-5
Hobbes 223, 225

Iklé, Fred Charles 22, 66
India: Assam conflict 32-3, 35; conciliation 265; conflicts with Bangladesh 115, 175-6, 210; conflicts with Pakistan 186, 266, 272, 298; perception of 14, 187, 203; social change 238, 288; *see also* International Commission for Supervision, Nehru
Indian Ocean 196
International Commission for Supervision and Control (ICSC) 64-5, 253-4, 265
International Court of Justice (ICJ) 227, 269-71, 275
International Monetary Fund (IMF) 203-5, 243
Iran 59, 66, 152; *see also examples*: Iran–Iraq war, Khomeini
Iraq 299, 303; *see also examples:* Iran–Iraq war
Ireland 151; *see also examples*: Northern Ireland conflict
Isik, Isar 124
Israel: arms sales 304; coalition government 190; creating facts 80, 197; nuclear weapons 231, 302, 308n11; perception: of security 34, 72, 127, 287, by others 14; refusal to recognise 82, 208, 283; *see also* Carter, Camp David negotiations
Italy 53, 151, 173, 230, 270

Japan 186, 203, 250, 288; *see also* voluntary restraint
Jenkins, Peter 181

Kennan, George F. 298
Khomeini, Ayatollah 59, 79, 286
Khruschev, Nikita 295
Kirkpatrick, Mrs Jeanne 57, 297
Kissinger, Henry 58, 182, 287, 290n2
Kolkowicz, Roman 17, 301

League of Arab States 234
League of Nations: cooling-off period 254; maintenance of peace 224, 230, 232; Permanent Court of Justice 228, 269
Lebanon 31, 210, 267, 287
Le Monde 57, 70n6
Le Pen, Jean-Marie 17
Liddell Hart, Basil 301
Lorenz, Konrad 29

Macmillan, Harold 245
Malinowski, Bronislaw 19
Malta *see* European Conference on Security and Co-operation, power to disrupt

Malvinas *see examples*: Falklands conflict
Mao Tse-tung 279, 280
Medawar, P.B. 12, 87, 89
Mexico 171-2, 173, 174, 240
Mitchison, Lady Naomi 309
Mitterand, President Francois 57
Montagu, Ashley 30
Montgomery, Field Marshal Viscount 303
Morocco 82, 208, 234, 283, 299
Moynihan, Daniel Patrick 66, 196
Multi-Fibre Agreement (MFA) 250, 251, 253

Namibia 82, 97, 191-2, 213, 271
Nash, J.F. 50, Appendix 312-13
Nehru, Jawaharlal 185
Nerlich, Uwe 292
New York Times 231, 237n4
Nicaragua 230, 268, 270
Nicholson, Michael 5, 8, 20, 21, 22, Appendix 313
Nixon, President Richard 195-6, 231
North Atlantic Treaty Organisation (NATO) 151, 182, 198, 231, 301; *see also* Montgomery
Northedge, F.S. 207, 276n2

O'Brien, Conor Cruise 292, 293
Oppenheim 223
Organisation of African Unity (OAU) 234
Organisation of American States 174, 233-4, 245
Organisation of Petroleum Exporting Countries (OPEC); discipline in 244; power of 186, 205; relations with: developed countries 33-4, 56-7, 193, 249, 294, 297, 304, developing countries 156

Pakistan: conflicts with India 186, 266, 272; withdrawal from the Commonwealth 198, 249; *see also* Carter, commitment to
Palestine Liberation Organisation *see* Israel, refusal to recognise
Perez de Cuellar, Javier 268, 286; *see also* United Nations, Secretary General
Permanent Court: of Arbitration 269; of Justice *see* League of Nations
Poland 267: *see also* International Commission for Supervision
Polisario *see* Morocco
Pol Pot 57
Pope, The 187, 266, 269
Popper, Karl 18
Portugal 180, 191; *see also* Salazar
Priestley, J.B. 31

Rapoport, Anatol 13, 21, 38, 44, 143
Reagan, President Ronald: attitude to: unions 76, USSR 295; nuclear policy 142, 284; on fairness 247; on negotiations 65-6; South Africa policy 97, 192-3; *see also examples*: Law of the Sea, American policy, United States, changing negotiators
regional organisations *see* League of Arab States, Organisation of African Unity, Organisation of American States
Rhodesia 191, 299
Richardson, Lewis 40, 303
Rowney, Edward L. 119

Sadat, President Anwar 267; *see also* Carter, Camp David negotiations
Safire, William 62
Salazar 74, 191, 280
Samuelson, Paul A. 45
Saudi Arabia 244, 267
Schelling, Thomas 6, 8, 16, 20, 26
Sen, Amartya 61
Solow, Robert M. 45
Somalia 234, 267, 270-1
South Africa: Apartheid 32, 215, 299; International Sugar Agreements 148; refusal to recognise SWAPO 82, 97, 208, 283; *see also* Namibia
South West Africa Peoples Organisation (SWAPO) *see* Namibia
Spain 180
Storr, Anthony 29
Strange, Susan 16, 18
Sudan 238, 266; *see also* Abboud
Syria 210, 234, 267

Textile Supervisory Body (TSB) *see* Multi-Fibre Agreement
Thatcher, Mrs Margaret 215, 263, 268, 286
Time Magazine 216
Treaties: Andean Pact 214; ANZUS

152; Bryan 265; Chicago 240; Congress of Vienna 228, 240; Danube Commission 240; European Coal and Steel 273; Hague Conventions 266, 269; Havana Charter 242; Locarno Pact 266; Mannheim Convention 240; on Pacific Settlement of Disputes 260, 266, 269; Panama Canal 214; Paris Congress 155, 236, 245, 250, 273, *see also* European Community; Smithsonian Agreement 4; Test-Ban 287-8, 301, 305; Versaille 3, 84; Vienna Congress 221, 247
Tuchman, Barbara 300
Turkey 185, 197, 240; *see also examples*: Cyprus conflict, Isik

Union of Soviet Socialist Republics (USSR): International Court of Justice 270; invasion of Afghanistan 211, 214, 230, 299; Law of the Sea 150; mediator 266; perception of 186, 292-3, 294-5; United Nations 198, 248, 265; wars 304; *see also examples*: arms control, Carter, commitment to Pakistan, Germany, natural gas purchase, Gromyko, Khruschev
United Nations: Conference on Trade and Development (UNCTAD) 205; General Assembly 139, 194-6; Secretary-General 183, 265, *see also* Perez de Cuellar; Security Council: maintenance of peace 232-3, 304, number of negotiants 139, veto 194, 202-3, 232, withdrawal of USSR 198; *see also* voting
United States: arbitration 269, 273; Bryan treaties 265; Central America 157; *see also* Guatemala, Mexico, Nicaragua; changing negotiators 198; chemical weapons 303; circumvention 250, *see also* voluntary restraint; Congress 142, 241-2; contributions to United Nations 203, 206n3, 248; Cyprus conflict 182, 268; dependence 188-9; fear of 293-4; free trade 296; International Commission for Supervision 65; International Commodity Agreements 59, 148, 157, 217-19, 242; internment of Japanese-Americans 298; Iran hostages 245-6, 298; labour disputes 175, 261; Law of the Sea 150, 193, 241; maintenance of international order 297, 298; military alliances *see* ANZUS, NATO; negotiating partner 242; power of 187, 293-4, in IMF 203-5, in UN 194-6, 283; Presidency 74, 192-3, 198; refusal to recognise 208, 283; South Africa 189, 192; super power conflict 186, 214-15; systemic perceptions 189, 192, 215; uranium cartel 56-7; wars 298, 304; *see also* Carter, *examples*: arms control, Middle East conflict; Haig, Kirkpatrick, Moynihan, Nixon, Reagan, Viet Nam

Vance, Cyrus 178
Vernon, M.D. 54-6, 58, 59, 65
Viet Nam: Chinese attack 231, 299; shape of the table 178-9, 208, 283; *see also* International Commission for Supervision
Von Neumann, John 37

Washington Post 231
Weinberger, Caspar 142, 212
Western Europe 292-3, 299; *see also* Britain, European Community, European Conference, France, Germany, Greece, Italy, Portugal, Spain
Wiener, Norbert 63, 279
Wilson, Edwin 29, 36n14
World Bank 266, 286
World Council of Churches 266

Yalta Conference 114-15, 140

Zuckerman, Solly 287, 300, 305

SUBJECT INDEX

absolutism 286, 295-6
Acts of God *see* environment, changes in
adjudication 261-4, 273-4, Table 16.1; *see also* arbitration, European Court of Human Rights, European Court of Justice
aggression 29-30
alignment *see* priority among dimensions
alliances 151-2, 157, 162; *see also* coalitions, North Atlantic Treaty Organisation
altruism 38, 61, 307
arbitration 261-4, Table 16.1; arbitrator 263; in international disputes 269-73; *see also* International Court of Justice
asymmetry 8, 45; *see also examples*: North–South, developing countries
auctions 5

bargaining *see* negotiation
bargaining population 91, 154; *see also* expansion, reduction
bargaining power 184; and bargaining skills 198; and coalition formation 144, 146; and dependence 188-9; and environment 80, 185, 282; and expansion 174-6, 210; and political will 213-15, 218; and possession 187-9; and secrecy 198; changes in 190-3, 196-8, perception of 193-6; disparities and international order 289; inequality and agreement point 160; measurement of 199-205; of developed countries 42, 210; two-person/one dimension 105-6; within an institution 140-1
bargaining skills 105, 142-3, 198
bargaining space 91, 96-7; and breakdown 210, 283; and environment 71-4, 282; *see also* contraction, enlargement
bluff 63
breakdown 83, 90; and conflict limitation 283-4; and levels of dissatisfaction 48; multidimensional negotiations Tables 8.1, 8.2, 8.3; reasons for 161, 208-211, Fig. 13.1; two person/one dimension 99, 100, 102, Figs. 7.2, 7.3
buying time *see* refusal to negotiate; *see also* intransigence

cartels *see examples*: uranium cartel; Organisation of Petroleum Exporting Countries
chance events *see* environment, changes in
choosing 10, 94-5, 114
circumvention *see* rules, disobedience
civil aviation 240
coalitions 161-2; and expansion 174, 179; formation of 143-5, psychological affinities 140, 151-2, shared interests 139-40, 145-51; survival of 155-7, 162; and minority party 152, 190; temporary 151-2; three negotiants/three dimensions Table 9.1; *see also examples*: husband and wife
codification 239
coercion 25-6, 35n9, 228; *see also* threats, unequal treaties
cold war 20; *see also* deterrence
collective self-defence 231; *see also* coalitions, formation, psychological
collusion 157-8, 162
common heritage 239
communication 64-6, 99-100, 114, 123-4, 159; *see also* feedback
comparability 40-1, 75
competence *see* bargaining skills
conciliation 260-1, 265-6, 285, Table 16.1
conflicts: analysis of 1-3, 20-1, 39, 89, 92, *see also* Nicholson, Rapoport, Schelling; resolution of 3, 9, 275; *see also* limitation of conflict, negotiation, and conflicts,

Subject Index

perception, in conflict situations, violence
containment 305; *see also* contraction, reduction
contraction 11, 168, 181-3; *see also* enlargement
cooling-off period 254, 289
covert action *see* war
creating facts *see* bargaining power, changes in
custom 227, 238

death *see* environment, changes in
dependence 33-4, 188-9, 217, 284; *see also* violence, sequence to
desperation *see* violence, sequence to
determination 254
deterrence 17, 25, 34, 300-2
differentials 75, 186
dimension 81, 94-5, 97; many: functional relationships 125-8, simultaneous negotiations 123-4; *see also* bargaining power, enlargement, linkages, priority among dimensions
disputes: avoidance of 252-3; settlement of 253-5, in treaties 274-5, 266
dissatisfaction 90, 160; and dispute settlement 254, 262; and enlargement 169; and game theory 7-8, 47, 51-2, 53; and law 229, 247; and limitation of conflict 280-5 *passim*; and political will 213; baby sitting group 68; cause of conflicts 39, 52n3; kinds of 27, 40, 47, 68-9; levels of 37, 47; unit of dissatisfaction 112, 131-2, 241; *see also* equality of dissatisfaction, residue of dissatisfaction, utility, violence, sequence to
division of the spoils 114-15; *see also examples*: dividing up
duration of negotiations: multi-dimensional negotiations 132-6, 160, Tables 8.1, 8.3; two person/ one dimension 109, Table 7.1, Appendix 311

economic integration 132, 214, 235
elections *see* environment, changes in
encounter *see* phases of negotiations, one dimension
enforcement *see* sanctions

enlargement: and breakdown 210; and immediate environment 77; consequences of 171-4; controlled *see* trade-offs; process of 11, 169-70; stages of 170-1, Table 11.1a; *see also examples*: going on holiday
entrapment 5
environment 9, 40, 91; and bargaining power 79-80, 190-3; and baragaining space 9, 71-4; changes in 78-80, 97, 106, 109, 211; immediate 74-77, 173, 176, 282; International Commodity Agreements 46; *see also* power
equality of dissatisfaction: and breakdown 210, 284; and coalition formation 144-5; and enlargement 169; in multi-dimensional negotiations 132, 136, 138, Appendix 314-15; in trade-offs 129; one person negotiation 50-1, 92-3; two person/one dimension 112-14, appendix 310-11; *see also* splitting the difference
equality of states 205, 226
equity *see* fairness
escalation 168; *see also* enlargement, expansion
escape mechanisms 251, 289
exceptions 251
expansion: and bargaining power 174-6, 210; consequences of 180; controlled 129; immediate environment 11, 77, 230; recognition and status 177-9; process of 11, 176-7; stages of 179-80, Fig. 11.1b
expectation: in the negotiating process 81, 91, 99-100, 121, many dimensions 123-4; of an institution 139, 143; unrealistic 116, 284; *see also* outcome

fairness 39, 44, 118, 228, 247
fear 189, 230, 285, 292; *see also* violence, sequence to, vulnerability
feedback 9, 63, 65, 281
free trade 247, 296; *see also* protectionism, voluntary restraint
frustration 29, 48, 275, 284 *see also* violence, sequence to
fundamentalism *see* absolutism

game theory 7, 37, 43-6, 50, 143; *see*

also examples: dividing up, Prisoner's dilemma

hypocrisy *see* rules, disobedience

immigration 171, 173, 240
individuals 185, 280; *see also* arbitration, arbitrator, mediation mediator, negotiator
insecurity 9, 280-1, 284, 286-8 *passim*, 296, 306; *see also* predictability, violence, sequence to, vulnerability
inspection 252-3
institutions 13, 140-3
interdependence 224, 234, 239, 284-5, 292, 297
international law: and municipal law 227-9; and sovereignty 225; enforcement in 228-9, 255; evolution of 223-4; obedience to 15, 243; war and international order 15, 224, 298-300; what is 223, 226-9; *see also* international order, peace, rules, obedience, sovereignty, treaties, sanctity of, war
international order: and limitation of conflict 15, 288-90; and rule systems 15, 234-7, 297-300; *see also examples*: North–South conflict, war
intimidation *see* threats
intransigence 230, 307
investigation 254

justice 230; *see also* adjudication, fairness, International Court of Justice

keeping up with the Joneses 40, 302, 304; *see also examples*: arms control, arms race, proliferation, nuclear

law creation 236, 239-40, 263, 270
limitation of conflict: and negotiation 4, 162-3, 279, 283; and politicisation 215-16; and uncertainty 281, 284, 306; between states 15, 234; changes in conflict 170; conciliation and mediation 285, 286, 287; containment 124, 183, 305; dependence 284-5; dissatisfaction 280-1, 285; entrenched violence 31; intransigence 283; numbers 203, 282, 285; political will 212, 214-15, 287-8; refusal to negotiate 179, 283; refusal to recognise 283; residue of dissatisfaction 282; trade-offs 307; *see also* contraction, reduction, resolution of conflict
limit position 71-2, 96-7, 99-100, 142, 212
linguistic problems 64-5
linkages 10, 129, 168-9; *see also* dimension, many

management *see* examples: board of directors, labour disputes
markets 57, 199; *see also* bargaining power, measurement of, *examples*: oriental market
mediation 260-1, 276n1, Table 16.1; and limitation of conflict 286; in international disputes 266-8; mediator: and feedback 65, as guarantor 266, 286, too many 286; rejection of 268, 286; see-saw cases 106; *see also* Carter, Camp David negotiations
memory 9, 45, 85, 92
multinational companies 187, 291
municpal law 223, 227-9, 242-3

national honour 31, 273; *see also* vital interests
nationalism 16, 224, 291
negotiant 23, 35n8; hierarchy among 152-3, 184; potential 177, 184; status of 177-9; *see also* negotiator
negotiation 21-3, 89; and conflicts 4-7, 24, 281-2, limitation of 162-3, 280; and third-party intercession 257; beginning of 37-41, 196; governmental 4-5, 14, 40, 49, 242; many dimensions 160-1, Appendix 314-15; one person 92-4; rationality in 6, 29, 284; two person/one dimension 96, Appendix 310-12, *see also examples*: buying potatoes; *see also* bargaining power, dimension, duration of negotiations, environment, negotiations about negotiations, phases of negotiation,

Subject Index

process of negotiation, tacit bargaining, types of negotiation
negotiations about negotiations 122, 208, 214; and limitation of conflict 183, 283; negotiation process 41-3, 83, 92; unrealistic expectations 116; *see also* refusal to negotiate, refusal to recognise, tacit bargaining
negotiator 23, 66-7, 69, 198; *see also* individuals, negotiant
nuclear proliferation: dissatisfaction as a cause 40-1, horizontal 302-3, vertical 288, 301
nuclear war *see* deterrence, *examples*: arms control, stress, war
numbers 139: increase in 203, 224, 291, optimum 153-5, 162, 282, 285; *see also* coalitions

obedience 25-6, 35n9; *see also* rules, obedience
one person negotiation 92-4
optimality 116; *see also* numbers, optimum
opting out 26, 83, 90, 106, 109, 198
order 9, 91, 237, 281; *see also* international order, predictability, uncertainty, reduction of
outcome 83, 92; and expectation 51; multi-dimensional negotiations 132-6, Tables 8.1, 8.2, 8.3; two person/one dimension 98-9, 106

package deals 130-2, 136, 210
past history 83-5
peace *see* League of Nations, United Nations, Security Council; *see also* disputes, settlement of, *examples*: arms control, war
perception 90; and communication 9; and political will 212-13; and trust 59-60; in conflict situations 54-9, 81, 282; of change in bargaining power 193-6; of civilisation 228; of dependence 189; of dissatisfaction 53-4, 92; of fairness 118, 247; of politics and power 187, 215-16; of security 212; systemic 212, 217; *see also* uncertainty
phases of negotiation: coalition formation 145; identification of 81-3, 92, 99, 109, 159, Table 7.1, stages of enlargement 170-1, Fig. 11.1a, stages of expansion 179-80, Fig. 11.1b; many dimensions 121, 126, 132-6, Tables 8.1, 8.3; one dimension 110, Table 7.1; *see also* negotiations about negotiations, refusal to negotiate, refusal to recognise
poker *see* types of negotiations
political will 19, 208; and bargaining power 9, 213-15; and limitation of conflict 287-8; and time 81; changes in 80, 214-15; elements of 211-13; in International Commodity Agreements 216-20; in North–South conflict 42
politics 215-16
possessiveness: and political will 213, 281; and power 187-9, 203, 297; vital interest 299
power 185-7, 289; to disrupt 189-90
preconditions 24-5, 82-3, 119, 208, 268; *see also* refusal to negotiate
predictability 63, 67, 91, 239, 281, 284; *see also* insecurity, uncertainty
priority among dimensions: alignment of 120-5; cause of breakdown 171, 274; coalition formation 145-51; realignment after enlargement 169
process of negotiation: and communication 63-6, *see also examples*: oriental market; multidimensional negotiations *see* Appendix 314-15, linkages, package deals, priority among dimensions, trade-offs; process 4-6, 12, 90; two person/one dimension 96-102, Appendix 310-14; *see also* dimension, equality of dissatisfaction, expectation, limit position, negotiations about negotiations, phases of negotiation, refusal to negotiate, refusal to recognise
propensity to obey 243-4, 274, 288-9
protectionism *see* European Community, voluntary restraint
psychological affinities *see* coalitions, formation of
public opinion 242

quick agreement *see* types of negotiations

Subject Index

rationality: and mediation 260; in game theory 45; in negotiation 6, 29, 123, 281, 284
recognition *see* refusal to recognise, status of negotiants
reduction 11, 168, 180-3, 285
refusal to negotiate: and alignment of priorities 123; and bargaining power 196; and limitation of conflict 179, 209; and non-starters 73; buying time 42-3, 46-8, 210; phase 82, 92; *see also* negotiations about negotiations, refusal to recognise
refusal to recognise: and bargaining power 196; and limitation of conflict 208, 283; by a mediator 267; postponing negotiations 82, 92; Viet Nam Paris talks 178-9; *see also* negotiations about negotiations, refusal to negotiate
repudiation *see* rules, disobedience
reservations 251
residue of dissatisfaction 8, 39, 47-50, 91, 246; and conflicts 37, 282; and fairness 118; in conciliation 260; in rule systems 246-7, 251-2; one dimension negotiations 115-16, Figure 7.9, Appendix 311-12; *see also examples*: going on holiday, selling a house
right to speak 253, 259
rules 91, 235, 247; disobedience: and dissatisfaction 247-9, and international order 289, circumvention 249-50, methods of 247-8, perception of vital interest 244-5; obedience: and dispute avoidance 252-3, in international law 15, 243-4, in municipal law 25, 228, 242, rights disputes 263-4; rule-making: international 236, 239-42, 289, law creation 239-40, 264, municipal laws 238-9, reduction of uncertainty 69; systems: characteristics 235-6, effective 250-5, in international order 234-5, 240-1, 288, 290; *see also* international order, order

safeguards 251
sanctions 228, 254, 255, 274, 290
sanctity of treaties *see* treaties
satisfaction *see* utility

secrecy 65, 70n16, 142-3, 198, 242
security *see* insecurity, vulnerability
see-saw *see* types of negotiations
self-defence 230; *see also* North Atlantic Treaty Organisation
self-preservation 231
sovereignty 224, 225-6
splitting the difference 7, 114-15, 130, 169, Appendix 312
status of negotiants 177-9
stress 66-7
super powers 291, 295, 297, 307n1; *see also* Union of Soviet Socialist Republics, United States
supervision 252
surveillance 252

tacit bargaining 22, 26, 43
technological progress 291; *see also* interdependence
terms of trade *see* examples: North–South conflict, commodity trade
territorial integrity 226
Theory of Games *see* game theory
threats 61-3, 281
time 5-10, 80-1, 91, 282; *see also* duration of negotiation, phases of negotiation
trade-offs: analysis of 119, 128-30, 210; and limitation of conflict 307; controlled enlargement 174; see-saw cases 106; *see also examples*: going on holiday
trade unions *see* examples: labour disputes
transparency 252
treaties 227; list of *see* Treaties; sanctions 255; sanctity of 229; *see also* rules, systems, unequal treaties
trust: and inconsequential agreements 287; and limitation of conflict 212, 253, 281; and perception 59-60; and survival of coalitions 157; in arbitration and mediation 263, 267; in see-saw cases 106
types of negotiations: equal bargaining power 106, Fig. 7.4; multidimensional 132-6, Table 8.2; poker 105, Figs. 7.4, 7.5; quick agreement 102-5, Fig. 7.4; see-saw 98, 106, 109, Figs 7.4, 7.7; two person/one dimension 102-9, 159, Table 7.1; unequal bargaining

Subject Index

power 105-6, Figs 7.4, 7.6, *see also* duration of negotiations, phases of negotiation

ultimatum 24
uncertainty 91; and absolutism 296; and bluff 63; and limitation of conflict 281, 284; and negotiating positions 100; in one-person negotiations 92; reaction to threats 61-3; reduction of 67-9, 91, 106, 224; *see also* insecurity predictability
unequal treaties 229, 246
utility: and dissatisfaction 39, 47, 51; and game theory 43-6; and satisfaction 7, 92; *see also* value of an agreement

value of an agreement 112, 116-7; *see also* outcome
veto *see* examples: United Nations, Security Council
violence 1-3, 26, 89; sequence to 30-5, 280; *see also* aggression
vital interests 201, 211, 244-5, 273, 283

voicing *see* phases of negotiation, one dimension
voluntary restraint 143, 249, 297
voting: denial of right 255; in the European Community 201-2, Table 12.2; in the International Monetary Fund 203-5; in the United Nations 202-3; *see also examples*: International Commodity Agreements, voting power
vulnerability 91; and coalition formation 151; and limitation of conflict 285; decline in power 196; deterrence 34-5; of countries 34, 156; perception of security 212; *see also* dependence, insecurity, violence, sequence to

waivers 252
war: and international order 298-300; covert action 20, 231, 299; Crimean 32; euphemisms for 231, 299; great powers 304; just and unjust 229-31; not negotiation 19-20, 23; *see also* United Nations, Security Council, maintenance of peace
work place 39, 48-9